The Conquest of North America

Introduction

Christopher Columbus landed on the island of San Salvador in the Bahamas on the morning of October 12, 1492. He thought that he was in the Orient, for he had set out across the Atlantic to find a new route to the rich countries of the East. Little did he dream that he stood on the edge of a vast new world, a world spanning two great continents, a world whose importance would, in the future, surpass that of the lands he had sailed to find.

Columbus was not the first European to reach the Americas—nearly 500 years earlier the Vikings had made several attempts to settle there. But the colonies of the Vikings never prospered, no record was kept of their voyages, and their new lands in the west were forgotten in time. Thus, for the first European explorers of the 1400's and 1500's, the Americas were indeed a New World. The great continents stretched unknown and mysterious into the distance, no one knew how far. In their vastness were hidden deserts and mountains, great rivers and rolling plains. There was gold there for the treasure seeker, furs for the trader, and land for the farmer. But when Columbus landed, all this had yet to be discovered. The story of that discovery is contained in this book.

The earliest New World explorers, whose adventures are recounted in the first part of the book, were the Spanish conquistadors. They sailed the Atlantic Ocean in search of treasure, conquest and fame. They found all three in abundance, for in Central and South America lay rich and mighty civilizations, and it was in the Spanish conquest of these empires that the Americas were first opened up. Within 50 short years after Columbus' landing, a trail had been blazed from northern Mexico south to Chile, and the way paved to a Spanish domination of those regions that would last for 300 years.

The Encyclopedia of Discovery and Exploration

The Conquest of North America

c.1

Doubleday and Company Inc.
Garden City, New York

Contents

This edition first published in
the United States of America in 1973 by
Doubleday & Company Inc., New York
in association with Aldus Books Limited
Library of Congress Catalog No. 72–93384
ISBN 0–385–04321–X

© 1971 Aldus Books Limited, London
Printed and bound in Yugoslavia by
Mladinska Knjiga, Ljubljana

Part 3 *Bridging a Continent*

Below: the final conquest of Tenochtitlán
as portrayed by an unknown Spanish artist
in the 1600's. During the 80-day siege, the
once magnificent capital was razed to the
ground. The fall of Tenochtitlán to Cortes
marked the end of the great Aztec empire.

PART ONE

God, Gold and Glory

BY NICHOLAS HORDERN

The New World

1

"It was easy going at first. The thinner air of 8,000 feet refreshed me. New summits slid into view on the far horizon. I felt utterly alone .... Then I rounded a knoll and almost staggered at the sight I faced. Tier upon tier of Inca terraces rose like a giant flight of stairs.... Each terrace, hundreds of feet long, was banked with massive stone walls up to 10 feet high ... what group of Incas had needed a hundred such terraces in this lofty wilderness? ... Suddenly breathless with excitement, I forgot my fatigue and.... I plunged once more into damp undergrowth ... fought my way forward through vines and foliage.... A mossy wall loomed before me, half hidden in the trees. Huge stone blocks seemed glued together, but without mortar—the finest Inca construction.... It was part of a ruined house. Beyond it stood another, and beyond that I could make out more houses encased in twining growth...."

So exclaimed Hiram Bingham, a young American historian, when he accidentally stumbled on the stone city of Machu Picchu high in the Peruvian Andes. The year was 1911. Bingham had been searching for the ruins of the last known Inca stronghold. Now before him lay

Left: the Inca fortress-city of Machu Picchu, situated in an inaccessible corner of the Peruvian Andes. Machu Picchu, the last stronghold of the Inca Indians, was never found by the Spanish conquistadors. With its rows of terraces, its imposing temples, and its handsome palaces, the city remains virtually intact. It was discovered by Hiram Bingham in 1911.

Right: a Peruvian warrior as pictured on a pre-Inca pottery vase, of about A.D. 600—800. The Indian warrior is dressed for battle. He wears a helmet and carries a shield on his right arm.

not just another collection of ruins, but an entire terraced city of palaces, temples, towers, military barracks, connecting stairways, and fountains fed by aqueducts. In this inaccessible corner of the Andes, some 400 years earlier, the last remnant of the once mighty Inca army managed to defy the Spaniards for over 30 years. The city of Machu Picchu, hanging atop sheer precipices 1,000 feet high and girt by rapids that were impassable for six months of the year, must have been ideal for their purpose.

Hiram Bingham's spectacular discovery rekindled popular interest in the archaeology of the Americas, not only of the Inca in Peru, but also in all those places where silent, mysterious citadels of stone told of once flourishing civilizations. Who were the people who had hewn cities out of solid granite with only hammers and short crowbars for tools? How had they learned the skills to turn each project into an object of lasting beauty? And, above all, where had these ancient architects come from?

Most experts agree that the American Indians are descendants of men from Asia who crossed the Bering Strait to North America at least 20,000 years ago. The first human discoverer of America was probably an Asian nomad clad in animal skins and armed with a club and stone-pointed spear. He was a hunter, and, like most hunters, was forced to follow the migration of his prey—the mammoth, the mastodon, and the giant bison. Until the end of the last Ice Age around 10,000 years ago, it is probable that he, together with successive waves of hunters, crossed from Asia to North America over a bridge of land that spanned the Bering Strait.

In their endless search for game—and, we can guess, for warmer, more hospitable regions—the descendants of this primitive hunter pushed south. Over a period of hundreds, or perhaps thousands of years, they reached the picturesque Valley of Mexico, an elevated tableland between the two ranges of the Sierra Madre Mountains. Then they continued on to the lowlands of the Yucatán Peninsula in Latin America. Crossing the Isthmus of Panama to South America, they moved into the towering Andes, spread out over the Amazon Valley, and finally reached Tierra del Fuego, the southernmost tip of the Americas.

For thousands of years, man in the Americas lived the life of the nomad hunter. When he killed a mammoth, he gorged himself on its meat. When his crude weapons proved inadequate or when game was scarce, he went hungry. But man survived in the New World. His was a lasting conquest.

Then, beginning about 5,000 B.C.—in the highlands of Mexico—man in the Americas turned to agriculture. The cultivation of crops freed him from the uncertainties of the chase. It provided him with a permanent home within a rapidly expanding community and afforded him leisure to explore social, religious, and artistic pursuits. This development in the Americas was closely paralleled in the Old World where farming began in the fertile crescent of the Near East along the banks of the Euphrates and Tigris rivers. In

Above: façade of the building of *Las Manjas* (the nuns) at Chichén-Itzá. The building is elaborately ornamented with figures and hieroglyphs and is typical of Maya architecture of the Classical Period. This sketch was made by the Victorian architect and historian, Frederick Catherwood.
Left: the Olmec civilization flourished on the eastern coast of Mexico until about A.D. 200. Some scholars believe Olmec ceramic figures, with their almond eyes and turned-down mouths, were influenced by early Asiatic visitors to the Americas.

both these regions, agriculture was introduced more than 5,000 years ago with wheat in the Old World and corn in the New. Some people see more than a coincidence between the two developments.

In the 1840's, when the American traveler John L. Stephens first glimpsed the stone ruins of the Maya civilization in the depths of the Honduran jungle, he felt compelled to comment: "savages never reared these structures." Stephens' opinion prevailed during the 1800's. Whenever vestiges of advanced civilizations were found in the Americas, they were attributed invariably to the direct influence of the Egyptians, Greeks, Phoenicians, Chinese, British, Irish, or

110°

Colorado
Gila
Phoenix • BALDY PK.
11,590

C. Gran
Desierto

SACREMENTO MTS.

Rio Gran

El Paso •
Juárez

Staked
Plain

U N I T E D

Forth Worth •

• Dallas

Red

S T A T E S

OUACHITA
MTS. Arkansas

90°

FALL LINE
HILLS

Birmingham •

FALL
HI

Colorado
GULF OF CALIFORNIA

Lower California

Río Bravo del Norte
DAM

Pecos

Colorado

Brazos

Mississippi

Alabama

APALACHE

San Antonio

• Houston

BIG
BURRO
MTS.

Bolsón
de
Mapimí

SIERRA MADRE OCCIDENTAL

Yaqui

Fuerte

C. S. Lazaro

OPIC OF CANCER

Río Grande

Corpus
Christi

Laguna
Madre

Galveston

Mississippi Delta

Pontchartrain

New Orleans

MOBILE BAY.

G U L F   O F

M E X I C O

Torreón •

MEXICO

CO. HUEHUETO
10,335

SIERRA MADRE ORIENTAL

• Monterrey

Mazatlán •

C. Falso C. S. Lucas

Río Grande de Santiago

C. Corrientes

Guadalajara •

Manzanillo •

SIERRA MADRE DEL SUR

Río de las Balsas

León •

L. de
Champala

Tampico •

C. Rojo

Mexico •

POPOCATÉPETL
17,887

Puebla • ORIZABA
18,701

Veracruz •

BAY OF CAMPECHE

Campeche •

C. San Anto
C. Catoche

COZUMEL I.

Yucatan

Isthmus
of
Tehuantepec

Grijalva

Belize
BR. HONDURAS
GULF OF
HONDURAS C. d

MAYA MTS.

0°

ISLAS REVILLA GIGEDO
(MEXICO)

Acapulco •

GULF OF
TEHUANTEPEC

SA. MADRE

GUATEMALA

Guatemala •

EL SALVADOR

Honduras

HONDURA

Tegucigalpa •

• San
Salvador

NIC

L. de Río Managua •
Managua •

P A C I F I C   O C E A N

Pena. d
Nico

0°

• CLIPPERTON I.
(FR.)

110°

0   100   200   300   400   500
Miles

100°

COCOS ISLAND
(COSTA RICA)

90°

Left: Mexico, Central America, and the Caribbean Sea, showing the principal physical features, the important cities, and the political frontiers as they are today.

ATLANTIC

OCEAN

TROPIC OF CANCER

WEST

INDIES

BAHAMA

ISLANDS
(BR.)

TURKS & CAICOS IS.
(BR.)

Charleston

Savannah

efen
kee
amp

Jacksonville

C. Kennedy

Tampa

Lake
Okeechobee

Miami

C. Sable

ey West

FLORIDA KEYS

STRAIT OF FLORIDA

ANDROS I.

ARCHO.
DE CAMAGUEY

GREAT
INAGUA

PUERTO RICO
(U.S.A.)

abana

C U B A

PINE
ISLANDS

G R E A T E R

Santiago
de Cuba

HAITI

Port-au-Prince

DOMINICAN
REPUBLIC

Santo
Domingo

WINDWARD PASS

H I S P A N I O L A

A N T I L L E S

Georgetown

CAYMAN IS.
(BR.)

JAMAICA

Kingston

C

A R I B B E A N   S E A

Laguna
Caratasca

C. Gracias á Dios

co

Mosquito Coast

UA

caragua

San José

CHIRRIPÓ GRANDE
12,861

TA
RICA

GOLFO
DE
CHIRIQUÍ

Peña de
Azuero

Isthmus Pta. San Blas
of Panama
PANAMA
CANAL ZONE
(U.S.A.)

Panama

P A N A M A

Panama
Canal

GULF OF
PANAMA

GULF OF
DARIEN

C. Corrientes

MALPELO
(COLOMBIA)

ARUBA

CURAÇAO (NETH.)

Willemsted

Peña de
Paraguaná

Punta Gallinas

Peña
de
Guajira

GULF OF
VENEZUELA

Barranquilla

Cartagena

PICO
CRISTÓBAL
COLÓN
18,950

SIERRA DE PERIJA

Maracaibo

Lake
Maracaibo

SIERRA MADRE DE MERIDA

LA COLUMNA
16,411

VENEZUELA

Meta

PARAMILLO
12,989

Cauca

Magdalena

Medellín

Bogotá

CORDILLERA OCCIDENTAL

CORDILLERA CENTRAL

CORD. ORIENTAL

NEV. DEL TOLIMA
18,452

Cali

NEV. DEL HUILA
18,865

Guaviare

COLOMBIA

EQUATOR

© Geographical Projects

80°

70°

30°

20°

10°

70°

80°

Norsemen—never, it seems, to the American Indians themselves.

No doubt America did have some chance contact with the outside world before its discovery by Christopher Columbus in 1492. Evidence of such contact is found in the early hybridization of wild American cotton with the cultivated Asian variety. Additional proof is seen in the ancient ceramics found recently on the coast of Ecuador. These ceramics are similar in detail to pottery made in Japan between 3,000 and 2,000 B.C. The logical explanation is that they were carried by hand across the Pacific Ocean.

But the American continents are separated from the rest of the world by the world's two largest oceans. Moreover, the Old World civilization was in many ways quite distinct from that in the Americas. Eurasian civilization was based on the wheel, domesticated cattle, wheat and rice, the plow, the written alphabet, and the use of metals—bronze, iron, and steel—for tools. With the exception perhaps of bronze, which was invented without contact with the

Above: the pyramid and Temple of the Inscriptions at Palenque in southern Mexico. Palenque was built during the Classic Period of the ancient Maya empire and represents the peak of Maya achievement in architecture and the arts. For hundreds of years after the decline of the Maya civilization, the city remained buried under dark, tangled rain forests. It was discovered by the Spaniards in 1773.

Right: a page from the Dresden codex, one of the three pre-conquest Maya codices that survived the zealous book burning of Spanish friars. The page contains elaborate astronomical calculations on the planet Venus.

Eastern Hemisphere, the New World was not acquainted with any of these. Quite independently, however, it cultivated food items that today comprise well over half the world's supply of agricultural products, such as corn, potatoes, chocolate, tomatoes, beans, squash, chili peppers, pumpkins, pineapples, avocadoes, papaya, and peanuts —all of which were unknown to the Old World.

It now seems entirely possible that the American pre-Columbian civilizations developed with only sporadic contact with Europe. And the people who created these separate civilizations did so with minimal contact among themselves. When the Europeans arrived in the Western Hemisphere, the three areas that had advanced the furthest were located in enclaves set physically apart from one another: the Maya in the lowland area of southern Mexico and Central America; the Aztec in the highland plateau of central Mexico; the Inca in the sealed desert and Andean kingdoms of South America.

The first Europeans in the New World encountered the most brilliant of all the pre-Columbian civilizations, that of the mysterious and enigmatic Maya. While Europe was in its "Dark Ages"—the period preceding the Renaissance—the Maya civilization was at its peak. From about A.D. 350 to the 800's, the Classic Period of the ancient Maya empire, the Maya built over 100 city-states in the highlands of Guatemala and Honduras, southern Mexico, and the Yucatán Peninsula. These towns were hewn out of dense jungle with primitive tools and without the aid of wheels or beasts of burden. They were centers for religious and civil events, rather than cities for habitation. Most of the Maya were farmers who lived in outlying agricultural communities within reach of the towns.

The thriving production of corn enabled the Maya to turn to the pursuit of science, art, and religion. Religion was the driving force behind their great achievements. All effort was directed toward gaining the indulgence of the gods whose favor regulated the abundance or paucity of the crops. To appease their gods, the Maya offered sacrifices (rarely human), and built magnificent temples, palaces, pyramids, and plazas in their honor. They studied astronomy so that planting and harvesting, sacrifices and other religious rituals, could be aligned with the day and hour most pleasing to the gods. They evolved a calendar based on these astronomical observations, as well as a system of numbers and a method of writing. Priests acted as intermediaries between the deities and the people, and were responsible for interpreting the gods' wishes. Their job was to provide for the future by teaching architecture, astronomy, astrology, chronology, writing, sculpture, and painting.

During the 700's, Maya architecture and art reached its peak. Then suddenly, and inexplicably, all collapsed. By A.D. 964, the disintegration of the Maya civilization was complete. What happened? Perhaps there was a series of disastrous earthquakes, a rampant epidemic, revolution, foreign invasion, or a severe change in climate. Until the hieroglyphs engraved on Maya pillars and temples can be deciphered, the mystery will remain.

The chances of ever finding out were rendered slim because of a zealous Franciscan friar, Diego de Landa. In the 1500's, De Landa consigned the ancient Maya library to the flames because he thought the books "contained nothing but superstitions and falsehoods of the Devil." Of the thousands of books painted on bark-cloth paper

Right: "Arraignment of the Prisoners," a scene from the wall paintings at Bonampak, an ancient Maya ruin. On the upper tier stand richly attired priests and nobles. Below them, awaiting sentence, sprawl the prisoners of war. Various minor officials and attendants are ranged on the lower terrace. The Maya were skilled in the art of narrative painting. The bright colors and absence of perspective create a rich, decorative effect.

Aztec Empire at time of Conquest
Maya Empire at time of Conquest
Inca Empire at its greatest extent

© Geographical Projects

Left: Mexico, Central, and South America, showing the areas dominated by the Aztec, Maya, and Inca empires at the time the Spanish conquistadors arrived and began steadily to overcome and crush them. The map also shows many of the other Indian tribes with whom the explorers came in contact.

(*codices*) only three fragmented specimens survive. The entire recorded history of a unique civilization was reduced to ashes.

The second period, known as the Mexican Period (about A.D. 900–1500), originated on the northern plains of Yucatán where the Toltec Indians formed a triple alliance of the city-states of Chichén Itzá, Uxmal, and Mayapán. The result was a vigorous renaissance of the Maya civilization. Architecture took on new dimensions of space and elegance that surpassed even that of the Classic Period. But in other respects the new empire fell short of its predecessor. Though more lavish, it introduced little that was really new. After 200 years of peace, the alliance of city-states dissolved. Civil wars dominated the life of the region. The first European visitors were to see the Maya empire in its final stages of decay.

The Aztec Empire

2

Left: turquoise mosaic knife carved in the shape of a crouched warrior. It was used at the sacrificial altar. Below: the Aztec practiced various forms of human sacrifice, the most common being the removal of the heart from a living victim. The man to be sacrificed was held by attendants while a priest tore open his chest and plucked out the still-beating heart. An early Spanish chronicler records that the number of men sacrificed in a single year exceeded 50,000.

In the late 1200's, a barbarian tribe from the north of Mexico moved south and entered the beautiful Valley of Mexico. They were the Aztec. Wherever the unwelcome intruders tried to settle, they were swiftly ejected by the already civilized Indian inhabitants. In about 1325, after years of struggle, the Aztec established their capital, Tenochtitlán, now Mexico City, on a forlorn little island in Lake Texcoco. Tradition states that here the tribal elders had seen the sign that their god, Huitzilopochtli, had told them to look for—an eagle (symbol of the sun and Huitzilopochtli) perched on a cactus and eating a serpent. That sign of the Aztec priests remains the Mexican emblem to this day. One hundred years later, the Aztec had conquered vast territories stretching from the coast of the Gulf of Mexico to the Pacific and as far south as Guatemala.

The meteoric rise of the Aztec can be more easily understood when it is seen as the culmination of a remarkable cultural sequence that began in the pre-Christian era and was continued by the archaic cultures of the Maya and the Toltec. What others had created, the Aztec adapted and refined. They were the inheritors, rather than the originators of their civilization. But, like the Romans, they were responsible for preserving and spreading that culture throughout the lands they conquered.

In certain aspects the Aztec culture never reached the excellence of its Maya neighbors. Their mode of writing was closer to elementary pictorial representation than to the hieroglyphic form. But like the Maya and other Mexican civilizations, the Aztec had a strong historic sense and fine tradition of picture writing. Painted books recorded their history, laws, rites, and ceremonies. The books were pictorial and were essentially only lists of events that served as memory aids to Aztec historians. Most pre-conquest manuscripts were systematically destroyed by the Spaniards, but the tradition continued during the colonial period and many early Spanish chroniclers based their writings on earlier Mexican manuscripts.

In art, science, agriculture, and architecture, the Aztec excelled in their own right. From European eyewitnesses, we hear of the sheer splendor of the temples and palaces, the flourishing state of the agriculture, and the exquisite nature of the works of art executed by highly skilled Aztec craftsmen.

The warlike Aztec established an empire that was constantly expanding. In less than 200 years, the once barbarian Aztec had

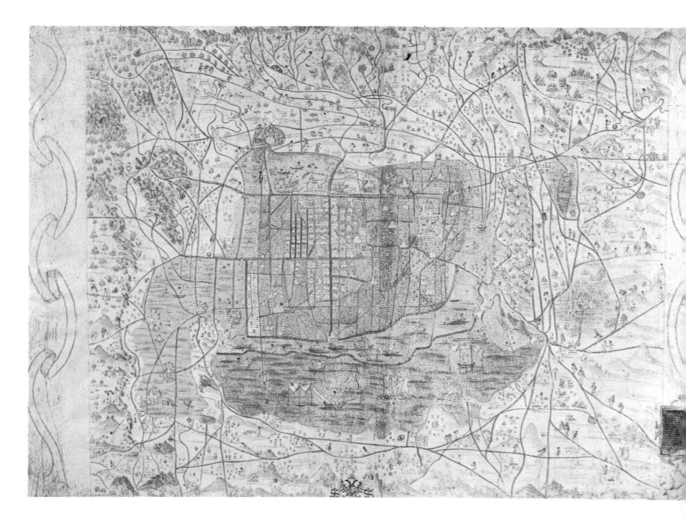

Above: the *Mapa de Santa Cruz,* an early plan of Mexico City and Lake Texcoco, shows the network of canals and causeways linking the city with the surrounding mainland. The Aztec artist has decorated the map with scenes of everyday Indian life. The lake is filled with boats and fishermen; the roads are crowded with Indian porters, hunters, and travelers.

Left: turquoise mosaic mask of the Aztec god Quetzalcoatl. The mask was placed over the effigy of the god at certain religious festivals and upon the death of a king. It was sometimes placed upon the dead after they had been dressed for burial. The exquisite workmanship of this mask is a fitting tribute to Quetzalcoatl, god of learning.

developed a civilization that caused the leader of the Spanish conquistadors to declare their capital Tenochtitlán: "The most beautiful city in the world."

By 1500, Tenochtitlán had developed into a giant stone metropolis with a population of about 100,000. Three wide causeways joined the island to the mainland, and stone aqueducts carried drinking water from the springs of Chapultepec three miles away. The city was brilliantly colorful. Noblemen's villas, administration buildings, and temples were painted either a dazzling white or dull red. The houses had cool inner courtyards or patios containing fountains at the center. Inside, curtains and tapestries hung from ceilings inlaid with cedar and other exotic woods. The Spaniards called the Aztec capital "The Venice of the New World." They had good reason. This glittering city, lying on a turquoise lake more than 7,000 feet above sea level and overlooked by snow-capped volcanoes, was a sight matched only by Venice itself.

The 20-square-mile city had been enlarged by the invention of "floating gardens," the *chinampas*, and by the driving of piles into the lake bed. Chinampas were rafts constructed of silt and masses of rushes and reeds which, in the course of time, took root in the soil

Above: skilled craftsmen displayed and sold their wares, such as this exquisite turquoise mosaic, in the great market at Tenochtitlán. Made in the shape of a double-headed serpent, this pendant was probably meant for the adornment of an Aztec noble.

of the shallow lake bottom, and became islands. Some were 300 feet in length, long enough to allow the cultivation of fruits, vegetables, and the flowers particularly loved by the warlike Aztec. Although most of the lake has since dried up, chinampas can still be seen today southeast of Mexico City at Lake Xochimilco.

Although they had neither wheel nor beast of burden, the Aztec found transportation no problem. The streets of Tenochtitlán were canals over which boats could glide. Through the maze of canals, produce-laden canoes headed for Tlatelolco, the great market square in the northern section of the city. The Spaniards told of the "plaza . . . where more than 60,000 souls gather daily, buying and selling . . . and where merchants from 60 cities would display, jewelry of silver and gold, and precious stones, skins of deer, jaguar, and puma, pottery, and textiles, beautiful mosaics made from birds' feathers, honey, fish, venison, turkey, fattened hairless dogs, dyes for fabrics, tobacco, rubber, and much else besides."

In 1502, at the age of 22, Montezuma II ascended the throne of the Aztec empire. Most of Mexico's 11 million Indian inhabitants now owed allegiance to the new young ruler. In reality his empire was no more than a loose federation of city-states linked through a common fear of an overlord who demanded tribute, but offered little in the way of protection or benefits of any kind. Some cities of

ancient Mexico, such as Tlaxcala and Tarascan, were never conquered by the Aztec. But other, less powerful cities that disputed the demands of the Aztec were raided—their men and women hauled off to the capital for slavery, or worse, for human sacrifice. The god Huitzilopochtli was ever hungry for blood. In 1487, no less than 80,000 captured warriors and members of subject states were sacrificed to celebrate the opening of a great temple.

Under Montezuma's rule, political power was held by a ruling class based on birth but open to talent. At the top of the social pyramid stood Montezuma, who held political and religious authority as supreme chief and High Priest. Contrary to the Spaniards' belief, he was not a hereditary ruler but an elected official who could be deposed if the high council grew dissatisfied with his performance. Of royal descent, Montezuma was well known before his election, both as a general in the army and as High Priest. So powerful was the priesthood in Aztec life that it was the latter of the two offices

Right: Montezuma on the occasion of his election. The emperor is dressed in the traditional manner of the Aztec nobility, with a richly decorated cape and elaborate arm and leg ornaments. The green quetzal feathers strapped to his back were the symbol or royalty and were identified with Quetzalcoatl, Aztec god of learning and of the priesthood.

Above: page from the Codex Zouche Nuttal, a Mixtec manuscript recounting the legend of an ancient Indian chief. Painted on a long strip of deerskin many years before the arrival of the Spaniards, the Codex Nuttal has been identified as one of the two books sent by Cortes to the Spanish king. It is perhaps the finest example of a pre-conquest Mexican painted book.

that proved more influential in his selection as emperor. In the chronicles of his Aztec contemporaries, Montezuma is described as "learned, an astrologer, a philosopher, and skilled in the arts."

Next in importance after the priests and nobles were the bureaucrats who handled the administrative chores of the state, and the merchants who traveled to all corners of the empire in pursuit of trade. Commerce was highly developed in the Aztec society. Often these merchants would combine diplomatic tasks with their own commercial ventures. They also provided information on new cities that could lead to an invasion of the territory. The artisans (sculptors, jewelers, weavers, masons) were next in rank. These were followed by the commoners and the peasants who tilled the land. The slaves—men captured in battle, or people sold into bondage for debt or other reasons—made up the lowest ranks of the Aztec social order. They were generally treated like the modern servant and their fate was quite different from the brutal and degrading

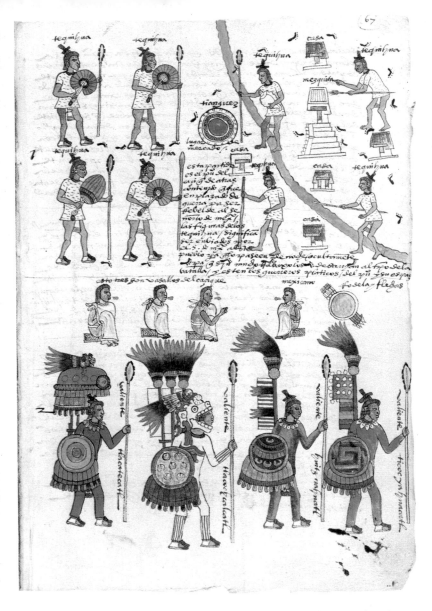

Left: an Aztec scouting expedition and punitive raid from the Codex Mendoza. This book was painted by an Indian artist after the Spanish conquest. Although it retains many of the characteristics of earlier Aztec manuscripts, it is a true "book" composed of folios and painted on European paper. The artist reflects the impact of European ideas in his use of perspective, line, and shading. (Bodleian Library, Oxford, MS. Arch. Selden A. 1. folio 67.)

treatment meted out to slaves in the later colonial era. The Aztec slave could marry at will and his offspring automatically assumed the full rights of a free citizen at birth.

Through all ranks of Aztec society, family and community were prized above all else, and a strong moral code prevailed. A surprisingly tender streak could always be detected beneath the warlike façade. A father counseled his son to: "Revere and greet your elders; console the poor and the afflicted with good works and words. . . . Follow not the madmen who honor neither father nor mother; for they are like animals, for they neither take nor hear advice. . . . Do not mock the old, the sick, the maimed, or one who has sinned. Do not insult or abhor them, but abase yourself before God and fear lest the same befall you. . . . Do not set a bad example, or speak indiscreetly, or interrupt the speech of another. If someone does not speak well or coherently, see that you do not do the same; if it is not your business to speak, be silent."

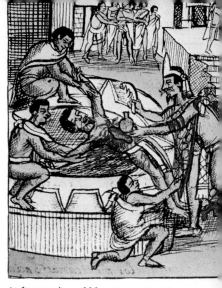

Left: drawing of Montezuma's palace depicts the emperor elevated and alone in his council chamber. Four judges sit in the Aztec court of appeal. Below them are the litigants. (Bodleian Library, Oxford, MS. Arch. Selden A. 1. fol. 69.)

Despite its domestic tranquility, the Aztec state was constantly at war. Disturbances and uprisings punctuated the first 16 years of Montezuma's reign as one province after another sought to break away from the Aztec's harsh rule. But the emperor did not concern himself very much with the affairs of state. Montezuma withdrew from the populace to devote more time to his religious offices and assumed an air of semi-divinity, which even extended to his dining habits. Thirty or more different dishes would be set before him, including turkey, quail, venison, pigeon, and hare. A favorite food was fresh fish, caught on the Gulf coast 200 miles away and brought by special couriers over the mountain passes. Beautiful, young handmaidens brought vessels containing water to bathe the

Above: Montezuma I (1390?–1464?)
attending a sacrifice in Tenochtitlán.
Below: Aztec warriors wage a
"flowery war" with their neighbors.
The object of this ceremonial warfare was the capture of warriors
for use as sacrificial victims.

emperor's hands between courses, and carefully placed a wooden screen before him so that he would be concealed from view while eating or while drinking from his golden goblets.

Cervantes de Salazar, a Spaniard, commented: "Toward his own people, Montezuma maintained a lofty majesty. With the exception of a few great lords of royal blood, Montezuma allowed no one to gaze upon his face, or to wear shoes, or sit down in his presence. He seldom left his chamber other than to eat, received few visitors, and conducted the bulk of his business through the members of his council. Even they contacted him through intermediaries. For the sacrifices at the temple of Huitzilopochtli, where he displayed great devotion, he made his way through his own quarters, remaining at some distance from the hierarchy, and returning downcast, deep in thought, speaking to no one."

Religion was the staff of life to the Aztec. The world seemed full of hostile natural forces whose power could be terrible if not assuaged. Drought, famine, thunderstorm, and earthquake was all occurrences fresh in the mind. The 40 or more deities in the Aztec pantheon were supposed to take care that these things did not

occur again. But the gods were hard to please. What they needed and wanted was the most valuable thing man could offer—life. The worse the predicament the more the gods needed propitiating. The sun was born every morning, and went to bed at night. He battled with the elements of darkness before sunrise. If the battle was not won, it meant the destruction not only of Tenochtitlán but of the whole world. If the sun did not rise, nothing would live. The strength necessary for the sun god's victory was best supplied by an offering of human hearts, for that beating, blood-driving muscle was obviously the seat of life itself. As the chosen people of Huitzilopochtli the holy mission of the Aztec was to fight battles to capture prisoners whose hearts would be offered to appease the god's desire for blood. This sacred mission went hand in hand with the profane political drive to expand territory. Under the Aztec, then, there could be no peace. With peace there were no captured warriors, and with no captured warriors, the sun would go hungry. Even "flowery wars" were resorted to. These were "friendly" battles between states, with equal numbers on each side. The fighting ceased when both had enough captives to satisfy the appetites of their respective gods. The sun god, Huitzilopochtli, was insatiable.

But the Aztec also venerated another god, Quetzalcoatl, the god with a white face and a dark beard. As god of learning and the priesthood, Quetzalcoatl abhorred human sacrifice. It was he who instructed man in agriculture, the arts, and industry. Huitzilopochtli and Quetzalcoatl were forever locked in a titanic power struggle for supremacy of the universe. Through deceit and trickery on the

Below: the title page of the Codex Mendoza depicts an eagle, symbol of the sun and of Huitzilopochtli, perched on a cactus. According to ancient legend, Huitzilopochtli led his people to the shore of Lake Texcoco where, on seeing this omen, they founded the city of Tenochtitlán. God of the sun and warfare, Huitzilopochtli was the principal deity of the Aztec Indians. (Bodleian Library, Oxford, MS. Arch. Selden A. 1. folio 1.)

part of his rival, Quetzalcoatl had been driven away. He went east across the sea vowing that he would return in the year *Ce Acatl* (one reed), to avenge his downfall.

Ce Acatl years fell in 1363, 1467, and 1519. The year was now 1518. During the preceding years, the superstitious Montezuma had been disturbed by a series of portents that his priests, soothsayers, magicians, and other prophets were at a loss to interpret: the temple of Huitzilopochtli suddenly ablaze; a vertical sheet of flame in the east at midnight every night for a year; enormous comets blazing fiery trails across the skies in broad daylight; the lake flooding its banks as if in some tempestuous storm when not a breath of air could be felt; a woman wailing each night, ceaselessly, an eerie and sinister lament.

Then one day, a breathless messenger rushed up to the emperor and reported that he had seen "towers or small mountains floating on the waves of the sea" off the Gulf Coast. A second report said that the vessels bore strange people who "have very light skin, much lighter than ours. They all have long beards, and their hair comes only to their ears." No sooner had Montezuma's messengers exchanged greetings with the strangers from the east than the latter seemed ready to depart Mexican territory, promising to return the next year. This would be 1519, the year of Ce Acatl. The riddle of the omens was solved. The only thing left for an apprehensive Montezuma to do was to sit back and let the omniscient power struggle unfold before his eyes. Quetzalcoatl, true to his word, was coming back.

Below left: an Aztec priest observes the fiery trail of a comet from his rooftop. To the Aztec people, comets signified imminent death and destruction. A year before the Spaniards' arrival in Mexico, a series of comets were sighted. When reported to Montezuma, they were interpreted as heralding the end of the Aztec empire.

Below: Quetzalcoatl, the "Plumed Serpent," was a former culture hero of the Toltecs who was absorbed into the Aztec pantheon as god of learning and the priesthood. He instructed men in farming and the arts. Quetzalcoatl had been driven out of Mexico by Huitzilopochtli, but had promised to return and claim his lost empire. Montezuma believed Cortes to be the returned god.

Right: Manco Capac, the first Inca
ruler, as pictured by the Inca
artist, Poma de Ayala. Manco Capac
is said to have led the Inca people
to the Valley of Cusco where he founded
the Inca empire around the year 1200.

Below: the towering snow-capped
peaks of the Andes Mountains stretch
along the entire coast of South America.
The Andes were the home of the Inca
Indians, one of the greatest of pre-
Columbian American civilizations.

The Land of the Inca

3

Far to the south of Mexico, centered in the Andes Mountains—the sturdy backbone of South America—the Inca empire stretched more than 2,500 miles from the Colombia-Ecuador border to central Chile. The Inca, like the Aztec, were latecomers. When they began their path of conquest that was to include parts of present-day Peru, northern Argentina, Bolivia, Chile, and Ecuador, they encountered civilizations that had been flourishing for hundreds of years. In the tremendous extremes of cold and heat, jungle, desert, and precipitous slope, the Inca came upon dwelling places which, through the resourcefulness and ingenuity of the inhabitants, had been made eminently habitable. Sophisticated networks of irrigation brought water to desolate wasteland. Agricultural terracing made farming possible on steep inclines. Aqueducts carried precious drinking water over distances of miles. The only domesticated animals in ancient America were tended on lofty Andean tablelands. Herds of llamas, distant relatives of the camel, grazed on the mountain slopes where the cultivation of maize was impossible. Roads swept to remote corners of the Andes, formerly inaccessible to man or beast. Nature rewarded this industry with a bountiful return of food, sunshine, and clear blue skies. It also provided awesome natural barriers that prevented the constant outbreaks of internecine warfare that had so often plagued the Mexican kingdoms to the far north.

The ancestors of the Inca Indians may have lived in Peru as early as 2,000 B.C. Until about A.D. 400, they were probably llama herders and potato growers in the high, inhospitable plains of the southern Peruvian highlands. As such they were indistinguishable from a host of other tribes in the vicinity. A popular Inca legend, however, gives a more colorful picture of their origin. The legend tells of four brothers and four sisters—the children of the Sun God—who emerged from a cave 18 miles southeast of Cusco. People from adjoining caves accompanied them. These were the Inca. Led by Manco Capac, one of the four brothers, the group set out in search of better lands. They were armed with a golden divining rod which, when plunged into the fertile earth would sink deep into the ground indicating the spot where a new city should be built. Their journey was a leisurely affair during the course of which the leader's three brothers were conveniently disposed of in one way or another. This left the only remaining son of the Sun God as the first Inca ruler.

CVSCO. REGNI PERV IN NOVO ORBE CAPVT.

To maintain the purity of his divine descent, he married his elder sister, Mama Oullo Huaca. This incestuous marriage established a precedent that was to continue throughout the Inca dynasty. The Inca emperor, like the Inca nobles, was polygamous. However, his *coya* (official wife) was generally a sister, and the successor to the throne had to be a male issue from this union.

The small band descended into the attractive Valley of Cusco, 11,440 feet above sea level. Because it is in the latitude of the tropics, the valley enjoys a delightful climate despite its high altitude. Here the soil is fertile, and the wooded, green meadows are watered by the Huatanay River. In this delightful spot, not surprisingly, the golden rod was put to work. According to one version of the legend, it sank so far down that it disappeared from view altogether. Thus, around A.D. 1200, the Inca capital, Cusco, was born. But the fertile Valley of Cusco was already occupied and the reception extended to the Inca was no less hostile than the one accorded to the nomadic, homeless Aztec who had entered the civilized Valley of Mexico much farther north at about the same time. They were unwelcome intruders. For the next 200 years the energies of the Inca were spent in warring with their neighbors.

In 1438, Pachacuti (all-teacher) became the ninth emperor in the Inca dynasty. In the course of the next 55 years Pachacuti (1438–1471) and his son, Topa Inca (1471–1493), conquered all of Peru and portions of Ecuador, Bolivia, and Chile. Pachacuti was more than just a conqueror. During his reign he founded a vast empire based on systematic lines. New cities that had been subdued by his armies were organized on Inca patterns, and administered by a hierarchy of officials directly responsible to the capital at Cusco. All positions of consequence were held by the Inca, and posts—such as governorship of a region—were reserved for those of Inca royal blood. In little over 50 years, at least 4 million people had been welded together by the strength of Pachacuti and Topa Inca. The Inca empire was made up of about 500 tribes, from very different geographic areas and often with separate customs, languages, occupations, and religions.

Cusco had acquired a population in excess of 100,000 people, and had become the focal point of the Inca empire. The main feature of the city was the central plaza, from which the narrow streets flowed. The plaza was encircled by the emperor's palace, the prominent buildings of the nobility, and the temple complex. The walls of many prominent buildings were adorned with gold plate. Thatched roofs in the adjoining areas were interlaced with straws of gold that caught the first rays of the morning sun as it rose from behind the rim of the surrounding mountains.

The gold-plated Temple of the Sun dominated the square of the city, underlining its central importance as the religious hub of the empire. Pachacuti was not only head of state but, as the Inca emperor in direct descent from the Sun God, was regarded by the people as a living god. His every whim became instant law. Even the highest nobles entered his presence only after showing marks of deep humility, with the head bowed and the symbolic laborer's "pack" on the back.

There is a saying that while the Maya dreamed and the Aztec worshiped, the Inca built. The Maya and the Aztec reached a higher intellectual level. The Inca, on the other hand, preferred to build houses, palaces, cities, roads, bridges, irrigation projects, and agri-

Below: modern travelers follow an ancient Indian highway in Peru. Inca roads were marvels of engineering skills. They crossed mountains and deserts, bringing remote corners of the empire within traveling distance.

Above: drawing by an Indian artist showing Inca builders placing stones in the construction of a wall. This illustration, and others in the same sequence used in this book, are taken from Felipe Guaman Poma de Ayala's *Nueva coronica y buen gobie-ino*, dated about 1600, and now in the Royal Library, Copenhagen.

cultural terracing—all items of earthly endeavor. Although religion was part of their daily life, it did not control it. And as for sacrificing thousands of human lives to propitiate the gods, when they could be regularly employed on any number of construction projects, this seemed not only impractical, but also totally self-defeating.

The Inca were undoubtedly the master builders of the New World. A feature of their buildings was a massive simplicity endowed with beautiful proportions. Their only external ornamentation was the occasional gold and silver plate, or feathered mosaic mural decorations. Their architects designed buildings in which walls often sloped inward from the perpendicular. The plain surfaces were

Above: the baths at Tambo Machay, Peru, testify to the Inca's skill in stone masonry. The baths are constructed of various-sized granite blocks, fitted together without cement. They are placed so exactly that it is impossible to insert the point of a knife between them.

The palace mayor in Hanan Cusco   The chief alguazil (constable)   The provincial corregidor (governor)   The provincial administrator

The inspector of the roads   The inspector of the bridges   The secretary of the Inca   The traveling inspector of the em

Above: the Inca evolved an elaborate and sophisticated bureaucratic system that enabled the vast empire to function smoothly. Hundreds of minor officials were appointed to take care of the everyday business of government.

broken up by slightly trapezoidal openings and niches that narrowed at the top. The close fitting of the gigantic boulders gave off a contrasting light and shadow effect, achieved from the hairline joints and the special texture of the rock itself. The result was not only decorative in effect but practical. The interlocking, mortarless pieces were capable of withstanding unusual stress and strain. The structures were impervious even to earthquakes that would shatter more recent and conventional masonry.

Pachacuti entrusted the active campaigning to his son, Topa Inca, and resolved to spend his last years in overseeing Inca construction. The versatile Pachacuti displayed as much foresight in his architectural feats as in his empire building. He was responsible for laying-out Cusco's streets on a grid system. He also began construction on what are considered the three most enduring monuments to Inca achievement in stone building: the Temple of the Sun at Cusco, the Sacsahuaman fortress, and Machu Picchu, the city-fortress high above the Urabamba River Valley.

The Sacsahuaman fortress, high up on a hill behind Cusco, was large enough to house the entire city. Hiram Bingham referred to

The royal courier

The Tahuantinsuyu supreme council

Above: a Mochica stirrup vase representing a Peruvian warrior. The Mochica-Chimu peoples were the last of the tribes of Peru to be conquered by the Inca. Their warriors were finally defeated by Topa Inca in 1461.

its northern wall as being "perhaps the most extraordinary structure built by ancient man in the Western Hemisphere."

In the aftermath of Cusco's devastating earthquake in 1950, the colonial superstructure of the Monastery of Santo Domingo collapsed into a pile of bricks, cement, and other rubble. Its foundations, however, consisting of ground granite blocks prescribing a graceful arc, remained as secure as the day Pachacuti saw them being laid.

While Pachacuti built, his son and successor to the throne, Topa Inca, increased the limits of the Inca empire. Advancing north up the highlands from Cusco to Ecuador, he defeated the powerful kingdom of Quito. Only one tribe of consequence was left to conquer, that of the advanced civilization of the Chimu in northern Peru. Having overcome the latter's northern allies, Topa Inca outflanked the fortifications built to ward off an attack from the south and soon crushed the lone rival to Inca glory.

The pattern of conquest began to acquire identifiable characteristics. First there was the diplomatic approach when prospective territories would be advised of the benefits of joining the Inca empire. If rhetoric or the sight of 200,000 lithe warriors on the

Above: the most famous of the Inca
bridges, spanning the precipitous
gorge of the Apurimac River. The
cables of plaited and twisted rope,
as thick as a man's body, were 148
feet long. Built in 1350, the Inca
bridge continued in use until 1880.

skyline were not persuasive, then hostilities commenced. Generally,
the opposing forces were overwhelmed, and an Inca garrison
stationed in the newly won territory. Teams of engineers and administrators followed quickly in the wake of victory. The learning of
the Quechuan language, the official language of the Inca and their
provinces, was made compulsory If the conquered people were
acquiescent, they were free to retain their own rulers and system of
government, but with an Inca advisor regulating policies. If
troublesome, the whole populace was liable for mass deportation
to a safer territory, and "friendly" citizens took their place in the
new outpost of the empire.

Vital to the success of Inca military operations was the rapid
communications systems based on its vast network of roads. As the
empire grew in size, it became doubly important to be in a position
to deploy large forces with utmost speed. Ten thousand miles of
paved roads crossed desert, jungle, and 15,000 foot Andean highlands alike. The largest of these was the Andean royal road that
stretched 3,250 miles south down the mountain chain. The coastal
desert road paralleled the highland, extending 2,520 miles to the
south. Numerous lateral roads linked the two major highways.
Bridges suspended by cable, or floating on pontoons (flat-bottomed
boats), were flung across marshes, chasms, or other obstacles in the
path of the long, straight roads. The most famous of these bridges
spanned a 150-foot-wide gap between the precipices of the Apurimac
River. Hung on rope suspension cables as thick as a man's body, the
bridge was in use from the time the Inca built it around 1350 until
1880.

On the main highways, *tampus* (rest stations), were distanced
12 or 18 miles apart, depending on the terrain. These tampus acted
as an invaluable logistical aid to armies on the move. They contained
abundant stores of arms and food—mostly dried llama meat and
dehydrated potatoes. Couriers were stationed about three miles
apart to provide a messenger service unmatched for speed. In all
types of terrain, these couriers averaged an incredible speed of a
mile in just over six minutes. The world record for this distance
today is just slightly under four minutes. Running in relays, Inca
couriers could cover 150 miles in a day!

Oral messages were often supplemented by a device known as the
quipu, the closest the Inca ever came to writing. The quipu consisted

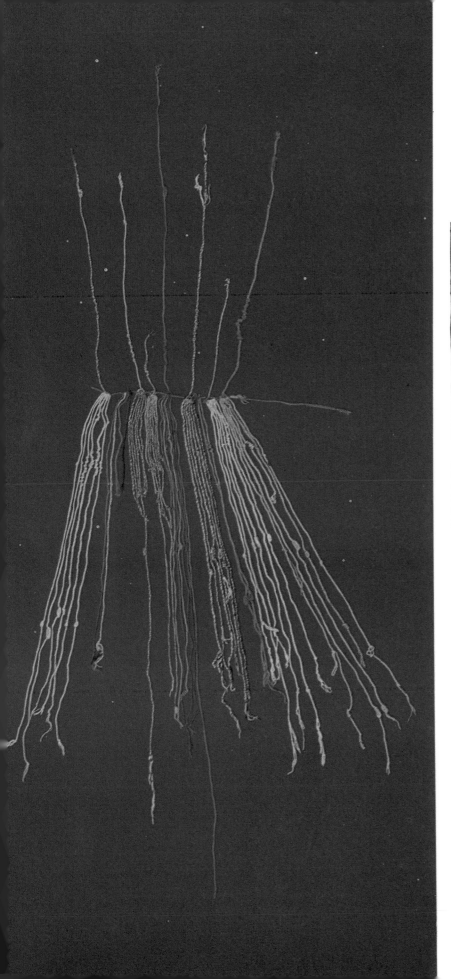

Above: an Inca official holding a quipu. A rapid communication system was vital to the vast Inca empire. Running in relays, messengers could cover about 150 miles a day, even over the most difficult terrain.

Left: the quipu was a device used by the Inca to keep accounts and to aid the memory in recording history and relaying messages. The quipu consisted of a main cord from which was hung many smaller strings, sometimes of different colors. Groups of knots, tied at intervals, indicated the number of a given item.

of one main strand of rope from which many smaller strings, sometimes of different colors, were hung. The position of the knots tied in the string would indicate the number of any given item, based on a decimal system. The strings indicated different objects, and even the way the thread was twisted or how the knot was tied, bore its special significance. Some claimed that it was even capable of conveying abstract ideas. Official court-appointed quipu readers (the best requiring a lifetime's familiarity with the technique) could catalog an entire inventory of a province down to the last head of llama or measure of maize. These keepers of the records would apply the quipu in their recitation of Inca history, an official version that camouflaged the existence of prior cultures in Peru.

In 1493, when Huayna Capac succeeded his father, Topa Inca, on the throne, he presided over a vast domain that was at heart an agricultural society. At the lowest rung, the bulk of the population were the farmers. Their life was organized from the cradle to the grave by a bevy of supervisors at the family, village, tribal, provincial, regional, and national level. The Peruvian was the most resourceful and scientific farmer known to the ancient world. He made extensive use of such devices as highland terracing, irrigation, and fertilization to ensure a productive soil even in the most inaccessible of regions. In the highlands he herded cattle, such as the llama and alpaca. And, where his maize and other staple crops could not be grown due to the high altitude, he developed and gave to the world the white potato, quinoa (a cereal grain), and other plants. Plants with medicinal properties—such as quinine and cocaine—that are used still in modern medicine, originated first in Peru.

Land belonged to the state but was loaned out to the people according to their needs. Each citizen was obliged to provide one-third of his produce to the state and another third to the temple The remainder could be used for his own consumption. The very young, the old, and the infirm were provided with food and other articles free of charge. As private property was non-existent, theft was a crime against the state and was punishable by death. But if, for example, the food was stolen to prevent starvation, then the person prosecuted was not the thief but his overseer, for failing in his duty to provide the basic amenities for living. The submergence of the individual for the benefit of the community as a whole was ingrained in the discipline of Peruvian life. The gulf between the privileged

Above: this early Indian drawing shows a farmer irrigating land in ancient Peru. Inca methods of agriculture were the most advanced of any pre-Columbian civilization. Below: modern farmers near Cajamarca, Peru still use the methods of irrigation developed by the Inca Indians.

Left: this Peruvian agricultural deity, wearing a moon headdress, dates from between A.D. 600–1000. The body of the deity is decorated with maize and squash, the traditional foods of pre-Columbian America. The majority of the Inca were farmers and worshiped gods of the land.

Above: genealogy from the late 1700's of Inca rulers and their Spanish successors. Manco Capac, the founder of the Inca dynasty, and his coya (official wife) stand in the two upper corners. The last of the Inca emperors, Atahualpa, and his successor, King Charles of Spain, are at the end of the second row.

and the common folk was very great, but none went hungry and military protection was guaranteed to all.

In 1525, the Inca encountered their first white man when the Chiriguano Indians attacked a southern Inca outpost. The Chiriguano attack was led by Alejo Garcia, a Spaniard who had been shipwrecked on the coast of Brazil. Garcia was killed before he was able to pass on the news of the fabulous kingdom of the Inca to other Europeans. Two years later, in 1527, an ailing Huayna Capac was greatly disturbed by reports of white men who had been seen sailing along the coast near Tumbes, a city in the northern part of his kingdom. But they sailed away again. Surprisingly enough, practically nothing had filtered through to Peru of the white man's exploits farther north, although Columbus had made his landfall in the New World 35 years earlier in 1492.

The Inca emperor had become increasingly attached to his northern district of Quito and had married a princess of the former Quito kingdom. He decided to break with tradition and leave four-fifths of his vast and somewhat unwieldy empire to Huáscar,

Right: a gold funerary mask, decorated with emeralds from northern Peru. News of the Inca empire's great wealth brought the Spaniards to Peru as it had earlier drawn them to Mexico.

the legitimate heir, who was his principal wife's (his sister's) child. The remaining northern segment he left to Atahualpa, his son by the Quito princess. With this one action he called into question the inviolable rule governing the divine succession of the Inca. On his sudden death from illness in 1527, a civil war broke out between the two sons. Huáscar and Atahualpa vied for total dominion of the Inca empire. The savage war lasted until 1532. Atahualpa, backed by Huayna Capac's army and with the generals on his side, eventually defeated Huáscar before retiring with a leg wound to Cajamarca, a little-known sulfur spa in the central Peruvian highlands.

At this precise moment, word came to Atahualpa that: "People have arrived by a big ship from out of the sea, with different clothing, beards, and animals like llamas, only larger." Atahualpa, on a whim, decided to stay at this rest place, and delay his triumphant entry to Cusco until he had met the strangers. Now that he had beaten his only rival to the throne, he was the most powerful man alive whose every word was obeyed to the last letter. The quipu told him that there were less than 200 in the strange party that was approaching. If there was any trouble, he could easily snuff them out, as he was surrounded by thousands of his faithful warriors.

The Return of the Quetzalcoatl

4

Above: portrait of Hernando Cortes at the time of the Spanish conquest by a Tlaxcalan artist. The conquistador is wearing a hat similar to that worn by the god Quetzalcoatl. The Mexican belief that Cortes was the god returning from exile was reinforced by the Spaniard's clothing and appearance.

Left: the giving of power to Quetzalcoatl as interpreted by an Indian artist. At the top of the picture, the bearded Quetzalcoatl sits among the temples and attributes being bestowed upon him by the heavens. In the lower part, he is seen descending to earth by means of a rope ladder. On his head he wears the high-crowned hat that was identified with the god.

News of the discovery of the New World by Christopher Columbus in 1492 surged through Europe with earth-shaking force. Nothing would ever be the same. The Renaissance, a rebirth of learning and culture that began in Italy in the 1300's, was now in full flower. An irresistible spirit of inquiry, speculative thought, and invention broadened man's horizons. There was a sharp increase in commerce. Man became eager to increase his knowledge of the world around him. He was at liberty to question all things. Columbus revealed that the habitable world was a much vaster place than ever conceived. Renaissance Europe was now offered the tantalizing prospect of spreading its new spirit of learning to distant lands.

In 1504, the same year that Columbus returned to Spain after his fourth expedition to the New World, a 19-year-old Spaniard by the name of Hernando Cortes arrived in Santo Domingo on the Caribbean island of Hispaniola (present-day Dominican Republic and Haiti). Cortes was in the vanguard of a new breed of conquistadors—explorers who were eager to earn personal glory and riches while opening up new kingdoms for the Spanish king.

In Hispaniola, Cortes discovered that the Spanish settlers were rapidly becoming disenchanted. Many of them had emigrated more than 10 years earlier to make their fortunes in the New World. The majority of settlers were obliged to earn a living by tilling the land. The only consolation—and that limited to those favored with the right connections—was a grant of land from which they could build up an estate, however modest, that would have been beyond their means in Spain.

Cortes became a popular figure in the small community. He showed courage in the irregular skirmishes with the Indians, and was "a great hand at games of cards and dice," enjoying himself whether winning or losing. He commanded an early following of people attracted to him because of his frankness and a disarming manner that rose above the trivia of island disputes.

For the next few years, Cortes was cast in the role of gentleman farmer, cultivating crops and raising horses and sheep. But his restless spirit yearned for more activity. The opportunity arose in 1511, when Diego de Velásquez set out to conquer Cuba and appointed Cortes as his private secretary. After displaying his customary valor in subjugating the Cuban Indians, Cortes was given a choice of desirable property, to which he applied himself with

45

Above: Indian slaves work at a Spanish sugar plantation on the island of Hispaniola. Spain's early colonies in the New World depended on Indian labor for both farming and mining.

some industry. He made farming, mining, and livestock raising into a highly profitable undertaking. He was periodically in and out of favor with the corpulent Velásquez, who had been appointed first governor of Cuba. Cortes' reckless love affairs were disruptive to the new colony and he was suspected of intrigue against the person of the governor.

On February 8, 1517, Velásquez sent Francisco Fernández de Córdoba to explore the west and search for treasure. Once in the open sea, a furious storm drove Córdoba off course. Three weeks later he made landfall on an unfamiliar shoreline. Clambering on land, he and his men were astonished to seé evidence of an Indian civilization that no one had till then imagined possible. Here were houses of stone and elaborately carved temples fashioned like pyramids. The inhabitants were colorfully dressed in finely woven cotton garments.

Córdoba had landed on the Yucatán Peninsula, directly west of

Cuba. There, the most brilliant of pre-Columbian American civilizations, the Maya, once held sway. Unlike the docile Arawak who inhabited the islands of the Caribbean, the mainland Indians were defiant. They drove Córdoba and his party away with a shower of stones and arrows. Rounding the cape of the peninsula and heading southwest to Campeche, a southeastern Mexican state, the party again encountered Indian hostility. Reluctantly, after suffering many casualties, Córdoba decided to return to Cuba, carrying with him some finely wrought specimens of gold.

The following year, on May 1, 1518, Velásquez sent out a second expedition to follow up Córdoba's discoveries. Under the command of Juan de Grijalva, the Spaniards sailed up the coast of the Yucatán Peninsula, rounded Cape Catoche and turned west into the Gulf of Mexico. Landing at Champoton, one of the cities where Córdoba's men had suffered heavy losses the year before, Grijalva beat off a strong attack from the inhabitants. He was as astounded as his predecessor had been by the stone temples and plazas, the large towns teeming with people, and the fields of cultivated maize. Resuming his westward path he now ventured into areas beyond Córdoba's route. In what is today the state of Tabasco, he found Indians prepared to parley. From them he first heard of a land called Mexico, a powerful inland state where there was a plentiful supply of gold.

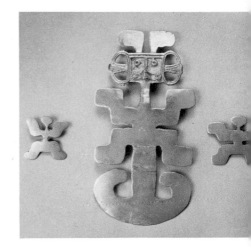

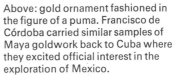

Above: gold ornament fashioned in the figure of a puma. Francisco de Córdoba carried similar samples of Maya goldwork back to Cuba where they excited official interest in the exploration of Mexico.

Left: Francisco de Córdoba's expedition sails along the coast of Yucatán after being blown off course by a storm. Córdoba was the first Spaniard to encounter traces of the Maya culture.

47

About 200 miles away, in Tenochtitlán, the Aztec capital of Mexico, Montezuma II had been following Grijalva's every move over the past month. Fleet-footed spies brought him details of the ships, the number of men-at-arms, and other descriptions by means of picture writing recorded on parchment. Montezuma was anxious to know more. These men answered in almost every detail the prophesied return of the god Quetzalcoatl. The white faces, the beards, and the supernatural weapons of the Spaniards corresponded to Indian legend.

The prophesy said that Quetzalcoatl would return in the Aztec year Ce Acatl. This was to be 1519, the following year. Surely this was the god come to reclaim his throne. The utmost hospitality must be extended, and if fate so decreed, the benign deity might be pleased to delay his return until Montezuma, who was now middle aged, had concluded his reign.

The emperor sent a trusted chieftain and his slave to the coast to report personally on the strangers. Their news was disturbing: "... in the middle of the water [we saw] a house from which appeared white men, their faces white and their hands likewise. They have long thick beards and their clothing is of all colors: white, yellow, red, green, blue, and purple. On their heads they wear round coverings. They put a rather large canoe in the water, some of them jump into it and they fish all day near the rocks. At dusk they return to the home into which they are gathered. This is all we can tell you about that which you wish to know."

Montezuma instructed his two emissaries to return to the coast. This time they were told to make contact with the strangers and give them gold, precious stones, and some styled feather work. "If it is really Quetzalcoatl greet him on my behalf, and give him these gifts. You must also order the governor of Cuetlaztla to provide him with all kinds of food, cooked birds, and game. Let him also be given types of bread that are baked, together with fruit and gourds of chocolate." And, presumably as an acid test of identity, the emissaries were ordered to "notice very carefully whether he eats or not. If he eats and drinks he is surely Quetzalcoatl and this will show that he is familiar with the foods of this land, that he ate them once and has come back to savor them again." Then Montezuma concluded: "Also tell him to allow me to die. After my death he will be welcome to come here and take possession of his kingdom, as it is his. ... Let

Above: Indian canoes attempt to capture one of Juan de Grijalva's ships in the Panuco River. Grijalva explored the Yucatán coast as far north as Tabasco where he first learned of the fabulous kingdom of Mexico.

Top left: Montezuma's emissaries carry gifts to the Spaniards.

Center left: the Indian ambassadors, unaccustomed to Spanish wine, "lost their sense" and were forced to spend the night aboard ship.

Left: the emissaries return to Montezuma with a gift of glass beads and report on the strange visitors and their ships, "more divine than human."

him permit me to end my days here. Then let him return to enjoy what is his!"

Shortly before dawn of the next day, the gifts and food were laid down on the beach and the two envoys waited for sunrise and the Spaniards. When Grijalva saw the Mexicans, he invited them aboard ship. The cabins and the rigging seemed to the Indians, "a thing more divine than human." The Spaniards thoroughly enjoyed the strange food. With "much laughing and sporting," they became the first Europeans to feast on turkey and chocolate. These must have been doubly welcome as Grijalva was nearing the end of his journey, and his supplies were low. Not to be outdone in hospitality, they offered the Indians the rather unappetizing ships' rations of jerked beef, bacon, and stale biscuits. Then Grijalva offered them some wine and after the first sip "their hearts were gladdened." But being unaccustomed to it, they "lost their sense" and had to spend the night aboard ship to recover. Before sailing away, the strangers intimated by sign language that they would return. In parting they gave the Mexicans a necklace to present to their sovereign.

The emissaries returned to Tenochtitlán and presented Montezuma with the necklace of glass beads, which he mistook for precious stones. Then they offered him the biscuit that the gods had given them. The king tasted it and said it was like tufa stone—a calcium carbonate deposit often found in river beds. He sent for a piece of the latter and solemnly weighed one against the other, discovering that the rock weighed less. He then summoned his dwarfs to taste it. Finally, Montezuma claimed that he was afraid to eat it as it

49

Left: the Aztec emperor, Montezuma, as pictured by a Spanish artist in the late 1600's. The crowned ruler is seen surrounded by the wealth and splendor of the Aztec empire, as he is borne by his nobles through the streets of Tenochtitlán.

"belonged to the gods and it would be sacrilege." The priests were instructed to bury it outside city limits. With due ceremony the biscuit was transported to Tula (or Tollan), ancient capital of the earlier Toltec civilization, where it was buried at the temple of Quetzalcoatl. On learning of the strangers' intended return, all the thinly suppressed fears, anxieties, and conflicting emotions returned to Montezuma. He needed no more reassurance that the god Quetzalcoatl was indeed returning on the scheduled date.

After naming the region he had explored *New Spain,* Grijalva returned to Cuba with samples of gold and stories of greater treas-

Above: the Temple of Quetzalcoatl at Tula, the ancient capital of the Toltec civilization. Believing that the biscuit sent to him by Grijalva "belonged to the gods." Montezuma ordered it to be carried to Tula and buried.

ures. Instead of a hero's welcome, Grijalva was subjected to a torrent of abuse from Velásquez. The governor was furious that he had adhered so rigidly to his instructions and had not established a settlement in the territory of his new discoveries.

Now that the rumor of a fabulous kingdom to the west bore some measure of authenticity, Governor Velásquez was anxious to stake his claim before others got around to it. He hurried preparations for a new, much larger, expeditionary force, while casting an eye around for someone to head it. His choice fell on his former secretary, Cortes, who had been waiting for just such an opportunity. By mortgaging his property, Cortes contributed the bulk of the cost of outfitting the expedition. Velásquez advanced the remainder. Soon, however, the unpredictable Velásquez thought he detected a change in his protégé's demeanor. He predicted with absolute certainty that Cortes would flout his authority. Velásquez was encouraged in this belief by relatives and others who coveted Cortes' command.

Cortes was warned that Velásquez was seriously considering an alternative choice to lead the expedition. But before his appointment could be revoked, Cortes led his tiny fleet clandestinely out of Santiago de Cuba Harbor on the southern coast of Cuba. He spent the next couple of months sailing along the southern coast of Cuba, picking up more recruits and supplies while ignoring Valásquez' summons to return. At last all was ready. On February 18, 1519, Cortes set sail with a force of about 550 soldiers, 11 ships, 16 horses, 10 brass guns, and 4 small cannons, called falconets.

Cortes headed for Cozumel Island off the coast of Yucatán. When he arrived, he discovered that several of his party had landed before him and had robbed the Indians of much of their possessions. Incensed at this irresponsible behavior, he upbraided the leader, the headstrong Pedro de Alvarado, and ordered all the looted goods be returned to the Indians. "We should never pacify the country in that way by robbing Indians of their property," Cortes declared.

Cortes was always at pains to adhere to proper diplomatic preliminaries. On Cozumel, his first act was to order the reading of the *requerimento* to the Indians. This was a rarely understood document from the King of Spain that invited Indians to become subjects of Spain and take up the true faith in peace. If they refused, the document ordered that "war shall be made on them with fire and sword,

and they shall be killed and enslaved." Before leaving the island, Cortes rescued a Spanish castaway, Jeronimo de Aguilar, who had been a slave to an Indian *cacique* (chieftain) for the past eight years. As Aguilar was fluent in the Maya tongue, he became a welcome addition to the party as an interpreter. In order to replenish food and water supplies, Cortes headed for Tabasco, the spot where Grijalva had met with friendly Indians the year before. But on this occasion the Spaniards' overtures were met with a rebuff. The Tabascans had been taunted by their neighbors for their cowardly behavior in not

Left: Malinche, an Indian princess who became Cortes' translator, interprets the words of a Mexican cacique to the conquistador. Called *Dona Marina* by the Spaniards, Malinche was presented to Cortes as part of the spoils from the battle of Tabasco. She became his loyal and devoted mistress.

Left: "Battle of Tabasco," by an unknown Spanish artist in the 1600's. Cortes and his men were met with angry defiance when they landed on the coast of Tabasco. In his first major battle on Mexican soil, the conquistador demonstrated his skill as a strategist by defeating an Indian army that outnumbered his forces by 30 to 1.

HERNAN CORES

Above: perhaps the most authentic likeness of Cortes, this drawing was made by Franz Weiditz in the 1500's. Weiditz is believed to have met the conqueror in Spain several years after the conquest of Mexico.

Left: portrait by an unknown artist of Hernando Cortes as a young man. This heroic likeness, painted many years after the conquistador's death, presents an idealized picture of what the conqueror of Mexico looked like.

attacking Grijalva's party. Fighting broke out and 12,000 Tabascan warriors took the field, outnumbering Cortes' small force 30 to 1. However, superior tactics together with advantages of musket, cannon, and steel sword prevailed over native spear, lance, and sling. The battle is vividly described by Bernard Diaz del Castillo, a member of Cortes' expedition who wrote an eyewitness account of the Spanish conquest of Mexico. "I remember," says Diaz, "that when we fired shots the Indians gave great shouts and whistles and threw dust and rubbish into the air so that we should not see the danger done to them, and they sounded their trumpets and drums and shouted and whistled and cried 'Alala! Alala!'" But the cavalry terminated the conflict abruptly. "Just at this time we caught sight of our horsemen," continues Diaz, "and as the great Indian host was crazed with its attack on us, it did not at once perceive them coming up behind their backs . . . they came quickly on the enemy and speared them as they chose. As soon as we saw the horsemen we fell on the Indians with such energy that with us attacking on one side and the horsemen on the other, they soon turned tail. The Indians thought that the horse and its rider was all one animal, for they had never seen horses up to this time."

The battle was won by the Spaniards. The caciques swore allegiance to the Spanish king and became Christian subjects. Food, gold, and other treasures were then brought to the victors. Among the valuable gifts presented to Cortes were 20 Tabascan girls. One of them, called Malinche, became his devoted and loyal mistress and later bore him a son, Don Martin Cortes. Diaz recalls that the Spaniards christened her Dona Marina, because "she was truly a great chieftainess and the daughter of great Caciques. . . ." Malinche spoke both *Nahuatl*, the Aztec language, and Mayan, the language Aguilar knew. Between the two of them, Cortes now had an interpreting team that could enable him to make contact wherever he went. Soon, the bright Malinche picked up Spanish and replaced Aguilar as Cortes' mouthpiece. Cortes was to rely more and more on her other qualities, her tact and counsel, which he was wise enough to heed from the start.

Cortes now continued along the coast until he reached a point on the coast near the island of San Juan de Ulua. Montezuma, anticipating Quetzalcoatl's return, had dispatched emissaries to the coast days earlier. They were waiting to greet the returning god. When the

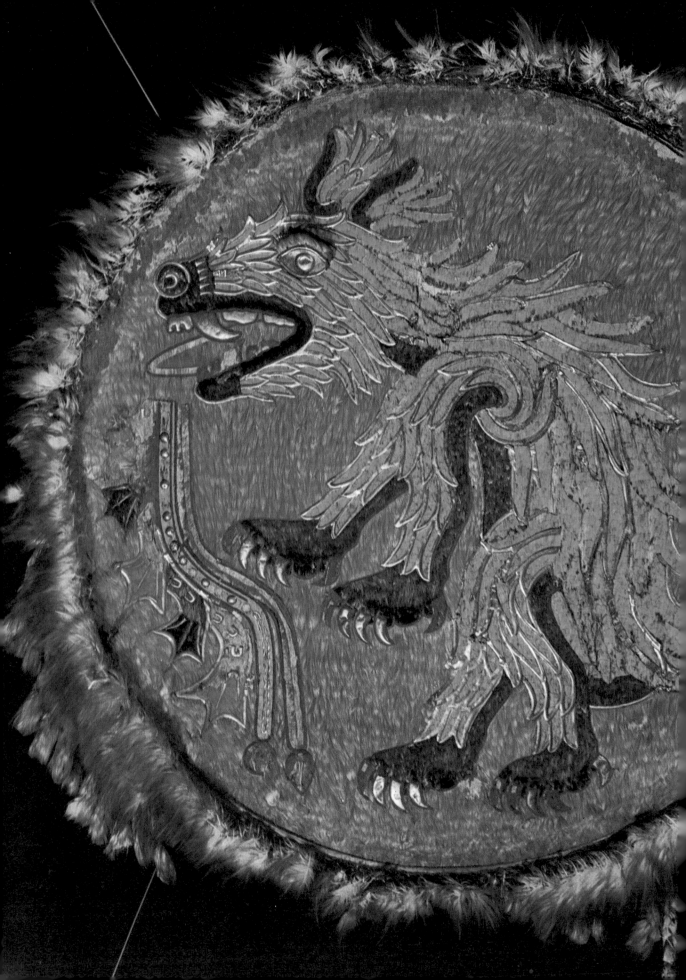

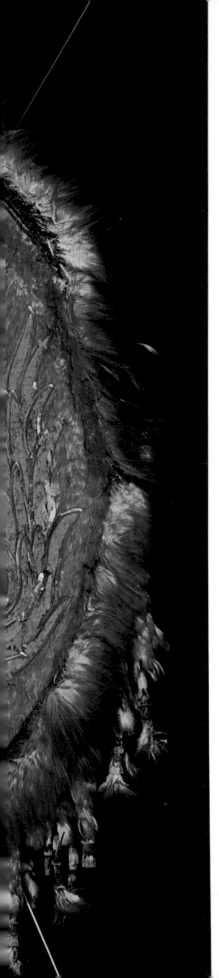

Spaniards appeared, the Mexicans went aboard and welcomed Cortes
in the name of their emperor. On Friday, April 22, 1519, Cortes gave
the order to disembark on the mainland. By an extraordinary coincidence, he had landed not only in the same year and month as
Quetzalcoatl promised to return, but also on the very day named by
the prophesy. The person who was the least surprised by this time
was Montezuma. Since Grijalva's appearance the previous year, the
Aztec emperor had been convinced that the deity would arrive at the
appointed hour.

Montezuma was in a quandary: to which of the two major gods
should he turn? Should he choose Quetzalcoatl, the gentle deity who
eschewed human sacrifice, or the god of war and sun, Huitzilopochtli, who demanded incessant human sacrifice and who had driven
out Quetzalcoatl? After much soul-searching and numerous con-
sultations with his ministers, priests, and soothsayers, Montezuma
decided he could not risk offending either god. Least of all, as emperor of the Chosen People of the Sun, could he afford to offend
their ancient tribal deity, Huitzilopochtli. Accordingly, he decided to
lavish goods on the god Quetzalcoatl whom he saw in the person of
Cortes. If not remorselessly bent on revenge, Quetzalcoatl might be
persuaded to leave.

When Cortes received the gifts intended for Quetzalcoatl he was
astonished at the treasures of which he was now the proud possessor.
As he did not yet understand the significance of these offerings, he
was overwhelmed by the generosity of the emperor. "The first
article presented was a wheel like a sun, as big as a cartwheel, with
many sorts of pictures on it, the whole of fine gold, and a wonderful
thing to behold, which those who afterwards weighed it said was
worth more than $10,000. Then another wheel was presented of
greater size made of silver of great brilliancy in imitation of the moon
with other figures shown on it, and this was of great value as it was
very heavy."

The royal gifts that were intended to hasten Quetzalcoatl's
departure had the reverse effect on Cortes. Nothing would be toler-
ated that stood in the way of his coming face-to-face with his ad
versary. "I intended," he wrote to his king, "to advance and see him
wherever he might be found," and vowed he "would bring him
either dead or in chains if he would not submit . . . to your Majesty's
crown."

The Fall of Tenochtitlán

5

Cortes and his men had landed on a melancholy strip of the Mexican coast. They called the low, sandy, mosquito-ridden area *Tierra Caliente* (literally, hot land). The army suffered severely from the hot, fetid swamps. Thirty men died, some from tropical fever, others from wounds received at Tabasco. Cortes led his force farther north to a more attractive spot and it was here that he threw off the yoke of Velásquez. He had himself elected captain and chief justice of a new colony, and the municipality of Veracruz, the first of its kind in New Spain, henceforth recognized the authority of none but the King of Spain (who as Charles V, was elected Holy Roman Emperor in 1519).

Cortes was careful to preserve the appearance of legality in his usurpation of Velásquez' control. He sent one of his ships back to Spain with a letter to the king explaining his action. He reinforced his claim by turning over the entire treasure he had received from Montezuma to the king.

Cortes was determined to march on the Aztec capital. To make certain that others would share his resolve he sank his entire fleet. Thus he removed the last opportunity for the fainthearted to return to Cuba. In the meantime he had been visited by emissaries from a cacique of the Totonac federation of cities in the area. They com-

Above: arrival of Cortes at Veracruz. Spanish horsemen gallop along the beach to the roar of cannons. In the upper left-hand corner, a delegation of ambassadors from Montezuma witnesses the landing of the Spanish forces.

plained of the intolerable burden of being a vassal state of the Aztec and asked for help against their oppressors. Diaz notes Cortes' reaction to this request. "As he stood there thinking the matter over, he said laughingly to some of us companions who were with him: 'Do you know, gentlemen, that it seems to me that we have already gained a great reputation for valor throughout this country . . . the people here take us for gods or beings like their idols.' "

The shrewd Cortes, preposterously outnumbered, now had the germ of a solution to Montezuma's vulnerability. If the Totonac Indians were smoldering with discontent, there might be many other tribute-paying states of similar disposition. Under his direction these combined forces could topple Montezuma and his loosely-knit empire. With an army consisting of 400 men, 15 horses, and 16 cannon, Cortes set off on the first leg of his 200-mile march to the Aztec capital. A small garrison was detailed to guard the new settlement at Veracruz. At Cempoala, the Totonac capital, the cacique provided the Spaniards with 100 porters and "40 chieftains, all warriors." The cacique advised Cortes to pass through Tlaxcala, where the inhabitants, hostile to the Aztec, might prove allies.

Above: the sinking of the fleet that had carried Cortes and his men to Mexico. Before setting out for the interior, Cortes gave the command for the ships to be scuttled. The conquistador was "determined to make my way in this land or die here."

The Spaniards left Cempoala in mid-August of 1519, and two weeks later crossed the borders into Tlaxcala. The Tlaxcalan Indians had never been subjugated by the Aztec. Cortes' dealings with Montezuma's emissaries and the Aztec vassal state of the Totonac, made the Tlaxcalan suspicious. Their attitude was blunt: "We will kill those *teules* (gods) and eat their flesh." And they attacked without negotiation.

There is no doubt that Cortes' tiny force was hopelessly outnumbered and this time they were faced by a people who were more warlike than the coastal tribes, and who made more effective use of their weaponry. They were particularly adept with the spear thrower, which, in the hands of a skilled warrior, was a devastating weapon.

During a lull in the fighting, 50 envoys of the Tlaxcalan came to the camp, ostensibly on a peace-making mission. When interrogated separately, they confessed to being spies. Cortes returned them all to their chieftains with their hands cut off. The fighting continued and the Spaniards were again victorious. The Indians submitted to Cortes, acknowledging: "We have done all we could to kill you and your companions, but our gods are worthless against you. We have determined to be your friends and serve you, and because in this province we are surrounded on all sides by our enemies, we beg you to protect us against them, and to come to our city of Tlaxcala to rest from the labors we have given you." The addition of the Tlaxcalan army was the turning point in Cortes' fortunes. Through all times, whether good or bad, he could not have found more steadfast allies.

It was while at Tlaxcala that Cortes heard from Montezuma again. This time Montezuma invited the Spaniards to come to Tenochtitlán, and suggested that they pass through Cholula on the way. Cholula was the sacred city of Quetzalcoatl. In addition to 400 temples, the city boasted a pyramid larger than the Great Pyramid in Egypt. Cortes' Tlaxcalan allies warned him that the Cholula route was a trap. When Cortes insisted that he would go anyway, he was given a bodyguard of 600 warriors.

Now only Cholula lay between Cortes and his ultimate goal, Tenochtitlán, 80 miles distant. The Cholulan who came out to greet him took exception to the presence of their sworn foes, the Tlaxcalan. Cortes ordered his allies to stay beyond the outskirts of the city while he and his men retired to quarters in the main temple precincts. After several days Malinche warned Cortes of a plot to wipe out the Spaniards. Cortes reacted quickly. He invited the city's warriors, caciques, and other leading dignitaries into the temple enclosure. At a given signal, the unarmed Cholulan were fired upon and then put to the sword.

The road now lay open to Tenochtitlán. One week and 60 miles separated Cortes from Montezuma. By this time, nearly all the Spaniards shared their leader's enthusiasm to complete the historic journey. Cortes turned down the offer of a fighting force of 10,000 Tlaxcalan warriors, requesting instead that 1,000 Indians accompany the Spaniards as porters.

Below: the Tlaxcalan sue for peace. After a fierce battle, Cortes defeated the Tlaxcalan army and made an alliance with them against the Aztec. The Tlaxcalan were to prove themselves the most steadfast and loyal of the Spaniards' Indian allies.

Below: massacre of Indians at Cholula. This watercolor shows both men and women being beaten and killed while struggling under the heavy burden of the Spaniards' luggage. Cortes ordered the massacre as punishment for a supposed Indian plot against the lives of the Spanish soldiers.

Above: valley of the Pasa Cortes through which Cortes marched on his way to Tenochtitlán. The pass lies between the twin volcanoes, left, Popocatépetl (smoking mountain) and, right, Ixtacihuatl (white woman). Below : an Indian artist depicts Cortes' forces emerging from the Pasa Cortes into the Valley of Mexico.

On November 1, 1519, the army took its leave of Cholula, a city in mourning. Towering before them, 20 miles distant, were the famous volcanoes, Popocatépetl (*smoking mountain*), and the two-breasted Ixtacihuatl (*white woman*). Cortes' route lay directly between the two giant snow-capped mountains, both soaring skyward to a height of over 17,000 feet above sea level. Slicing through the pine trees, icy gusts of wind swept down the mountain slopes as the army climbed higher up the rugged terrain. The battle-hardened soldiers shivered in their cotton-quilted jackets. The horses became unnerved. Ice, snow, and sleet slowed them to a crawl. When dusk fell, Cortes ordered his men to halt for the night. They camped about six miles short of the top of the pass.

The next morning they continued to the top. Crossing the last ridge, the Spaniards stopped short and gazed in awe at the spectacle confronting them. Below, thirty cities were evenly sprinkled in all directions. The jewel of all was the island-city of Tenochtitlán. Its gleaming white temples and white plastered houses were interspersed with trees and surrounded by the shimmering blue waters of Lake Texcoco. Their wonder increasing at every step, the Spaniards made their way to the gates of Tenochtitlán.

Montezuma came out to meet the Spaniards. Nobles lined the sides of a broad avenue as Montezuma was borne past on a golden, jewel-

Above: The Old World meets the New. A Spanish painting of the 1600's shows the epic confrontation between Cortes and Montezuma—the explorer dressed in the armor of medieval Europe and the emperor of the Aztec clothed in the riches of Mexico.

studded litter. A green canopy, decorated with tail feathers of the sacred Ouetzal bird, shaded the emperor from the sun. Courtiers swept the ground, laying down cotton cloths before the path of the royal litter. The nobles averted their eyes as the emperor passed, not daring to look him in the face as he readied to greet the heavensent strangers from across the sea. Montezuma was richly attired. While his nobles went barefoot, the emperor wore gold sandals encrusted with precious stones.

Cortes and Montezuma at last met face-to-face. The Mexican version of this historic confrontation is recorded in Bernardino de Sahagún's *General History of the Things of New Spain*.

" 'Is it true that you are the king Montezuma?' asked Cortes. And the king said: 'Yes I am Montezuma.' Then he stood up to welcome Cortes; he came forward, bowed his head low and addressed him in

these words: 'Our lord, you are weary. The journey has tired you, but now you have arrived on earth. You have come to your city, Mexico. You have come back to sit on your throne, to sit under its canopy. The kings who have gone before, your representatives, guarded it and preserved it for your coming. . . . Do the kings know the destiny of those they left behind, their posterity? If only they are watching! If only they can see what I see! No, it is in my dreams. . . . I have seen you at last! I have met you face to face! I was in agony for five days, for ten days, with my eyes fixed on the Region of Mystery. And now you have come out of the clouds and mists to sit on your throne again. This was foretold by the kings who governed your city, and now it has taken place. You have come back to us; you have come down from the sky. Rest now, and take possession of your royal houses. Welcome to your land, my lords!'

Above: map of the city of Tenochtitlán made under the supervision of Cortes. It shows the three main causeways leading into the city. At the center is an enlargement of the temple area— the heart of the Aztec capital.

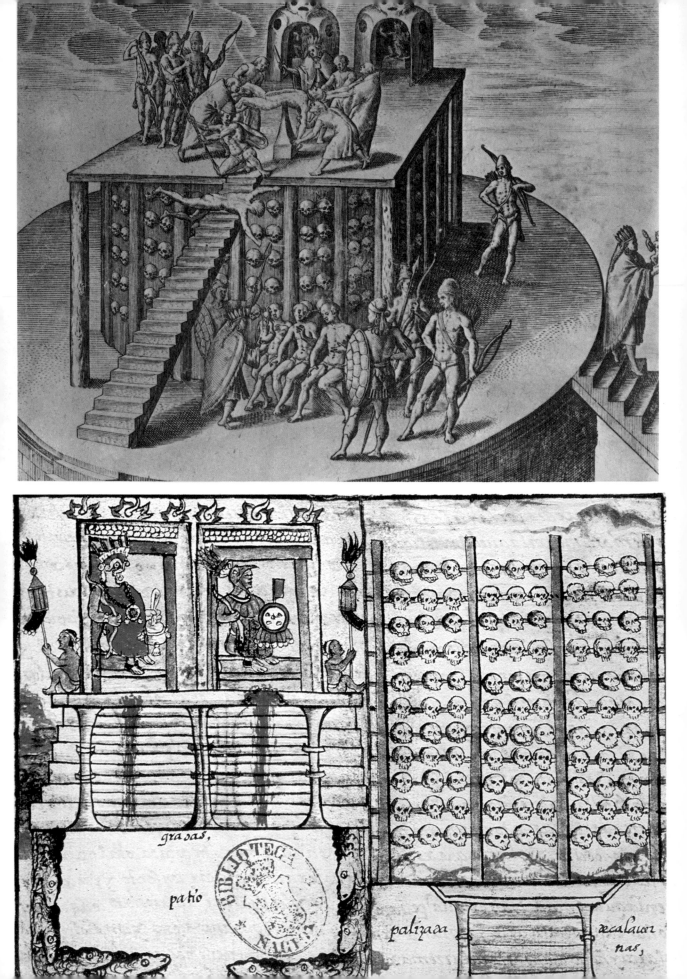

grasas,

patio

palizaa

æcalacoa
nas,

"Cortes replied: 'Tell Montezuma that we are his friends. There is nothing to fear. We have wanted to see him for a long time, and now we have seen his face and heard his words. Tell him that we love him and that our hearts are contented.' "

The Spaniards were housed in a magnificent palace fronting the main plaza of Tenochtitlán. The temple of Huitzilopochtli that dominated the city separated the newcomers from the emperor's palace. Here, each day, the Spaniards were obliged to witness the horrors of human sacrifice. The dead victim, his heart excised, was hurled from the top of the temple. Choice limbs were saved for the repasts of priests and nobles while the torsos were tossed to the hungry beasts in the adjoining zoo. A skull rack, called a *tzompantli,* stood nearby. It contained 136,000 human skulls—victims of this religious sacrifice.

Cortes was treated graciously by Montezuma, but was always on the alert. Despite the hospitality of his host, he disliked the idea that his very existence hung on the slender thread of the emperor's caprice. And although Montezuma seemed well disposed at the moment, he could easily change his mind. After one week, Cortes decided on a daring maneuver: He would take the emperor prisoner and at once achieve dominion over the Aztec. Montezuma would remain as ruler in name only, a puppet-king.

To accomplish this bold plan, Cortes took 30 armed soldiers, his most trusted captains, and the loyal Malinche, to the emperor's palace. He declared that he had come to take the emperor to his lodgings for surveillance. At first the emperor was incredulous that anyone—god or not god—could behave with such audacity. But Malinche's quiet insistence that he would be killed on the spot unless he complied stopped all further remonstrations on his part. The emperor was borne away on his litter, seemingly resigned to his fate, while vainly attempting to reassure his weeping nobles that all was well and everything would be back to normal shortly. Though Cortes encouraged Montezuma to conduct government business from his new domicile, the emperor suffered no illusions that his status was anything but a crude version of house arrest. His subjects, unused to acting without a leader, were stunned into submission. Montezuma was made to undergo a ceremony as humiliating to his councilors as the abduction from the royal palace. He was forced to swear allegiance to the Spanish king.

Above: Montezuma, in captivity, receives Cortes and his officers. Although surrounded by the semblance of power, Montezuma was reduced to the status of a puppet ruler and forced to swear allegiance to the Spanish king.

One day Cortes, struck by the priests' insolent mocking of his explanations of Christianity, could contain his evangelical wrath no longer. "Oh God! Why do you permit such great honor paid the Devil in this land? Oh Lord, it is good that we are here to serve you." An eyewitness account then describes what followed, as Cortes addressed the temple priests. " 'It will give me great pleasure to fight for my God against your gods, who are a mere nothing.' Before the men he had sent for arrived, Cortes took up an iron bar that was there and began to smash the stone idols."

With this single action, Cortes dashed all hopes of ever gaining the Aztec empire by peaceful means. He had undone the incredible gains he had achieved by skill, courage, diplomacy, guile, and luck. He had committed the unpardonable sin of meddling with the gods who controlled the cosmic forces. Each blow delivered at Huitzilopochtli struck at the very core of Aztec belief. Montezuma, horrified at Cortes' sacriligious excess, and brooking no further nonsense on this score, warned that he had only to lift one finger and the whole populace would storm the building. Cortes believed him. As the

Above: Montezuma leads the Spaniards to the treasure of the Aztec kings. A contemporary account of the conquest states that in their search for gold, the Spaniards "did not leave a corner or chamber unsearched or undisturbed." Below left: besieged by Aztec warriors, Alvarado and his men seek refuge in their quarters after brutally massacring unarmed Aztec men and women during a religious festival.

priests were already inciting the people to rebellion, Montezuma continued, the Spaniards' only chance of survival was to leave the city immediately.

With the Aztec on the point of uprising, events now took a turn for the worse from an unexpected quarter. A messenger on the coast reported that a substantial force had arrived from Cuba to overthrow the rebel. The situation was dangerous because many of Cortes' soldiers were in distant provinces collecting gold. Leaving Alvarado in charge at Tenochtitlán, Cortes set out with 70 men to Cempoala where the Cuban force was encamped. Under the twin covers of night and a heavy rainfall, Cortes' men took the rebels by surprise and defeated them. Cortes had only a few moments, however, to enjoy his victory. Messengers brought the news that Alvarado was besieged in the capital.

During Cortes' absence Alvarado had given permission for the Mexicans to celebrate the solemn feast of Toxcatl, during which the idol of Huitzilopochtli was moved from one temple to another. On the day of the feast, thousands of Aztec men, unarmed and dressed only in rich plumes and precious jewels, gathered in the city's main square to begin a ritual dance. Whether in fear of so large an assemblage of warriors, or aroused by the great wealth that adorned the dancers, Alvarado gave his soldiers the signal to attack. The brutal massacre that followed has been called "the most atrocious act ever committed in this land: the end of the flower and nobility of Mexico." Alvarado and his men took refuge in the palace where they were besieged by the outraged population of Tenochtitlán.

When Cortes returned to Tenochtitlán, the city was deathly still. On the whole, Cortes was in a good frame of mind. He had not had to fight his way back into the capital as expected. Many soldiers from the Cuban force had defected to Cortes, and strengthened the Spanish army threefold. Having achieved the near impossible with but 400 men, Cortes felt confident he could handle almost any crisis from now on. But what he failed to understand was that the one man who could guarantee his immunity was now powerless. The high council was already deliberating on a successor to Montezuma.

Below: from the roof of his palace, Montezuma begs the Aztec to make peace with the Spaniards. Roused to fever pitch, the Indians responded with a hail of arrows and stones, one of which is believed to have fatally wounded the Aztec emperor.

In an attempt to negotiate the reopening of the market, Cortes released from custody the emperor's brother Cuitlahuac. Unwittingly, he had provided the Aztec with their next leader. Led by Cuitlahuac, the Aztec attacked the following day. The Spaniards were surprised at the fury of their assailants. "Neither cannon nor muskets nor crossbows availed, nor hand-to-hand fighting, nor killing 30 or 40 of them every time we charged, for they still fought on in as close ranks and with more energy than in the beginning. . . ." noted Diaz, the Spanish commentator.

On the fifth day of hostilities, Cortes summoned Montezuma to address his people, giving the assurance that the Spaniards would leave if granted safe conduct out of the city. Montezuma reluctantly agreed to appeal to his people but knew in his own heart that it would be useless. His authority had been transferred to his brother, Cuitlahuac. For this event, he dressed himself in his imperial robes. All fighting ceased when he stood on the palace rooftop. His presence still commanded a respectful silence. But as soon as reference was made to the Spaniards, who stood on either side of him there arose an angry roar. A volley of arrows, stones, and darts was let loose at the odious intruders. Montezuma was struck by three stones, one on the temple wounding him fatally.

Cortes realized that his chances of survival were growing slimmer the longer he stayed in the capital. The only alternative was to attempt a breakthrough to the mainland. The shortest route was to the west to Tacuba, a distance of only two miles. The causeway, however, was linked by eight bridges that had all been removed. Cortes ordered the construction of a portable bridge, with the idea of transporting it to cover the gaps as they advanced. On the day Montezuma died, Cortes drew up his final plans.

Shortly before midnight, on June 30, 1520, afterward known as *La Noche Triste,* the army stole out of the palace. Under the cover of darkness the Spaniards crossed the deserted city. The alarm was soon sounded. Priests banged on snake drums, and the great booming sounds reverberated throughout the valley. Suddenly the city came alive. The lake was a mass of canoes speeding toward the causeway to cut off the escape route. The portable bridge had to be abandoned. By now arrows, stones, darts, and javelins were hurled from canoes. Plunging down off the side of the causeway, the lucky Spaniards drowned, the others screamed as they were hauled off for sacrifice. Swords hacked through flesh. The yells, whistles, and shrieks were deafening. Carcasses of horses, human bodies, cannon, and treasure formed the inanimate bridge over which the soldiers passed from one gap to the next. Cortes was now on the mainland, and like the others, streaming blood from his wounds. Malinche, too, was safe.

But Alvarado and the rear section were in trouble. Cortes galloped back and plunged into a sea of canoes. Struggling on to the causeway and across the next gap, he saw his comrade on the other side. Alvarado was surrounded by the enemy. The Aztec recognized with glee the man they had nicknamed *Tonatio* (the sun). Suddenly,

Above: on June 30, 1520, Cortes and his men began their retreat from the Aztec capital. The Spaniards called it *La Noche Triste,* "the sad night," because so many of their number perished at the hands of frenzied Aztec warriors. The streets and canals of Tenochtitlán were choked with the mangled bodies of men and horses. According to one Spanish chronicler, on that night "Cortes lost seven hundred men, all of them cut to pieces mercilessly."

Left: Indian drawing showing Spanish soldiers tossing the bodies of Montezuma and one of his chiefs into a canal. Many Aztec sources claim that Montezuma was murdered by the Spaniards, and not by his own people.

Alvarado took his lance, plunged it into the melee of bodies and canoes, and vaulted to safety. Together, Alvarado and Cortes fought their way back to the mainland. The gray light of dawn exposed the wreckage of their flight. While his army regrouped, Cortes looked back toward the city and saw the utter desolation left in their trail. More than two-thirds of his force was destroyed. He turned and wept sad, bitter tears, under a cypress tree, *El Arbol de la Noche Triste,* which still stands in this sector of Mexico City to commemorate the incident.

The Spaniards' troubles, however, were far from over. They had more than 100 miles of Aztec territory to cross before reaching Tlaxcala, the land of their allies. Cortes rallied his men, although all were drained of energy through hunger and exertion. After a final clash with the Aztec forces, during which they overcame incredible odds, the Spaniards crossed into Tlaxcalan territory.

They received a warm welcome from their allies, whose admiration for the white strangers was further increased by their having escaped with their lives from the island-fortress of Tenochtitlán.

Cortes immediately began to make preparations for an all-out assault on the Aztec capital. Ten months later he was ready. In May, 1521, he attacked Tenochtitlán, his tactic being to lay siege to the city in the lake by severing its links with the mainland. To achieve this involuntary embargo that would prevent canoes bringing merchandise to the island, he built brigantines (small vessels) and at once gained control of the lake. Then he cut off the fresh water supply from Chapultepec. Now followed the most ferocious fighting of the Spanish incursion into the New World as the courageous Aztec defended their city to the last man, preferring death to surrender.

For 80 days the Aztec held out as one by one the beautiful buildings, palaces, and houses were razed to the ground. Montezuma's 22-year-old nephew, Cuauhtémoc, was now the emperor. (Cuitlahuac had died of smallpox after reigning only four months). Cortes was nearly captured on two occasions but managed to escape the fate reserved for his less fortunate comrades, who every day were offered to the gods. The ominous sound of the snake drum would signal the commencement of this ghastly rite, the platform above the temple steps elevated so as to be in full view of the watching conquistadors. The captive Spaniard, adorned in feathers, was made

Right: Cortes began his seige of Tenochtitlán in May of 1521. Refusing to surrender to the Spaniards, the Aztec saw their city burned to the ground. In this drawing from the Codex Azcatitlan, Indian warriors are seen defending the sacred temple —the last Aztec stronghold.

Below: capture of Cuauhtémoc, last emperor of the Aztec. According to Indian history, Cuauhtémoc begged his captors to "tell the captain [Cortes] that I have done my duty. . . . But I have failed. Now that I am his captive, let him take this dagger and kill me with it."

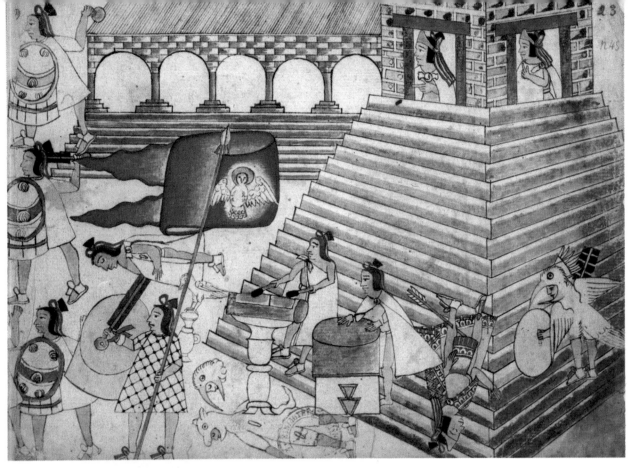

to perform a grotesque dance in front of the idols before he was stretched over the sacrificial stone.

But in the surrounding city of Tenochtitlán itself, conditions were wretched beyond belief. Disease ravaged the entire island community. The city was in ruins except for a small enclave around the market precinct of Tlatelolco. Women and children clawed their way across the causeways, swaying and collapsing, to strip the trees for bark, or grovel in the ground for insects or worms, anything to satisfy their desperate pangs of hunger. Cortes begged the Aztec to surrender, but Cuauhtémoc still would not give in. "I know not how to free ourselves without destroying their city—the most beautiful city in the world... we found them more undaunted than ever... the plan was to demolish every house as we penetrated into the city and not to advance a step until all was level with the ground." Finally, on August 13, 1521, Cuauhtémoc was captured. Nothing but masonry rubble remained to remind the onlooker of the glories of the Aztec past.

Cortes began to rebuild the city. He erected a cathedral on the site where the temple of Huitzilopochtli with its sacrificial altar had stood. Fourteen months later, his titles and honors were confirmed by the Spanish king. He was appointed governor and captain general of New Spain. He devoted his energies to making the Mexican empire a model Spanish colony. Cattle and plants were imported from Europe. Spaniards were allocated estates, but Cortes

was vigilant that abuses accorded the Caribbean Indians should not be repeated in New Spain. Tribes that cooperated with the new government were treated with consideration. The rest were subjugated ruthlessly.

Cortes' captains opened up territories beyond the boundaries of the old Aztec empire. Pedro de Alvarado penetrated deep into the south, and after two years subdued the highland Maya. As a reward, he was given the governorship of Guatemala. Cristóbal de Olid, a captain in Cortes' army, was sent to the Yucatán. After penetrating

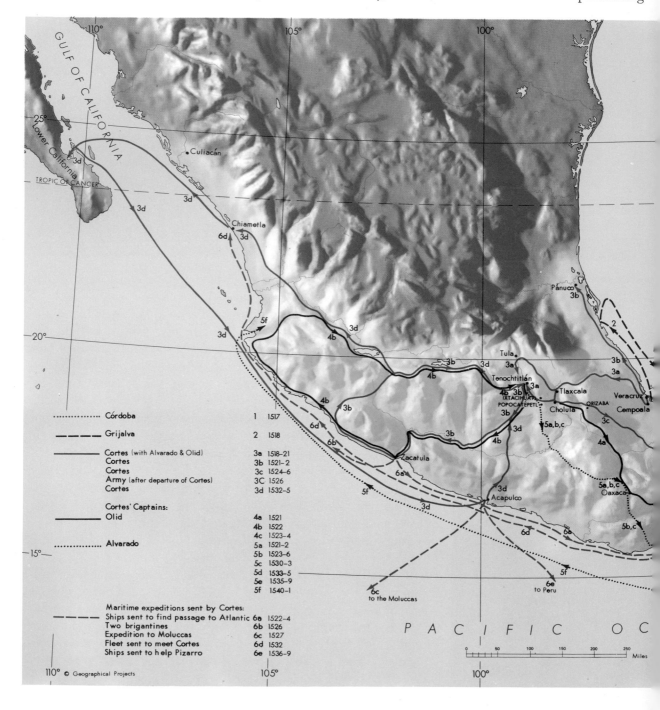

	Córdoba	1	1517
	Grijalva	2	1518
	Cortes (with Alvarado & Olid)	3a	1518-21
	Cortes	3b	1521-2
	Cortes	3c	1524-6
	Army (after departure of Cortes)	3C	1526
	Cortes	3d	1532-5
	Cortes' Captains:		
	Olid	4a	1521
		4b	1522
		4c	1523-4
		5a	1521-2
		5b	1523-6
	Alvarado	5c	1530-3
		5d	1533-5
		5e	1535-9
		5f	1540-1

Maritime expeditions sent by Cortes:
Ships sent to find passage to Atlantic	6a	1522-4	
Two brigantines	6b	1526	
Expedition to Moluccas	6c	1527	
Fleet sent to meet Cortes	6d	1532	
Ships sent to help Pizarro	6e	1536-9	

110° © Geographical Projects   105°   100°

Honduras, he promptly disavowed Cortes. In an achievement some rank as phenomenal as the conquest of Mexico, Cortes marched 1,300 miles overland in pursuit of Olid. He had to negotiate a terrain of unimaginable difficulty, tropical forest, fever-ridden swamp, and range upon range of mountains. Olid paid for his mutiny on the executioner's block. Cortes was away from the capital for more than two years. When he returned, he equipped four maritime expeditions along the Pacific coast, to search for a strait to the Spice Islands, and in the process discovered what is now Lower California. The land

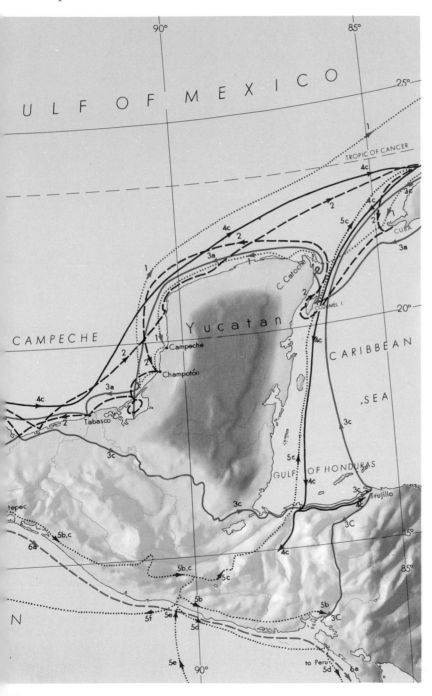

Left: this map of what is now Mexico shows the movements of Cortes and his armies and fleets during the 20 or so years that they took to destroy the Aztec empire. The green areas pick out the regions that became known, as the men from Spain marched, rode, and sailed around the rich, sophisticated empire they found and crushed.

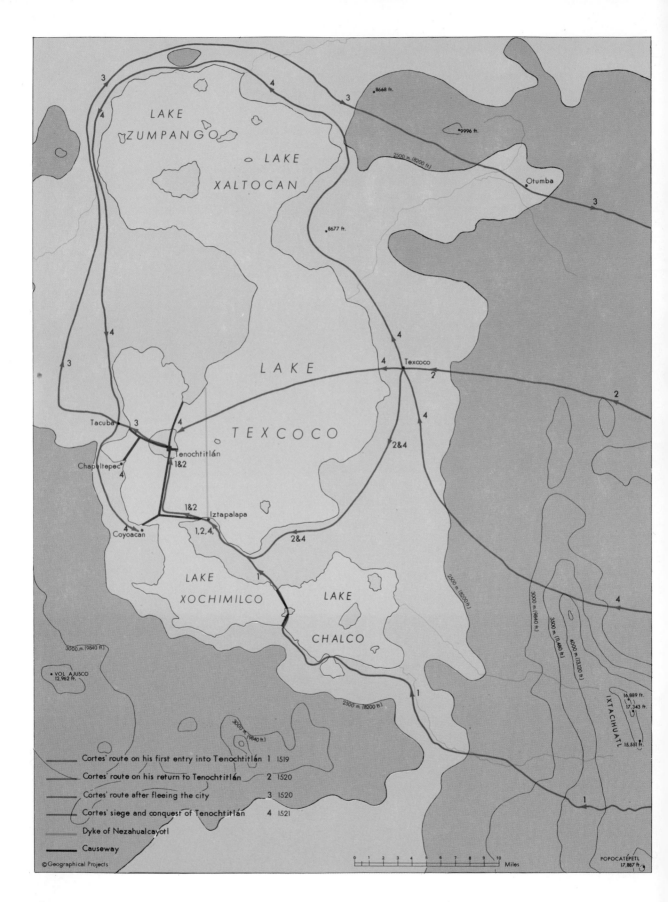

LAKE
ZUMPANGO

LAKE
XALTOCAN

• 8668 ft.

• 9996 ft.

2500 m. (8200 ft.)

Otumba

3

• 8677 ft.

LAKE

TEXCOCO

4

4   Texcoco
4   2

2

Tacuba   3   4

Tenochtitlán
1&2

Chapultepec
4

2&4

4

1&2   Iztapalapa

Coyoacan   4   1,2,4,   2&4

1

LAKE
XOCHIMILCO

LAKE

CHALCO

2500 m. (8200 ft.)

3000 m. (9840 ft.)

3000 m. (9840 ft.)

3500 m. (11,480 ft.)

4000 m. (13,120 ft.)

• VOL AJUSCO
12,962 ft.

2500 m. (8200 ft.)

16,889 ft.
17,343 ft.

15,551 ft.

IXTACIHUATL

1

POPOCATÉPETL
17,887 ft.

———— Cortes' route on his first entry into Tenochtitlán 1 1519
———— Cortes' route on his return to Tenochtitlán   2 1520
———— Cortes' route after fleeing the city   3 1520
———— Cortes' siege and conquest of Tenochtitlán   4 1521
———— Dyke of Nezahualcayotl
———— Causeway

© Geographical Projects

0 1 2 3 4 5 6 7 8 9 10
Miles

Left: this map of the Aztec capital city of Tenochtitlán, the lake on which it was built, and the surrounding countryside shows the movements of Cortes and his army in the years leading to the three-month siege and final conquest of the city in 1521. The 10-mile long Dyke of Nezahualcoyotl, also shown on the map, was built by the Aztec in the mid-1400's. It protected the city of Tenochtitlán from the floodwaters of the surrounding Lake Texcoco.

was thought to be an island and was given the name *Isla de Cortes*.

Returning to Spain in 1528, Cortes was received with full honors by the king, and awarded the title of Marquess del Valle de Oaxaca. But his career was already on the wane. The king, fretful lest Cortes' powers and independence become too great, appointed an *audiencia* (a court of judges) to supersede his authority as governor. In 1535, Cortes' pride was damaged irreparably when he discovered that Antonio de Mendoza, the first Viceroy of New Spain, had the right to terminate the conquistador's office as captain general whenever he liked. Humiliated by these diminutions in his authority and the failure to establish a colony in California, Cortes sailed for Spain in 1540 to obtain redress for his grievances.

But this time the king turned a deaf ear to the former conquering hero. Spain had no more use for him. Many a subsequent conquistador, who had financed an expedition and taken all the risks to incur new possessions for the motherland, was to be accorded similar treatment. The effective power in overseas territories was invariably turned over to an intimate of the royal circle whose obedience to royal edicts could be relied upon without question. Attention was beginning to focus on the new territories in South America. Gold and treasure from Peru were fattening the Spanish treasury in amounts that eclipsed those derived from Cortes' New Spain. The most famous of all conquistadors was never to return to the scene of his many triumphs. One of his missives to his monarch reposed in government files for three years, unanswered. Written on the back were the words "no need to reply." Cortes died at the age of 63, embittered and broken in spirit.

Right: Indian laborers erecting a building under Spanish supervision. Mexico City, capital of New Spain, grew up on the ruins of the Aztec city of Tenochtitlán.

Coronado and the Seven Cities

6

Left: for many years after the conquest of Mexico, the conquistadors believed that to the north of Mexico there were rich cities comparable to Tenochtitlán. Drawn in 1558, this map of New Spain pictures castles and fabulous cities scattered throughout what is today the American Southwest.

In April, 1536, a squad of Spanish cavalry was slave raiding in the region of the Sinaloa River, some 700 miles northwest of Mexico City. This distant outpost of New Spain, whose inhabitants were unused to Spanish ways, had been selected as a likely area for recruiting slave labor. But the Indians had taken to the hills, leaving the soldiers to chase one false trail after another. Suddenly, on the horizon, the troopers espied a group of stragglers ambling along at a leisurely pace. They galloped forward to make the capture. But on overtaking the unsuspecting victims, the Spanish soldiers halted in amazement. There were Indians certainly, 11 of them, but also a white man and a Negro. What were they doing in this out of the way place? Burned dark by the sun, and bone thin, the gaunt Spaniard, Álvar Núñez Cabeza de Vaca, looked more dead than alive. "They stood staring at me a length of time so confounded that they neither hailed me nor drew near to make an enquiry." Shortly after, he was joined by two more Spaniards in the same emaciated condition.

This dramatic encounter was the first news of an expedition that had set out from Florida eight years before, in 1528. The expedition under the command of Pánfilo de Narváez had long been presumed lost. But here, 2,000 miles from their starting point, were four survivors out of the original 400-man party. One was Cabeza, who had been the treasurer of the ill-fated expedition. His servant, Estevanico, a Negro slave of Moroccan origin, Captain Alonzo del Castillo, and Captain Andrew Dorantes made up the foursome. All the others had perished. These four had crossed two-thirds of the unexplored North American continent on foot. From Florida, on the Atlantic Coast, all the way to California, on the Pacific, they had made their way through swamp, earth-scorched plain, and mountain ranges peopled by hostile Indian tribes.

Instead of curbing the Spaniards' curiosity about the land to the north, Cabeza's tale of misadventure had the reverse effect. Coming at the time it did, it focused attention on an area that seemed ripe for Spanish domination. Why should one or two preliminary disappointments halt these glorious adventures? No conquistador had any real doubt that to the north there were kingdoms as rich as Mexico.

One legend in particular, that of the *Seven Cities of Cibola,* had a strong hold on the Spanish mind. The legend told of seven fabulously rich cities somewhere to the north in what is now the

Below: portrait of Antonio de Mendoza, first Viceroy of New Spain. Anxious to establish Spanish domination in the New World and win greater treasures for his king, Mendoza sent Fray Marcos de Niza and later Francisco de Coronado to explore the vast region to the north of Mexico.

Above: an Aztec tribute list from the Codex Mendoza. The first column lists the Mexican towns that paid an annual tribute to the Aztec. The remaining illustrations show the types of tribute paid—among them cloth, warrior costumes, and cacao beans. Viceroy Mendoza commissioned the painting of the codex to explain Aztec culture to the Spanish court. It is a valuable source of information on pre-conquest life. (Bodleian Library, Oxford, MS. Arch. Selden A. 1. folio 52.)

Southwest United States. The Spanish imagination played havoc with fact. Knowledge of the continent north of New Spain was very sketchy. Only the Atlantic coast of North America had been mapped. The uncharted west coast was a mystery. And what lay inland? The question was compelling. Obviously the first man to come up with the answer to the riddle of the north would be rewarded by vast new possessions.

Antonio de Mendoza, Viceroy of New Spain, decided to send a small party into the north. Two candidates immediately sprang to mind. One was Fray Marcos de Niza, a Franciscan priest who had spent much time among the Indians on the remote northern borders of New Spain. A second was the Moor, Estevanico, one of the four survivors of Cabeza's party. Estevanico's firsthand acquaintance with the religions and superstitions of the Indian tribes would be especially useful.

On March 7, 1539, with a small band of Pima Indians, the two hopefuls set off from Culiacán—which today is the capital of the Mexican state of Sinaloa. No more unlikely couple could have been chosen to lead the expedition. The two leaders almost parodied their differences. Fray Marcos, the soft-spoken priest, was dressed in plain, rough garb well-suited to his calling. The ebullient Estevanico, with his infectious grin and raucous laugh, had chosen a costume more suited for his role as magician and god. He sported plumes and feathers of brilliant hue, and to his arms and legs were attached little bells that tinkled with every movement he made. Remembering his days with Cabeza, Estevanico carried a magical gourd to which were attached red and white feathers. The gourd, when carried in advance by one of the Pima, was often accepted as a symbol of authority by the Indians.

As they progressed up the coast, the Indians they met instantly

Above: a Spanish friar baptizes a Mexican Indian. Large numbers of priests accompanied the conquistadors to the New World in order to convert the Indians to Christianity. Fray Marcos, the first white man to travel into the Southwest United States, spent many years working among the Indians on the frontiers of New Spain.

recognized Estevanico as their long-lost friend and both he and Fray Marcos were eagerly welcomed as "Children of the Sun." Throngs of Indians clung to the small procession. The group was a welcome contrast to previous Spanish slave-raiding parties. Proceeding up the western coast of Mexico, they crossed the Yaqui River, and then turned inland through the lovely valley of the Sonora River. Here Fray Marcos halted his men in a small village. He then dispatched several Indians of his original retinue to survey the coast. While waiting for their return, he agreed to Estevanico's request to go ahead into the unexplored regions of the north as pathfinder. Fray Marcos stipulated that on no account was Estevanico to go farther ahead than 150 miles. The Moor was to send back

Left: a page from the Codex Azcatitlan depicts the work of the Spanish friars as seen by their Mexican converts. Although the tonsured friar in his simple brown robe was a common sight in Mexico, the Indians of Arizona and New Mexico greeted Fray Marcos as a god.

reports via his scouts as soon as he discovered anything of import. A cross would indicate the relative significance of the find. One the size of a hand would indicate "but a mean thing found," twice the size would show the discovery to be of some "great matter," and "if more important than New Spain," a very large cross should be sent.

After only four days, an Indian from Estevanico's escort appeared bearing a cross the size of a man. The news was electrifying. The Seven Cities of Cibola had been located! Not in his wildest hopes had the friar expected such providential news so early in their journey. Estevanico had found someone who had actually been to the very metropolis hinted at by Cabeza. It was only 30 days distance to the north.

Estevanico had already set out for Cibola and by now had 300

Above: view of the Colorado Plateau— a barren, broken country of deep canyons, sharp cliffs, and rugged, flat-topped hills. Fray Marcos crossed parts of the Colorado Plateau in his search for the Seven Cities of Cibola.

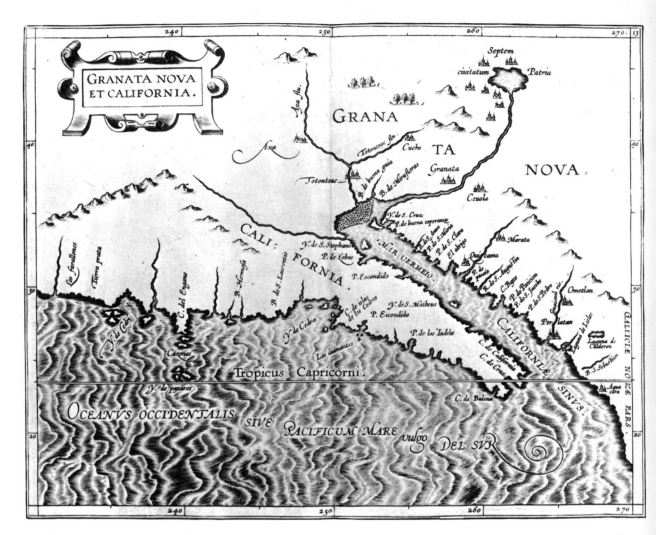

The map contains the following labels:

GRANATA NOVA ET CALIFORNIA.

Septem / cuitatum / Patria

Gxa flu.

GRANA / TA / NOVA

Axa

Totonteac flu. / Cucho / Granata

B. de buena guia / B. de Miraflores

Totonteac / Ceuola

V. de S. Cruz / P. de buena esperance

CALI: / FORNIA

V. de S. Stephano / P. de Lobos / S. Anna / P. de S. Salaria / P. de S. Clara / El abrigo / Marata

B. Hermofa / R. de S. Laurentio / P. Escondido / MAR VERMEIO / Quiuira

C. del Engano / C. de islas / de los Cedros / V. de S. Matheus / R. de / R. de S. Augustin / B. Baço / P. de Poniente / P. de S. Iacob / Ometlan

Los Farellones / Tierra grata / V. de Cedro / P. Escondido / P. de los Iudios / P. de S. Pedro / Per. Maten / Guanaual riu.

V. de Cobi / Caçones / Los diamantes / C. de California / C. de Cruz / Laguna de / Calderon / GALLICE NOVE PARS.

Tropicus Capricorni. / CALIFORNIE SINUS. / B. S. Sebastian

V. de pyaros / Aqua clara

OCEANVS OCCIDENTALIS SIVE PACIFICUM MARE vulgo DEL SVR / C. de Balena

Indians in his train. Fray Marcos lost no time in following the Moor's path. He traveled north into present-day Arizona and then northeast into what is today New Mexico, in the territory of the Zuñi Indians. Here he ascended the high Colorado Plateau between the Little Colorado and the Rio Grande rivers.

It was at this point, when he was but three days short of his destination, that he espied an Indian making haste in his direction. Something terribly wrong must have happened. The messenger "came in great fright, having his face and body all covered with sweat, and showing excessive sadness in his countenance." A calamity had fallen. The Moor was dead. Surrounded by a wide circle of admirers Estevanico had reached the gates of Cibola. Just at the moment that was to be his greatest hour, Estevanico's magic had deserted him. The reception he received from the townspeople was openly hostile. He was detained in a small hut on the outskirts of the city for two days. On the third day, the puzzled Moor was told he could go. It was his death sentence. He walked straight into a merciless hail of arrows. Estevanico is assured of his place in history. The Moor had traveled the full width of the United States. At the

Above: the fabled Seven Cities of Cibola are seen in the top right-hand corner of this map of New Granada and the California Peninsula made in 1598.

Above right: the Taos Pueblo in present-day New Mexico is similar to the Zuñi village first seen by Fray Marcos. The terraced houses, made of boulders or adobe, were sometimes four or five stories high. From the distance, Fray Marcos mistook the simple stone buildings for elaborate and rich temples.

Right: this portrait of Francisco Vasquez de Coronado, although not historical, agrees with contemporary descriptions of the conquistador. Coronado was sent by Mendoza to find and conquer the Seven Cities of Cibola.

time of his death, no man had covered more ground of the unexplored regions of the United States.

Fray Marcos resolved not to return to New Spain until he had seen Cibola, even if he should die in the attempt. With a handful of Pima, more frightened than loyal, the determined priest continued north. From a hilltop, Fray Marcos first glimpsed the legendary city framed against the backdrop of the Zuni Mountains. Across the shimmering plain, in the deceptively bright light of an altitude that magnifies distant objects, he saw a collection of stone buildings, some rising higher than others. These latter he took for palaces and temples. This was undoubtedly the Cibola of the legend. Dedicating the discovery to Saint Francis, he claimed possession of the land for Spain. This done, Fray Marcos hitched his skirts above his knees, and, in his own words, "with much more fear than victuals," sped for home.

The fair city that the priest had merely caught a glimpse of soon became in the telling the equal of Tenochtitlán. Fray Marcos did little to discourage such speculations. As for Mendoza, he already considered this new territory as won. The only decision left was to

		Córdoba	1	1517
		Grijalva	2	1518
		Cortes (with Alvarado & Olid)	3a	1518–21
		Cortes	3b	1521–2
		Cortes	3c	1524–6
		Army (after departure of Cortes)	3C	1526
		Cortes	3d	1532–5
		Expeditions by Cortes' captains	4	1521–41
		(Alvarado & Olid)		
		Maritime expeditions sent by Cortes	5	1522–39
		Coronado	6	1540–2
		Alarcón (with fleet)	6A	1540–1
		Díaz (in search of Alarcón)	6B	1540
		Cárdenas	6C	1540–1

ATLANTIC

OCEAN

BAHAMA

ISLANDS

TROPIC OF CANCER

ANDROS I.

CUBA

Santiago
de Cuba

HISPANIOLA

C. Catoche

Yucatan

COZUMEL

CARIBBEAN

JAMAICA

SEA

Mississippi
Delta

Florida

OF

CO

peche

potón

GULF OF
HONDURAS

Trujillo

Isthmus

of Panama

GULF OF
PANAMA

SOUTH

AMERICA

Left: this map of Mexico and Central
America shows the routes traveled by
the early Spanish explorers, from
Córdoba and Cortes in the 1510's to
Coronado in the early 1540's. The
conquistadors pushed north into what is
now the American Southwest, and south
along the Pacific coast of the Americas,
all the time hoping to find another Indian
empire as rich and rewarding as the Aztec.

appoint a commander to lead an expedition of conquest. He bestowed this honor on his young friend Francisco Vásquez de Coronado, the 29-year-old governor of New Galicia, the northwest province of New Spain.

On February 23, 1540, Coronado set out from New Galicia with 300 young men newly arrived from Spain. Many were of the aristocracy. Their blue blood, however, did not prevent them from being, as one observer noted, "for the most part vicious young gentlemen who did not have anything to do." They were accompanied by Indians, some Negroes, and 1,000 horses. Two ships under the command of Hernando de Alarcón conveyed the heavy equipment and stores on a parallel course up the west coast of Mexico. Alarcón was also instructed to survey the Pacific coast, and endeavor to locate Cibola from the sea.

Above: Coronado leads his men across the deserts of New Mexico and Arizona in search of the legendary Cibola. Although he found no civilization comparable to that of the Aztec, Coronado explored much of the American Southwest before returning to New Spain.

Right: a New Mexican Zuñi Indian practices the craftsmanship of his ancestors. The handsome turquoise and silver jewelry made by the present-day Zuñi is similar to that first seen and described by the conquistadors.

Advancing up the coastal strip, Coronado's large army made only sluggish progress. They spent three comfortable weeks at Culiacán. Frustrated at the slow pace of the cavalcade, Coronado decided to lead a flying column and make straight for Cibola. On April 22, 1540, he set out with his most trusted captains at the head of a small party of soldiers. Fray Marcos was also in the party.

The vanguard proceeded up the Sonora Valley and over the mountains into southern Arizona. Continuing north they crossed miles of parched deserts and rugged mountain ranges before reaching the high Colorado Plateau. Cibola lay just over the New Mexico border.

The ever-watchful Zuñi signaled their approach to Cibola by smoke signals. In July, 1540, they reached the Indian city. Coronado gazed eagerly across the plain and saw at once that it was nothing like the "silver city" that Fray Marcos had described. It resembled, rather, a collection of huts of varying height, all jumbled haphazardly together. The sight was a bitter blow to all. They had been on the march for the best part of five months and had covered 1,500 miles of torturous country. They had been in constant danger from hostile Indians and starvation. They had been promised glory, honor, and riches at the end of their journey. The humble Zuñi pueblo before them fulfilled none of their hopes.

The disappointed Coronado requested permission to enter the city peaceably. When this overture was rebuffed, the *requerimento* was delivered in all solemnity. When the Zuñi realized that they were being asked to give up their settlement without a fight, they were angry and bewildered. What sort of fools did the strangers take them for? They began to taunt the outnumbered Spaniards, thinking that they were too afraid to fight.

Coronado had no alternative but to attack. His men had not eaten for days and would starve unless they obtained provisions from the town. It took the conquistadors less than one hour to seize Cibola. But the Zuñi put up a fierce and bitter defense. "For myself," wrote Coronado, "they knocked me down to the ground twice with countless great stones which they threw down from above, and if I had not been protected by the very good headpiece which I wore, I think that the outcome would have been bad for me."

It was time to break the dismal tidings to Mendoza. "It now remains for me," wrote Coronado, "to tell about this city and kingdom

Above: "The Battle of Pueblo Oa-Quima,"
painted by Jan Mostaert about 1545.
The picture is probably based on Coronado's report to the Spanish king on
his expedition in search of Cibola.
The landscape is a mixture of fact
and fantasy. The Spanish soldiers,
seen advancing from the right, are
met by naked Indians trying to defend
their strange clifftop dwellings.
The animals in the foreground are
reminiscent of a typical European
pastoral scene of the same period.

and province of which [Fray Marcos] gave your Lordship an account.
In brief, I can assure you that in reality he has not told the truth in
a single thing that he said, but everything is the reverse of what
he said, except the name of the city and the large stone houses. For,
although they are not decorated with turquoises, nor made of lime
nor of good bricks, nevertheless they are very good houses. . . ."

Coronado's attempts to open negotiations with the vanquished
Zuñi were unsuccessful. The Indians remained in hiding in a
neighboring pueblo. They did not understand the Spaniard's request

to meet with their "prince" or "ruler." The Zuñi had no history of princes, kings, rulers, or statesmen. "They do not have chiefs as in New Spain," observed one of Coronado's officers, "but are ruled by a council of the oldest men. They have priests who preach to them, whom they call 'papas'. These are the elders. They go up on the highest roof of the village and preach to the village from there, like public criers, in the morning while the sun is rising, the whole village being silent and sitting in the galleries to listen. They tell them how they are to live, and I believe that they give certain com-

mandments for them to keep, for there is no drunkenness among them . . . nor sacrifices, neither do they eat human flesh nor steal, but they are usually at work."

The Indians of the adobe pueblos had plenty to eat, the land belonged to everyone, and what they built, they built to last. Unlike the majority of Indian tribes on the North American continent, the Zuñi were not nomads. They were a sedentary people with fixed traditions and a strong sense of duty to family and community. They worked hard for their stability but they had no understanding of the value of material things in the European sense. To them, a turquoise was valuable because of its sparkle and luminosity. There was no marketplace set up to determine its value. Why put a price on a thing of beauty?

The Spaniards, on the other hand, had come looking for gold and treasure and they were bitterly disappointed when they found there was none. Their disappointment soon turned to anger and in their fury they cared little for the finer points of the Zuñi culture—a culture that appeared backward and heathenistic to them.

By this time, the main body of the army had arrived at Cibola. But still there was no word of the ships commanded by Alarcón. Coronado sent Melchior Diaz to see if he could locate the vessels.

Fray Marcos, whose life was threatened by the angry soldiers, took this opportunity to slip away from Cibola.

Diaz accompanied Fray Marcos as far south as the Sonora Valley. Then taking 25 Spaniards and some Indians, he headed northwest. Near the mouth of the Colorado River, Diaz found letters from Alarcón buried near the foot of a tree. Alarcón had sailed north along the coast of Mexico as far as was possible. He had confirmed beyond a doubt that the so-called "Isla de Cortez" was not an island but a peninsula, later known as Lower California. There, where the Colorado River empties into the Gulf of California, Alarcón had waited for news of the army. When no word came he decided to move farther north.

Crossing the treacherous shallows, Alarcón took some small boats and proceeded up the Colorado River. It is thought he reached a point beyond the Gila tributary, in which case he could be said to be the true discoverer of California. But the farther inland he penetrated, the more desolate the surroundings became. One moment there was nothing but barren stretches of desert, the next they would be going "between certain very high mountains, through which this river passes with a narrow channel." It was from the Indians that he had heard of Coronado's exploits in Cibola.

Above: the 1,450-mile-long Colorado River, one of the major waterways in the United States. The river takes its name from the Spanish word *colorado* meaning "colored red," because it flows through canyons of red stone. It was first discovered by Alarcón in 1540.

Left: drawing of an American buffalo from a contemporary account of Coronado's expedition. Coronado was the first white man to encounter the American "crooked back oxen," and was quick to recognize its importance to the American Indian, who looked to it for food, clothing, and shelter.
Below: Coronado and his men on the banks of the Kansas River. After crossing the American Great Plains, Coronado abandoned his search for Quivira and returned to New Spain.

Alarcón returned to New Spain without achieving a link-up with the land forces. Nevertheless, he had accomplished a great deal. He was the first to map the Gulf of California with any accuracy, and the first to discover and explore the Colorado River, the mightiest waterway in the Southwest United States. It was not until 300 years later that anyone would equal his efforts in the area.

Meanwhile, at Cibola, high on the Zuñi Plateau, Coronado dispatched search parties to see if a more attractive province could be located. Captain Pedro de Tovar went due west and after 45 miles came across the Hopi Indian pueblo of Awatapi in northeast Arizona. The inhabitants refused to surrender. After bitter fighting the Indians were defeated. There was no gold.

About the same time that Alarcón had reached his farthest point up the Colorado River, García López de Cárdenas, another of Coronado's officers, was following its course from the opposite direction. Neither was destined to meet, due to the virtually impassable natural obstacles. Cárdenas and his men were the first white men to gaze upon one of the seven natural wonders of the world. Crossing the Colorado Plateau, they were suddenly confronted by that immense rent in the earth's crust that is now known as the Grand Canyon. The conquistador had met his match. One look at this strange land, and Cárdenas knew it was unconquerable.

Coronado and the main body of the army waited at Cibola for news of some rich territory, the conquest of which might justify their expedition. One day, a young Indian chief with an extraordinary handlebar mustache, strode into Coronado's quarters. After presenting him with some handsome gifts, the chief offered to lead a Spanish party to his pueblo in the east where the inhabitants, he promised, would look upon them as friends. The Spaniards were quick to nickname the agreeable young man "Whiskers." Coronado ordered Hernando de Alvarado to proceed at once to Whiskers' pueblo of Cicuye situated by the Pecos River.

Alvarado's small band traveled 80 miles to the east before coming

ALFRED RUSSELL

across a pueblo of any size. Then they headed northeast. As they neared present-day Bernalillo, in New Mexico, the desolate land changed to one of fertile, green pastures. The Spaniards called the area *Tiguex*. Here, a cluster of 12 pueblos, sheltered on the east by the Sandia Mountains, and watered by the upper reaches of the Rio Grande River, offered a refreshing contrast to the lands they had been journeying through. It was September and winter was fast approaching. Because Cibola was too small and remote to accommodate the entire army and its livestock, Alvarado sent a messenger to Coronado recommending that they set up their winter quarters at Tiguex.

Guided by Whiskers, the party continued on its northeast path. When they arrived at the chief's village, high up in the Santa Fe Mountains, they received a tumultuous welcome. While at Cicuye, Alvarado became acquainted with a man known as *El Turco* (The Turk). He was a servant of the Cicuye, a stray member of one of the Plains Indian tribes. El Turco told Alvarado that there was an abundance of gold in his kingdom of Quivira to the east. In Quivira, "there was a river in the level country which was two leagues [five miles] wide, in which there were fishes as big as horses, and very big canoes, with more than 20 rowers on a side, and that they carried sails, and that their lords sat on the poop under awnings, and on the prow they had a great golden eagle. . . . He said also that everyone had their ordinary dishes made of wrought plate, and the jugs and bowls were of gold."

With the wily El Turco in tow, Alvarado hurried his departure from Cicuye to bring this good news to Coronado. At Tiguex, where the army was now camped, El Turco told Coronado that when he was first captured by the Cicuye they had stolen some gold bracelets he was wearing. If only he could lay his hands on the bracelets, he could show the Spaniards the quality of the gold in Quivira.

Eager for the sight of gold, the Spaniards returned to Cicuye to track down the ornaments. Brushing aside the effusive welcomes, Alvarado demanded that Whiskers bring him the gold bracelets. Whiskers was perplexed by the sudden change in those he took to be his friends. He told Alvarado that there was no gold and that El Turco's story was a lie. But so intent were the conquistadors in believing in the wealthy kingdom of Quivira, that they preferred to take the word of El Turco. Alvarado arrested Whiskers and one of the oldest and most respected men of the pueblo. He took his captives back to Coronado at Tiguex. As one observer remarked, "This began the want of confidence in the word of the Spaniards whenever there was talk of peace from this time on."

On April 23, 1541, the Spanish army left Tiguex and headed directly for Cicuye, where they released Whiskers. The expedition then swung southeast from the Pecos to the Brazos River and made a loop due north across unending stretches of prairie where herds of wild buffalo grazed. In northeastern Texas, the Spaniards encountered the Tejas Indians from whom Texas derives its name. When Coronado asked them of Quivira, they could not corroborate El Turco's story.

It was now the end of May. Coronado had led his men over 600 miles of unexplored territory. The food supply had dwindled dangerously. He decided to lead a flying squadron to Quivira, due north, taking with him 30 horsemen, a few foot soldiers, and some Tejas as guides. The rest of the army were to stay where they were. Within a week Coronado promised to send back word whether they were to join him or return to Tiguex. When the orders came, the army was directed to make their way back to the winter camp.

Coronado's force pushed north into present-day Oklahoma. They crossed the Canadian River and continued to the Arkansas. They were now in Kansas, at a point just east of the future site of Dodge City. The general then wheeled the column in a northeasterly direction. Finally, having traveled 500 miles since leaving the main army, they came across El Turco's Quivira on the Kansas River. It was a modest Wichita Indian encampment where the inhabitants, terrified at the sudden arrival of the conquistadors and the strange animals on which they were mounted, cowered in their huts of grass and thatch. El Turco received instant justice. He was strangled.

Coronado took possession of this disappointing kingdom in the name of the Spanish king. He then led his men, dispirited and weary, back to Tiguex. The plan was to rest for yet another winter, then head north past Quivira in the spring of 1542. But an accident changed these plans. While taking part in a horse race, Coronado was thrown under the hoofs of an oncoming steed. The horse trampled over the leader who at one point was thought to be on the verge of death. Coronado recovered slowly, but, weary of the northern plains, he feigned illness in order to cut short the abortive expedition.

Leaving nothing but hate, fear, and violence in its wake, the Spanish army returned to New Spain. Many soldiers deserted as soon as they neared their homesteads. The bedraggled army was less than 100 strong when it drew up its ranks to face the displeasure of the viceroy at Mexico City. Mendoza had expected much more from the young Coronado. Cárdenas wrote, "Coronado came to kiss the hand of the viceroy and did not receive so good a reception as he would have liked, for he found him very sad . . . because this was the outcome of something about which he had felt so sure."

Coronado can hardly be blamed for failing to find something that

Below: Spanish friars are slain by embittered Indians. Because Coronado's forces had burned and plundered countless Indian villages, they left behind them a legacy of misery, suffering, and hatred. The result was the torture and death of many of the Spanish friars who chose to remain with their new converts.

was not there in the first place. His achievements were considerable. He had blazed a trail across the Southwest United States, from Mexico to Kansas. His men had discovered the Grand Canyon and the Colorado River. He had reported competently on the customs and habits of the various Pueblo communities. Nevertheless, for Mendoza's purpose, he had come back empty-handed. The whole expedition had been a fiasco. The northern continent had become anathema to the gold-hungry conquistador and no one was to make a move in that direction for another 40 years.

Explorers, Conquerors, and Colonizers

7

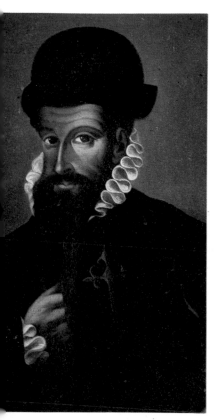

Above: portrait of Francisco Pizarro, the conqueror of Peru. Pizarro was almost 50 years of age when he set out with a handful of men to topple the largest empire in the New World.

Left: Pizarro's dress sword, with its velvet handle and delicate filigree, was acquired only after the conquest of Peru had made him a rich man. It probably bears little resemblance to the rough steel sword with which the impoverished adventurer drew his famous line and initiated the conquest of the Inca empire.

Taking his sword, Francisco Pizarro traced a line in the sand and straightened up to address his men. "Friends and Comrades! on that side are toil, hunger, nakedness, the drenching storm, desertion, and death; on this side, ease and pleasure. There lies Peru with its riches; here, Panama and its poverty. Choose, each man, what best becomes a brave Castilian. For my part, I go to the south." This said, he stepped over the line. On that day, in 1526, on the island of Gallo off the coast of Ecuador, 13 Spaniards elected to stand by the side of their leader.

The man with whom the 13 valiant soldiers had irrevocably linked their fate was an elderly man by the standards of the times. Francisco Pizarro was almost 50 years old. But his utter disregard for personal comfort while following a course of action with almost obsessive single-mindedness won him the respect and allegiance of both young and old. Before his death he was to conquer, without the aid of Indian allies, an empire stretching more than 2,500 miles down the South American continent.

Pizarro was born about the year 1478 in Trujillo, Spain. His birth was the result of what the Spaniards delicately refer to as a *desuedo* (negligence). His father was a retired army officer, Colonel Gonzalo Pizarro, and his mother a woman without rank. The colonel was to be "negligent" on at least two other occasions, the results being Gonzalo and Juan Pizarro. But he did have legitimate offspring, the proud Hernando Pizarro, who reckoned himself socially superior to his brothers.

In 1502, Francisco Pizarro went to the West Indies to make his fortune. He lived for some time on the island of Hispaniola (present-day Haiti and Dominican Republic) before joining the colony of Darien in what is now Panama. About the year 1520, Pizarro entered into a bizarre partnership with Diego de Almagro, an illiterate adventurer. Short and ugly, the middle-aged Almagro combined fantastic energy with a flair for business. He was immensely likeable, generous, and gay. The two adventurers were joined by a priest, Fernando de Luque. De Luque later earned the nickname *Fernando El Loco* (the crazy) for associating himself in what were thought to be hairbrained schemes. De Luque was on friendly terms with Panama's governor, Pedro Arias de Avila (Pedrarias), and possibly through his influence, the three prospered in their joint mining and farming ventures.

About this time, rumors of a vast southern kingdom on the western side of South America reached Panama. The first official government survey to the south of Panama had taken place in 1522 under the command of Pascual de Andagoya. Andagoya sailed south of the Gulf of San Miguel and reached the Biru River where he met Indian traders who told him of the rich and powerful Inca empire. It is thought that the name they gave the fabulous land was garbled by the Spaniards and came out as Peru.

Governor Pedrarias appointed a captain to search for the rich kingdom and, if possible, make contact with the Indian ruler. But the officer died without fulfilling his commission. Pizarro's group applied for and were granted the right to explore the area. Without delay the trio sold their estates and properties to raise capital for the enterprise. Pedrarias did not contribute a penny but declared himself in for an equal share.

In mid-November, 1524, Pizarro sailed from the newly established city of Panamá on the country's Pacific coast. He was accompanied by 100 men. Almagro followed later in a second ship. Both men explored the Pacific coast of Colombia. They found tropical forests

Right: French map of part of Mexico, and Central and South America drawn in the year 1550. Less than 20 years after Pizarro landed in Peru, the coasts of South America were relatively fixed. Only the interior, with its mountains and mythical cities, remained a mystery.

Below: Francisco Pizarro, Diego Almagro, and Fernando de Luque lay their plans for the conquest of Peru. The bizarre partnership between the two illiterate adventurers and the Catholic priest was to have a lasting effect on the history of South America.

Above: Pizarro's arrival on the Peruvian coast as depicted by a European artist in the 1500's. Crowds of hostile Indians are seen threatening the Spanish force.

and mangrove swamps housing hostile Indians but little gold. In the end they ran out of supplies and were forced to return to Panamá. The expedition was a total financial loss.

Far from being dismayed at this setback, the ambitious trio immediately set about organizing another expedition. Gaspar de Espinosa, mayor of the city of Panamá, agreed to finance this second undertaking. Pedrarias, convinced that the search was doomed to failure, was glad to sell his interest to Espinosa. With 2 vessels, 160 men, and 5 horses, Pizarro sailed from the Isthmus for the second time on March 10, 1526. This time he had been fortunate in securing the services of Bartolome de la Ruiz, a distinguished navigator. Ruiz immediately headed west out to sea and thus avoided the currents and the contrary southerly winds that had troubled and slowed the progress of the preceding journey. This time they landed in a more favored spot on the Colombian coast. Immediately inland they found settlements where richer samples of gold could be plundered.

Almagro was sent home with the treasure to gather more men and materials. Ruiz was to sail farther south to survey the coastal land.

Pizarro himself led a party inland in a frenzied search for gold and treasure. There was little to plunder and the old enemies—disease, hunger, and hostile Indians—took a steady toll in lives. But Pizarro's disappointment turned to elation when Ruiz returned.

Ruiz had sailed down the shoreline for several hundred miles to a point just below the equator. As he progressed farther south he had noticed increasing signs of civilization. There were towns, irrigated fields, people dressed in beautifully woven cotton garments, and substantial-looking houses of adobe brick. The high point of his survey had come when he encountered a large balsa raft quite far out to sea. The Indians aboard the raft wore beautifully made ornaments of gold and silver and were dressed in decorative garments of skillful weave. He had made the first contact with the Inca. Two of the Indians on board had told him of the Inca city of Tumbes, with its impressive buildings and its temple walls plated with gold.

This was the news Pizarro had been waiting for. When Almagro turned up with new recruits and stocks of provisions, the expedition resumed their exploration in high spirits. Ruiz' descriptions were accurate. They soon saw enough to know that they had stumbled

Above: this cross on the coast near Tumbes, Ecuador, marks the spot where Pizarro and his forces landed and began their march into the interior.

onto a kingdom worth exploiting, a second Mexico. But they were stalemated in proceeding farther. Despite the addition of new men they had not nearly enough troops to exploit these discoveries. At this stage, Almagro suggested he should return to Panama once more. With the impressive articles of gold and silver from their recent plundering, he would have no difficulty in raising an army of the size needed to bring the affair to a successful conclusion. Pizarro and Almagro nearly came to blows over this. Pizarro complained bitterly that it was always his lot to be left stranded in the most inclement

Above: map of the South American coast showing the island of Gallo. Pizarro and his men spent five months on the barren island awaiting supplies and reinforcements from Panama.

Left: mosaic ceiling and wall over Pizarro's tomb in Lima Cathedral. The artist portrays the conquistador's heroic stand on the island of Gallo, when, drawing a line, he chose to continue south to Peru rather than return to Panama. Thirteen soldiers decided to accompany their leader.

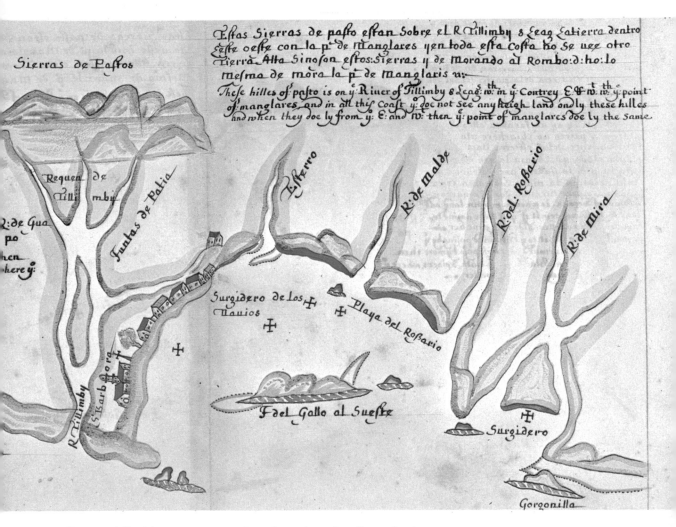

Sierras de Pastos

Estas Sierras de pasto estan Sobre el R Tillimby 8 Leag tierra dentro este oeste con la pᵗᵃ de manglares yen toda esta Costa no Se uee otro Tierra Alta Si no son estos Sierras y de morando al Rombo:d:ho:lo mesma de mora la pᵗᵃ de manglaris

These hilles of pasto is on y̆ Riuer of Tillimby 8 Leag: to: in y̆ Contrey E & w: th y̆ point of manglares and in all this Coast y̆ doe not see any heigh land only these hilles and when they doe ly from y̆: E: and w: then y̆: point of manglares doe ly the same.

surroundings, while Almagro returned to the colony in all comfort. The argument was patched up for the time being and, when Almagro left for Panama, Pizarro sent the other boat after him containing some of the disaffected elements of his party. The old conquistador and the remaining soldiers camped on the island of Gallo, off the coast of Ecuador.

When Almagro reached Panama, he found that Pedrarias had been replaced by a new governor, Pedro de los Rios. De los Rios had no interest in these excursions along the coast of South America. He believed they were all doomed to failure and refused to take any responsibility for the lives lost on the ventures. The governor dispatched two vessels to Gallo with orders to bring Pizarro and his men home.

When the ships arrived at the island, Pizarro boldly refused to return to Panama. It was at this time that he made his dramatic appeal. Thirteen stalwarts defied the governor by standing firm beside their chief. The ships sailed away, leaving Pizarro and his small party stranded on the shores of Gallo. Almagro, however, managed to prevail upon the governor not to abandon the tough old con-

Above: Pizarro at the Spanish court appealing for permission to conquer Peru. When the governor of Panama refused his consent for the venture, Pizarro sailed to Spain to appeal to the king personally. He carried with him gold and silver treasures he had looted on his earlier trips to Peru. The royal agreement was signed on July 26, 1529.

quistador. He argued that Pizarro and his men were only doing their duty for Spain and Saint James. The governor relented. He gave Almagro permission to join Pizarro insisting that they return within six months.

Pizarro, however, was to wait five months before Almagro's sails hove into view. The party, at last reunited, proceeded southward. Sailing 350 miles below the equator they entered the Gulf of Guayaquil and landed at the city of Tumbes. When he went ashore, Pizarro saw large, well-constructed buildings. The busy populace went about their affairs dressed in fine apparel. It was by far the most civilized center he had seen since his arrival in the Americas almost 20 years earlier. But it was the temple, sheathed in gold, that made the old warrior's heart leap with joy.

After sailing farther south, to what is now Trujillo, Peru, Pizarro returned home, eager to outfit an expedition. At Panama, they had been given up for lost. Instead of six months, Almagro had been away for 18 months. Unimpressed by Pizarro's treasures and stories of an Andean kingdom, De los Rios still refused to give his blessing to the enterprise. Faced with the governor's obstinate refusal,

Pizarro decided to go to Spain and appeal to the king himself.

Once Pizarro penetrated the royal circle his reception was un-usually favorable. He paraded llamas and samples of gold and silver ornaments before the court, regaling it with stories of gold-plated temples. The conquistador convinced his sovereign that what had come about in New Spain could easily be repeated in Peru.

The royal agreement was signed on July 26, 1529. Pizarro was made governor and captain general of the lands he had yet to con-quer. Almagro was appointed governor of Tumbes with less than half Pizarro's salary. Fernando de Luque was to be bishop of Tumbes and the faithful Ruiz was appointed grand pilot of the Southern Seas. Before his departure, Pizarro stopped at Trujillo and recruited his brothers—Hernando, Juan, and Gonzalo—and his half-brother Martin de Alcantara, to take part in the enterprise.

Pizarro's return from Spain was not an unqualified success. Almagro was furious at his downgrading. Hernando Pizarro treated the illiterate Almagro with a haughty attitude that did little to alleviate the troubled situation. But the differences were smoothed over. To placate the distrustful Almagro, Francisco Pizarro

Above: a silver llama, an alpaca, and the figure of a woman, all dating from pre-conquest Peru. These are among the few pieces of Inca metal workman-ship that were not destroyed by the Spaniards. They are typical of the orna-ments Pizarro carried with him to Spain and displayed before the Spanish court to impress the king and his ministers.

EL DECIMO CAPITAN
CHALLCO·CHIMA

Above: Peruvian warriors in battle, by an Indian artist. Pizarro arrived in Peru at the end of a civil war that had deeply divided the Inca empire and that was to facilitate the Spanish conquest.

promised that he would be amply rewarded after the conquest.

In January, 1531, Pizarro led his third and final expedition to Peru. His force consisted of 3 ships, 183 men, and 37 horses. Almagro, as usual, would follow later, but first he had the difficult task of enrolling recruits.

Pizarro's plan was to head straight for Tumbes in the Gulf of Guayaquil. But severe headwinds and storms forced them to put in at San Mateo Bay, 350 miles short of their objective. Impatient to begin his conquest, Pizarro disembarked his armor-clad troops and led them south through some of the worst terrain imaginable. The Spaniards attacked defenseless coastal settlements, gaining little, and assuredly losing any element of surprise. In the district of Coaque, however, they managed to loot a respectable haul of gold, silver, and emeralds. Pizarro's strategy now became clear. He sent back his ships to Panama, hoping that the sight of the treasure just won might act as an inducement for others to join. There was nothing for it but to advance to Tumbes by foot.

Left: the rival Inca emperors, Atahualpa (far left) and his brother Huáscar. The two sons of Huayna Capac waged a five-year civil war for control of the empire that their father had divided between them.

Since Pizarro's first visit to Tumbes, the city had been sacked and stripped of many of its treasures. At first the conquistadors were disappointed but when the reason for the state of affairs became known, the hopes of the whole party began to rise. A civil war had been raging throughout the Inca empire for the past few years. The Inca were now sharply divided into two camps. Pizarro immediately realized that the war-torn empire would be far easier to overcome than one united and strong.

At this point, Hernando de Soto (who would later explore the North American continent) arrived with much needed reinforcements. This enabled Pizarro to leave a garrison at Tumbes while he advanced 65 miles farther south to found the city of San Miguel, which afforded an excellent natural harbor at the mouth of the Chira River. There he learned from the Indians more details of the civil war. His timing could not have been better.

The war had been a struggle of succession between rival claimants for the Inca throne. The last emperor, Huayna Capac, had precip-

itated the crisis by dividing his kingdom between two sons. Atahualpa, his son by a Quito princess, was to govern the northern section of the Inca empire—what is today Ecuador. Huáscar, his legitimate heir (because he was the issue of his legal marriage with his sister), would rule over the rest of the mighty kingdom.

Huayna Capac died in 1527. An uneasy truce between the two brothers lasted for only a few months. Then a savage five-year war broke out. Pizarro had arrived at Tumbes shortly after Atahualpa's final crushing victory over his brother. Huáscar was in jail in Cusco, and the usurper Atahualpa now considered himself ruler of the entire empire. He planned to make his triumphal entry into the capital when he had fully recuperated from a leg wound inflicted during battle. To hasten his recovery he had retired to a sulfur spa, high in the Andes. The name of the town was Cajamarca.

Above: the baths at Cajamarca, a sulfur spa high in the Andes. Atahualpa was resting with a leg wound at Cajamarca after his final crushing defeat of Huáscar, when his couriers brought news of the Spanish landing in Peru.

Right: conquistadors on the march. Determined to capture Atahualpa in his mountain retreat, Pizarro urged his men on through the biting cold and rarified air of the Andes. Strangely, the outnumbered Spaniards met little opposition along the way.

Cajamarca, 350 miles distant from where Pizarro and his men were assembled, could be reached in 12 days' hard marching. Cusco, on the other hand, was 1,300 miles away and would take weeks to reach. When Pizarro learned that his quarry was camped in a relatively small town, and not the fortified capital of Cusco, he was elated. He decided to act at once, without waiting for Almagro's reinforcements. With a force of 106 infantry, 62 cavalry, and a few cannon, Pizarro set out to conquer an empire.

In their heavy armor the conquistadors began a march of incredible difficulty. Leaving 80 men at the garrison in San Miguel, Pizarro led his soldiers southeast across the scorching Sechura Desert and then east, toward the ice-capped mountains. He would not allow his men to slacken their pace although their breathing became more difficult with the steep inclines and rarified atmosphere. They must not miss Atahualpa on any account.

Soon the Spaniards were ascending the Andes. It was the rainy season in the mountains and the party made perilous progress through the ravines. They advanced slowly along narrow paths overhung by heavily barricaded fortresses. A handful of Inca warriors could have destroyed them at any time. The horses began to suffer from frostbite and the altitude made the men gasp for breath. Yet they met only scattered opposition. Apart from a few light skirmishes there had been no hostility along the route. Had the civil war destroyed all effective opposition in these parts? Soon they were to find the answer. An Inca nobleman advanced on the party and bade Pizarro and his men welcome. Atahualpa would gladly receive the Spanish strangers as his guests at Cajamarca.

For some weeks now, Atahualpa had been watching the progress of the Spaniards with interest. He had no reason for fear. Whatever their intentions, hostile or otherwise, the Spanish soldiers were at his mercy. Atahualpa, secure after his great victory, could allow himself the luxury of waiting and seeing what happened before taking any precipitate action. His messengers had confirmed that their numbers were insignificant. Other reports indicated that their weapons were not particularly out of the ordinary. This would be a pleasant diversion before his journey to Cusco.

Early on the morning of November 15, 1532, six weeks after setting out from San Miguel, Pizarro and his men arrived at Cajamarca. The Inca encampment was spread out on the slopes above. Pizarro

found the town suspiciously quiet. No one came out to greet them. The leader cautiously led his men forward. When they reached the central plaza he sent his brother Hernando and Hernando de Soto to seek out the emperor. They were to invite Atahualpa to come "to meet his brother."

The Spaniards found the Inca ruler seated on a small stool attended by nobles and numerous officials. Cieza de Leon, a Spanish historian, records a description of the emperor's appearance as recalled by a member of the party: "Atahualpa was a man of 30 years of age, good-looking, somewhat stout, with a fine face, handsome and fierce, the eyes bloodshot. He spoke with much dignity, like a great lord. He talked with good arguments and reasoned well, and when the Spaniards understood what he said they knew him to be a wise man. He was cheerful; but, when he spoke to his subjects, he was very haughty, and showed no sign of pleasure."

At first, Atahualpa did not reply to the visitors' request. Only when Hernando Pizarro repeated his invitation in the politest of terms, did the emperor speak. He informed them that he was observing a fast that did not end until the following day. When his fast was over he would dine with the Spaniards. Hernando de Soto, an excellent horseman, chose this moment to impress the Indian ruler and his entourage. Wheeling his horse, he galloped at full

Left: a European engraving of De Soto's and Hernando Pizarro's meeting with Atahualpa. During the interview, the flamboyant De Soto wheeled his stallion at the Inca emperor. The Inca nobles, who had never seen a horse before, recoiled in terror. Only the emperor remained impassive.

Right: a drawing by the Inca artist Poma de Ayala of the same scene. An Indian account of the incident states that De Soto's horse brushed so close to the emperor that he "felt the breath of the beast on his face."

Above: Atahualpa, advancing on a golden litter to meet Pizarro, is accompanied by his household and court. Nobles swept the road of pebbles and straw as the unarmed emperor and his court entered into Cajamarca.

speed toward Atahualpa, stopping so close to the seated monarch that the horse's nostrils almost brushed the Indian's face. Atahualpa, who had never seen a horse before, sat impassive and dignified. His attendants—not supported by royal dignity—had involuntarily shrunk back in horror. Some say that those who had shown fear were executed for displaying cowardice in front of the strangers.

The two captains returned to their leader, disappointed that the Inca, unlike the Aztec, had no superstitious dread of the foreigners. According to their calculations, there were 30 or 40 thousand warriors encamped on the hill. The Spaniards slept lightly that night.

At noon on the following day, Atahualpa advanced slowly toward the town. He was carried by his nobles on a golden litter. Attendants swept the ground over which he was to pass. The emperor had accepted Pizarro's invitation and had let it be known that he and his men were coming as guests, bearing no arms.

Pizarro was almost beside himself with joy at this last news.

La conquista del Peru. ☙
llamada la nueua Castilla. La q̃l tierra por diuina vo
luntad fue marauillosamente conquistada en la felicis
sima ventura del Emperador y Rey nuestro señor: y
por la prudencia y esfuerço del muy magnifico y vale
roso cauallero el Capitan Francisco piçarro Gouerna
dor y adelantado de la nueua castilla: y de su herma
no Hernando piçarro: y de sus animosos capitanes
z fieles y esforçados compañeros, q̃ con el se hallaron·

Left: Atahualpa is met, not by Pizarro, but by a Spanish friar with a bible and crucifix. Annoyed at the friar's impudence, Atahualpa threw the book to the ground. At a signal from Pizarro, Spanish soldiers, concealed in the city, rushed the royal procession. The soldiers put all to the sword, brutally massacring the Inca nobles who tried to protect their emperor.

Atahualpa was playing into his hands more easily than he had imagined possible. And having no doubt as to whose side God was on, the Inca's intimation that neither he nor his men would carry weapons seemed a divine answer to his prayers. He briefed his soldiers on a variation of the Montezuma kidnap. On the prearranged signal, the Spaniards concealed in the buildings surrounding the square were to open fire and then rush the imperial entourage. Twenty soldiers were detailed to seize the emperor and see that he came to no harm. The remainder were to be wiped out.

Atahualpa made his way into the square with his attendants numbering between three and four thousand. His entrance into Cajamarca had been strangely similar to Pizarro's on the previous day. The procession wended its way through the empty streets to the plaza in an eerie silence. There was no sign of the Spanish force. "Where are the bearded ones?" asked the Inca ruler. But it was a friar named Valderve, not Pizarro, who came forward to greet the

Inca emperor. Valderve carried a bible and crucifix and immediately began a long discourse on the Christian faith. He demanded that Atahualpa declare his allegiance to the Catholic Church and the King of Spain. Annoyed at the impudence of this lowly man who was insisting that he renounce his own divinity in favor of a crucified god, Atahualpa is said to have tossed the bible to the ground and with a proud gesture toward the sun to have exclaimed "My god still lives." At that moment Pizarro gave the signal. Soldiers and cavalry charged the unarmed Inca, slashing their way through the bodies. The massacre was over in 30 minutes. Atahualpa was Pizarro's prisoner. His bodyguard was dead or scattered. One of those who took part in the battle later commented: "As the Indians were unarmed they were defeated without danger to any Christian." The royal procession bedecked with gold, jewels, and feathers now lay dead, an inextricable tangle of blood-spattered bodies.

Atahualpa, under Spanish guard, continued to hold his court in miniature. In a desperate bid for freedom, Atahualpa made a fantastic offer to Pizarro. He promised to cover the floor of the room in which they were standing, an area 22 feet long by 17 feet wide, with gold. Pizarro, probably stupefied, did not reply at once. The Inca immediately raised his ransom bid saying that he would fill the room with gold and silver as high as he could reach (about seven feet) and he would do this in two months! Pizarro drew a red line marking the height. From that moment, streams of porters from all over the empire began piling one golden masterpiece on top of another.

In February, 1533, when Almagro arrived at Cajamarca with much needed reinforcements, Atahualpa had spent three months in captivity. The Inca emperor had fulfilled his side of the bargain. The room was filled with a golden treasure estimated as worth anything between $8 and $20 million. Now the thorny questioned remained—what to do with the royal charge? Honor demanded that Atahualpa be released on fulfilling his part of the bargain. Pizarro, however, recognized the strength of the man. Set at large the proud chief was capable of rallying his empire and wiping out the Spaniards.

Rumors began to multiply that the Inca army was massing in the south to attack the Spanish camp. Atahualpa denied that any such movement was in operation, but the Spaniards became increasingly nervous. They implored their leader to kill the emperor and thus end the threat of rebellion. Hernando de Soto and Pizarro's own brother Hernando protested against such a flagrantly dishonorable solution.

As the months passed, the strain began to tell. The Spaniards, who had the riches of a lifetime, were in the paradoxical position of not being able to take advantage of their changed circumstances. Because supplies of iron were short, horseshoes were cast of silver. A piece of armor or a gun was worth a fortune in gold. The officers and men made fresh remonstrations to Pizarro to execute Atahualpa as a way out of all their troubles. Pizarro at first demurred, or for the sake of appearances, pretended to do so. Then he agreed to a trial.

The ruler of the Inca was accused of "treason," of trying to raise

Above: in a desperate bid for freedom, Atahualpa promised to fill a room seven feet high with gold and silver. Magnificent objects, such as this golden toucan (a common bird in Peru) were brought from all over the empire.

Above: the dark line marking the height of the treasure can still be seen in the ransom room at Cajamarca. The size of the ransom was unparalleled in history. Most of the best of Peru's artifacts were brought here, melted down by the Spaniards, and shipped to Spain.

Left: Indian messengers bring fine gold ornaments, stripped from temples and palaces throughout the Inca empire, to fulfill Atahualpa's ransom promise.

The following labels appear within the painting:

DIFUNTO ATAHUALLP

CAPILLA DELA CA[T]

GUAINA CCAPAC PADRE DEL DIFU[N]TO.

JUAN D PISARR[O] HERNANDO PISARRO ...CONDE...CELE[N]S ALSARA[DO] HERRERA MAMA QUACHAIOZA MADRE DEL DIFUNTO

F. FRANCISCO PISARRO

MAMA OCLLO.

HUASC[AR] YNGA [HER]MANO DEL DIF[UNTO]

FR. UICENTE BALUERDE

D. JUAN ATA GUALL PA.

forces to overcome the Spaniards. However much Atahualpa denied this, he faced other accusations such as incest (the recognized legal marriage with his sister), usurpation of the Inca throne, and just about anything else the Spaniards could think of. The court was assembled on August 29, 1533. Prudently, Pizarro had sent his brother Hernando and De Soto to investigate a false rumor of troops congregating some distance from the town. When they returned to the camp, the deed was already done. Atahualpa had been found guilty and sentenced to death by fire. Just before the execution, his sentence was commuted from burning at the stake like a heretic, to strangulation. The judicial murder of the man who had kept his side of the bargain and who had given no intimation that he would have

Above: the trial and death of Atahualpa, by an unknown artist of the Cusco school. After fulfilling his promise and amassing a fortune in gold for the Spaniards, Atahualpa was tried on trumped up charges, sentenced to death, and murdered by the Spaniards.

120

harmed the Spaniards, was a simple measure of brutal expediency rather than justice.

Pizarro now resolved to move on the capital. Resistance was minimal. The Inca seemed completely demoralized by the swift turn of events. On November 15, 1533, just one year after his arrival at Cajamarca, Pizarro entered Cusco with a force of 480 Spaniards. The restraint that the soldiers were forced to exercise on the march was abandoned as soon as they reached the capital. The beautiful city of Cusco, over 300 years old, was stripped bare of everything of pos-

sible value. Temples, palaces, and homes were plundered. In some buildings, the Spaniards found planks of silver 20 feet long. Even the sacred mummies of earlier Inca emperors were looted of their jewels.

The Spaniards helped themselves liberally to everything. The Inca's ingrained obedience to whichever hierarchy was in power was mistaken for cowardice on their part. The inhabitants were tortured and raped at will. Their engineering marvels, such as the irrigation canals that had rendered wastelands into fertile havens, were allowed to fall into decay. The fields became fallow and llamas were killed off at such a rate that the breed was threatened with extinction.

When the rape of Cusco was complete, Pizarro set about establishing order in the chaotic city. He appointed a new Inca emperor,

Above: Pizarro marched into Cusco in November of 1533. The inhabitants were tortured, raped, and put to the sword, while the city itself was systematically stripped of everything of value.

CARIBBEAN SEA

ATLANTIC

OCEAN

Isthmus of Panamá

GULF OF DARÍEN

Panamá

Orinoco

Magdalena

Santa Fé de Bogotá

Orinoco

T. OF GALLO

SAN MATEO BAY

Caquetá

Quito

EQUATOR

EQUATOR

Napo

Amazon

GUAYAQUIL

Tumbes

Chira

San Miguel

Sechura Desert

Cajamarca

PACIFIC

Lima

Cusco

Lake Titicaca

OCEAN

A N D E S

Atacama Desert

Tupiza

TROPIC OF CAPRICORN

Copiapó

La Serena

from Valparaíso

to Santiago

.... Andagoya	1	1522
———— Pizarro, Francisco (followed by Almagro)	2a	1524-5
Pizarro, Francisco (with Almagro & Ruiz)	2b	1526-8
Pizarro, Francisco (with his 3 brothers & half-brother & followed by Almagro)	2c	1531-5
– – – – Alvarado	3	1533-5
———— Benalcazaar	4	1534
.... Almagro	5	1535-7
·········· Jiménez de Quesada	6a	1536-7
Supply ships	6A	1536
Jiménez de Quesada	6b	1569-72
———— Pizarro, Gonzalo (with Orellana)	7	1540-8
———— Orellana	8	1541-3
———— Valdivia	9	1540-7

© Geographical Projects

Miles

100 200 300 400 500

80°   70°   60°   50°

30°

Above: this equestrian statue of Francisco Pizarro, the conqueror of Peru, stands in the plaza at Trujillo, Spain, the conquistador's birthplace.

Left: this map of northern South America shows the routes of Francisco Pizarro, Almagro, Valdivia, and the other Spanish conquistadors as they explored the rugged western side of the vast continent. It also shows Orellana's amazing journey eastward down the Amazon to the Atlantic Ocean in 1541–1543.

Manco Capac, as puppet ruler. Real authority, however, was vested in a town council consisting of eight *regidors,* two of whom were his brothers Juan and Gonzalo. Every Spaniard was allotted a house, a grant of land, and Indian servants.

Cusco, located high in the Andes, was too far inland to serve as the center of Spanish trade with the mother country. Leaving his brothers in command at the ancient Inca capital, Pizarro traveled to the coast where he founded the new *City of the Kings* on January 18, 1535. The future Lima, located near the mouth of the Rimac River, was to serve as the headquarters of the Spanish government in South America for the next 200 years. With characteristic vigor Pizarro exchanged his sword for the tools of an artisan and began the planning and construction of his capital.

Everything was quiet. The victory was complete. Or was it? Little undercurrents began to ripple the smooth surface of everyday life. These were not discernible to the new masters of the Inca empire. But they soon would be. The peace was illusory.

Below : Spanish soldiers ill-treating
their Indian slaves. After the conquest of
Peru, the Indian population was reduced
to slavery by the introduction of
the brutal encomienda system, the basis
of the Spanish colonial empire.

The Quest for an Empire

8

By 1535, the conquest of Peru was complete. This should have been the end of the epic adventure. But the spirit of the conquistador was a restless one and his appetite for gold was not easily satisfied. The vast South American continent held promises of still richer kingdoms for those who were willing to look for them. Thus began a period of exploration, during which the conquistador was to reach into the most inaccessible corners of the Andes Mountains and the almost impenetrable growth of the Amazon jungle. The conquistadors found no kingdoms equal to those of the Aztec and the Inca, but in the course of their search, they opened up the whole of South America.

Diego de Almagro was the first to look beyond the lands of the Inca. In reward for his part in the conquest of Peru, Almagro was appointed *adelantado* of the region stretching 500 miles below the southern extremity of Pizarro's lands. After an abortive attempt to claim Cusco as part of his grant, Almagro began preparations to explore the lands farther south.

In July of 1535, accompanied by 570 Spaniards and several thousand Indians, Almagro left Cusco. Herds of llama and swine, which were to provide food during the outward-bound journey, trailed behind the column of marching men. The first leg of the trip, along the Inca highway, was made quickly and with relative ease.

But 150 miles southeast of Cusco, the Inca military road winds out of the highland valleys and ascends the Bolivian *altiplano,* a high, wind-swept plateau that is bordered on two sides by parallel ice-capped ranges of the towering *Cordillera* of the Andes. Almagro led his men along the western shore of Lake Titicaca—the world's highest inhabited lakeland area that today forms part of the border between Peru and Bolivia. The Spaniards were astonished to see the remains of elaborate stone buildings and huge megalithic structures whose precision-measured blocks weighed sometimes 100 tons. Here and there on the bleak altiplano stood tall columns with decorative friezes. The ruins were the last remnants of the Tiahuanaco Indians who had flourished in the area from the A.D. 300's to the 900's. In the 1200's, the Inca had extended their rule throughout the plateau and, in consequence, Tiahuanaco architecture had profoundly influenced subsequent Inca construction.

As the Spaniards trudged along the barren altiplano, about 12,500

feet above sea level, they suffered severely. The soldiers struggled for breath and were blinded by the dazzling light of the rarefied atmosphere. As they made their way south through what is now Bolivia, food and water became scarce. Most of all they complained of the excruciating cold. It was midwinter and the treeless steppe offered no protection to an army on the march. Augustin de Zarate, a Spanish historian of the 1500's, states: "No clothes or armor were sufficient to keep out the icy wind which pierced and froze them." Men and horses began to drop out, undergoing agonies of frostbite from which many never recovered. "The ground was so cold, too, that when Don Diego [Almagro] returned to Cusco 5 months later he found in various places men who had died on the way out frozen hard to the rocks with the horses they were leading; and their bodies were as fresh from corruption as if they had only just died."

At Tupiza, in southwest Bolivia, they reached the southern limit of the altiplano. The depleted force made its descent into the

Left: Inca reed boats on Lake Titicaca, the world's highest navigable inland lake. Almagro and his men marched along the shores of Lake Titicaca on their way south to Chile. There they encountered traces of the ancient Tiahuanaco civilization (A.D. 300–900). Below: early Spanish woodcut of Lake Titicaca. The artist has pictured an imaginary European city on its shores.

Left: Almagro and his forces crossing the Chilean Andes. Although the Spaniards suffered from the bitter cold and thin air of the Andes peaks, it was the Indian porters who underwent the greatest hardship. Unaccustomed to the extreme cold, unprotected by warm clothing, and struggling under their heavy burdens, 1500 Indians died during the crossing.

Above: the "Peruvian sheep" or llamas as depicted in Zarate's *History of the Discovery and Conquest of Peru.* The llama was to prove invaluable to all Spanish explorers in South America.

secluded valley of Salta, in northwest Argentina. There they rested for the remaining winter months before resuming their march. The most difficult part of the journey lay ahead. The conquistadors now had to cross the towering peaks of the Andes that separate Chile from eastern South America. The casualties increased sharply as Almagro led his men through freezing mountain passes to Copiapó, in northern Chile. More than 1,600 men, mostly Indians, died during the march.

One of the stoutest members of the expedition was the llama, the animal peculiar to the Andes, which the conquistadors referred to as "Peruvian sheep." Zarate's account of the expedition gives a detailed description of the llama. "In all these wild places where there was no snow there was a great shortage of water, which the Spaniards carried in sheepskins, each living sheep carrying the skin of a dead

one on its back filled with water. One of the characteristics of these Peruvian sheep is that they can carry a load of 50 or 60 pounds, like camels, which they much resemble in build though they have no hump. The Spaniards have since used them as horses, for they can carry a man 4 or 5 leagues [10 or 13 miles] in a day. When they are tired and lie on the ground, they will not get up even if beaten or pulled; the only thing to do is to take off their load. If they grow tired when ridden and the rider urges them on, they will turn their heads and spatter him with a very evil smelling liquid which they seem to carry in their crops . . . these animals are of great use and profit, for they have very fine wool, especially the kind that they call alpaca, which have long fleeces. They require little food, especially those that work; they eat maize and can go for three or four days without drink. Their flesh is . . . clean and succulent."

Above: the Pacific coast where Almagro and his men rested before continuing south. The mild, subtropical climate offered a welcome respite after the freezing cold of the Bolivian altiplano and the Andes Mountains.

From Copiapó Almagro led his men south through a subtropical belt of the Chilean coastal strip. The soft breezes and abundant vegetation made a refreshing contrast to the savage cold they had endured on the barren Bolivian altiplano and the freezing Andean Cordillera.

Almagro halted the army near what is now Santiago in central Chile. By a circuitous route he had covered a distance of about 2,500 miles since leaving Cusco. Nowhere had he seen a kingdom to rival that of the Inca. Because of the barrenness of the soil and the lack of easy treasure, Almagro was merely perfunctory in claiming title to the region in the name of the Spanish king. He was certain by this time that he would not settle in the lands in which he had been appointed *adelantado*. He determined to return to Peru and demand from Pizarro his proper share in the fruits of a venture in which they had set out as equal partners.

Before heading north, however, Almagro sent a reconnaissance party farther south in the hope that some rich kingdom might yet be discovered. The scouting party went as far south as the Maule River—the southern boundary of the former Inca empire. They encountered only savage and hostile Indians. There was no gold whatsoever. Although the land was green and fertile they preferred to tell their leader that it was drab and uninteresting and not worth pursuing. The soldiers were as anxious to return home as was their commander. The journey had been hard and the returns negligible. When news was brought that an Indian uprising had sparked a countrywide revolt in Peru, and that the Spaniards were in imminent danger of losing everything they had so recently won, Almagro hastened his departure north.

Profiting from the bitter lesson of the outward journey, Almagro resolved to avoid the peril and discomfort of the highland route by keeping as close to the coast as possible. The first stage of the journey, as far as Copiapó, was over familiar ground and was covered briskly and in comparative comfort. The soldiers were pleased to be going home.

Advancing north of Copiapó, the Spaniards found themselves on the threshold of the Atacama Desert, one of the most forbidding regions in the world. As they struggled forward, the sun beat down mercilessly with temperatures of over 100°F. No vegetation relieved the monotonous brown landscape. Hovering in the background,

Left: Inca warriors under Manco Capac rebel against Spanish rule. On receiving news of the Inca uprising in Peru, Almagro hastened back to Cusco.

Below: from their stronghold on a mountain peak, Indian warriors hurl stones and uprooted trees at the Spanish soldiers approaching below. The Inca, familiar with the terrain, were better equipped for mountain warfare than the Spaniards who were encumbered by their horses and heavy armor.

HISTORIA GENERAL
DE LOS HECHOS
DE LOS CASTELLANOS
EN LAS ISLAS Y TIERRA FIRME
DEL MAR OCEANO
Escrita por Antonio de Herrera
Coronista
Mayor de SU MAGESTAD
de las Yndias y Coronista de Castilla
y Leon
DECADA QUARTA
AL REY Nuestro Señor

El Adelantado Capitan Liberal. Don Diego de Almagro

El Marqz Don Francisco Picarro de Truxillo

Franco Pizarro y sus compas estan en la ysla Gorgona

Franco Picarro Sale de Panama a descubrir

Franco Pizarro de la Puña pasa a Tumbez

Los Castellanos llegan a la Baya de san Mateo

Los de Tumbez debaxo de Seguro dan en los Castellanos

Los Castellanos pasan a la Isla Puña

Edified el primer templo en S. Miguel de piura y Her de Soto pelea con los yn

los Castellanos pelean con los Indios en la puña

El Adelantado Don Pedro de Alvarado de Badaxoz

El Capitan Diego de Ordas del Reyno de Leon

la Batalla de Vtlatlangz dio don Pedro de Alvarado a los yndios

Diego de Ordas Reconoce el Volcan de Tlaxcala

Left: page from Herrera's *General History.* In the top left-hand corner is the conquistador Diego Almagro, on the right Francisco Pizarro. Other drawings show incidents from their conquest of Peru. At one time close friends, Almagro and Pizarro fell out over the division of their spoils. Their quarrel resulted in a civil war among the invading Spaniards that lasted for 11 years.

Right: Almagro and his followers lay siege to the city of Cusco, from Gomara's *History of the New World.* The former Inca capital is portrayed as a medieval European town with towering castles and drawbridges.

the ice-capped western Cordillera of the Andes seemed to mock the soldiers as they trudged through the blistering heat of their present route.

In April of 1537, Almagro's force reached the outskirts of Cusco. There they learned that Manco Capac, the puppet-ruler, had escaped and rallied the Inca nation to rise up against the Spaniards. Hernando and Gonzalo Pizarro, with 200 Spanish soldiers, had been besieged in their mountain camp at Cusco almost from the very moment Almagro had left for Chile some two years earlier. Francisco Pizarro was at Lima on the coast and was powerless to help the beleaguered fortress. His own force was relatively small in numbers, and the lines of communication between Lima and Cusco had been cut by Manco Capac's forces.

The Inca were far more experienced in mountain warfare than were the Spaniards. As they darted from their clifftop fortresses and laid their ambushes in narrow mountain passes, the Indians attacked with relative impunity. Encumbered by their heavy armor, breathless from the high altitude, and separated from supplies and reinforcements by miles of mountainous territory, the Spaniards were no match for the Inca warriors. Augustin de Zarate described the Inca's successful tactics. "The Indians let the Spaniards enter a very deep and narrow valley, and blocked both the entrance and the way out with great numbers of men. Then they hurled so many stones and boulders down on them from the slopes that they killed almost all of them without coming to close quarters; and from the dead, who amounted to more than three hundred, they took great quantities of jewels and arms and silk clothing."

Foolishly, the Inca allowed themselves to be drawn into open battle by Almagro and his men. The battle took place on the plains near Cusco and the Inca were soundly defeated. It was a decisive turning point in the conflict. From that time on, organized resistance to the Spaniards petered out into sporadic raids from mountaintop fortresses such as Vilcapampa and Machu Picchu. Almagro entered Cusco both as liberator and conqueror. He chose this moment to make good his previous claim to the city.

The Inca were now treated to the spectacle of a civil war between their conquerors, as the followers of Pizarro fought the Almagro faction for supremacy. On April 6, 1538, Almagro's forces were defeated on the plain of Las Salinas near Cusco. The aging conquistador was brought before Hernando Pizarro for trial. Almagro begged for mercy: "I was the first ladder by which you and your brother mounted up. When I held you as you now hold me and all counselled your death, I alone gave you life." Hernando rebuked Almagro saying that these were no fit words for a man of courage and that he should prepare to meet his death "like a Christian and a gentleman." "I am human and may fear death, since Christ himself feared it," was the reply. The old adventurer, who had played a large part in the conquest of Peru and had explored hundreds of miles of unknown territory, was summarily tried and executed in July, 1538.

Almagro's death was only the first step in a power struggle that was to last for 11 years. Three years later, on June 26, 1541, Almagro's death was avenged when a band of his followers murdered Francisco Pizarro in his palace at Lima. The conquistador's death is described by Augustin de Zarate: "They all fell on the Marquis with such fury that he was too exhausted to brandish his sword. And so they finished him off with a thrust through the throat. As he fell, he cried for a confessor. But his breath failed him. Making a cross on the floor, he kissed it and so gave up the ghost." "Thus one sees,"

Right: capture and death of the conquistador Diego Almagro. Defeated by Hernando Pizarro at the Battle of Salinas, Almagro was tried and executed in July of 1538

Below: Francisco Pizarro is murdered at the palace in Lima. Although the conquistador was killed by Almagro's followers three years after their leader's death, the Indian artist has depicted Almagro himself thrusting his sword through Pizarro's heart.

Zarate continues, "the way of the world and the varieties of fortune: that in so short a time a gentleman who had discovered and governed great lands and kingdoms . . . should be killed . . . yet none of them came to his aid."

While the power struggle between the supporters of Pizarro and the followers of Almagro raged in Peru, the search for new sources of gold and glory continued. Rumors of mysterious kingdoms in the interior of present-day Colombia and Venezuela flourished. The most haunting of the legends that grew up was that of the *El Dorado*—a mythical South American king who supposedly powdered his body with gold dust each morning and washed it off every evening in a lake. The name El Dorado also referred to a fictitious kingdom located somewhere on the Amazon. During the search for the kingdom of El Dorado, northwest South America was opened up.

In April of 1536, Gonzalo Jiménez de Quesada set out to explore the forbidding interior of Colombia. He traveled overland through the swamps and jungles of the coastal region and finally reached the Magdalena, Colombia's chief river. Penetrating farther inland, Jiménez de Quesada came upon hints of a superior civilization. He was nearing the kingdom of the Chibcha Indians who lived on the high plains of the central Colombian Andes. The Chibcha were a highly advanced civilization with stone temples, statues, roads, and suspension bridges that almost rivaled those of the Maya, Aztec, and Inca. They worked gold, drilled emeralds, made pottery and basketry, and wove textiles. Their's was the last kingdom of any great wealth to be found in South America.

Politically divided, the Chibcha fell easily to Jiménez de Quesada's forces, and the valuable Colombian highlands, rich in minerals and emeralds, was incorporated into Spain's empire in the New World. On August 6, 1538, Jiménez de Quesada founded the town of *Santa Fé de Bogotá*, which became the capital of the Spanish Viceroyalty (province) of New Granada (present-day Panama, Colombia, Ecuador, and Venezuela). Today, Bogotá is the capital of Colombia.

The discovery of the kingdom of the Chibchas focused attention on the northern segment of South America. No expense was spared as one expedition followed another in an effort to capture the glittering prize of El Dorado. Wily Indians fired the conquistadors' insatiable desire by luring the strangers in the one direction left

Right: title page from Book VI of Herrera's *History,* depicting several incidents from the civil war that raged between the followers of Almagro and Pizarro. The page includes a portrait of Gonzalo Jiménez de Quesada in the upper right-hand corner. Jiménez de Quesada explored the interior of Colombia while searching for the legendary city of El Dorado. He conquered the Chibcha Indians and founded the city of Bogotá in 1538.

El Mariscal ✠ Alonso de Alvarado

Prision de Atahualpa Rey del Piru

El Licenciado Gonzalo Ximenes de Quesada descubrio el Nuevo Reyno de Granada ✠

Batalla de Benalcazar

Almagro y Alvarado se conciertan

HISTORIA GENERAL
DE LOS HECHOS
DE LOS CASTELLANOS
EN LAS ISLAS Y TIERRA FIRME
DEL MAR OCEANO
Escrita por Antonio de Herrera
Coronista
Mayor de SU MAGESTAD
de las Yndias y Coronista de Castilla
y Leon
DECADA SESTA
AL REY   Nuestro Señor

Batalla de Abancay

Batalla de las Salinas

Sitio del Cuzco

El Mariscal ✠ Rodrigo Orgoñes

Adelantado ✠ Sebastian de Benalcazar

unexplored. To the east of Peru an enormous basin drained the chief river of South America—the 3,900-mile-long Amazon. The impenetrable jungle stretching the length of the river was rumored to hold not only the fabulous kingdom of gold, but large tracts of cinnamon trees.

In 1540, Gonzalo Pizarro set out from Cusco to find the riches that had so far eluded everyone. Early the next year, accompanied by Francisco de Orellana and a large cavalcade of soldiers and Indians, Pizarro left Quito in a blaze of triumph. The expedition crossed the

Left: the Amazon River winds sinuously through the jungles of Brazil. The longest river in South America, the Amazon takes its name from the legendary female warriors said to have been seen by Francisco de Orellana, the first white man to navigate the river to its mouth.

eastern Cordillera of the Andes and descended into the dense jungle growth of the Amazon basin. In order to make their way through the solid blanket of green, the Spaniards were forced to cut a path with their swords. In November 1541, they reached the banks of the Cocoa River, which flows into the Napo, one of the tributaries of the Amazon. When they reached a point where the river became navigable, Pizarro ordered the construction of a small boat to carry the sick and the heavy supplies. The march along the swampy river bank continued. Food became scarce and the men were forced to live off

Above: Pedro de Valdivia, conqueror and first governor of Chile. The young conquistador was appointed by Francisco Pizarro to found a colony to the south of Peru. Valdivia led his expedition to Chile in 1540.

wild roots and nuts. Hostile, primitive Indians sporadically attacked the weary men.

Near the junction of the Cocoa and Napo rivers, Pizarro halted the army and sent Orellana ahead in the boat to forage for food. It was Christmas when Orellana set out with about 50 men and most of the supplies and weapons. He made rapid progress downstream. The small craft, swept onward by a strong current, passed the juncture of the Cocoa and Napo, and raced on toward the Amazon. Finally, having covered 500 miles in 8 days, Orellana landed at a small village where there was a supply of food. The problem now was how to carry the food back to Pizarro. The current was so strong as to make an upstream voyage virtually impossible. Abandoning Pizarro and his men to their fate, Orellana continued to the mouth of the Amazon, thus becoming the first white man to explore the full course of South America's longest river.

Pizarro and his men waited in vain for Orellana's return. Desperate with hunger and exhaustion, the men "leaned against the trees and begged for food, but [they were] so thin and weak that they died of starvation." Deprived of his boat, and without adequate weapons or supplies, Pizarro was forced to fight his way back through the difficult terrain he had just covered. Finally, the tattered remnants of the once hopeful expedition reached the vicinity of Quito. A Spanish commentator described the pitiful condition of Pizarro and his men as they neared the city. "They were traveling almost naked, for their clothes had rotted long ago with the continuous rains. . . . Their swords were sheathless and eaten with rust. They were all on foot, and their arms and legs were scarred with wounds from the thorns and bushes. They were so pale and disfigured that they were scarcely recognizable."

While Gonzalo Pizarro was planning his ill-fated search for the kingdom of El Dorado, a smaller expedition set out quietly from Peru. Led by Pedro de Valdivia, this expedition to the south excited none of the enthusiasm or support that characterized Gonzalo's venture. Valdivia had been commissioned to found a colony in Chile. Because of Almagro's report that Chile held no treasure and that the routes south were of indescribable difficulty, Valdivia had a difficult task recruiting men for his expedition. "All fled from it as from the plague and many sane men thought I was insane." By January, 1540, however, he had accumulated sufficient numbers to

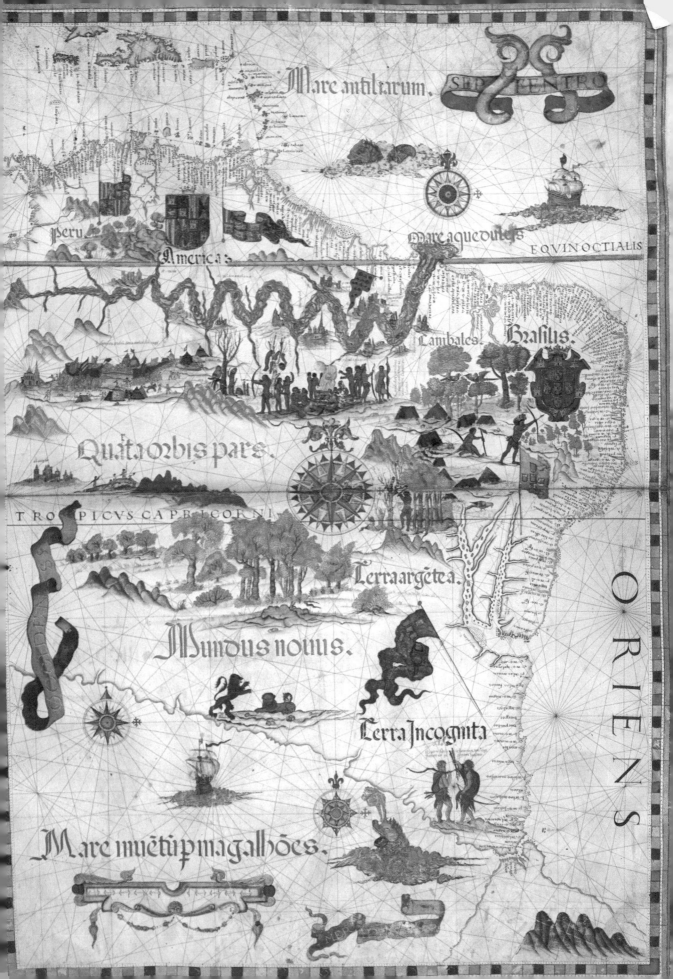

Above: Spanish laborers construct a
building in Santiago, the city founded
by Pedro de Valdivia in 1541.
Below: an early prospect and plan of
the settlement of Santiago.

make a start. The expedition consisted of 150 Spaniards, 100 Indians,
and horses and swine.

Profiting from Almagro's experience, Valdivia led his men south
along the Peruvian coastal strip and across the Atacama Desert into
Chile. The Indians, angry at this new invasion by the Spaniards,
concealed foodstuffs from the passing convoy, making the trek
even more difficult for Valdivia and his men. It was a year before
the exhausted Spanish force reached Copiapó—the first habitable
settlement after the barren wastes of desert lands.

Continuing south for another 400 miles, the Spaniards found
themselves in a beautiful, fertile valley at the foot of the Andes
Mountains. There, in February, 1541, Valdivia traced out the plans
for a city. The streets, main plaza, and sites for the town hall,
church, and prison were in the grand Spanish style. He allotted
each Spaniard land and *encomiendas* (Indian labor) to work it. As
wooden huts with thatched roofs sprang up in the beautiful green
turf, Valdivia's settlement took root. Such was the humble beginning
of Santiago, the capital of modern Chile.

Due to his extraordinary powers of leadership, Valdivia was able
to avert one crisis after another that plagued the colony in its early
years. The land itself was isolated from Peru. Not only distance but
the natural physical barriers of desert and mountain cut off Chile
from the rest of South America. The unusual ferocity of the Indians
frustrated early attempts on Valdivia's part to erect a permanent
base of operations. The Spaniards themselves were by no means
united in their desire to live and work peacefully in the fertile valley.
Many had come solely to find another Mexico or Peru and to win
immediate riches. They took the first opportunity to complain at
the land grants allocated to them by Valdivia and demanded huge
numbers of Indians to work for them. Dissension among the
colonists rose to mutinous levels.

Four months after the establishment of Santiago, Valdivia
received news of Pizarro's assassination. Almagro's son had illegally
claimed title to all Pizarro's offices and estates. The legitimacy of
Valdivia's grant was called into question by the unexpected events
in Peru. The newly constituted town council of Santiago decided to
settle the issue in its own way. It nominated Valdivia as governor
and captain general of Chile, pending ratification by the Spanish
king. Valdivia immediately made it clear that he would deal with no

Right: despite fierce opposition from the Araucanian Indians, the city of Santiago flourished. By the 1800's, it had become one of the most important centers of trade in South America.

Below: today Santiago is the capital and largest industrial city in Chile. Replacing earlier colonial buildings, skyscrapers now rise in the shadow of the snow-capped Chilean Andes.

usurpers in Peru and would recognize only those representatives legally appointed by Spain.

Anxious to keep informed of events in Peru, Valdivia decided to establish a sea link with the northern country. He led a detachment of men to a harbor site, 60 miles from Santiago, that he had noticed on his journey south. There, at what is modern Valparaíso, he ordered that a ship be constructed. A sea route would be infinitely preferable and faster than the overland alternatives. While on the coast a plot to overthrow the leader and seize control of the Chile expedition was revealed in Santiago. Valdivia quelled the rebellion by returning at once to the capital and executing the ringleaders.

No sooner had he returned to Santiago to cope with the dissident elements within his own ranks, than Valdivia was confronted with the news that the small garrison he had left at Valparaíso had been wiped out by the Indians. Only two survivors had escaped the massacre. The Indians, encouraged by the success of their first strike against the white intruders, concentrated all their efforts on driving the Spaniards out of the land completely. Waiting until Valdivia and the main body of the army were engaged outside the town, they attacked Santiago in full force. The 50 Spaniards trapped inside the fort were heroic in its defense and the Indians were put to flight. But by the time Valdivia and the army had returned, the town had been reduced to rubble and smoldering embers. "Not one post standing: we had nothing but our arms and the old rags which we wore in the fight."

There was nothing to do but to start rebuilding the city from scratch. The conquistadors became farmers and construction workers as the settlers engaged in a desperate attempt to keep the colony alive. Help was sought from Peru, and a party of five men, carrying as much gold as could be mustered, was dispatched north to secure supplies and reinforcements. Three of the party were killed by Indians at Copiapó but the remaining two men eventually reached Lima. They arrived in Peru just after Vaca de Castro, the new viceroy from Spain, had defeated the Almagrist army.

The desperate force at Santiago were compelled to wait two years before relief came. In September, 1543, a ship arrived in Valparaíso bringing food, supplies, and a relief force of 20 men. From that time forward, ships and men began to dribble into the isolated colony.

Above: present-day Valparaiso, Chile's main port and fishing center. Lying 60 miles west of Santiago, Valparaiso was founded by Valdivia in 1541.

Left: an early map of Valparaiso. The bustling port was a vital link in Chile's communications with the rest of Spain's colonies in South America.

Gradually, Valdivia began to broaden his sphere of operations. To the north, in the Coquimbo Valley, Valdivia built a town in 1545, and named it La Serena after his birthplace in Spain. A reconnaissance party to the south reported that the area was ideal for settlement. The land was fresh and green, suitable for both farming and grazing.

But before Valdivia could establish settlements in the south, he was called back to Peru to aid in putting down yet another rebellion. In 1544, Gonzalo Pizarro had challenged the legitimate viceroy's authority by declaring himself governor of Peru. Valdivia defeated

Pizarro's forces at Sacsahuana—the Inca fortress at Cusco. The viceroy rewarded him by confirming his title to Peru and extending the area of his governorship.

Valdivia returned to Chile in the early part of 1549, arriving in the aftermath of a serious revolt in the northern part of his domain. The uprising was severely put down and for the next few years all was comparative peace and quiet. Fields of corn and wheat flourished and the livestock multiplied. Chile was becoming a land of plenty. Valdivia established more towns to the south of Santiago, where the

Above: an Araucanian family in their traditional dress. The Araucanians in southern Chile successfully resisted Spanish domination for 300 years. They finally signed a peace treaty with the Chilean government in 1883.

Right: the Araucanians took horses from the Spaniards in the mid-1500's and moved freely between Argentina and Chile, fighting the Spaniards on the coast and fleeing to the mountains for refuge. Secure in their mountain retreats, the Araucanians found time for sport and recreation. Here, a group of Araucanian boys are seen playing a form of hockey.

green fertile land was watered by crystal clear streams and shaded by large forests. Concepción, which was soon to rival Santiago in importance and size, was founded in 1550.

But the period of grace for the Spaniards was running out. The Araucanian Indians of southern Chile particularly resented the presence of the strangers. Their resistance continued for 300 years. The Araucanians were a proud, fierce, and warlike tribe who refused to be enslaved by the white men. The atrocities of the Spaniards (400 Indian prisoners were mutilated by cutting off their right hands

and noses) infuriated the Indians who closed ranks against the oppressors. Their knowledge of the impenetrable forests and other peculiarities of the terrain gave them an advantage over their foe.

In December, 1553, while riding in the region of Concepción, Valdivia came across a Spanish fort that had been raided by the Indians. Accompanied by only a small force, he determined to seek out the perpetrators of the deed at once. The Araucanians were waiting for him.

Valdivia attacked, but the terrain was unfavorable for his horses and the attack was turned into an undignified retreat. It is said that Valdivia could have made good his escape but, when he saw his chaplain in difficulties, preferred to stay at his side. He was captured and tortured to death.

The Indians followed up their victory by storming Concepción and other southern towns. The inhabitants fled to Santiago. For three years, the Indians made devastating attacks, and reinforcements and supplies from Peru could barely keep up with the minimum supply needed to fight off the relentless strikes. Eventually, in April 1557, the Spaniards won a key victory and Chile was saved for Spanish domination. For the next 300 years, however, the Bío-Bío River in southern Chile remained the frontier of their dominion. The Araucanians were undisputed masters below this line. After a huge expenditure in lives and money had been wasted in attempting to subdue the belligerent tribe, the Spaniards left them to their own devices.

By 1550, most of South America had been conquered and explored by the Spanish conquistadors. Only Brazil, which Orellana had described as uninhabitable and which legitimately belonged to Portugal, remained outside Spanish rule. In less than 25 years since Pizarro's first landing in Ecuador, Spain's coffers had been filled with a fortune in gold and treasure. More important, the basis of continued Spanish control had been firmly established in the form of settlements and towns scattered throughout the continent. In their quest for gold and glory, the conquistadors had won for Spain a vast and sprawling empire that was to last for almost 300 years.

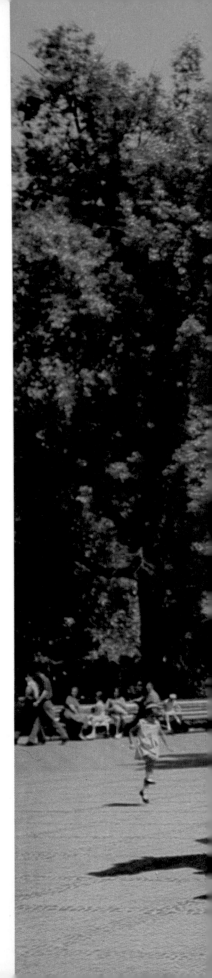

Right: this statue of Pedro de Valdivia stands in Santiago's main square – the Plaza de Armada. Valdivia died at the hands of the Araucanians in 1553.

End of an Era

9

"Broken spears lie in the roads,
We have torn our hair in grief.
The houses are roofless now . . .
And the walls are red with blood. . . ."

(Elegy for Tenochtitlán)

Tenochtitlán is dead. Four hundred and fifty years ago the passing of the Mexican city was mourned by an unknown Aztec poet. He saw it razed to the ground before his eyes. We shall never see it, this city of palaces and pyramids, of raised causeways across the lakes, of stone statues and turquoise masks. We shall never view the royal processions of priests and kings ablaze with jewels and plumes. We shall never follow the colorful canoes laden with fruit and native Mexican flowers as they glide silently in the watery streets. The city of the Aztec is gone. Only the snowy peaks of the Sierra Madre Mountains remain impassive and unchanged by the Spanish intrusion.

A thousand years before Columbus arrived in the New World, the Mexican high tableland had witnessed the rise and fall of many civilizations. But when the Spaniards arrived, the greatest of all Mexican empires was in the making—a colossus stretching from the arid steppes of northern Mexico to the burning jungles of the southern isthmus. The city of Tenochtitlán was barely 100 years old when it fell to the echo of steel blades against swords of volcanic glass, guns against arrows and spear-throwers, iron helmets against feather headdresses.

How did the Spaniards, so greatly outnumbered and with such dangerously extended supply lines, uniformly win the battles of conquest? Part of the answer lies in their weapons and horses. The explosion of a gun terrorized the Indians, while men on horseback were at first taken to be single creatures, awesome in their power. Imaginative campaigning, as in Cortes' use of brigantines on the waters of the Valley of Mexico, contributed to particular campaigns. The Indians were weakened psychologically through their superstitious myths, that sometimes foretold defeat at the hands of white and bearded strangers coming from the east. The Spanish policy of alliances with rival Indian tribes often equalized or minimized the initial imbalance in numbers. Thus, Cortes profited from the long-established hostility of the Tlaxcalan toward the Aztec. And Pizarro could hardly have made his way so readily through the Inca

Above: the brutal reality of the Spanish conquest of the Americas is illustrated by this simple Inca drawing of a Spaniard ill-treating his Indian servant.

Right: Santiago (Saint James), patron saint of the conquistadors, from a painting by an unknown artist of the Cusco school. The archetypal soldier-saint is pictured with upraised sword crushing his enemies beneath him. The battle-cry "Santiago!" rang out on every field of battle as the conquistadors fought their way to victory over the American Indians.

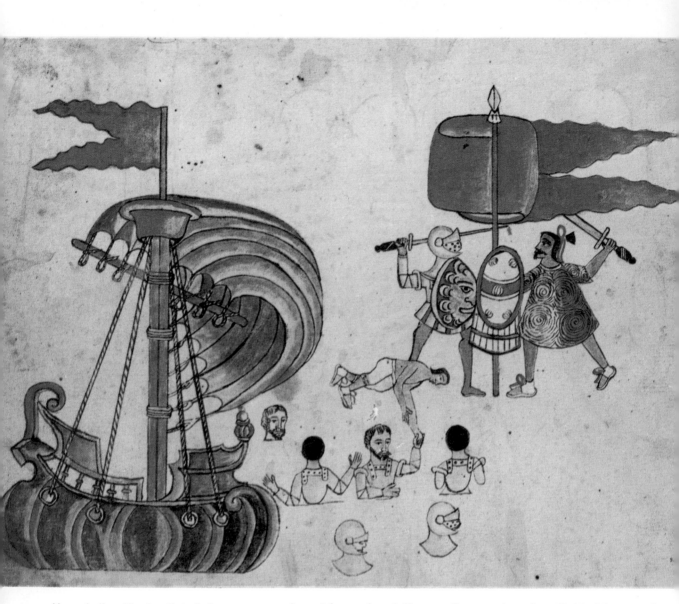

Above: Indian allies, hostile to their Aztec overlords, played an important part in the Spanish conquest of Mexico. In this Indian drawing, a Tlaxcalan warrior is seen pulling the armor-clad Cortes from a canal in Tenochtitlán.

empire without the civil war of succession that divided its people. Finally, Indian allies provided and transported goods, thus reducing the threat of overextended supply lines.

The confrontation between Aztec and Spaniard was more than just a meeting between two expanding nations—it was a clash between two radically different cultures. The Spaniards thought the Indian was an inferior species, a creature more animal than human, destined by God for slavery and serfdom. Moreover, he was guilty of tyranny, human sacrifice, cannibalism, idolatry, and other sins. The Aztec, on the other hand, thought the strangers represented Quetzalcoatl and other gods returning from over the sea. The Spaniards—despite their astonishment at the magnificent temples, palaces, and gardens of Tenochtitlán—considered the Aztec no better than barbarians.

The Europeans were not even sure that the Indians were human

Above: Indian laborers lay the cathedral foundation in Mexico City. Below: a Spanish friar instructs the Mexicans in the Christian religion. The Church's interest in the Indians' spiritual welfare did not deter them from exploiting Indian labor in the building of churches and monasteries.

beings. Did they have immortal souls? Should they be baptized? These were not idle questions. For Columbus and the powerful Spanish nation that he served, the spreading of the Christian gospel was an integral part of national policy. The theologians soon decided that the Indians did in fact have immortal souls and were proper subjects for conversion. Unfortunately for the Indians, they wore gold ornaments and jewels. The Spaniards had set out not only to spread the gospel but also to trade in the spices of the East. The prospect of finding gold and jewels softened their disappointment at failing to find the spice routes. The slight regard the Indians had for the ornaments they wore seemed to prove conclusively that the land was full of riches.

As Spain's need for more and more gold to maintain its naval supremacy increased, the Spanish adventurers were required to send vast stores of wealth back to the mother country. They were their own judges of the methods they used to get them. To find these realms of gold, adventurers probed along the coast and up the rivers, led expeditions into the interior, and built bases from which to organize systematic searches. In their minds, gold and glory were always uppermost. They had not left Europe, as many North American colonists had, to escape war or persecution, nor did they propose to carve a new home from the virgin territory. But while seeking gold and glory they had to eat, and that meant that food had to be grown. Gradually, as the illusion of ready-made wealth faded, many cut their dreams down to size and adjusted to living off the land.

Nevertheless, they still refused to work with their hands. Instead, the conquistador—both nobleman and commoner—continued to make the Indians do the work. The Indians found it less convenient. They lacked the physical stamina for steady exertion. They died off like flies in the gold mines of Hispaniola, under brutal Spanish overseers. On the great estates, too, the Indians were victimized by cruel overseers.

To the burdens imposed by this lay aristocracy were added those of supporting the Church. Christianity was represented at first by government-paid friars, who accompanied every expedition. The holy fathers often won the affection of the Indians by protecting them from the cruelties of the conquistadors. But even the friars could be harsh in the interests of God. Pagan temples had to be replaced as rapidly as possible by Christian churches. Indian laborers were made to quarry the stones, while Indian craftsmen carved them and set them in position under Spanish supervision. Every valley in central and southern Mexico was dominated by the towers and domes of churches—12,000 were built in Mexico alone during the colonial period. The churches testified not only to the triumph of Christ over Huitzilopochtli, but to the skill of his missionaries in obtaining unpaid labor from the Indians.

The most disastrous result of the Spanish conquest, however, had little to do with the cruelty of the conquistadors. The Spaniards had brought with them European diseases—smallpox, measles, influenza—against which the Indians had no natural immunity. Smallpox was rampant even before the fall of Tenochtitlán. Another disease, which first appeared during the viceroyalty of Mendoza, killed the Indians by the hundreds of thousands and then swept

Above: an early map showing the profusion of churches that sprang up after the Spanish conquest. During the colonial period, about 12,000 churches were built in Mexico alone.

Right: La Antigua, the oldest church in the Americas, was founded by Hernando Cortes at Veracruz shortly after the Spaniards' arrival in the New World.

Below: Indians suffering from smallpox, from a contemporary illustration. The Spaniards brought new diseases and infections with them to the New World. During the 1500's epidemics of smallpox, measles, and influenza swept through the Americas killing hundreds of thousands of Indians.

across New Spain again and again during the following 200 years. At the time, the disease was attributed to the influence of a comet or to volcanic fumes. It was, apparently, a strain of influenza. In turn, the Indians infected the Spaniards with syphilis—a kind of biological revenge. The result of these diseases was a heavy decrease in population. For hundreds of years, Mexico was never so thickly inhabited as before the Spanish conquest.

Spain, in contrast to the English colonies to the north, regretted the depopulation caused in Central and South America. The Spaniards—in spite of the practices that killed Indians by the tens of thousands—depended on them to exploit the riches of the conquered lands. In Spanish America, the Indians were regarded from the start as subjects of the Spanish king, and the authorities in Spain did their utmost to ensure that they should be protected, converted to Christianity, and instructed in useful crafts.

Bartolome de las Casas, the first monk to protest effectively

Above: Indian representation of the encomienda system from the Kingsborough Codex. Under the system, Indian labor was leased to the Spaniards who, in turn, were responsible for the physical and spiritual well-being of their charges. Not unnaturally, the system led to unjust exploitation of the Indians. Addressed to the Royal Audiencia, the Kingsborough Codex complained of the excessive duties imposed by Spanish overseers.

against Spanish cruelty, spent a long lifetime working among the American Indians. He and others had the legal status of the Indians spelled out. The basic institution created to protect them was the *encomienda* that introduced the European feudal relationship of lord and vassal. The Indians were to be brought together in villages where they would be under the authority of a Spaniard. They were not slaves but free men in the eyes of the law, entitled to certain rights in return for specified services.

The Spaniard undertook to "convert, civilize, and educate" the Indians in his service, while guaranteeing them possession of the lands owned by the village. In return, the Indians had to work in his fields or mines. In practice, there was nobody to see that the Spaniards carried out their part of the bargain. Despite the protests of Las Casas and other missionaries, the Spaniards gradually established rights over the village lands and reduced the Indians, in effect, to slaves. Large numbers, nevertheless, survived and were gradually incorporated into the Spanish culture, forming the basis of the modern population. The process of incorporation was facilitated by the intermarriage of Spanish men and Indian women.

The New World was conquered by conquistadors. But most of the men whose qualities had made such extraordinary achievements possible were not of the stuff of empire-builders. Even the role of explorer had been purely incidental. Their business was fighting. Success did not break them of the habit and most of them died violent deaths in the power struggles that followed upon each new conquest. Consolidation of the empire they gained was left to others.

The conquistadors and their lands were controlled by a bureaucracy whose members were sent out from Spain. At the top of the administrative pyramid was a viceroy who lived in royal magnificence and

Above: this painting of the 1700's shows the double wedding of two Inca ladies and two Spaniards. The woman on the left is robed in the traditional Inca ceremonial dress, while the bride on the right wears European costume. Intermarriage between Spanish men and Indian noblewomen was encouraged in colonial Spanish America. The descendants of such marriages make up the majority of the population of most Latin American countries.

 QHAZE·TEGR·RO   PORFVERZACASA   CASTIGACRVELMEN   MALACONFICION

How they make their women work   How they marry the Indians   How they confess them   How they apply penitence

SOBERBIOSO·P·COLERICO   COMBIDAELPALOSBORA   CRISTIAVICIMO·PÕEV   FRAILEFRAÑ·S·ÕT

They fight   They get drunk with half-castes   There are also some good Christians   The Franciscans are charitab

Above: the misconduct and cruelties of Spanish priests in Peru are irreverently depicted in a series of drawings made about the year 1613 by the Inca artist Poma de Ayala. The last four drawings show that there were also good men among the clergy, especially the Franciscan mendicants who were "poor and beg like the rest of the poor."

was treated with royal honors The viceroy was assisted by an *audiencia*—a civil court—and an advisory body. The smaller administrative divisions were headed by governors and mayors. All these officials, as well as the higher officials of the Church, were usually Spanish-born.

The Viceroy of New Spain held court in Mexico City. His authority reached from Texas to Panama. The Viceroy of Peru, with his palace in Lima, controlled almost the whole of South America (with the exception of the Portuguese territory of Brazil).

In theory, as well as in practice, the authority of the King of Spain was supreme in the Americas. His wishes were transmitted to his American kingdoms by the Council of the Indies—a powerful body whose functions included the issuing of laws, the supervision of the Church, justice, and finance, and the direction of trade and shipping.

It was the end of an era. The swarm of officials that had plagued Cortes in New Spain now had access to South and Central America as well. But the new laws they introduced came too late to save the Indians. Manco Capac, the Inca puppet ruler, who had so nearly succeeded in destroying the Spaniards at Cusco in 1536,

hey cruelly punish little children

They gamble

ICARIOGENERALSO

ood aged vicar of eighty years

HERMITAÑOSS.DEEUS

A pious hermit begs for the poor

Above: religious procession in modern Lima. Ninety out of a hundred Peruvians belong to the Roman Catholic Church. But even today, many Indians cling to the religion of their ancestors.

carried on a guerilla resistance until his death at the hands of Spanish forces eight years later. Thereafter, the few Indians who continued to resist were forced to retreat deeper and deeper into the Andes Mountains. Their last strongholds were in the mountains between the Urubamba and the Apurimac rivers. Machu Picchu was almost certainly one of them. The impenetrable nature of these mountains offered no incentive to Spaniards intent upon the rapid acquisition of wealth, and it was their failure to penetrate this area that gave rise to rumors of lost cities and hidden hoards of Inca gold. The majority of Indians, however, passively accepted the destruction of their civilization and the condition of virtual serfdom that followed.

The first Spaniards who came to the Americas were conquerors. They were men of a feudal age not yet ended, who stood on the threshold of an age of discovery. Individually they were adventurers who financed their own expeditions and staked everything on one throw. They knew with great exactness what they wanted. They wanted gold, and they sought it ruthlessly. In the cases of Mexico and Peru, they knew they could win only through desperate meas-

ures. They were willing to risk their lives to achieve their ends. Something of the pain they caused they also endured.

The natural abilities of the conquistadors, as well as their luck, varied widely. Some of them were obvious incompetents. Others gave hints of genius. They ranged from the illiterate Pizarro (perhaps the boldest adventurer of them all), to the cultured and sophisticated Cortes. But none of them deviated from the broad pattern. All had those qualities that in the circumstances made for their short-term success—an overpowering lust for gold, a religious fanaticism, a hardness toward self and toward others, and a heroic discipline.

With the assassination of Pizarro in 1541, the age of the conquistador was drawing to its end. The period of discovery and conquest had been relatively short. Within 50 years a whole new world, vast in size and spanning two continents, had been opened up.

Acknowledgments

PART TWO

Rivers of Destiny

Rivers of Destiny

BY SIMON DRESNER

Right: an Indian from the Nipissing region, Canada, done by an anonymous artist, 1717.

Foreword

The Aztec capital Tenochtitlán lay in ruins. The last survivors of the Inca had withdrawn into their lofty mountain retreats gradually to die out, forgotten but unconquered. Then it was that the Spanish conquistadors began to look north. Reports of mariners who had sailed the Atlantic had revealed that the Americas stretched far to the north of Mexico and, in such a great continent, so the Spanish believed, there were bound to be riches to rival the Aztec and Inca wealth. So, relentlessly pursuing their dream of treasure, the Spanish took the first steps north.

The North American continent, however, held none of the riches the Spanish were seeking. Its treasures were of a different kind. They lay in furs to trade and in land to farm, in freedom from the hatreds and persecutions that were rife in so many of the countries of Europe, and in the opportunity for any man who was strong and willing to carve out a new life. In pursuit of these goals, the European pioneers crossed the Atlantic, the French to trade in the St. Lawrence Valley, the English to colonize the east coast. As time passed, the European nations established themselves firmly on North American soil.

Here is the story of the pioneers of North American exploration, of the men who made the first forays into the interior of that land. It tells of their first meetings with the Indian peoples, and of the first struggles between them, during which the seeds of long years of discord would be sown. It is a tale, too, of political rivalry, as the European nations set up their colonies and maneuvered for supremacy in North America, and of the struggles by which the disputes between them were solved. During those exciting years of discovery and of colonizing, the foundations of the great American nations would be laid.

The First Americans
1

In the early hours of October 12, 1492, three small, weather-beaten ships moved slowly westward through the waters of the Atlantic. The night was calm, but the men on board the three vessels tossed restlessly in their sleep. They had been sailing through uncharted seas for more than a month, and most of the crew shared a deep and fearful conviction that they were doomed. Their commander's promises that they would find "lands to the west" had begun to sound like the words of a madman, and mutiny was brewing. . . .

Suddenly, at 2 A.M., a hoarse shout rang out from the watch on board the *Pinta*. "Land!" cried the lookout, "Land! Land!" The ship's master, Captain Martin Pinzon, hurriedly made his way to the rails and peered through the mist. It was not the first time that "land" had been sighted in the last two weeks, and he feared what the crew might do if their frail hopes were dashed again. But this time there could be no mistake. Land lay ahead, a pale but distinct line low on the horizon. He could just make out a row of white cliffs shining far away in the moonlight.

News of the sighting quickly passed from ship to ship. As the excited crews made preparations for a landing, Admiral Christopher

Left: the people of the vast new world that Columbus discovered were not mere savages, who had no experience of any culture but their own, as reported by the early explorers. American "Indians" were in fact an enormously varying people, with patterns of life adapted harmoniously to the conditions in which they lived. In this painting George Catlin shows the Chippewa dancing their snowshoe dance, singing in thanksgiving to the Great Spirit for the first snowfall, when hunters could track their quarry more easily.

Right: Christopher Columbus, in a portrait by Sebastiano de Piombo, painted in 1519, probably from a life portrait. It shows Columbus in his vigorous and commanding middle age.

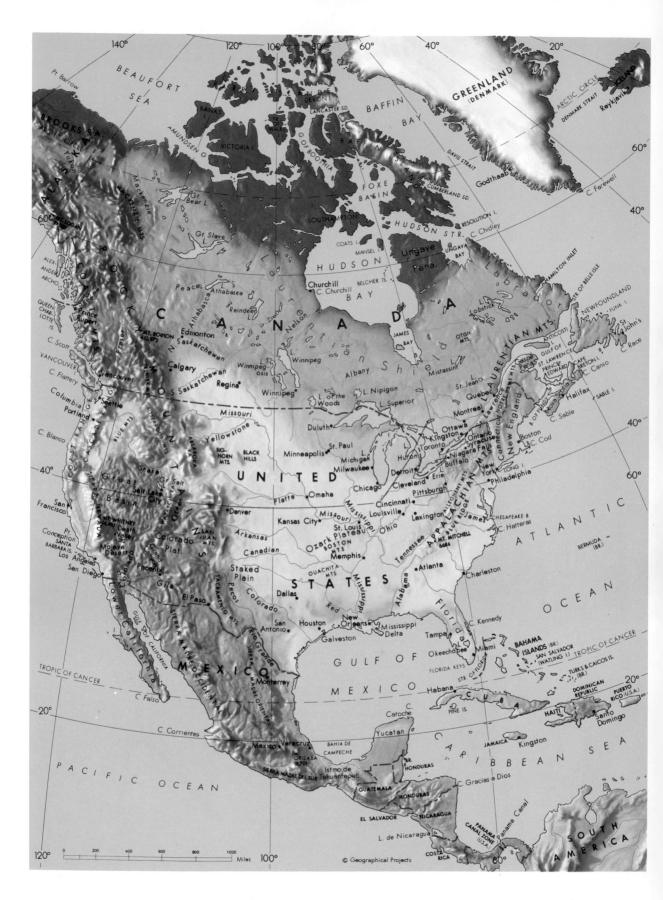

Columbus paced the deck of the Spanish flagship *Santa María* in eager anticipation. Not for a moment did either he or his men doubt that the island now looming up before them was an outpost of the fabled Indies, the Eastern world of spice and treasure, luxury and culture so glowingly described by Marco Polo.

That the world he had discovered was utterly different from what he believed it to be would not in fact be fully realized for almost a decade. Columbus himself would never know that he had found the New World and that, in so doing, he had inaugurated a period of exploration, conquest, and colonization that would completely alter the course of history.

But if Columbus was ignorant of the real significance of his voyage, so too were the peoples who would ultimately be most affected by it. As the three ships moved slowly, fatefully, toward the island of San Salvador in the Bahamas, neither its inhabitants nor those of the immense continent beyond it had any inkling of the dramatic

Above: Osceola, the young warrior of the Seminole tribe, shows all the pride and distinguished bearing of the native Americans in this portrait painted by George Catlin in 1837–38.

Right: the Indian village of Secoton, Virginia, showing the tidy arrangement of fields and houses. The watercolor drawing is by John White, the leader of the ill-fated colony of Roanoke.

changes that lay in store for them. On that continent in the early hours of October 12, 1492, the descendants of the New World's first discoverers and settlers slept quietly. They would not know about Columbus for decades, in some cases for centuries. And had they known, they could not have guessed that the three tiny ships now making for a Caribbean island were the harbingers of a new era —an era in which they and their way of life would be threatened, and in many tragic cases destroyed.

Who were these million or so people who occupied the North American continent at the time of Columbus' arrival? In his mistaken belief that he had reached the Indies, Columbus called the islanders "Indians," and the term was later applied to the native inhabitants of North and South America as well. In fact, the American Indians *are* related to the people of Asia but only distantly, and far back in the mists of time.

The original ancestors of the American Indians came from northeast Asia. They were primitive hunting peoples who, more than 20,000 years ago, began crossing from Siberia into Alaska over a broad land bridge now covered by the waters of the Bering Strait. Successive waves of these nomadic peoples gradually moved farther south and east in search of better hunting grounds. Over thousands of years, their descendants ultimately spread out across North America and down through Central and South America. Gradually, each group's adaptation to the climate, geography, and food resources of its own particular region affected not only the type of tools, clothing, and shelter it developed, but also its social organization, customs, beliefs—even its appearance. So, by the time Columbus arrived, the two continents contained not one, but many separate peoples. In North America alone, there were at least 600 different tribes, speaking over 200 distinct languages, and following ways of life as richly diverse as the regions they occupied.

A great many of these North American tribes inhabited the extensive forests that covered almost the entire eastern half of the continent. Collectively, they are known today as the Eastern Forests Indians, but because they followed a number of distinctly different life styles, they are often divided into three major groups.

The most northerly of these groups, the Subarctic Hunters, were nomadic tribes like the Beaver, Carrier, Kutchin, and Cree of west and eastern Canada. Following the seasonal migrations of caribou and moose, they were constantly on the move, traveling in large, light birchbark canoes, or on foot—using snowshoes or toboggans in wintertime. The subarctic Indians were a proud and independent people who inhabited a harsh and inhospitable world. The terribly cold winters and ever-present threat of death by starvation made some of them ruthlessly practical. It was common among some of the northern tribes, for example, to abandon the old and the sick when they could no longer keep up with their families.

A very different group of Eastern Forests Indians lived south of the Canadian border. These, the Northeastern Woodsmen, are

Above: the Indian method of hunting deer, as reported by Jacques le Moyne de Morgues, one of the members of the French expedition to Florida in 1564. He explained that the hunter's head fitted into the head of the animal, peering out of the holes where the deer's eyes had been "as through a mask."

Left: the ingenuity of the American Indians in finding practical methods of catching food, lacking the metals so common in Europe, fascinated the early visitors to America. Here John White carefully recorded how the Indians he saw in Virginia in 1585 caught fish.

among the best known of America's Indians, for they played a crucial role in its early exploration and colonization. It was to this group of tribes, too, that one of the most interesting prehistoric Indian peoples belonged. These were the Hopewell Indians, who flourished in the Ohio Valley region from about 1000 B.C. to about A.D. 1300, and formed part of the so-called Mound Builder culture. Farmers, traders, and skilled craftsmen, the Hopewells operated an extraordinary network of trade that brought them into contact with other tribes from coast to coast. It was the Hopewells who built the many dome-shaped burial mounds and curious animal-shaped mounds that can still be seen in the Ohio Valley states today.

Above: fortitude in suffering was one of the most highly prized virtues for many Indian tribes. The Mandan had a grueling religious torture ceremony, shown here, in which their young men took part to prove their courage. When George Catlin, who painted this scene, reported the ceremonies his account was so horrifying that for years many people simply refused to believe him.

Right: a wampum belt and two bracelets. For the Iroquois, as for some of their neighboring tribes, these were not for decoration, but were used as money.

But in 1492, the region once dominated by the Hopewell people had long since been occupied by other tribes, such as the Shawnee. Around the Great Lakes, dwelt the Menominee, Fox, Illinois, Sauk, Winnebago, and Potawatomi. Most of these Great Lakes Indians spoke variations of the Algonkian tongue, a language also spoken by the tribes who lived along the Atlantic coastline from present-day Maine to the Carolinas. These tribes—the Micmac, Penobscot, Massachusett, Pequot, Delaware, and Powhatan—were the very first Indians met by the early explorers.

Between the Algonkian-speaking Indians of the Great Lakes and those of the Atlantic seaboard lived five tribes who spoke another language altogether. These were the famous Iroquois—the Cayuga, Oneida, Seneca, Mohawk, and Onondaga—who made their homes in upstate New York. In addition to their distinctive language, the Iroquois had developed a unique type of dwelling. Unlike the round or oval bark-covered *wigwams* of the Algonkian, the Iroquois had rectangular bark lodges, called long houses. These they arranged inside their stockaded villages in regular rows, like streets inside a walled town. But many customs were common to both the Iroquois and their Algonkian neighbors. One of these was the practice of using *wampum* (white, purple, or black beads made from shells and woven into a belt) as money. Another was the smoking of a long-stemmed peace pipe as a symbol of agreement at tribal councils.

Throughout the deep and quiet forests of the east roamed large numbers of deer, bear, beaver, and wildfowl. All the Northeastern Woodsmen hunted these animals for food and clothing. Fish were also plentiful in the region's many lakes and rivers, and could easily

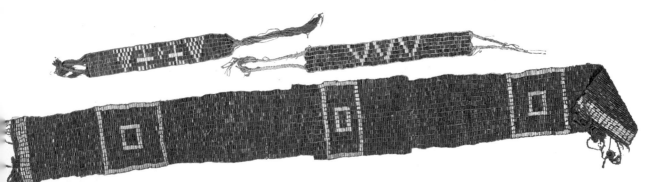

Below: a battle, a facsimile of a drawing by an American Indian on a buffalo robe.
For many tribes, war was part of the fabric of life, giving the young men a chance to
prove themselves or to revenge their tribe's honor after an insult.

be caught by shooting stone-tipped arrows into the water. Along the
Atlantic coast, where cod, flounder, and shellfish abounded, Algonkian fishermen used bone hooks fastened to lines made of milk-
weed fiber.

But the Algonkians and Iroquois did more than hunt and fish for
their food. Outside their villages were well-tilled garden plots—
sometimes covering as much as 20 acres—where they grew squash,
corn, beans, and pumpkins. To clear these fields, the Indians used the
slash-and-burn technique. They would "ring" (cut away a strip of
bark around the trunk) the trees so that they would ultimately die and
fall. The area would then be burned, and later, crops planted.

Like Indians throughout the American continent, both the Algonkian and the Iroquois believed that the land and its produce, like the

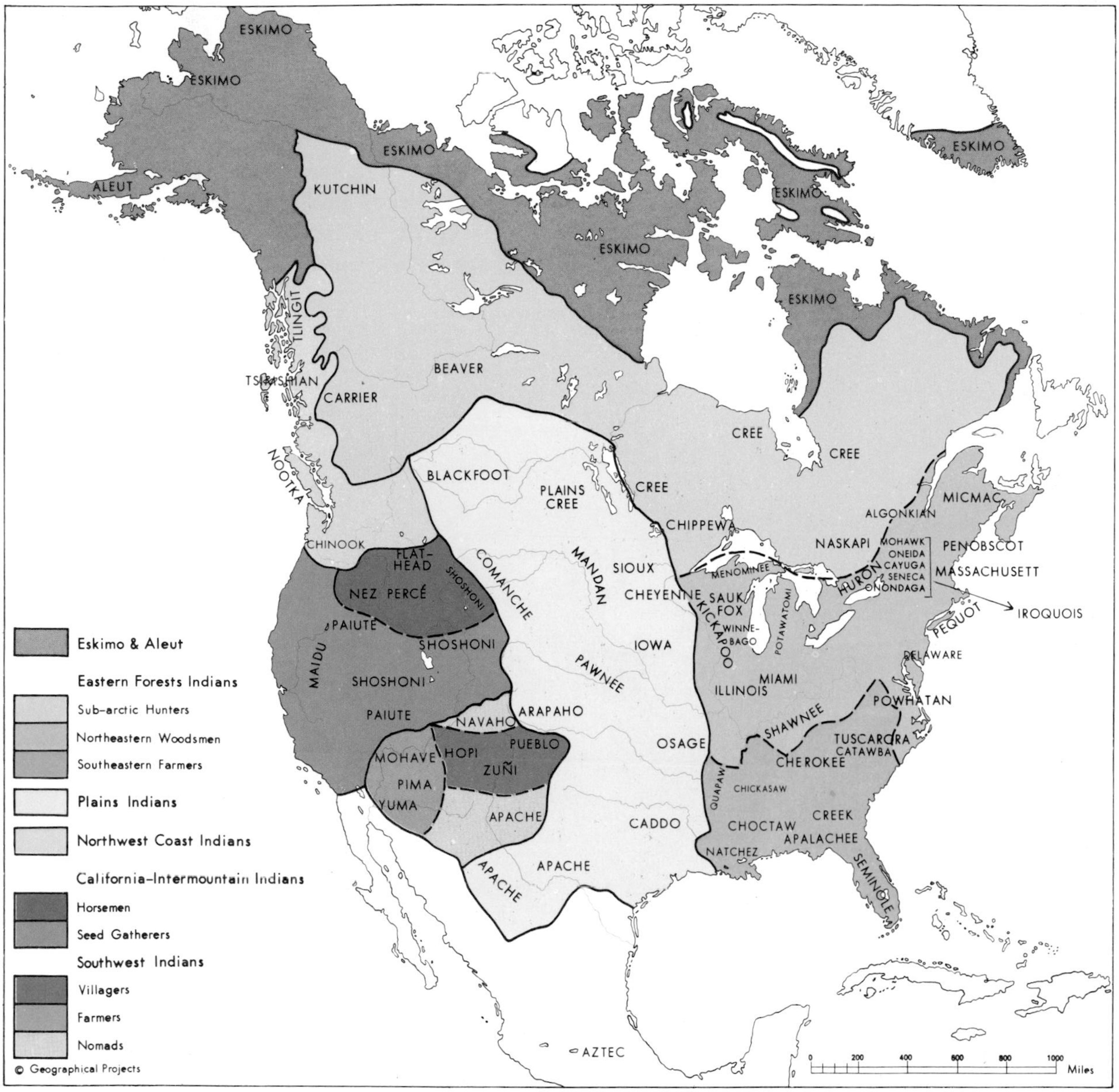
ESKIMO
ESKIMO
ESKIMO
ESKIMO
ESKIMO
ESKIMO
ESKIMO
ALEUT
KUTCHIN
TLINGIT
TSIMSHIAN
CARRIER
BEAVER
NOOTKA
CHINOOK
CREE
CREE
CREE
BLACKFOOT
PLAINS CREE
CHIPPEWA
ALGONKIAN
MICMAC
NASKAPI
MOHAWK
ONEIDA
CAYUGA
SENECA
ONONDAGA
PENOBSCOT
MASSACHUSETT
IROQUOIS
HURON
MENOMINEE
PEQUOT
FLAT-HEAD
NEZ PERCÉ
SHOSHONI
COMANCHE
MANDAN
SIOUX
CHEYENNE
SAUK
FOX
KICKAPOO
WINNE-BAGO
POTAWATOMI
PAIUTE
SHOSHONI
MAIDU
SHOSHONI
IOWA
PAWNEE
MIAMI
ILLINOIS
DELAWARE
POWHATAN
PAIUTE
ARAPAHO
NAVAHO
SHAWNEE
TUSCARORA
CATAWBA
CHEROKEE
MOHAVE
HOPI
PUEBLO
ZUÑI
OSAGE
PIMA
YUMA
APACHE
CADDO
QUAPAW
CHICKASAW
CHOCTAW
CREEK
APALACHEE
NATCHEZ
SEMINOLE
APACHE
APACHE
AZTEC
Eskimo & Aleut
Eastern Forests Indians
Sub-arctic Hunters
Northeastern Woodsmen
Southeastern Farmers
Plains Indians
Northwest Coast Indians
California-Intermountain Indians
Horsemen
Seed Gatherers
Southwest Indians
Villagers
Farmers
Nomads
© Geographical Projects
0
200
400
600
800
1000
Miles

Above: North America, showing the probable location of the more important Indian tribes at the time that Columbus arrived in the New World. North American Indian tribes are generally divided into a number of *culture areas,* or regions in which all the tribes shared about the same *culture* or way of life. These areas are indicated on the map by colors. The regions inhabited by the Aleut and Eskimos, who are not Indians, are also shown.

air and the water, could not be "owned" as personal property. A tribe would claim a certain area as its territory for farming or hunting, but it was held in common by the entire tribe. Again like other American Indians, Northeastern Woodsmen possessed a deep respect and reverence for nature, and believed in supernatural forces that linked human beings to every other living thing. They thought that each animal and tree, each natural element, had its own spirit, and some believed that there was a higher force, or Great Spirit, that shaped and guided all events.

Living close to nature, and believing in its power, the Northeastern Woodsmen strove to live in harmony with it. They sincerely believed that illness, misery, and misfortune would result if that harmony were disrupted. In addition to the chiefs and tribal councils

Below: "The Indian Council" by Seth Eastman. Many tribes had the tradition of a tribal council to settle any quarrels within the tribe and decide on a common policy toward outsiders, but the confederation of Iroquois tribes known as the Five Nations was the most highly developed form of all the North American Indian organizations. Women, too, played an important part in tribal affairs. Some, as in Eastman's painting, became chiefs and took part in tribal councils.

that led the tribes, there was always a medicine man, or *shaman*, who was believed to possess special powers. It was his duty to cure the sick, ensure good crops or good hunting, call on supernatural forces for aid against an enemy, and maintain the tribe's harmony with the spirit world.

The Iroquois were among the most warlike Indians on the whole of the American continent. Feuds among the tribes led to frequent raids—for honor, for revenge, or in defense of tribal lands. The Iroquois men carried spears and tomahawks as well as bows and

arrows, and often wore a single long "scalp lock" over the top and down the back of their otherwise shaven heads to taunt their enemies. Intertribal wars were generally limited by mutually-accepted rules, but enemies were scalped, burned, or slaughtered without remorse. To the Iroquois, pain and death were regarded as a test of courage, and those unfortunate enough to be captured often died singing or whistling in order to prove their bravery. Scalping was a ritual of warfare. The victim could be alive, unconscious, or dead, it did not matter. The scalp—a strip of skin torn from the crown of the head— was a battle token, to be displayed with pride in the scalp dances that followed victory.

The Huron Indians of southern Ontario and the Iroquois of New York were frequently at war. About 1570, a Huron refugee named Dekanawidah and the Mohawk Indian chief, Hiawatha, persuaded the chiefs of five Iroquois tribes—the Mohawk, Seneca, Oneida, Cayuga, and Onondaga—to unite themselves in a tribal federation. He urged them to renounce war, at least among themselves, and to present a united front against any other tribe outside this federation, or league, which was to be called the Five Nations. In preparing the code of the confederacy, its creator stated: "I, Dekanawidah, and the chiefs of the tribes in this League, now uproot the tallest pine tree and into the cavity left in the earth we cast all weapons of war. We bury them from sight, deep in the ground, and plant again the tree. Thus shall the great peace be established."

The chiefs and elders of the Five Nations met each summer at the largest village of the Onondaga, near what is now the city of Syracuse in New York state. Fifty peace chiefs, selected by the mothers of the leading families in each tribe, made up the central council. Certain women chiefs also had a place in this council, where issues were discussed and decided by vote. Each tribe had only one vote, and difficult problems were debated until a solution agreeable to all could be found and approved unanimously.

The Five Nations—which became the Six Nations when the

Tuscarora Indians of North Carolina joined them later on—was able only rarely to unite all its members against a common enemy. Nevertheless, it did succeed in ending the conflicts among its member nations, and was, both in theory and in practice, the most highly developed Indian union north of Mexico. Despite the ravages and turmoil that came to the region with the advent of the white man, the league remained unbroken for over 200 years. Ultimately, its democratic principles and structure may have shaped the ideals of the men who created the United States Constitution.

Above: one of the constructions of the Hopewell people—a serpent mound in Ohio. Although by the time the white men arrived the Hopewell Indians had given way to other people in the Ohio River Valley that had once been the center of their remarkable culture, these huge ceremonial animal-shaped mounds and the dome-shaped burial mounds stand as a reminder of their accomplishments.

Below Tennessee and North Carolina, in the region that we now call the Deep South, lived the third major group of Eastern Forests Indians: the Southeastern Farmers. These included the Tuscarora, Creek, Apalachee, and Seminole of the South Atlantic coast; the Cherokee of Tennessee; and the Quapaw, Chickasaw, and Choctaw in the lower Mississippi Valley.

Many of the southeastern tribes practiced a distinctive way of life developed by a group of mound-building Indians in the lower Mississippi River Valley. These, the so-called Mississippian Indians, had begun flourishing about A.D. 1000, and had swiftly developed a strong, agriculturally-based society composed of village-states. The Mississippians possessed a complex religious system, and built their communities around special religious centers—large, earthen mounds topped with wooden temples—where their leaders conducted elaborate rites and ceremonies.

By the time the white men came in large numbers, the Mississippi Valley culture had begun to decline. This was possibly as a result of the epidemics of European diseases that originated from the white men, wiping out large numbers of the Indian people before they even met the explorers. As late as the 1600's, however, small groups of these people could still be found. One of the surviving groups was the Natchez Indians, some 6,000 of whom were discovered by French explorers in 1682. They lived in nine towns along the Mississippi River. Ruled by a single, despotic leader who was believed to be descended from the sun, the Natchez were strictly divided into classes, or castes, ranging from the "Great Sun" and all his relatives

Below: feuds and wars between indian tribes were frequent, but within the tribe, around the common fire, life was generally ordered and tranquil. Here Indians in Virginia gather to celebrate a victory around their fire.

at the top, to the "Stinkards," or common people, at the bottom.

Not all the farming people of the Southeast adhered as strictly to the old Mississippian way of life as the Natchez, however. In Georgia and Alabama, the mound-building Creek tribes had established a more democratic unity in the form of a loose confederacy of almost 50 towns divided into two categories: the Red (warrior) towns, and the White (peace-keeping) towns. And in southern Florida and the Keys, where farming was unknown, each of the various tribes proudly went its own way.

Wherever farming was done in the Southeast, corn was the primary crop. From it the Indians made corn soup, hominy (corn mash), and flour for the loaves of bread that they baked over the fire

Sioux Indians of the plains playing a form of lacrosse, as painted by Seth Eastman around 1847. The Sioux were one of the tribal groups whose pattern of life was most changed by the coming of the white men. Then they acquired horses and guns, which made it possible for them to hunt buffalo with such skill and efficiency that the vast herds of the western prairies were dwindling long before the white men came onto the plains to join the hunt.

and sometimes "buttered" with bear fat. Wild cane—in thickets called cane-brakes—also grew abundantly in the fertile soil of the southern river valleys. The Indians used sharply cut stalks from the brakes to spear single fish, or drew cane baskets across the rivers to catch dozens of fish in one sweep.

West of the Mississippi River, in the broad expanse of prairie that stretched from the Mississippi River to the Rocky Mountains, and from Canada's Saskatchewan River to central Texas, dwelt the hard-riding, buffalo-hunting Plains Indians. Perhaps it is they who have left behind the most enduring image of the American Indian. But surprisingly enough, the colorful and exciting way of life we think of as so characteristic of the Plains Indians came about chiefly as a result of the Europeans' entry into North America.

For at least 1,000 years before the coming of the white man, large numbers of the Plains tribes had been farming peoples, living in semipermanent villages of earthen lodges. Among these tribes were the Osage in Missouri, the Mandan in the Dakotas, and the Caddo in eastern Texas. These Indians supplemented their diet of home-grown food with buffalo meat, but did not make buffalo-hunting their way of life.

The tribes whose existence did center around the buffalo lived in

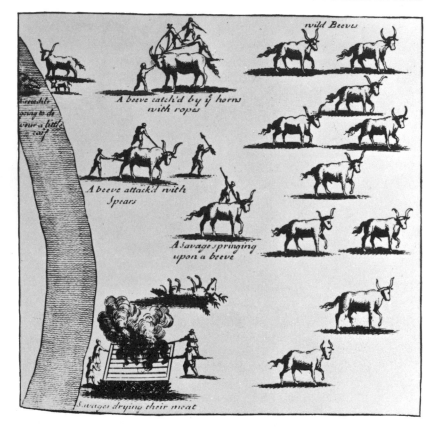

Above: George Catlin painted this scene of a Sioux buffalo chase in 1832. He described the Sioux tribesmen as "a bold and desperate set of horsemen." Left: a 1703 drawing showing Indians hunting "beeves," or buffalo, as they did before the arrival of the horse. The European artist obviously imagined buffalo would look like ordinary cattle.

the more westerly regions of the Plains. Among these tribes were the Blackfoot of southern Canada; the Comanche and Arapaho of Wyoming and Colorado; and the Apache of Texas. These nomadic tribesmen followed in the wake of the immense herds of shaggy bison that roamed the prairies. They lived in cone-shaped *tepees* covered with painted buffalo hide, and transported their belongings by means of *travois* (two-poled frames with a bundle suspended between them) originally drawn by dogs, and later by horses. They hunted single buffaloes by creeping up on them dressed in animal skins, and sometimes killed large numbers of them at one time by stampeding them over a cliff. When they killed more animals than they needed right away, they preserved some of the meat in the form of *pemmican,* a combination of dried and pounded beef mixed with hot fat. Berries were added to give it flavor. In common with other North American Indians, the men wore buckskin breechcloths,

leggings, and moccasins, while the women wore leather skirts or dresses. Chiefs well-known for their bravery had the right to adorn themselves with tall feathered war bonnets.

The way of life of the western Plains Indians came to be adopted by all the peoples of the prairie lands when they acquired two prized European possessions: the horse and the gun. Horses had inhabited North America in prehistoric times, but became extinct on the continent during the Ice Age. They were reintroduced by the Spanish explorers and colonists who came to the Southwest in the mid-1500's and early 1600's. Although at first the Spaniards tried to prevent the local tribes from learning how to handle their horses, the Indians soon taught themselves to ride them. And it was not long before raids on the Spaniards' Southwest ranchlands, and trading among the tribes spread the animals throughout the Plains.

Meanwhile, firearms had begun appearing among the Plains tribes to the north. Originally given to the tribes of the Northeast by French and English traders, guns quickly passed westward from tribe to tribe, reaching the Plains Indians before the white man did.

By the late 1700's, both guns and horses were in wide use by the Indians of the grasslands. Increasing numbers of tribes moved into the area—Cheyenne and Sioux from the east, Comanche from the west, Blackfoot from the north, and Pawnee from the south. Some

An American Indian man and woman eating together, drawn by John White. He reported that the Indians were "very sober in their eating and drinking." In fact many tribes lived on the perilous edge of starvation. When hunting was good and food was plentiful, they ate richly, but a hard winter left them struggling to survive.

were fleeing from the encroachments of the white men to the east. Others were drawn by the dynamic and profitable way of life then in full swing on the Plains. Horses and firearms greatly facilitated bison hunting and the nomadic pattern of existence that went with it. Often many tribes would meet for a communal hunt. At such gatherings there would be games, foot and horse races, and intertribal council meetings. Sometimes as many as 20 different language groups would gather together, communicating with one another by a sign language of hand gestures.

The acquisition of horses and firearms increased the restlessness and aggressiveness of the Plains tribes. Tribal warfare—for glory, captives, horses, or revenge—became more and more common. But the object of a war was never mutual slaughter. Often the fighting would break off after the first casualties. And one of the most highly honored battle exploits was to touch a live enemy without harming him, and get away safely.

West of the Plains Indians, beyond the Rocky Mountains and along the Pacific coastline from southern Alaska to northern California, lived another major group, the Northwest Coast Indians.

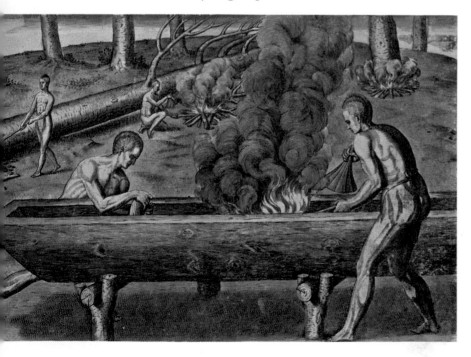

Left: the tribes dependent on fishing from rivers and lakes became adept canoe-builders. Some made light birch-bark canoes; others, such as the Indians in the Virginia region shown here, used fire to fell and hollow out tree trunks.

Right: Canadian Indians making music, from a history of America published in Paris in 1722. Music with chanting and dancing was part of many rituals.
Below: the Sioux bear dance, by George Catlin. Prospective hunters would dance for several days before the hunt, with songs to the Bear Spirit. The dance was led by the chief medicine-man, dressed as a bear, and the dancers—some wearing bears' heads—would circle, imitating a bear to the accompaniment of drums.

Among them were the Tsimshian, Tlingit, Nootka, and Chinook. In this region of misty mountains and rushing streams, farming was unknown, but salmon, halibut, cod, and shellfish abounded. Life was relatively easy here, and the Northwest Indians had time and leisure to develop arts and crafts. They made ornamental wooden masks, built gabled plank houses, and carved lofty wooden poles, called *totems*, which they stood outside their doors. Totem poles depicted their owners' guardian animal spirits, and symbolized wealth and prestige. The Indians of this area were, in fact, inordinately concerned with wealth and social status, and devoted much of their time to making and acquiring possessions. To demonstrate his riches, a man of property would hold a feast or celebration called a

187

The Southwest Indians, living in a hot, dry climate, developed a high degree of cooperation in their societies, working together to bring water to their crops, and living together in city-like pueblos, such as the cliff dwelling here, Montezuma's Castle National Monument in Arizona.

potlatch, in which he would ostentatiously give away or destroy his possessions. As he freed his captives, distributed his household goods, and burned his house down, he would sing boastful songs about himself and make fun of his rivals. A man rich enough to hold a series of potlatches became known as a noble.

In California, and in the area of plateaus and deserts between the Rockies and the Sierra Nevada, lived the Indians who are collectively called the California-Intermountain Indians. But the Indians of this region followed different ways of life. The Paiute and southern Shoshoni of Nevada and the Maidu of California, for example, were Seed Gatherers. They lived a nomadic life, gathering various kinds of seeds, nuts, and berries as they ripened. The seed-gathering tribes were loosely organized, but possessed a rigid social code. Many, for example, practiced an intricate system that required a man who had injured the property, person, or feelings of another to recompense him with an elaborately worked out payment for damages. In common with many other tribes, the Indians of California were fond of making music. They played flutes, eagle-bone whistles, and rattles, and used halves of large hollow logs placed over a pit to form drums upon which they danced out the rhythm of their songs.

Another group of western tribes, called the Horsemen, are also classed among the California-Intermountain Indians. The Horsemen tribes, most notably the Nez Percé, Flathead, and northern Shoshoni, combined some of the ways of the seed gatherers with a number of customs—like riding and buffalo-hunting—that they had learned from the Plains Indians.

Of all the North American tribes, few possessed as stable and highly developed a culture as the Southwest Indians. Here, in the region noted for its canyons, deserts, and high, rocky mesas, dwelt the peoples who, more than any other Indian group, were to be successful in retaining their identity and way of life after the coming of the white man.

Despite the aridity of the region, the people of the Southwest began farming almost 2,500 years ago. Using irrigation techniques that by A.D. 600 had developed into vast networks of canals, they were able to obtain enough water for their large plots of corn, cotton, squash, and beans. By about A.D. 700, one of these farming groups, the Pueblo (from the Spanish word for "village") had begun building large many-storied dwellings in northern Arizona, New Mexico, Utah, and

Colorado. About A.D. 1000, they began to build their homes on the tops of mesas, or in the arched hollows of cliffsides. About A.D. 1300, something—perhaps a drought or increased enemy attacks—caused many of the cliff dwellers to abandon their homes and settle farther south, near the Zuñi and the Hopi in Arizona and New Mexico. Together, these three groups are known as Villagers.

When the first Spanish explorers arrived in the region, they found the Pueblo Indians following a complex way of life in compact communities of multistory buildings. Each village was an autonomous political unit ruled by a council of advisers, and all decisions were made on the basis of what was best for the group as a whole. Religion played an important part in the life of the community, and the men spent a large part of their time engaged in elaborate and regular ceremonial rites.

Like all the American Indians, the peoples of the Southwest reared their children with the utmost gentleness. But unlike other Indian groups, they took care to instill in their offspring an abhorrence of all violence, aggression, and competitiveness. Indeed, the Pueblo, Zuñi, and Hopi were the most peace-loving and orderly of all the American tribes. Conservative, even conformist in temperament, they took a commonsense approach to life. Marriage, for example, was a practical arrangement, and could be ended by the wife whenever she chose. She simply put her husband's belongings outside the door, and he went back to his own family.

Another group of southwestern tribes, called Farmers, lived a less complicated existence than the Hopi, Zuñi, and Pueblo Indians. Although they, too, grew crops, these tribes—the Yuma, Pima, and Mohave of Arizona—moved about more than the Villagers, and dwelt in big houses built of brush and dirt.

Still another group of tribes, the Nomads, included the Navaho and Apache Indians who first began moving into the Southwest from the Northwest around A.D. 1000. Fierce warriors, the Apache carried out frequent raids on the peaceful desert dwellers for captives, horses,

Above: the interior of a Cree Indian tent, drawn in 1820. A forest people, the Cree were hunters and fishers, continually on the move through the woods of North America. Their tents, like the rest of their possessions, were therefore necessarily portable.

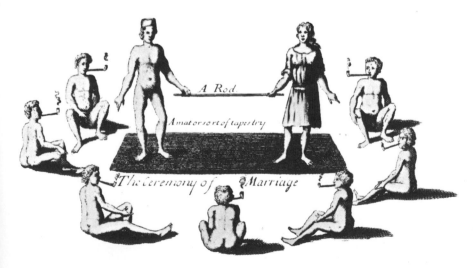

Left: "The Ceremony of Marriage", as imagined through European eyes, from an account of American life written by Baron de Lahontan, at one time the lord-lieutenant of Newfoundland. He wrote his book as a series of letters from Canada between 1684 and 1687.

and other booty. The Navaho, on the other hand, came to stay. Living in cone-shaped *hogans* made from poles covered with earth, they gradually adapted to the ways of the Hopi, Zuñi, and Pueblo.

Far, far to the north of the desert dwellers, in the Arctic regions of Canada, lived a very different group of people, the Eskimo and Aleut, descendants of the last waves of migrating peoples from Asia. Living in skin-covered tents in summer, snow-banked igloos in winter, these hardy people were skilled hunters and fishermen, who had developed a wide variety of bone and ivory tools to help them in their struggle for survival. One of their most ingenious inventions was the *kayak,* a one-man canoe consisting of a light wooden or bone frame covered with tightly sewn skins. The rigorous demands of the cold, white world they lived in made the Eskimo and Aleut a tough and independent people, although family life in their isolated clan groups was warm and easygoing.

Above: an Eskimo hunting, showing him in his kayak. From the Arctic wastes inhabited by the Eskimo, to the tropical heat in which the Mayan Empire flourished, the inhabitants of the two continents skillfully adapted themselves to their different environments.

There could be no greater contrast·to the Eskimos' self-reliant way of life than the highly regimented existence of the Indians of Latin America. Here, at the time of the Spaniards' arrival in the 1500's, there flourished two mighty empires—the Aztec of Mexico, and the Inca of South America. Militaristic and expansionist in outlook, both empires were founded on a strong agricultural base. The peoples of each lived in sophisticated urban centers and possessed elements of culture that rivaled many of the developments of the Old World. Their magnificent temples, their elaborate road and irrigation networks, their achievements in mathematics and astronomy (which echoed the even more brilliant Mayan culture that was then on the decline), and their elaborate religious and political systems, continue to astonish modern archaeologists and historians.

But in the 1500's it was something else about the two great Indian

Above: Chac-Mool, the Mayan Rain God, a statue in the Temple of the Warriors, Chichén Itza, Yucatan, dating from about 1300. He holds a dish awaiting the sacrifice of human hearts.

empires that impressed the Spaniards: the immense hoards of Aztec and Inca gold. And it was the search for yet more gold that led the Spaniards to begin exploring the American South and Southwest in the early 1500's. Meanwhile, not to be outdone by the Spanish, French and English ships began scouring the north Atlantic coast in search of a passage to the riches of the East.

All these activities sprang directly from Columbus' first fateful voyage to the New World in the autumn of 1492. But the tribes who lay asleep there in the early hours of October 12 could not know or imagine the events that lay ahead. Dreaming, perhaps, of corn rustling in the wind, of flashing salmon, or of stampeding herds of bison, the Indians of America slept on in the forests and grasslands, the rainy mountains, and wind-swept deserts, unaware that with the dawn would come the start of a dramatic and shattering new era.

The Lure of Gold
2

Spain was swift to exploit Columbus' spectacular find in the western Atlantic. Now was her chance to challenge Portugal's long and aggravating monopoly on exploration, trade, and treasure. For almost a century, Spain had looked on as Portugal's daring navigators worked their way down the west coast of Africa, forging the first links in an eastern sea route to the Orient. The Portuguese had secured exclusive trading rights wherever they had stopped along the way, and it was clear that they would do the same when they reached the Eastern lands of spice and treasure.

But now, with Columbus' momentous discovery, Spain, too, had a claim to make and defend. In 1494, Spain's King Ferdinand V and Queen Isabella, with the aid and support of the pope, made an agreement with Portugal that safeguarded Spanish rights in the western Atlantic. According to this agreement—called the Treaty of Tordesillas—an imaginary north-south line was drawn 370 leagues west of the Cape Verde Islands, dividing the unexplored regions of the world into two equal halves. Portugal was given the rights to all lands east of that line (including the eastern bulge of Brazil). Spain was granted the rights to all lands west of it.

In effect, Spain had been given almost the whole of the New World, though, of course, at that time she did not know that it *was* the New World, or that it encompassed two vast continents. None-

Left: the Spanish passion for gold first bewildered and then embittered the Indians whom they interrogated, enslaved, and murdered during their relentless search for the precious metal. Here in a drawing of the 1600's Indians take their revenge—pouring molten gold down the throats of the Spaniards, "throwing their greed at them with these words: 'Eat gold, eat gold, insatiable Christians.' "

Right: a gold pendant of the 1400's, representing the Aztec god of the dead, Mictlantecuhtli. A remnant of a dead civilization, it is one of the few golden objects still surviving, having escaped being melted down by the rapacious Spanish conquistadores.

A Mexican painting of about 1550, showing the Spanish entering Mexico. The figure in the dark suit without a helmet is Cortes. With him is the famous Moor soldier Estevanico. In spite of the humid climate, the soldiers wore their full armor on ceremonial parade as well as during battles.

theless, she lost no time in calling on her citizens to explore her western claim, to colonize it, convert its heathen peoples, and uncover its wealth. The men who answered this call were the rough and ready *conquistadors,* eager to win fame and fortune through conquest and adventure. Gold had already been found on the island of Hispaniola, where Columbus had established a colony in 1493. Who knew how much more gold might lie elsewhere in these western lands? So the conquistadors swept north, south, and east from Hispaniola, exploring, conquering, colonizing—and always seeking gold.

By 1512, the Spanish had established themselves in Jamaica, Cuba, Puerto Rico, and the Isthmus of Panama, where, in 1513, Vasco Núñez de Balboa first sighted the mighty Pacific. The same year, a 63-year-old Spaniard named Juan Ponce de León, seeking a legendary isle where a magic mountain was said to make old men young again, discovered the Florida peninsula.

Meanwhile, Spanish exploration along the coast of Latin America had turned up some information that was far more tantalizing to the young conquistadors than any mythical "fountain of youth." In 1518, an expedition led by Juan de Grijalva had explored the Mexican coast from Yucatán to what is now Veracruz and come back with stories about a fabulously wealthy people living somewhere in the interior. Within the next three years the truth of these stories became abundantly clear with Hernando Cortes' discovery and conquest of the Aztec. Here at last was the gold and silver Spain had dreamed of. But the treasure of the Aztec was only the beginning. Francisco Pizarro's conquest of most of Peru in 1532 uncovered an even more magnificent hoard of gold and silver—that of the Inca empire. The riches of Mexico and Peru began flowing back to Spain by the shipload, and soon the wealth of the New World was adding some $30 million a year to the coffers of Spain.

But the search for gold and silver did not end with the discovery of the Aztec and Inca. If anything, it intensified. Other conquistadors, their imaginations reeling with dreams of gold and glory,

Right: Pánfilo de Narváez being chained before Cortes, his blinded left eye bandaged. Behind, the soldiers of Cortes assault Narváez' stronghold with cannons. Narváez was held by Cortes for two years before he could escape.

looked to the lands north and east of Mexico as a possible source of further riches. No one had yet found the fabled "Seven Cities of Cibola"—said to be even wealthier than the cities of Mexico and Peru—but every conquistador believed that they existed, and hoped that he might be the one to find them.

One such man was Pánfilo de Narváez, a soldier and explorer who had taken part in the conquest of Cuba in 1511. In 1521, he had been sent by the Cuban governor to arrest Cortes, whose brutal excesses in Mexico had begun to alarm the Spanish authorities. But Cortes had got wind of the mission before Narváez arrived, and met him at Veracruz, where he put out one of his eyes and imprisoned him for two years. When Narváez at last escaped and returned to Spain, he was rewarded by the king with a grant to conquer and establish a colony in Florida.

On June 17, 1527, Narváez sailed from Spain with 5 ships, 600 men, and 100 horses. When the fleet reached the Caribbean, it was struck by a fierce hurricane, in which two ships and scores of men were lost. Frightened by this experience, 140 of the men refused to continue with the expedition, preferring to remain behind in the West Indian colony of Santo Domingo. Undaunted, Narváez collected his remaining men and sailed on to Tampa Bay, halfway along Florida's west coast. From here, in 1528, he decided to proceed by land, taking with him the 42 horses that had survived the voyage, and 300 of his men. He left the others behind to man the ships,

Indians collecting gold in about 1563, as reported by Jacques le Moyne de Morgues who was in Florida with the French at that time. The picture, first published in Frankfort in 1591, was titled "How gold is gathered in the rivers descending from the Appalachian Mountains." The sight was to prove elusive to Narváez and his followers.

with orders to follow the coast and meet him at a point farther north.

One of Narvácz' officers, Álvar Núñez Cabeza de Vaca, strongly opposed the idea of splitting up the party and leaving the relative safety of the coast. But Narváez overruled all opposition. He had seen flakes of gold in an abandoned Indian fishing net, and was convinced that the fabulous Seven Cities lay in the interior. Cabeza had no choice but to follow his commander inland.

The men made slow progress as they marched north through Florida's glades and marshlands. All along the way they were sniped at by Indians who had developed a fear of white men because of Spanish slave raids along the coast. Using powerful bows, the Indians shot at Narváez' troops with flint-tipped arrows that went right through the soldiers' armor. But when the mounted Spaniards wheeled and charged their assailants, the Indians simply disappeared

The Florida swamplands, virtually the same as they were when Narváez and his men splashed their way northward. With dwindling supplies and under constant harassment from the Indians, Narváez and his men eventually abandoned their quest for gold.

into the woods. On one occasion, the soldiers did manage to capture an Apalachee chief and questioned him closely about the golden cities they were seeking. But the chief could only tell them that the peoples beyond were much poorer than those of his own region.

Despite these gloomy tidings, Narváez continued to push on through the wilderness. At last, however, dwindling supplies forced him to give up his quest and return to the coast. But he did not find his ships there to meet him. After sailing up and down the Florida coast for many weeks looking in vain for some sign of the expedition, the crews had given up the search and sailed back to Spain. Narváez and his followers found themselves marooned.

Desperate, Narváez ordered his men to start building boats. All the metal that could be spared—from stirrups, spurs, crossbows, and weapons—was forged into nails, saws, and axheads. Trees were felled and planks hammered together to make five crude barges whose seams were caulked with palmetto fiber and pine tree resin. The horses were killed for food and their manes and tails used to make rope. Despite persistent Indian attacks, the men at last finished the makeshift boats, and the 250 weary survivors clambered aboard. "The boats were so crowded that we could not move," wrote Cabeza later. "With the gunwales only six inches above the water, we went into a turbulent sea, with no one among us having a knowledge of navigation."

Helped by the currents, and occasionally by the wind that filled the boats' crude patchwork sails, the little fleet inched its way along the coast under the watchful eyes of the armed Indians on shore. Because they could not land without placing themselves at the mercy of these hostile observers, the Spaniards soon ran short of food. But the worst was yet to come. Sometime after passing the mouth of the Mississippi River, the flotilla was caught in a storm. Narváez' boat was blown out into the Gulf of Mexico and disappeared. Others of the frail craft capsized. A mere 85 exhausted men survived the shipwreck, dragging themselves ashore on the barren coast of southern Texas.

The castaways had escaped with their lives, but nothing else—without food, clothing, tools, or weapons. Too weak to fish, they grubbed for roots and berries. Many of them died in the weeks that followed. Others were taken captive by local tribes who treated them as slaves, kicking, beating, or working them to exhaustion,

"Cabeza de Vaca stranded in the Texas desert," by Frederic Remington. After the shipwreck in which most of his companions were killed, De Vaca was taken captive by an Indian tribe, and was held by them for nearly six years.

MEXICO.

MEXICO, REGIA
ET CELEBRIS
HISPANIAE NO
VAE CIVITAS.

Cum Privilegio.

and occasionally killing them at will. Only a few of the Spaniards fell into the hands of friendly Indians. One of these fortunate individuals was Álvar Núñez Cabeza de Vaca. He won the trust and admiration of his captors and ultimately become one of their traders, traveling to other tribes to exchange and acquire articles such as seashells for cutting, ocher for war paint, cane for arrows, sinews for bowstrings, and flint for arrowheads. Cabeza lived among the Indians for nearly six years, sharing with them the frequent hunger and starvation that was part of life in this desolate land. He wrote later that, "Occasionally they kill deer or fish, but the quantity is so small and the famine so great, that they eat spiders and the eggs of ants, worms, lizards, salamanders, snakes, and vipers: they eat earth and wood, the dung of deer, and other things that I omit to mention."

Finally, Cabeza and three other men—among them a Moor named Estevanico—were able to escape from their captors. Heading in the direction of Spanish Mexico, the four struggled through deserts, grasslands, and mountains for many months. At long last, they reached the fringes of a Spanish settlement in Mexico. There, on an April day in 1536, they were sighted by a troop of Spanish cavalry, who stared in amazement at the four exhausted men who were staggering toward them out of the wilderness.

The four were treated as heroes in Mexico City where, according to Cabeza, they found it somewhat difficult to readjust to the trappings of civilization. "I could not wear any [clothes] for some time," he writes, "nor could we sleep anywhere but on the ground."

Cabeza's return to Mexico stirred fresh interest in the regions to the north of Mexico. Though the Indians who had befriended him had themselves been dreadfully poor, they had spoken of rich tribes farther north. When Cabeza reported this, he raised the hopes of those who believed that the Seven Cities of Cibola might still be found. Accordingly, Estevanico, the Moor who had escaped with Cabeza, was sent northward again on a reconnaissance mission, this time in company with a Franciscan priest named Fray Marcos de Niza. When they reached one of the Zuñi settlements in New Mexico, Estevanico somehow managed to offend the community, and was killed. Fray Marcos, however, escaped unharmed, and returned to Mexico City. There, for some unknown reason, he not only confirmed, but exaggerated Cabeza's report of riches to the

The title page decoration from Cabeza de Vaca's book. the rumors he reported of rich Indian tribes living farther north led more men to chance their lives on more expeditions seeking gold.

north. No further encouragement was necessary. The Viceroy of Mexico set the wheels in motion for a major expedition to find and capture the wealth of this fabled northern kingdom.

Francisco Vásquez de Coronado was put in charge of the expedition, which consisted of no fewer than 300 Spanish soldiers and noblemen and several hundred Indians. Setting out in 1540, Coronado kept his men at a fast pace, convinced that immense treasure lay before him. The expedition marched into what is now Arizona, reaching the Grand Canyon before turning eastward into New Mexico. Here Coronado discovered the Zuñi pueblo of Hawaikúh. This, he thought, must be the "silver city" described by Fray Marcos. He ordered his men to attack. Uttering the traditional

war cry used before a battle with infidels—"Saint James! Spain! blood! fire!"—the Spanish troops stormed the fortress, and at last captured it, along with the stores of food they badly needed. But to their great disappointment, they found no treasure in the pueblo.

But perhaps, Coronado thought, the fabled Seven Cities lay farther on. Still hoping, he pressed on until he came to the Pueblo Indian settlement of Tiguex on the Rio Grande. Here the expedition was granted peaceful entry into the town. Once inside, however, the Spaniards began stripping the blankets off the very backs of the Indians, and fighting broke out. But the Pueblos' war clubs were no match for the Spaniards' muskets and lances, and the Indians were soon defeated. To celebrate the victory, Coronado's captains

Francisco Vásquez de Coronado and his enormous expedition, which started out in 1540. In spite of the numbers of his men, and his ruthlessness in dealing with the Indians, Coronado returned to Mexico in 1542, no more successful than his predecessors.

A pottery jug in the shape of an owl, from a Zuñi Indian pueblo. Coronado's men, hoping to find gold, were bitterly disappointed to discover nothing they considered of value in the pueblos they ransacked. They were contemptuous of the men who had mastered the gentle art of molding clay into practical, decorative, everyday objects.

cruelly burned 30 Pueblos at the stake and slaughtered 60 more.

But carnage and pillage had not brought the Spaniards one step closer to the mythical Seven Cities. Coronado led his men as far north as Kansas, all to no avail. The treasure still eluded him. In the course of the journey, he, or members of his party, had explored the Rio Grande River, the Grand Canyon, the Southern Rockies, and the Great Plains. They had traveled farther into the American wilderness than any white men before them. Nevertheless, because they had found no gold, their expedition was held to be a failure and Coronado returned to Mexico in 1542, a ruined man.

While Coronado and his men were marching through the South-*west*, a rival expedition, led by Hernando De Soto, was exploring the South*east*. De Soto had taken part in the conquest of Peru in 1532, and his share of the Inca gold had made him so rich that, back in Spain, even the king had borrowed money from him. Spending lavishly and living the life of a Spanish *grandee*, De Soto had become a symbol of the success to be had in the New World.

The grateful king of Spain made Hernando de Soto governor of Cuba and gave him a free hand to explore and conquer Florida. De Soto needed no urging to undertake the task. He believed that Álvar Núñez Cabeza de Vaca had been hiding the truth about the wealth of the peninsula, and he was certain that he would find the legendary Seven Cities there.

As a well-known conquistador, De Soto had little trouble raising an army for his expedition. He had his pick of soldiers, and chose only the fittest men with the best weapons and the finest armor. He bought seven ships, fully equipped, and sailed for the New World. After a stop in Cuba, he set out for Florida, reaching the Tampa Bay area in May, 1539. With him were 600 men, 213 horses, a pack of dogs, and a herd of swine, brought along to provide a continuing food supply.

Soon after the ships landed, Indian smoke signals appeared up and down the coast, warning of the white man's presence. The Indians guessed that De Soto would prove as unpleasant an intruder as any of the other white men who had appeared on their coast. Tragically, they were all too right. De Soto was casually, inhumanly cruel to the Indians he encountered as the expedition marched northward. He hunted them for sport, sometimes throwing them to his dogs to be torn to pieces, or having them beheaded by the

Above: Hernando de Soto. He launched his expedition into the Southeast on a wave of glory generated by his success in Peru. Hoping to repeat the Peruvian triumph, he took a lavishly equipped expedition to Florida in 1539.

Right: De Soto was well-known for his cruelty to Indians even before the expedition into Florida, where all his atrocities did not help him find a single grain of gold. Instead, he found himself in situations such as that pictured here, when Indians, afraid to tell him there was no gold when he demanded to be taken to gold mines, would lead him on long marches. When no gold was to be found, De Soto, enraged, would have their hands cut off.

score to test his men's swordsmanship. When the expedition reached an Indian village, the Spaniards would loot and burn it, torturing the chiefs and massacring the inhabitants. Those they spared were turned into slaves and dragged along behind the soldiers in chains attached to collars around their necks. If they complained, they were burned at the stake, or punished by having their hands cut off.

But this unmitigated cruelty produced no treasure. De Soto found no gold in Florida, nor in Georgia, nor in the Blue Ridge Mountains of North Carolina and South Carolina. The only valuable article he collected was a pearl necklace given to him by a woman chief of one of the Creek tribes along the Savannah River. In the course of the march northward, he met a lone survivor of the ill-fated Narváez expedition, a man called Juan Ortiz, who had been living as a slave of the Indians for almost 10 years. Ortiz had heard no reports of gold and silver. But perhaps, De Soto thought, this was only because the man's captors had kept him in ignorance of

Above: those of De Soto's men who decided to stay with the Creek Indians were typical of many Spaniards in the New World. Their children were the first mestizos (mixed Indian/white), now the racial majority in the former Spanish colonies in South America.

the Seven Cities. So De Soto pushed on—minus a few of his men, who had found the land so rich, the life so comfortable, and the Indian girls so attractive that they opted to remain among the tribes of the Creek confederacy in Georgia. Certainly, life among the Indians seemed preferable to the hardships of interminable marches in search of elusive golden cities.

De Soto now turned westward, marching into Tennessee, and then southward into Alabama. Here, some of his soldiers were boldly attacked and put to flight by a band of Indians. Seeing this, the Spaniards' Indian slaves broke free of their captors and ran to

the village of their fellow Indians, who smashed their chains and armed them. In retaliation, De Soto attacked the village in force, killing 2,500 men, women, and children.

At this moment, word reached De Soto that his fleet was waiting for him on the Gulf coast, only six days' march away. But he kept the news a secret from his men. He was not yet ready to leave. He did not want to return empty-handed and lose his reputation. A year of exploration had yielded only a handful of pearls and the loss of scores of men. Without sending word to the waiting ships, he turned northwest, away from the Gulf. In May, 1541, while making

"De Soto at the Mississippi." This painting, by W. H. Powell, shows the Spanish force in vigorous strength. In fact, they arrived at the river exhausted and worn after months of struggling through unknown, difficult territory, beset by hostile Indians.

his way through northern Mississippi, he discovered the great Mississippi River and crossed over it into Arkansas.

Months passed, and De Soto found himself still struggling through deep forests and bayous (small rivers), still fighting Indians, and still looking in vain for the golden cities. At last, in northeastern Louisiana, he returned to the Mississippi River. There, after routing a large force of hostile Indians, De Soto had four large boats built. The expedition floated downstream to the treacherous bogs and bayous of the lower Mississippi Valley where, in 1542, worn out

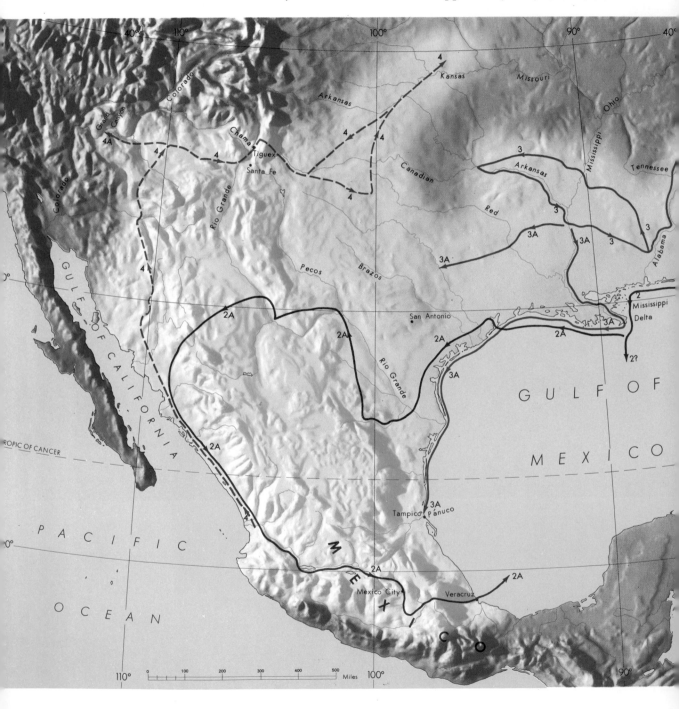

and sick with fever, De Soto died. His men, fearful that the Indians would mutilate the body if they found it, weighted his body with stones and dropped it into the depths of the river during the night.

Before he had died, De Soto had named as his successor a man called Luis de Moscoso. Under his leadership, the expedition briefly explored northeast Texas, finding nothing but impoverished Indians who fled at the sight of the white men. Recognizing the truth of Cabeza's bleak description of these lands, Moscoso retraced his steps to the Mississippi River. Here he decided to build boats

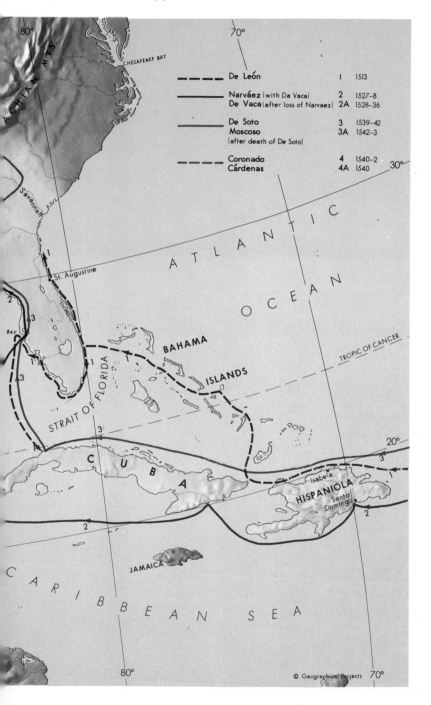

Left: the southern United States and Mexico, showing the routes of the Spanish explorers searching for gold in Mexico and the southern states in the early 1500's.

De León		1	1513
Narváez (with Da Vaca)		2	1527–8
De Vaca (after loss of Narvaez)		2A	1528–36
De Soto		3	1539–42
Moscoso (after death of De Soto)		3A	1542–3
Coronado		4	1540–2
Cárdenas		4A	1540

© Geographical Projects

and sail down the river to the Gulf of Mexico. Using all the available iron—including the chains and collars that had shackled the Indian slaves—the men hammered together seven crude brigantines. The remaining 322 Spaniards set out in these boats in the spring of 1543. Somehow, despite constant Indian attacks, most of them managed to survive the 700-mile journey to the Gulf of Mexico. Then they sailed on until they reached Tampico on the Pánuco River, about 200 miles north of Veracruz. Here they sighted Indians wearing European clothes, and realized that they had reached the safety of Spanish Mexico.

De Soto's expedition had long since been given up for lost, and the Spanish settlers in Mexico stared in wonder at the 300-odd men who had miraculously survived four years in the American wilderness. Nevertheless, the expedition was considered a total failure. No gold or other treasure had been found, and the Indian inhabitants had resisted conquest, so the land could not be brought under the Spanish flag. The only mitigating factor was De Soto's discovery of the Mississippi River. Moscoso's voyage down the great river to the Gulf of Mexico had demonstrated that the Mississippi was a navigable waterway leading directly into the heart of the North American continent.

The expeditions of Narváez, Coronado, and De Soto put an end to Spanish dreams of finding the Seven Cities of Cibola, but Spanish colonial ambitions remained undimmed. Throughout the 1500's, continued efforts were made to secure a Spanish foothold on the

Left: Indians fighting a Spanish force. De Soto's expedition of 1539–42 was under continuous attack by Indians, who had the advantage of knowing the country and quickly learned to use the weapons that they took from the slain Spaniards. The sense of the Indian presence, lurking in the background, must have added to the strain on the surviving men, even when they were not actually being besieged.

Right: a map of Spanish America, from a mariner's atlas with maps of the whole known world, made in Portugal probably in 1573. This map has the Spanish coat of arms to indicate which areas were Spanish possessions.

Atlantic coast, and numerous Jesuit missions were founded from Florida to Chesapeake Bay. The only eastern outposts to endure however, were those in Florida, where the missionaries were able to convert the Apalachee and Calusa and establish a permanent settlement on the east coast at St. Augustine in 1565.

Meanwhile, the Spanish were making plans to colonize the Southwest. Under the leadership of Juan de Oñate, a group of settlers, soldiers, and priests traveled to New Mexico in 1598 and founded a colony at the Pueblo of San Juan de los Caballeros near the Chama River. But the Pueblo Indians they enslaved to work their land rose up against them in 1680, and it took almost 12 years of fighting to reassert Spanish rule. Sante Fe was established as the capital of the Spanish province of New Mexico in 1610, and courageous Spanish missionaries founded outposts throughout the Southwest. But the fierce Apache and other warlike tribes of the Southern Plains prevented the Spanish from extending their rule farther north. The Spanish colonists had more success in Texas, where they founded the Mission of San Antonio de Valero, now called the Alamo, in 1718. And in California, Franciscan missionaries, under the able leadership of Father Junípero Serra, set up no fewer than 21 missions between 1769 and 1823. Among these were San Diego, Santa Clara, San Gabriel, and San Francisco.

But long before Father Junípero built his California missions, the fortunes of Spain had begun to wane. The treasure of Mexico and Peru was not inexhaustible, as the Spaniards found out in the late 1500's, when the golden harvest began to dwindle noticeably. And to make matters worse, French, Dutch, and English pirates had begun waylaying gold-laden Spanish galleons on their way back to Spain. As early as 1526, a French corsair named Jean Fleury had commandeered some of Cortes' treasure ships in mid-Atlantic and sailed home with them to his own king. Despite official Spanish protests, piracy on the high seas rapidly increased in scale during the century. In 1580, the daring English seaman Francis Drake triumphantly returned home in the *Golden Hind* with some $40 million in New World gold and silver taken from Spanish vessels.

And what of the treasure that did reach Spain? Much of it went to finance a series of wars against the French and the Turks. Much of it, too, was squandered by Spain's devout Catholic king, Charles, in a futile effort to stem the tide of Protestantism then sweeping through Spain's holdings in Germany and The Netherlands. Charles vowed he would not spare his "dominions, friends, body, blood, life, or soul" in the fight against heresy. But even his determination was surpassed by that of his son, Philip II, who came to the Spanish throne in 1556.

Philip zealously stepped up his father's crusade against Protestantism on the European continent. But his own particular grievance was against England, where the state religion of Catholicism had been replaced by Protestantism. England's Queen Elizabeth I added insult to this injury by rejecting Philip as a suitor, by aiding the

Right: St. Augustine, Florida, in 1760. The modern city is the remnant of the Spanish attempt to establish an empire on the Atlantic coast. Only in Florida, where the Jesuits converted the Apalchees and Calusas, did they build a permanent settlement.

Right: not only were the treasure ships ripe for pirates swarming over the sea, but Spanish towns found themselves vulnerable. In this engraving French pirates plunder the Spanish town of Chiorera on the island of Cuba in 1556

Protestant Dutch when they rebelled against their Spanish masters in 1568, and by actually knighting Francis Drake for his wholesale robbery of Spanish gold on the high seas. In 1587, the Protestant queen consented to the execution of her Catholic cousin, Mary, Queen of Scots. This was the last straw. Philip swore vengeance, and, in 1588, launched a war fleet—the mighty Armada—to teach England a lesson. Unfortunately, the lesson was Spain's, for almost the entire Armada was vanquished by a combination of English naval power and a severe storm at sea.

By now, Spain's treasury was almost empty and the country

deeply in debt. No further major efforts of conquest could be made in the New World. Missionary work and colonization continued, particularly in South America, where Spanish plantation owners, often mercilessly exploiting the native population, ruled with an iron hand. But over her vast northern claims, Spain could exert little or no control. Helpless to defend her interests there, she was forced to stand aside while the explorers, traders, and colonists of other nations strode through her forests, sailed up her rivers, and established mastery over lands whose real riches the Spanish conquistadors had never even dreamed of.

Above: the English launch fireships against the Spanish Armada anchored at night off the coast of Calais in August, 1588. The defeat and destruction of the Armada was a severe blow to the power of Spain. The riches of the New World – taken at such a price in both Indian and Spanish lives – were dwindling, and the most that Spain could do was develop the areas that were already conquered.

Seeking the Northwest Passage

3

Early in the 1500's, the Treaty of Tordesillas became a thorn in the side of King Francis I of France. It seemed grossly unfair to him that a mere piece of parchment should give Spain and Portugal exclusive rights to all the world's newly discovered lands. Soon after coming to the throne in 1515, Francis wrote a scathing letter to the King of Spain saying, "Show me, I pray you, the will of our father Adam, that I may see if he has really made you and the king of Portugal his universal heirs."

As if to add fuel to Francis' envy and frustration, Spain proceeded to top Portugal's control over Eastern spice and treasure with her own conquest of the glittering Aztec empire in 1521. This was too much for the French king to bear. Treaty or no treaty, he declared, he would break his southern neighbors' unjust monopoly over trade and treasure. He would send explorers of his own to find and claim the western sea route to the Orient.

From about 1504, French fishermen had been sailing into the North Atlantic Ocean to fish for cod in the Grand Banks off the coast of Newfoundland, and rumor had it that somewhere along that coast there was a strait that led to China. If Francis' mariners could locate that strait, then France, too, could enter the inter-

Left: a map of Canada drawn by a Portuguese cartographer before 1547. (North is at the bottom: to orient the map turn it upside down.) The map shows Cartier, but it is disputed whether it shows him leaving France or arriving in Canada with his settlers.

Right: "Francis I of France," painted by Titian in about 1536. It was he who challenged the pope's division of the newly discovered lands between the Spanish and Portuguese crowns.

national race for riches. Accordingly, in 1524, Francis sent a highly skilled Italian navigator named Giovanni da Verrazano to seek out this fabled "Northwest Passage."

Verrazano followed a somewhat southwesterly course and may have reached the shores of North Carolina. Then he sailed north along the New England coast, reaching Newfoundland before returning to France. Historians believe that in the course of the voyage, he spent some time near the mouth of the Hudson River, which he later described to the king as being "very large and pleasant." He went on to report that, "We greatly regretted having to leave this region, which seemed so delightful and which we supposed must also contain great riches."

King Francis was pleased with Verrazano's report. The voyage, though it had failed to produce any significant information about the much-desired strait, did allow the king to make certain grandiose claims to the region Verrazano had explored, and it was not long before the northeast coast of the mysterious northern continent was being referred to as "New France."

Wars in Europe forced Francis to abandon his quest for the Northwest Passage for almost 10 years. Then, in 1533, he received a petition from one Jacques Cartier, proposing a new exploratory voyage to the American coast. Cartier, born in the French town of St. Malo, had sailed and fished in the waters of the North Atlantic, and had spent a few adventurous years as a corsair, pirating Spanish vessels. Inspired by reports of Verrazano's voyage, he was now eager to try his hand at finding the fabled shortcut to China. Francis willingly granted Cartier's request, and in 1534 outfitted him with two small vessels and a crew of 120 men.

Cartier reached Newfoundland after 20 days at sea, and made a brief stop at tiny Funk Island to replenish the ships' larder with the murres, gannets, and great auks that abounded there. The men soon found that they were not the only hunters on this rocky "Island of Birds." Cartier noted in his journal that "although the island is 30 miles from the mainland, bears swim there to eat the birds, and our men found one as large as a cow and as white as a swan, swimming as swiftly as we could sail."

Leaving Funk Island, Cartier's ships sailed up and around the northern tip of Newfoundland and passed through the Strait of Belle Isle into the Gulf of St. Lawrence. Rounding the eastern tip

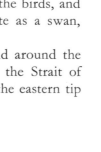

Above: the Gulf of St. Lawrence, with Percé Rock on the Gaspé Peninsula. Neither Verrazano, nor Cartier on his first voyage, recognized the importance of the gulf as the opening to the sea of one of America's greatest waterways.

Left: a glazed terra-cotta bust, by an unidentified Italian artist, of Giovanni da Verrazano, the mariner who probably discovered the mouth of the Hudson River, where New York City now stands.

of Anticosti Island, the vessels crossed the gulf—completely missing the mouth of the St. Lawrence River—and anchored off Gaspé Peninsula. Suddenly, as they lay at anchor there, Cartier saw a fleet of 50 birchbark canoes approaching them, bearing Indians who began "making signs of joy as if desiring our friendship and saying in their tongue *napeu tondamen assurtah*." This was the Micmac Indians' phrase for "we wish to have your friendship."

The next day the Micmac returned, holding up furs as a sign that they wished to trade. Cartier obliged by giving them some knives and a red hat for their chief. When the Frenchmen went ashore, they were greeted by the other men and women of the tribe. The women sang and danced, "rubbing our arms with their hands, then lifting them up to heaven and showing signs of gladness." In exchange for the white men's knives, hatchets, and beads, the Indians traded every pelt they had—even to the furs they were wearing—"until they had nothing but their naked bodies."

Before leaving Gaspé Peninsula, Cartier and his men erected a 30-foot cross and fixed to it a shield bearing the French emblem, the fleur-de-lis. Below the shield they printed in large bold letters the words "LONG LIVE THE KING OF FRANCE!" Then, while the puzzled Micmac stood gazing at this monument to an unknown faith, king, and country, Cartier took two captives, young braves named Domagaia and Taignagny.

In his report to King Francis, Cartier included the information—learned from his captives—that there was a great river leading westward from the gulf he had discovered. Could this be the Northwest Passage? To find out, Francis commissioned Cartier to make a second voyage, this time with three vessels. So, on May 16, 1535, Jacques Cartier set out once more for the New World. With him on the flagship *Grand Hermina* went Domagaia and Taignagny, to serve as interpreters.

Again Cartier passed through the Strait of Belle Isle. But this time he continued westward until he reached the mouth of the great river. He named it the "St. Lawrence," because he first saw it on August 10, St. Lawrence's feast day. He sailed up the St. Lawrence to the Huron village of Stadacona, near the site of present-day Quebec City. The Huron leader, Donnacona, was called the chief of "Canada" (the Indian name for that part of the St. Lawrence Valley). At first, Donnacona welcomed Cartier with ceremonial

Above: Jacques Cartier. He had gained his early sailing experience fishing in the North Atlantic. It was due to his navigational skill that his three ships were able to sail some 800 miles up the uncharted St. Lawrence River.

orations and other signs of friendship. But then the chief's attitude abruptly changed. Domagaia and Taignagny, no doubt bitter about their year of captivity, had taken Donnacona aside and warned him not to let the white men proceed any farther up the river.

But how was the chief to prevent them? Donnacona tried sending three of his braves dressed in black and white dog skins, with blackened faces and horns on their heads, to frighten the white men. But the wild shrieks of the Indian "devils" only made Cartier's men laugh. Donnacona threatened and pleaded with Cartier to no avail. On September 19, the Frenchmen hoisted sail on the ship's pinnace (tender) and sailed up the St. Lawrence, leaving Domagaia and Taignagny behind at Stadacona.

After traveling 150 miles up the river, they came to the Indian village of Hochelaga. Here they were met by 1,000 men, women and children, who gave them a joyful welcome and provided them with a feast of fish and cornbread. When darkness fell, the sailors returned to their boats, while the Indians continued dancing and singing around the great bonfires they had lighted to celebrate their arrival.

Early the next morning, Cartier and some of his men were taken on a tour of the village. The Algonkian, believing Cartier to be a medicine man, brought all their sick and wounded to him to be healed. Even their chief, an old man shaking with palsy, was carried

Below: Jacques Cartier erecting the cross at the entrance to the Gaspé harbor, as painted by Samuel Hawksett. With the cross, Cartier claimed the newly discovered territory for France.

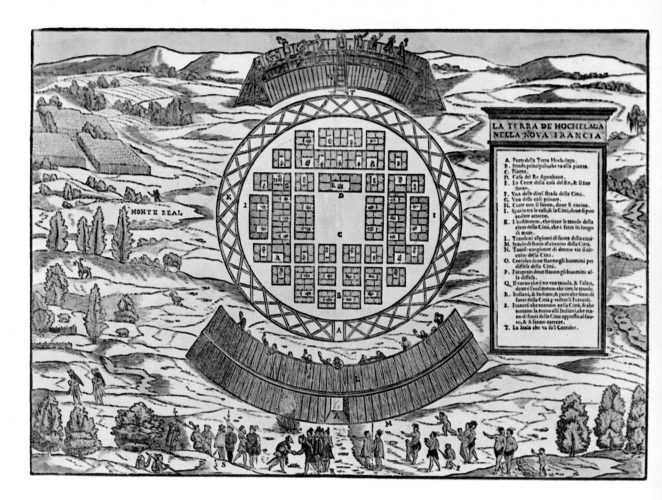

LA TERRA DE HOCHELAGA
NELLA NOVA FRANCIA

A. Porto della Terra Hochelaga.
B. Strada principale che va alla piazza.
C. Piazza.
D. Casa del Re Agouhanna.
E. La Corte della casa del Re, & il suo focere.
F. Vna delle dieci strade della Città.
G. Vna delle case prinate.
H. Corte con il focere, doue si cucina.
I. Spacio tra le case & la Città, doue si puo
  andare attorno.
K. L'ordimento, che tiene le tauole della
  cinta della Città, che é fatta in luogo
  di muro.
L. Tauole si fceno di fuora della città
M. Spacio di fuora al circuito della Città.
N. Taui congiunte di dentro via il cir-
  cuito della Città.
O. Corridor doue stanno gli huomini per
  diffesa della Città.
P. Parapetto doue stanno gli huomini al-
  la diffesa.
Q. Il vacuo che é tra vna tauola, & l'altra,
  doue é l'ordimento che tien le tauole.
R. Indiani, & Indiane, & parte che sono di
  fuori della Città p vedere i Francesi.
S. Francesi che entrano nella Città, & che
  toccano la mano alli Indiani, che era-
  no di fuori della Città appresso al fuo-
  co, & si fanno carezze.
T. La Scala che va su'l Corridor.

to Cartier on the shoulders of 10 braves. But the French captain resisted the temptation to play healer, and instead solemnly opened his Bible and read out to the bewildered populace a passage from the Gospel of St. John.

Cartier and his men then climbed the mountain that rose high above Hochelaga. It was almost sunset, and the forests he could see for 60 miles around were ablaze with autumn colors. Cartier was enthralled by the view from the summit of this peak, which he named Mont Réal (Mount Royal). The city, Montreal, takes its name from the mountain. To the southeast, over the shining ribbon of the St. Lawrence, he could make out broad, fertile valleys and the Green Mountains of Vermont, "a country," he wrote later, "which is the loveliest a man could see." But to the west he saw a series of swift rapids churning up the river a short distance beyond the point where he had anchored. The Indians told him that there were still more rapids beyond these. This was disheartening news, for it destroyed Cartier's hopes of using the St. Lawrence as a waterway to the East. With bitter irony, he named the foaming waters "Sault La Chine" (or Lachine)—the Chinese Rapids.

Cartier then sailed back down the St. Lawrence to Stadacona, where he decided to spend the winter. It proved a grim experience,

Above: the plan of the Indian village of Hochelaga, on the site of Montreal. The earliest known picture of the place, it comes from a book published in Venice in 1565. The rapids that prevented Cartier from going farther west were just beyond the village.

for he and his men fell prey to scurvy, a vitamin-deficiency disease. They became weak, with swollen joints, shrunken sinews, and rotting gums. At one point there were only three men strong enough to bring food and water to the entire ship's company. Fearful that the Indians would attack them if they knew their weakness, the feeble men forced themselves to make noise and look active whenever the Indians drew near. Twenty-five men died before Cartier learned by accident from his one-time captive Domagaia about a cure for the disease—a potion made from the boiled bark of the white pine, which contains vitamin C.

When at last the winter ended, Cartier returned to France to report his findings to the king. Although he had not found a

Above: "A View of the City of Montreal, taken from the top of the Mountain, the 15th October 1784," a watercolor by James Peachey. The mountain is Mont Royal, which Jacques Cartier named.

Below: the modern city of Montreal. as viewed from Mont Royal. The Indian village that Cartier found has become an internationally important city and a vital symbol of the French contribution to present-day Canada.

Above: Cartier and his followers in Canada, from a manuscript map by Pierra Desceliers, drawn either in 1536 or 1542. It is possibly the only contemporary and authentic picture of Cartier. This is only a section of the map which shows the whole world.

Left: the detail showing Cartier.

navigable waterway to the East, Cartier, like his sovereign, continued to believe in its existence. There was no doubt in either man's mind that it would be found. The only question was when, and by whom? Cartier himself made another voyage to Canada in 1541. Again, he sailed up the St. Lawrence and again failed to locate the fabled waterway to the East.

French ambitions to find and claim the Northwest Passage were baulked during the late 1500's by a series of bloody civil wars between the French Huguenots (Calvinists) and the French Roman Catholics. Until this internal conflict was finally resolved in 1593, nothing more could be done about exploring New France.

Meanwhile, a lucrative trade in furs had been started by the French fishermen who sailed yearly to the Grand Banks off the coast of Newfoundland. The coastal Indians, they discovered, were only too eager to part with their rich pelts for such things as beads, guns, or whiskey. And back in France, the furs fetched a handsome price. The profit to be made from beaver pelts was particularly high, because at that time beaver hats were in fashion everywhere in Europe. By the late 1500's, this fur trade had become so obviously profitable that other Frenchmen were anxious to cash in on it. At the same time, the French authorities were beginning to think seriously about planting colonies in New France to strengthen their claims there. As a result, the king took to granting individual men short-term monopolies on the St. Lawrence fur trade in return for their promise to settle a certain number of colonists there. But the Laurentian monopoly-holders were always more interested in fur trading than in colonizing, and one grant after another was revoked when they failed to keep their bargain. In fact, the 1600's might have seen little French progress in North America had it not been for the Herculean efforts of one remarkable man—Samuel de Champlain.

Above left: Samuel de Champlain, 1567 ?–1635. He was responsible for establishing the French in North America, proving with his unquenchable enthusiasm that it was possible for French settlers to live in the American wilderness.

Above: astrolabe used by de Champlain during his exploration of North America. The astrolabe is an instrument for measuring the altitude of heavenly bodies, from which latitude can be calculated. It was replaced by the sextant in the 1700's.

Champlain had grown up an ardent Catholic in the little French harbor village of Brouage. Prompted by a love of adventure, he had accompanied his uncle, an officer in the Spanish navy, to the port of Cádiz in 1598, and soon after had entered the service of the King of Spain. As captain of a Spanish vessel, he had toured the West Indies and sailed along the coast of Central America for two years. On his return he had written an account of his travels for his own king, Henry IV of France. Included in his report were some 60 detailed maps of the Spanish colonies, and an ingenious suggestion for a canal across the Isthmus of Panama.

King Henry was grateful for the young captain's loyalty and impressed by his skill in mapmaking. To reward Champlain, he made him his Royal Geographer, granted him a small pension, and gave him a noble title. But after spending two years at the French court, Champlain became restless again, and when an opportunity for travel presented itself in 1603, he seized it gladly. That opportunity was a chance to serve as official geographer on an expedition to New France.

The expedition, sponsored by the man who possessed the current monopoly on the Laurentian fur trade, sailed from France in 1603. When the party's two ships reached the North Atlantic, they sailed directly up the St. Lawrence River to the site of Hochelaga. But the Indian village visited and described by Jacques Cartier in 1535 had vanished. The Algonkian who once lived there had long since fled to escape the ravages of the aggressive Iroquois to the south.

In the course of charting the region, Champlain encountered several groups of nomadic Indians and from them learned about the existence of a great waterfall to the south—Niagara Falls. Champlain and his comrades traded for furs with these Indians and, when the expedition returned to France in September, 1603, their ships were heavily laden with a valuable cargo of pelts.

In 1604, Champlain sailed again to New France, this time in company with Pierre du Guast, Sieur de Monts, a French explorer who had secured the fur-trading rights along the North Atlantic

Above: an Indian war party landing in a canoe, while Champlain was exploring the New England coast in what is now Massachusetts. It was on this journey that Champlain succeeded in mapping the whole eastern coast of North America from Nova Scotia to Cape Cod.

Left: the Habitation of Port Royal, from Champlain's book published in 1613. It was here that the French colonists came after the first grim winter in Nova Scotia's Bay of Fundy.

coast on condition that he settle 100 colonists in the region. Again, Champlain's assignment was to serve as the expedition's official geographer and chartmaker.

Sieur de Monts, Champlain, and the party of colonists chose to settle on the island of St. Croix near the mouth of the St. Croix River in Acadia. But the French flag they raised so bravely in the little settlement on June 25, 1604, came down again sadly the following spring. Winter in Acadia, as the French then called the Nova Scotia area, had been a harrowing ordeal and many had died. The survivors —Champlain among them—moved in 1605 to Port Royal, a harbor on the Nova Scotia side of the Bay of Fundy. The next winter proved so "mild" that only a quarter of the people died —a blessing, considering the usual death rate in the New World colonies of this period.

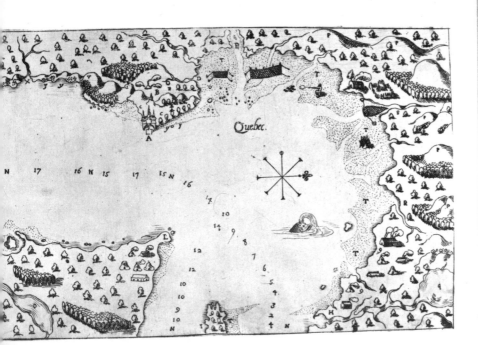

Champlain then set off to explore the coastline to the south. Passing Mount Desert Island and Penobscot Bay, he reached the site of present-day Portland, Maine, where he noted that "large mountains are to be seen to the west"—the White Mountains of New Hampshire. He then proceeded south to Massachusetts Bay, where he explored the mouth of the Charles River, site of present-day Boston. Continuing along the coast, he visited Plymouth harbor—where some 15 years later, the Mayflower would land its band of Pilgrims—and explored the bay side of Cape Cod's long crooked arm. Then, in 1607, having explored and mapped the entire North Atlantic Coast from Nova Scotia to Cape Cod, Champlain sailed back to Port Royal, and from there returned to France.

The next year, he was back in New France, this time as Sieur de Monts' representative in the Laurentian region. Sieur de Monts had just been granted the fur-trading monopoly there, and wished to establish a trading post at a strategic location along the St. Lawrence River. Accordingly, Champlain led a small expedition up the river to a place not far from the old Huron village of Stadacona. Here he ordered that a fort, a warehouse, and three small huts be erected. On July 3, 1608, the trading post was officially opened. It was called Quebec.

Champlain was convinced that the St. Lawrence would one day prove to be more than a convenient fur-trading route. He believed that the legendary Northwest Passage branched off from it somewhere, and that little Quebec would become famous as the first stopping point on the fabled water route to the Orient. He could not guess that Quebec's future greatness would rest, instead, on its being a cornerstone of the Canadian nation

From the first, however, Champlain realized the value of maintaining good relations with the local Indians. Only with their help

Above left: a map of Quebec and the surrounding area, from a book by Samuel de Champlain published in 1613. This is the first picture of Quebec.

Above: "A View of the City of Quebec the capital of Canada taken from the Ferry House on the Opposite side of the River, October 3rd, 1784," an aquatint painted by James Peachey.

Right: the skyline of modern Quebec at sunset, photographed by M. Milne. Sited spectacularly on the St. Lawrence River, Quebec is one of the world's most beautiful and elegant cities.

could the French hope to acquire pelts from the interior. Early on, Champlain won the confidence of the region's Huron and Algonkian tribes. He got on well with the proud and eloquent Huron braves, and relished the company of the comfort-loving Algonkian. Soon Quebec became the object of regular visits from Indian fur traders, and in the fall of 1608, Champlain sent some of his men back to France with a heavy cargo of pelts. He and 28 others remained behind to man the fort at Quebec.

In the spring, a group of Huron braves came to Champlain and

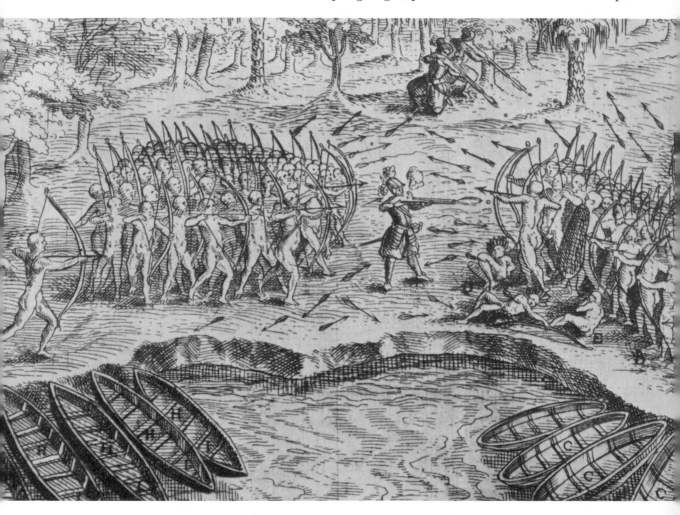

begged his assistance in a raid they were planning against their Iroquois enemies to the south. Rashly, Champlain agreed to help them. Taking two of his own men, he set off with the war party in early summer. In birchbark canoes, the group paddled west along the St. Lawrence River and then, after a journey through the thick woods, traveled south via the Richelieu River to the lovely lake which now bears Champlain's name. Here, near the site of what would one day be Fort Ticonderoga, the party met a group of Iroquois braves paddling along the shore. A canoe from either side cautiously advanced and drew together for a brief discussion.

Right: Zacherie Vincent, a Huron brave, in a self-portrait. Born in 1812, he described himself as the last of the full-blooded Hurons.

Above: Champlain firing his arquebus at Iroquois Indians. The French were to pay dearly for Champlain's quick decision to help the Huron warriors. Not only were the French settlements along the St. Lawrence River constantly harried by raids, but also the Iroquois eventually joined forces with the English in their wars with the French.

Because dusk was falling, it was agreed to begin the fight the next day. Both sides spent the night in warlike song and dance, loudly defying each other.

With the dawn, the adversaries joined battle. Facing Champlain's companions were 200 Iroquois warriors. The Huron had kept the three white men hidden until the very last moment. Then, as the early morning mist cleared, the Iroquois suddenly saw Champlain, clad in gleaming armor, stride forward and take his place at the head of the Huron braves. Champlain describes what happened next: "When I was within 20 paces, the enemy, halting, gazed at me; as I also gazed at them. When I saw them move to shoot I drew a bead on one of the chiefs. I had loaded with four bullets and hit three men at the first discharge, killing two on the spot. When our Indians saw this they roared so loudly that you could not have heard it thunder. Then arrows flew like hail on both sides. But when my companions fired from the woods, the Iroquois, seeing their chiefs killed, turned tail and fled."

It was a glorious moment for Champlain and his Huron friends. But in later years, his siding with the Hurons against the Iroquois turned out to have been a grave tactical error. Once the Iroquois learned that their enemy's white allies were Frenchmen, they never

The land carriage

Savages setting boats along

Savages setting boats along

A cataract

Savages rowing in a great Canow and standing upright

Above: an early drawing of Canadian Indians with their canoes, published in 1703. It was supposed to demonstrate the method of portaging and paddling the canoes. In fact, the painting by Cornelius Krieghoff, opposite, is based on more accurate observation.

forgot it. Nursing their grudge against the French, they launched countless raids on subsequent French settlements along the St. Lawrence. Ultimately, the Iroquois joined forces with the British, and played a vital role in the struggle that won Canada for Britain in the 1700's.

Before Champlain returned to France in 1610, he persuaded the Algonkian to take a young French boy, Étienne Brulé, with them to their winter home west of Hochelaga, so that he might learn more about the region. The plan worked well, for when Champlain returned in the spring of 1611, Brulé was able to describe to him a route west over the Ottawa River to a great lake, the Huron. Champlain was anxious to follow up this lead, but he was prevented from doing so by trouble in Quebec. Sieur de Monts had lost his monopoly on the Laurentian fur trade, and a motley crew of greedy men had come over from France to make a quick profit in beaver pelts. These rough opportunists were hard to control, and the

brandy they brought with them as a trading commodity made the Indians equally wild. Champlain had to use all his diplomatic skill to keep the peace. In desperation, he returned to France to try to obtain some authority over the region. There, he finally persuaded a French nobleman to act as viceroy for the region, with Champlain himself as lieutenant governor.

Returning to Canada in 1613, Champlain found that most of the Huron Indians had left the St. Lawrence region. Two thousand braves had waited in vain for him in 1612. Their disappointment at his failure to return, plus the traders' brandy and treachery, had driven them back into the interior. All of Champlain's painstaking Indian diplomacy had been unraveled.

But at this moment, he met Nicholas Vigneau, a Frenchman who claimed to have found the water route from the St. Lawrence to the sea. Champlain accepted this fantastic story at face value, and immediately set off up the St. Lawrence to see for himself. After a

Above: an 1858 painting by Cornelius Krieghoff showing Indians portaging furs. In the Canadian wilderness, where most of the rivers were fast and shallow, with large numbers of rapids, any long-distance travel was likely to involve a succession of these portages.

calamitous journey up the Ottawa River, during which he almost drowned in the churning rapids, Champlain reached an Indian village whose chief soon exposed the unreality of Vigneau's story. Discouraged, Champlain began the long trip back, slowed by difficult portages through mosquito-infested country and dense forests. Only the 60 canoes loaded with furs that followed him downriver to the trading post saved the expedition from being a complete loss.

Champlain returned to France once more in 1614, and sailed back to Canada the following year with a number of missionaries of the Franciscan order. He hoped that the missionaries would help to pacify the Indians as well as keep the peace among the unruly traders. On his return he found that his Indian friends were once more begging for help against the Iroquois, who had now crossed the St. Lawrence and were boldly ambushing the Algonkian along the lower reaches of the Ottawa River. Champlain decided to set

Below: the French employing siege techniques against an Iroquois fort. This was the battle that took place near Lake Oneida, to the northeast of present-day Syracuse, New York.

out and enlist the aid of more distant tribes against the Iroquois.

His search for Indian allies led Champlain to discover important new territories. Following the Ottawa River for some 300 miles, his expedition crossed by portage to Lake Nipissing, then continued southwest to Lake Huron's Georgian Bay. By so doing, Champlain and his men forged a northern water route to the Great Lakes, a route that was to be used by French traders and settlers for decades to come. After paddling the length of Georgian Bay, the expedition traveled to the eastern end of Lake Ontario, and then proceeded

Above: a storm over Georgian Bay, Ontario. It was this bay that the French crossed on the expedition into Iroquois territory near Lake Oneida.

237

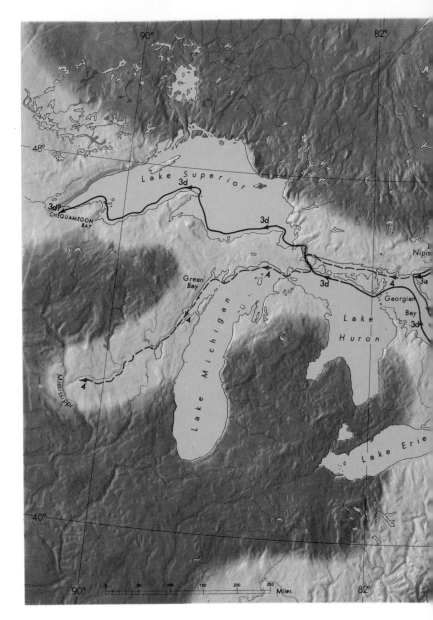

Right: the Great Lakes, showing the routes taken by Cartier, Champlain, and other French explorers in the century between 1534 and 1634. These enterprising men penetrated deep into the heart of the North American continent, along the waters and shores of the St. Lawrence River and the lakes themselves.

south into Iroquois territory near Lake Oneida. There Champlain's band of Indian warriors launched an attack on an Onondaga fort but, despite Champlain's shouted directions and European tactics, they failed to take it. Champlain himself was wounded twice and had to be carried from the scene of battle by his braves. Because the Iroquois controlled all southern approaches to the St. Lawrence, the defeated French and Indians were forced to take the long way back to their homes, via Lake Ontario, Lake Huron, Lake Nipissing, and the Ottawa River.

Champlain wanted desperately to learn more about the region west of Lake Huron, and in about 1620 he sent his young friend Étienne Brulé to explore it. Brulé traveled as far as the Upper Michigan Peninsula—becoming the first white man to visit the area. Champlain himself, however, was prevented from making any

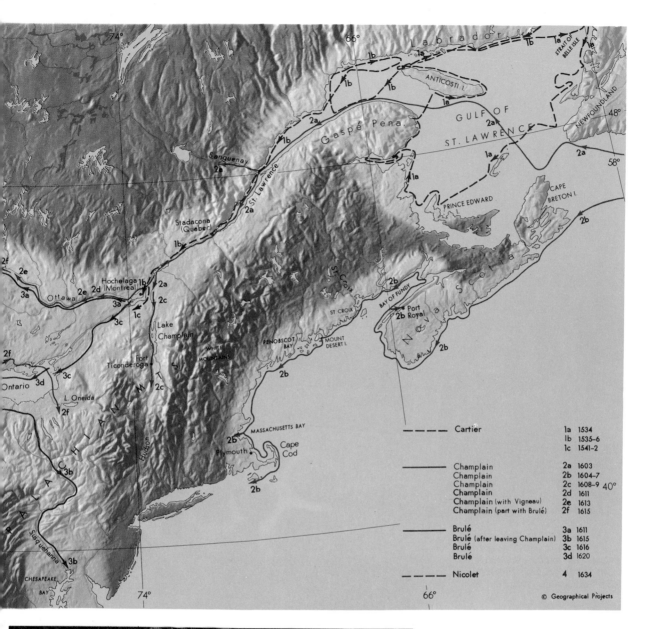

------ Cartier		1a	1534
		1b	1535-6
		1c	1541-2
——— Champlain		2a	1603
Champlain		2b	1604-7
Champlain		2c	1608-9
Champlain		2d	1611
Champlain (with Vigneau)		2e	1613
Champlain (part with Brulé)		2f	1615
——— Brulé		3a	1611
Brulé (after leaving Champlain)		3b	1615
Brulé		3c	1616
Brulé		3d	1620
— — — Nicolet		4	1634

© Geographical Projects

Left: the arrival of Champlain's wife in Canada. She arrived July 2, 1620, after a voyage of almost two months. For some time Champlain's family and the family of Louis Hébert were the only permanent settlers in Quebec.

239

further journeys of exploration by his duties in Quebec. He was determined to build up the size and strength of the colony. But, although the fur business continued to flourish, the traders came and went, anxious to make their profit and return to the comforts of their native land as quickly as possible. In the early 1620's, Quebec had only two families of permanent settlers. One was Champlain's own (he had brought his wife over in 1620). The other was the family of one Louis Hébert, a Parisian druggist who in 1617 had gladly seized the opportunity to own his own land in the New World. But

Above: David Kirke taking Quebec, after a siege of the city that lasted for several months of the winter of 1628–29. Champlain had finally been forced to surrender to the English.

Right: Jean Nicolet's landfall on the shore of Lake Michigan in 1634, by E. W. Deming. Nicolet was the *coureur de bois* who was probably sent by Champlain to find out if there was a "sweetwater sea" beyond Lake Huron as had been reported to him. Nicolet, who put on a Chinese robe in honor of the "Asians" he expected to meet, found only Winnebago Indians.

back in Europe, the traders' reports about the hard Canadian winters and the ferocity of the neighboring Iroquois tribes discouraged other Frenchmen from following Hébert's example. Among the other 80-odd souls who dwelt in New France at this time were the dedicated Catholic missionaries who had come over in the service of their faith.

War broke out between France and England in 1627. The French authorities, realizing that the English in North America would probably use the pretext of war to attack New France, dispatched a

fleet of colonists and supplies to strengthen Quebec in 1629. But it was already too late. Before the fleet could reach its destination, it was captured in the St. Lawrence by David Kirke, a Scots merchant-pirate in the employ of England. Rightly guessing that Quebec could not last out the winter without fresh supplies, he sailed up the river and demanded the colony's surrender. Champlain refused, believing that the French supply fleet was on its way. For several winter months, Kirke played a waiting game, living comfortably off the French provisions while the people of Quebec slowly starved. Eventually, Champlain was forced to surrender, and Kirke's 150 men took over the colony. Champlain was taken to England as a prisoner, where he waited out what he was sure would be a conquest of short duration. His prediction was borne out in 1632 when, with the cessation of hostilities between the two countries, Quebec was restored to France.

Back in Canada once more, Champlain worked hard to rebuild the fort and buildings of Quebec. At the same time he sought to repair the alliances with the Indians engaged in the fur trade. Quebec began to grow again under Champlain's guiding hand, and the little fortress became firmly established as an outpost of French civilization in the Laurentian wilderness.

About this time, a new type of adventurer began to flourish in New France. This was the "forest runner," or *coureur de bois*. Drawn as much by the mystery of the virgin hinterlands as by the profits to be made from the fur trade, the coureurs de bois were young men with a taste for solitary adventure and a readiness to adopt the Indians' self-reliant way of life. Preferring the challenge of the wilderness to the comforts of civilization, they roamed far and wide through the Canadian forests gathering furs from the Indians.

It was to one of these coureurs de bois, Jean Nicolet, that Champlain turned in 1634 when he sought confirmation of reports about the great "sweetwater sea" beyond Lake Huron. It was his hope that, from this sea, a waterway to Asia could be found. Nicolet had heard tales of a certain tribe, living on the shores of this sea, who had flat faces and yellow skin. Surely, Champlain thought, these must be the people of the Orient. Accordingly, he equipped Nicolet with a Chinese robe, so that the young man might make a favorable impression when he met these "Asians."

Nicolet probably set out in 1634, traveling up the Ottawa River and overland to Lake Huron. He is believed to have paddled along the north shore of the Lake, and to have passed through the Strait of Mackinac into Lake Michigan. When he reached the clay cliffs of Green Bay, Wisconsin, he thought that he had found the mainland of China. He landed, donned his silken robes, and fired two pistol shots. But, when he scrambled to the top of the cliffs, he found only the Winnebago Indians. These were the "people of the sea" he had been told of! Although Nicolet was very disappointed, he made friends with the Winnebago, who entertained him royally. Then, after traveling a short distance inland via the Fox River, he made his

Above: the statue of Jean Nicolet at Green Bay, Wisconsin. When Nicolet saw the clay cliffs of Green Bay, he thought that he had reached China.

way back to Quebec to report his findings to Champlain. Alas, when he reached the settlement, he found it in mourning. The great "Father of New France" had died, on Christmas Day, 1635.

Champlain had devoted his life to establishing the French in North America. His dauntless energy, sweeping vision, and persistent efforts had enabled him to rise above the greed of his fur-trading patrons and gain a substantial foothold for France in the New World. All the storms of life—and there were certainly storms ahead for the French-Canadians—could never remove the stamp of French civilization he had imprinted on the St. Lawrence Valley.

ECOTAN

Pasquenoke

Dasamonguepeuc

Roanoac

Trinety harbor

Hatorasck

The English Venture West
4

England was a step behind France and Spain in the exploration of North America. English mariners did not really begin probing the east coast of the great continent until the late 1500's—almost half a century after the exploits of Cartier, Narváez, and De Soto. Yet, curiously enough, the English flag had been planted on American soil before the banners of either France or Spain.

In 1497, a full 27 years before Verrazano set off to find the Northwest Passage for France, another Italian, one Giovanni Cabotto, had gone in search of it for England. Cabotto had emigrated to England as a young man and, after changing his name to John Cabot, had become a captain for the Merchant-Venturers of Bristol. It was with their backing—and a special license from King Henry VII—that Cabot, no doubt inspired by Columbus' voyages, set out to find the East Indies in 1497.

In a little ship called the *Matthew,* Cabot made his first landfall on the coast of Newfoundland or Nova Scotia. There he landed and, believing that he had reached an outpost of Asia, unfurled the royal standard and claimed the region for the King of England. Then, after sailing around Newfoundland, he returned to England with news of its rich fishing grounds.

But the English king was not pleased with the results of the voyage. Cabot had brought back no spices, no treasure, no emissary from the Great Khan of China—nothing, in fact, to prove that he had reached the East. Henry VII granted Cabot a small pension for his efforts, but warned him that if he intended to make any further voyages westward, he would do so without a royal blessing.

Cabot was undeterred. Apparently, like Columbus, he was convinced that a further voyage would bring him to his goal. In 1498 he set out once more, this time with four or five ships. Again he traveled west, possibly sailing north as far as Greenland and south as far as North Carolina. His own ship went down during a storm on the return voyage, and the crews of the remaining vessels could give only sketchy accounts of the southern coasts they had seen.

Cabot's voyages had given England nothing but a flimsy legal claim to the area he had explored, and English interest in the New World remained almost nonexistent for the next 78 years. England was concerned with other, more pressing matters during this period. At home, the nation was wracked by political and religious strife. And abroad, England was embroiled in conflicts with France and Spain. Meanwhile, English sailors such as Francis Drake—with the blessing of Queen Elizabeth herself—remorselessly plundered Spanish treasure ships on the high seas, an activity that only served to heighten the mounting hostility between the two countries.

Ultimately, it was the conflict and rivalry with Spain that led England to take a fresh interest in the New World. In the late 1500's, a number of Englishmen began urging the queen to carry the battle against Spain to the New World. An English settlement there, they argued, would not only serve as a base from which to launch

Left: Elizabeth I of England, in the portrait by Nicholas Hilliard. During her reign Sir Francis Drake made his great voyages, and enriched not only himself but his queen with the gold snatched from Spanish treasure ships. The ermine on the queen's sleeve is a symbol of virginity, alluding to Elizabeth's popular title "Virgin Queen."

attacks on Spanish holdings in the Americas, but would also act as a check on further Spanish expansion in North America. And, they added, who could tell what riches might lie north of Spain's current holdings on the continent? An outpost in America might one day provide England with vital raw materials, even treasure.

Two of the men who argued for such a colony were Humphrey Gilbert and his half brother Walter Raleigh (or Ralegh, as he spelled it). Both were firmly convinced of the strategic value of an English base in North America. But no individual could simply set off and

establish a colony at will. A charter granting royal permission had to be obtained first. In 1576, 1577, and 1578, an English navigator named Martin Frobisher had received the queen's permission to make voyages in search of the Northwest Passage—voyages which had taken him to Greenland, Labrador, Baffin Island, and Hudson Strait. In 1578, Humphrey Gilbert, following Frobisher's example, petitioned the queen for permission to seek "a passage by the north to go to Cathay." But Gilbert's charter also provided for the founding of a settlement, whose colonists were to have the "privileges of free denizens and persons native of England."

Gilbert set out for the New World in 1578. But his ships were beset by storms in mid-Atlantic, and he was forced to return to England. In 1583, he made a second attempt, and this time succeeded in reaching Newfoundland, which he claimed for Elizabeth I. He set up a colony there, near St. John's, and then sailed for home. But on the return voyage his ship went down in a storm. And the little colony in Newfoundland soon had to be abandoned.

After Gilbert's death, the royal patent was transferred to Raleigh, who was given the right to "discover, search, find out, and view such remote, heathen, and barbarous lands, countries, and territories not actually in possession of any Christian prince." Like Gilbert, Raleigh was granted permission to establish a colony in these lands. But unlike Gilbert, Raleigh dreamed of something more than a mere strategic base in the New World. He wanted nothing less than to found a new England, an overseas empire where English homes,

Above: the French explorer René de Laudonnière with Chief Athore standing before a decorated column at the mouth of the St. Johns River, Florida, 1564. This is the only surviving painting by Jacques le Moyne de Morgues, who was on the expedition. This view of "the land of plenty" is said to have given Sir Walter Raleigh the idea of establishing a colony in America. Below: Sir Walter Raleigh, 1552–1618.

English speech, English culture, and English law might prevail.

In 1584, Raleigh equipped and sent out two ships on a reconnaissance mission to the shores of America. Sailing west-southwest, the vessels reached the sandy beaches of North Carolina, then followed the coast north to Cape Hatteras. They entered Pamlico Sound, and came to an island that the Indians called Roanoke. The island's inhabitants gave the sailors a royal welcome. Arthur Barlowe, who, with Philip Amadas, was in charge of the expedition, later reported that the chief's wife "cheerfully came running out to meet us and commanded her people to pull our boats ashore. When we arrived at her house, she sat us down by the fire, took off our clothes, and washed and dried them. . . .She herself dressed meat for us, and brought us venison, fish, melons, and wine mixed with ginger. . . .We were entertained with all love and kindness and found the people most gentle, loving, faithful, and free of guile and treason, living in the manner of the golden age."

Barlowe's report to Raleigh also included a glowing account of the beauty of the countryside, with its tall trees, wild vineyards, and abundant deer, rabbits, and birds. Raleigh was delighted, and named the newly-found land "Virginia," in honor of the "Virgin Queen," Elizabeth I. Elizabeth, too, was pleased, and knighted Raleigh, instructing him to inscribe his coat of arms with the legend "Walter Ralegh, Lord and Governor of Virginia." In 1585, Raleigh dispatched a second expedition to Virginia. This expedition, led by Sir Richard Grenville, carried colonists. But the little settlement on Roanoke Island fared badly. The colonists, desperately short of provisions, almost starved to death waiting for their meager crops to ripen. The next year, when Sir Francis Drake's fleet made a stop at the outpost, the settlers gladly accepted his offer to take them back to England.

Raleigh's last and most serious attempt to establish a colony in Virginia was launched in 1587, when he sent 117 settlers to Roanoke under the leadership of John White. Soon after the passengers had landed and chosen a site for their settlement, White's daughter, Ellinor Dare, gave birth to a daughter. The infant was named "Virginia," as she was the first English child to be born in America. White's orders were to sail back for additional supplies, and, when he set off, his daughter and her husband, together with little Virginia, were among the 91 men, 17 women, and 10 children left at Roanoke.

The naval battle with the Spanish Armada took place soon after White reached England, and it was three years before he could return to Roanoke. Alas, when he did finally reach the island in 1590, he found it deserted. No trace of his family or their fellow-colonists remained, save for the word "Croatoan" the name of a neighboring island, carved on a tree. Friendly Indians in the region suggested that all the settlers had been massacred on the orders of Chief Powhatan, leader of the confederacy of Powhatan tribes along the coast.

In 1603, a few months after James I became king of England, Sir

Above: the wife and child of an Indian chief in Virginia in about 1585, a watercolor drawing by John White. He was the leader of the Roanoke colony and the grandfather of Virginia Dare, the first white child to be born there.

Above: a map of Virginia drawn by John Smith and published in 1624. In the upper left hand corner is a picture of Powhatan in state. Although called Chief Powhatan by his tribes, his name was actually Wahunsonacock.

Right: an idyllic view of the pastimes a knight could enjoy in Virginia, from an account of 1619. Although hunting and fishing were certainly part of the life in the new colonies, this picture does not reveal that they were less practiced as sports than as a matter-of-fact way of providing food to eat. This kind of propaganda may have been part of the reason that recruits to the colonies found real life in Virginia so desperately hard.

Walter Raleigh was suspected of treason, charged, and imprisoned in the Tower of London. There he remained for 12 long years. But Raleigh's dream of a Virginia colony did not languish there with him. In 1606, the English merchants who had helped finance Raleigh's efforts formed a colonizing association of their own, and were granted the colonial privileges previously enjoyed by Raleigh. The association, called the Virginia Company, was divided into two groups. The Virginia Company of Plymouth (or Plymouth Company) was to colonize the northern portion of the Atlantic coast (from Maine to Maryland), while the Virginia Company of London (or London Company) was to colonize an overlapping section of the mid-Atlantic coastline (from New York to the Carolinas).

In December, 1606, the Virginia Company of London dispatched its first expedition to the New World. Aboard the *Susan Constant,* the *Goodspeed,* and the *Discovery* were about 100 colonists. Among them was one Captain John Smith, a remarkable man who was later to play a vital role in the fledgling colony's fight for survival against the ravages of hostile Indians, starvation, disease, and sheer despair.

John Smith was no stranger to hardship and danger when he set out for Virginia at the age of 26. Indeed, he was already a past master at the difficult art of survival among alien people in alien lands. At 15 he had begun traveling through Europe seeking challenge and excitement, and he had found it in abundance—as a mercenary soldier in the armies of The Netherlands, France, and Hungary, as a slave of the Turks in Constantinople, and as a prisoner of the Tartars in Russia. Romance and adventure had been part and parcel of his life for almost 10 years when he finally escaped from his Russian master and returned to England in 1604. But his wanderlust was still unsatisfied, and when he learned of the Virginia undertaking, he signed on at once.

Before the ships set sail, the London Company had secretly selected six men to serve as the colony's governing council. The list of names was placed in a locked box that was not to be opened until

Left: long before John Smith came to America he had proved himself capable of surviving desperate situations triumphantly. Here he is shown in one of the episodes from his early career when he took on three Turkish knights in single-handed combat and defeated each of them in turn. The illustrations come from his book *The True Travels, Adventures, and Observations of Captaine Ione Smith, In Europe, Asia, Affrica, and America,* which was published in London in 1630.

Right: the coat of arms that Smith was awarded after his victory. It shows the heads of the three knights.

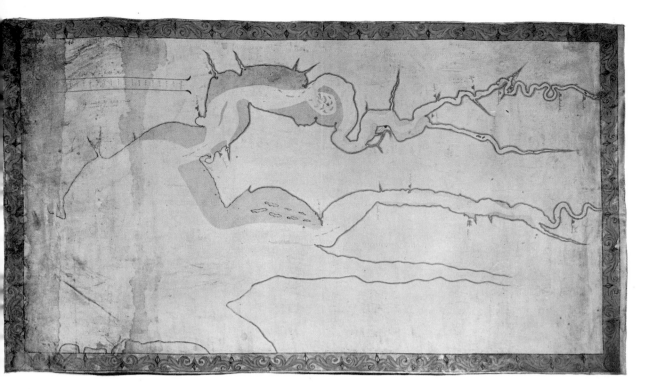

Above: the James River, a vellum map drawn by "Robarte Tindall of Virginia, anno 1608." The colonists dispatched by the Virginia Company of London established their settlement, Jamestown, about 60 miles up the river.

the fleet reached its destination. As the vessels neared the Virginia coast, the box was opened and the names read out. Smith's was among them. But the other council members distrusted the youthful adventurer, and refused to accept him. When the party went ashore to choose a site for the settlement, Smith remained aboard ship—accused of mutiny.

The London Company had specified that the colony was to be built on good land, and in a location that might easily be defended against Indian attacks. These conditions were hardly fulfilled by the site chosen: a mosquito-infested strip of swampland 60 miles up the James River in the very heart of Powhatan country. Here, amid the little cluster of rude dwellings they called "Jamestown," the colonists laid out garden plots under the direction of Edwin Maria Wingfield, the president of the council. John Smith urged Wingfield to put up a fort of wooden logs like those he had seen in Russia, but the president insisted that a mere brushwood fence would serve to keep out the Indians. But, soon after the fence was built, 400 Powhatan braves attacked the settlement, breached the flimsy fortifications, and wounded many men before being frightened away by cannon shot. Wingfield had learned his lesson. Captain John Smith was admitted to the council and a wooden fort was built under his guidance.

But the colony did not prosper. Three months after its founding, 46 men were dead from starvation, malaria, pneumonia, and dysentery, and those alive were so weak that they barely had strength enough to bury the dead. In desperation, the council turned to John Smith, begging him to go out and trade for food with the Indians.

How they tooke him prisoner
in the Oaze 1607

C. Smith bindeth a saluage to his arme,
fighteth with the King of Pamaunkee and
all his company, and slew 3 of them.

Their triumph about him

C: Smith bound to a tree to be shott to death
1607

Above left: Captain John Smith being taken prisoner by Powhatan Indians.

Left: the Indians triumph at Smith's capture, from his 1624 book. He had gone up the James River hunting food for the colony, hoping to trade with the Indians. When he went ashore, he found himself surrounded by warriors.

Above left: Pocohontas in 1616, the
year her husband, John Rolfe, took her
back to England with him. It was then
nine years since she had saved John
Smith's life in the Powhatan village.

Above: the illustration that appeared
in John Smith's book, showing how
the 12-year-old girl Pocohontas had
saved his life. Smith lies facing upward,
with the two Indians with clubs ready
to strike as the chief's daughter comes
and kneels beside the condemned man.

Smith made his way along the James River. When he had traveled
about 50 miles, he suddenly found himself confronted by 200
Powhatan warriors. After a brief skirmish, Smith was taken prisoner.
But he was cunning as well as brave, and managed to convert their
hostility into curiosity—first by writing a letter to the council at
Jamestown, and then by showing them his compass. The magic of
the "talking paper" and the little needle under the clear "ice" that
always pointed in the same direction gave him a reputation as a
medicine man. He was taken to the Powhatan's leader, Wahunsonacock, known to his tribes as Chief Powhatan. There, in the presence
of the great chief and all his council, Smith's fate was debated. At
last, after much deliberation, it was decided that the white man
should die, and Smith was forced to put his head between two large
stones so that the warriors could beat out his brains with their clubs.
But at the very last moment, according to Smith's later account of the
incident, Powhatan's young daughter, Pocahontas, ran forward and
placed her head upon his to save him from death.

Perhaps Pocahontas was truly smitten with John Smith—though
the bruised and half-starved man in tattered clothing must have
presented a sorry sight. Perhaps shrewd old Powhatan had urged his
daughter to throw herself upon Smith, knowing full well that his
hot-headed braves would not dare to lay a hand on a child of the
chief. Powhatan may have feared reprisals from the force of English
soldiers that Smith had told him were on the way.

It may seem strange today that a 12-year-old girl could intervene
in such serious tribal decisions and have her wishes obeyed. But
some Indian women had a strong voice in tribal affairs, especially
among the tribes of the Iroquois Indians. Women could own pro-

perty, speak in councils, and even serve as chiefs. They were often sent on peace missions to other tribes, and in general were accorded greater respect and allowed more personal freedom than the women of Europe during this period.

After Pocahontas had rescued John Smith, Powhatan adopted the Englishman, gave him an Indian name, and sent him back to Jamestown with provisions. In fact, the Indians helped the colonists with gifts of food many times in the ensuing years. But despite their aid, the Virginia settlement almost collapsed during the first few years. Of the 900 colonists who were brought over in successive waves from 1607 to 1609, fewer than 100 remained alive in 1610. In large part, this was because the settlers were not only inexperienced but almost incurably lazy. During his term as president of the colony, from 1608 to 1609, John Smith forced the Jamestown residents to work hard for their survival, imposing harsh punishments on those who did not give their best efforts to the settlement. Smith himself set the pace, toiling every day in the fields, or hacking down trees for firewood and new buildings. Anyone who refused to work hard was left to starve on the other side of the river, and all deserters were shot.

Above: the earliest known picture of a tobacco plant, a woodcut from a book published in Antwerp in 1576. The struggling settlement of Jamestown was given a new lease on life when John Rolfe produced a mild variety of tobacco that would suit Europeans.

Right: tobacco was a familiar part of Indian life, used mainly for ceremonial occasions. This portrait of Chief Tishcohan, one of the chiefs with whom William Penn signed a treaty, shows his tobacco pouch around his neck.

Above: "Boors Carousing," a picture painted in 1644 by a Flemish artist, Teniers the Younger. Within a few years of its introduction, the craze for smoking tobacco had spread through all classes of the European population.

Such brutal discipline seems to have been necessary, for after Smith returned to England in 1609, having been wounded in a gunpowder accident, the colony foundered. Doctor Simons, who remained in Jamestown, wrote that "the savages no sooner realized that Smith was gone, than they all revolted and murdered any white man they met. . . . Now we all cried for the loss of Captain Smith, even his greatest enemies cursed his loss, for we had no more corn or contributions from the savages, but only mortal wounds from clubs and arrows. Of the 500 people left behind after Smith's departure, six months later there remained only 60 men, women, and children, most miserable and poor creatures, who survived on roots, herbs, acorns, walnuts, berries, and now and then a little fish. So great was our famine that a savage we slew and buried was dug up by some and eaten. . . . This was the time we called the starving time, which was too vile to describe and scarce to be believed. . . ."

Indeed, the colony was but "10 days from death," when the fleet of England's Lord De la Warr, the colony's governor, appeared on the coast, bearing 150 colonists and a store of provisions. Despite the Jamestown survivors' pleas to be taken back to England with him, De la Warr forced them to stay on in the colony which, as one of the new settlers remarked, looked more like the "ruins of some ancient fortification, than that any people living might now inhabit it."

HUDSON BAY

The Great Lakes

GULF OF
ST. LAWRENCE

NEWFOUNDLAND

Nova Scotia

SABLE I.

APPALACHIAN MTS.

St. Lawrence

Kennebec R.
PENOBSCOT BAY

New England

Connecticut

Salem
Boston
Plymouth
Providence
RHODE I.
NANTUCKET
MARTHA'S VINEYARD
ELIZABETH IS.
LONG I.

Hudson R.

ATLANTIC

DELAWARE B.

Virginia
CHESAPEAKE BAY

Ohio

James
Williamsburg
Jamestown
Roanoke
ROANOKE I.
PAMLICO SD.
Hatteras

OCEAN

Mississippi

Mississippi
Delta

Florida

GULF OF MEXICO

BAHAMA
ISLANDS

CUBA

TROPIC OF CANCER

HISPANIOLA

Miles
100 200 300 400 500

— — — Gilbert	1	1583
Raleigh's expeditions under:		
——— Barlow (with Amadas)	2a	1584
Grenville (with Lane & White)	2b	1585-
White	2c	1587
·········· Gosnold	3	1602
— — — Waymouth (with Rosier)	4	1605
——— Smith (for the London Company)	5a	1606
——— Smith (for the Plymouth Company)	5b	1614

© Geographi

For the next nine years, the Virginia colony grew slowly under the harsh rule of one of Governor De la Warr's deputies, Thomas Dale. For a time, the settlers continued to suffer the agonies of extreme privation and isolation. In 1612, however, Jamestown's future was saved by a man named John Rolfe, who developed a new cash crop: tobacco. Rolfe probably brought tobacco seed from South America and improved the curing of tobacco leaves until he produced a sweet variety that suited European tastes. A craze for smoking Virginia tobacco soon developed in England, and Jamestown began to show signs of becoming an economic success. The momentous consequences of Rolfe's development were accelerated later on, when the first Negro slaves were sold to the colony by Dutch traders. Using this forced labor, Virginia was soon exporting 500,000 pounds of tobacco every year.

Rolfe celebrated the success of his invention by marrying Pocahontas. The wedding took place in April, 1614, with the full approval of Powhatan, who sent three of his relatives to witness the ceremony. Afterward, diplomatic relations between the Powhatan confederacy and the Virginia colony were resumed. With the return of peace, trade flourished between the Indians and the Jamestown settlers.

In 1616, Rolfe took Pocahontas to England, where she was described as "the Lady Rebecca, alias Pocahontas, who was taught by John Rolfe, her husband, and his friends, to speak English and

Left: the eastern United States, showing the routes of the first Englishmen who explored and began to settle on the Atlantic seaboard between the years 1583 and 1614.

Right: the Jamestown massacre of 1622. Powhatan's brother, Opechancanough, and his warriors attacked all the English plantations simultaneously, killing more than 10 percent of the settlers.

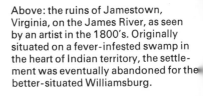

Above: the ruins of Jamestown, Virginia, on the James River, as seen by an artist in the 1800's. Originally situated on a fever-infested swamp in the heart of Indian territory, the settlement was eventually abandoned for the better-situated Williamsburg.

learn English customs and manners. She also had a child by him, and the Treasurer [of the London Company of Virginia] took responsibility for the welfare of both mother and child; besides there were many persons of great rank who were very kind to her." But at the age of 21—just as Rolfe was about to return with her to Virginia— Pocahontas contracted smallpox and died.

Back in Virginia, Pocahontas' fellow tribesmen fared little better. As tobacco became a source of profit, a number of wealthy noblemen and stockholders in the Virginia Company of London were given large grants of land along the James River. Tobacco was the chief crop on all of these "plantations," but it used up the soil and fresh fields were required every few years. Instead of clearing their own land, the plantation owners drove the Indians from their cornfields and took over the land they had cleared. The Indians grew angry and resentful, and war became inevitable. In 1622, under Opechancanough, probably Powhatan's brother, the Indians launched a lightning

Above: Wren Building, at the College of William and Mary in Williamsburg, Virginia. The oldest American academic building in use, it was erected at Middle Plantation—where Williamsburg now stands—in 1695 from plans said to have been made by Christopher Wren.

attack on all the plantations simultaneously, killing 347 of the 3,000 or so settlers. The English retaliated, and over the next two decades, the combined might of the Powhatan tribes was broken by the Europeans' superior military tactics. The victorious settlers then split up the Powhatan confederacy, and drove the remnants of the various tribes westward.

Meanwhile, the uncompromising rule of Thomas Dale had been replaced, in 1619, by a more democratic form of government, the House of Burgesses. It was the first representative legislative body in America, and continued to play an important part in governing Virginia even after 1624, when King James I made the settlement a royal colony with a governor appointed by himself. Meanwhile, Virginia continued to grow and prosper as more and more colonists flocked to its shores to seek their fortune in the New World. Raleigh's dream of an "Inglishe nation" in America was well on its way to fulfillment.

New England's Bays and Rivers

5

While the London Company was busy sending wave after wave of settlers to Jamestown, the Plymouth Company had not been idle. Under the terms of the 1606 agreement that had divided the Virginia Company in two, the Plymouth group was entitled to found a colony in the region between Maine and Maryland. Intending to get a head start on their London associates, the Plymouth merchants had already dispatched one expedition when the first Jamestown settlers left England in December, 1606. But the first Plymouth expedition fell prey to the Spanish in the West Indies. And the second, which set out in May, 1607, did not fare much better. True, the little band did succeed in reaching the coast of Maine, and even established an outpost, called the Popham Plantation, near the mouth of the Kennebec River. But, after one "extreme, unseasonable, and frosty" winter, the Maine settlers gave up and sailed for home.

The New England region, or "northern Virginia," as it was called then, was almost wholly unknown territory in the early 1600's. That the English knew anything at all about it was due to the efforts of two merchant-adventurers, who had explored its coastline shortly before the Plymouth Company was founded.

The first of these merchant-adventurers was Captain Bartholomew Gosnold, who sailed to northern Virginia early in 1602 in search of sassafras. Tea made from the bark of the sassafras tree—which grows throughout the eastern half of North America—was then believed to be a general cure for many types of diseases. A cargo of sassafras was sure to bring a high price in Europe, and Gosnold hoped to make his fortune. He was taking a risk in making the voyage, for he sailed without the permission of Sir Walter Raleigh, who at that time was still governor of all of Virginia. The penalties for infringing on another's royal charter could be stiff, but Gosnold was willing to take a chance in order to earn a quick profit.

On May 14, 1602, after a stormy voyage of nearly two months, Captain Gosnold's ship, the *Concord,* reached the rocky shores of Maine. Great was the surprise of both captain and crew when,

The Pilgrim Fathers leaving Plymouth in 1620. From all reports, the actual departure was a much quieter affair, with the Pilgrims embarking without ceremony and quietly slipping away from the harbor to the open ocean.

Left: Gosnold was able to win the friendship of the local Indians by presenting them not only with trading trinkets but with steel knives, which were much more valuable to them. This engraving shows sailors landing and offering the gifts to the Indians.

shortly after their arrival, they sighted a small European fishing boat manned by six Indians, whose leader was dressed in a sailor's coat and breeches! From this unusually-garbed Indian, Gosnold learned that French fishermen-traders had recently been in the area to fish for cod. Gosnold himself discovered the rich bounty of New England's coastal waters when, a few days later, having sailed south into a large bay, he and his men did some fishing of their own. "Within five or six hours," wrote one of his seamen later, "we had filled our ship with so many cod fish that we threw many of them overboard again, and I am convinced that in March, April, and May this coast has better fishing than in Newfoundland." Appropriately, the arm of land that forms this bay was later named "Cape Cod."

Gosnold rounded the cape and made landings on the islands of Nantucket and Martha's Vineyard where his crew found "straw-berries, red and white, as sweet and much bigger than ours in

England, raspberries, gooseberries, and grapes on every tree so that it was impossible to walk without treading on them." Sailing west to the Elizabeth Islands, they found the soil so fertile that seeds of barley, wheat, and oats sowed at random grew to a height of nine inches within two weeks. They also found an abundance of trees—cedars, beeches, and elms, as well as the special tree whose bark they had come in search of—the sassafras.

Gosnold quickly won over the local Indians with gifts of knives and trinkets. In return for this gesture of goodwill, the Indians obligingly helped the sailors cut the sassafras bark from the trees and load it onto the ship. When the hold was full, Gosnold set sail for England, but not before giving his Indian friends a farewell salute with a blast of trumpets.

Back in England late in 1602, Gosnold made a fine profit from his cargo, much to the annoyance of Sir Walter Raleigh, who ordered a full investigation of this illegal voyage to northern Virginia. But at length, the two men made peace, and Gosnold later became one of the first colonists to sail to Jamestown.

In 1605, a second exploratory voyage to the New England coast was made by one Captain George Waymouth. This voyage was sponsored by two wealthy Englishmen, Sir Ferdinando Gorges and Sir John Popham, who had become greatly interested in the possibilities of founding a colony on the coast of Maine.

Captain Waymouth's ship, the *Archangel,* sailed from London in March, 1605, and followed a west-southwesterly course for five weeks. In early May, while still out of sight of land, the crew sighted

A
TRVE RELATION
of the moft profperous voyage
made this prefent yeere 1605,
by Captaine *George Waymouth,*
in the Difcouery of the land
of *Virginia*:

Where he difcouered 60 miles vp
a moft excellent Riuer; together with a moft
fertile land.

Written by IAMES ROSIER.
*a Gentleman employed
in the voyage.*

LONDINI
Impenfis GEOR. BISHOP.
1605.

Above: the title page from the book that James Rosier wrote about the voyage to the New England coast with Captain Waymouth on the *Archangel.*

Left: a river in the prosperous, green territory that is now called Maine, along the coast of which Waymouth and Rosier were exploring. The rivers, woods, and virgin meadows stretching off into the unmapped interior seemed to promise inexhaustible riches and a safe place of refuge for dissenters.

a churning rip tide: the *Archangel* had reached Nantucket Sound. Waymouth sailed on to the coast of Cape Cod. Then, rounding the cape, he sailed north to an island off the coast of Maine, where he made a landing. Here he and his men were approached by a group of Indians. According to James Rosier, a seaman on board the *Archangel,* the English sailors greeted them with gifts of "bracelets, rings, and peacock feathers, which they stuck in their hair, [and with] brandy, which they tasted but would not drink, [although] they like sugar candy and raisins." Rosier went on to report that Waymouth's trade with these Indians was very profitable: "For knives, glasses, combs, and other trifles worth four or five shillings, we received 40 good beaver skins."

Captain Waymouth gave the Indians a demonstration of magnetism. "His sword and mine having been touched with the lade-stone," writes Rosier, "they attracted a knife and held it fast. . . . The sword made the knife spin on a block, and when we touched it, the knife in turn attracted a needle. This we did to make them believe that we had some great power, so that they would love and fear us." The Indians were then invited aboard the ship, where they "behaved themselves very civilly, neither laughing nor talking all the time, and at supper did not eat like ignorant men, but ate and drank only enough to satisfy them." This restraint seems to have especially impressed the Englishmen, for in Europe at that time it was common for men to make themselves sick by overeating.

Leaving the island, Waymouth explored the Maine coast, and discovered the Kennebec River, of which Rosier wrote: "I would boldly call it the richest, most beautiful, largest, and most secure river and harbour in the world." In so extolling the Kennebec, Rosier was probably thinking of the river's deep and quiet water, which made it much more navigable than the shallow River Thames back in England.

Along the southern coast of Maine, the sailors encountered some hostile Indians who tried to lure them into an ambush. The Englishmen not only avoided the ambush, but succeeded in capturing five of the Indians, whom they took back to England with them. One of the captives was a man named Squanto, who found life in England very much to his liking, and remained in England—by choice—for several years before returning to his native land.

On his return to England, Waymouth gave his employers a glowing report of the Maine region. Popham and Gorges were delighted and, acting on behalf of the Plymouth Company, dispatched a colonizing expedition to the Maine coast in 1607. This was the ill-fated Popham Plantation on the Kennebec River, which had to be abandoned after the first year.

Others besides Gorges and Popham had been interested in Waymouth's report about Maine. English Catholics who were suffering religious persecution at home had begun to seek ways and means of establishing a colony of refuge in the New World. For a time, they considered founding such a colony on the Maine coast. But in the

Above: Squanto, the Indian captured by Waymouth who later became a good friend to the Pilgrims, teaching them a great deal about the wilderness.

Below: "Mrs. Penobscot at the Court of Queen Elizabeth," reputedly the portrait of one of the four Indian women that Sir Ferdinando Gorges brought back from America to the court in the 1500's.

end, it was not Maine, but Maryland that provided an American haven for the persecuted Catholics. In 1632, a Catholic peer named Lord Baltimore was granted a tract of land around Chesapeake Bay, and soon after, established the new colony of Maryland there.

Meanwhile, what of the Plymouth Company's holdings in "northern Virginia"? In 1614, Sir Ferdinando Gorges, annoyed at his fellow merchants' failure to do anything more about exploration or colonization in the New World, contacted Captain John Smith. Smith had returned from Jamestown some five years earlier, and Gorges commissioned him to investigate the shores of northern Virginia. Soon after, Smith sailed west, and explored the coast from Cape Cod to Penobscot Bay. He returned with an enthusiastic report of the Massachusetts coast. "Of all the four uninhabited parts of the world that I have seen," he wrote, "I would rather live and plant a colony here than anywhere else. . . . Plymouth Bay has an excellent harbour, good land, and needs only industrious people."

Delighted, Gorges sent Smith off the following year to plant a colony in this promising land. But his ship never reached America. It was captured by French pirates on the way over. John Smith himself was kept a prisoner by the French for some six months, a period of enforced inactivity that he put to good advantage by making a detailed map of the coast of northern Virginia, which he had renamed "New England." This map was to prove of vital importance to a historic little band of colonists who set out for America some four years later in a vessel called the *Mayflower*.

The Catholics were not the only religious group being persecuted in England at this time. Certain Protestant sects were also under

Above: the capture of John Smith by the French. In the upper left corner he is shown making his landfall on French territory. He was on his way to set up a colony in the land of Massachusetts, about which he had made such an enthusiastic report in 1614.

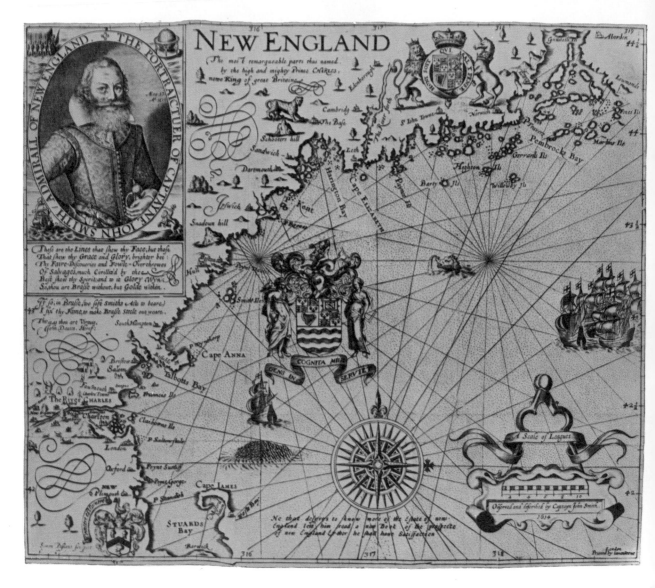

Above: John Smith's map of New England, which the Pilgrims used in 1620 to find their way along the coast and into Plymouth Harbor.
Below: a Delft tile of the early 1600's, with a ship the size of the *Mayflower*.

attack. Although the Church of England had freed itself from papal control and become a strongly Protestant institution, some of the English Calvinists—the "Puritans"—were still dissatisfied with it. They resented the control over the church exercised by the king and his bishops, and wanted a "purer" form of Protestantism—one that upheld a rigorous moral code and relied solely on the teachings of the Bible. Some groups of Puritans were known as "Separatists" because they believed in separating themselves entirely from the Church of England. These views made them very unpopular in England.

In 1608, a group of Separatists, under the leadership of William Brewster, had emigrated to Leiden, in The Netherlands, seeking refuge from the persecution they suffered at home. But, after several years there, they found themselves disenchanted with the life in a foreign country. Deciding that their best hope lay in founding a new community where they could worship as they pleased *and*

Right: the patent of Plymouth Colony. Issued in 1621, it gave the Pilgrims actual title to the lands they had taken. Up until then legally they had been squatters. This patent gave no powers of government, which only the king could grant, and so the only basis of government organization in the colony was still the *Mayflower* compact.

Below: the Pilgrims going to church, walking through the snow carrying their Bibles. The guns were for protection against hostile Indians. Presumably this would be during their first winter, before they had established their friendship with Chief Samoset.

keep their English way of life, they made plans to sail to the New World. They found financial backing from a group of like-minded London merchants and, on September 16, 1620, set out from Plymouth, England in the *Mayflower*. On board were 102 passengers, of whom about 50 were "strangers"—that is, tradesmen, craftsmen, and soldiers (such as Miles Standish) who had been recruited to help in the building of the new colony.

The intended destination of the Pilgrims, as they called themselves, was southern Virginia. But, after 65 storm-tossed days at sea, they found themselves off the coast of New England. Concluding that God's will had brought them to this spot, they decided to found their colony along New England's shores. They had with them a

copy of John Smith's map of the region, and after some searching, found the "Plimouth harbour" he had indicated on the map (now Plymouth, Massachusetts). Here, on December 26, 1620, they went ashore and began building a cluster of rude dwellings, a storehouse, and a place for meetings and worship.

Even before they landed, the Pilgrims had addressed themselves to the problem of how they should govern themselves. They knew that difficulties lay ahead because they possessed no charter. They were, in fact, illegal immigrants in a land that by rights belonged to the Plymouth Company. Moreover, cut off from English law, the group knew that they would need some rules of internal organization. Accordingly, they drew up an agreement called the *Mayflower Compact*, which provided for the enacting of "just and equall" laws "as shall be thought most meete and convenient for ye generall good of ye colonie." The Pilgrim leaders persuaded 41 men on board to sign the compact. By agreeing in advance on a mode of

Above: the first Thanksgiving. Now a traditional holiday in American life, the first Thanksgiving was a simple celebration of the Pilgrims' first corn harvest and an expression of gratitude to the Indians who had taught them how to plant and fertilize their crop.

Right: John Winthrop, 1588–1649, the governor of the Massachusetts Bay colony. He took advantage of an oversight in the community's charter to set up the headquarters in the colony itself, rather than back in England.

self-government, the Pilgrims not only decided how their little society would function, but also gave their enterprise a semblance of legality that might prove useful in any future conflicts with the English authorities.

The Pilgrims' first winter at Plymouth was an agonizing ordeal. The intense cold permeated their primitive houses, and they found themselves desperately short of food. Almost half the colonists died, and of those who were left by spring, few would have survived another winter had it not been for the kindness shown them by Indians of the region.

During the winter of 1620–1621, the Pilgrims had been aware of the presence of Indians, who, they knew, often watched their activities from the nearby woods. No doubt the Indians were simply observing these intruders to see if they intended any harm. But the colonists believed that the Indians' watchfulness was but a portent of a full-scale attack to come. They braced themselves for such an onslaught, but it never came. Instead, one day in March, 1621, a tall Indian strode into the settlement and hailed the colonists with two words: "Welcome Englishmen!" The speaker was Samoset, a chief of the Pemaquid Indians. He had learned English from fishermen along the coast. Samoset informed the Pilgrims that he was sending for two friends, Massasoit, the chief of the Wampanoag Indians who lived around Plymouth and Squanto, the Indian who had been captured by Captain Waymouth and lived in England for several years.

When Massasoit arrived, the Pilgrims concluded a treaty of peace with him—a treaty that lasted until he died 40 years later. Samoset's friend Squanto was given a warm welcome by the settlers, and soon became a regular visitor, often staying as a guest in the home of the colony's governor, William Bradford. In return for this hospitality, Squanto showed the Pilgrims how to plant corn, where to fish, how to fertilize the soil with fish, and how to stalk and trap wild game.

Squanto's teachings proved invaluable to the Pilgrim settlers. The following fall, to celebrate the bountiful harvest he had helped make possible, they held a three-day festival of thanksgiving, to which they invited all their Indian friends. The Indians—who themselves held annual harvest celebrations—came gladly, bringing gifts of meat and corn. Together, Pilgrims and Indians prepared the feast, sang songs, and played games. Out of this happy occasion grew the American tradition of celebrating Thanksgiving Day.

Some years after the Pilgrim colony began to flourish, another Puritan community, the Massachusetts Bay Colony, was planted in New England. This settlement, established at Salem in 1628, was greatly increased in size in 1630, when 1,000 Puritans came to settle there. The new settlers' leader was a lawyer named John Winthrop and, possibly because of his legal knowledge and skills, this second group of Puritans had been able to obtain a royal charter, which gave them the right to settle and govern a colony in the Massachusetts

Bay area. Like other colonial charters, the Massachusetts Bay Company's patent stipulated that the colony be administered by a governor, assisted by a council. But the charter neglected to mention that the company's administrators should be located in England. Seizing on this oversight, the settlement's governor, John Winthrop, transferred the company's headquarters to Massachusetts itself, and initiated a system by which the citizens of the new colony could have an active say in the settlement's political affairs.

Below: a chart of the coast of New England, drawn in about 1680. As with most new territories, it was the coastal region that was the best known for many years, and the interior that was only gradually mapped accurately as trappers, soldiers, and adventurers probed deeper inland.

Right: one of the early groups to leave the Massachusetts colony, Hooker's party is shown here arriving at the site of Hartford, Connecticut, in 1636.

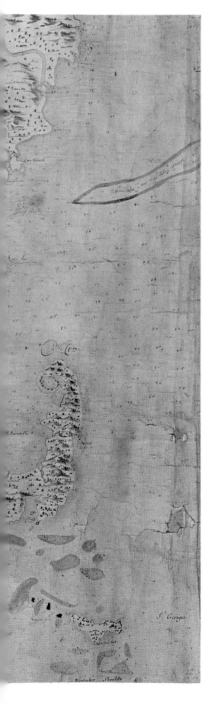

Right from the beginning, the Massachusetts colony prospered. In 1630, 1,000 picked settlers joined their compatriots there, and by the end of the decade, the Massachusetts Bay Colony had about 10,000 settlers. Towns sprang up quickly throughout the region. By the early 1630's, there were 15 such towns, of which the biggest was Boston, the colony's capital. The Puritans were industrious, and worked hard to establish themselves in the new land as farmers, merchants, craftsmen, fishermen, and shipbuilders.

Politically and economically, the Massachusetts colony was a going concern, but it soon developed religious problems. The Massachusetts Puritans who had sought refuge from religious persecution were themselves persecutors. Dissent from their rigid Puritan beliefs was held to be a crime, and a strict censorship of speech and conduct was set up. One man who dared to raise his voice in protest against this heavy-handed restriction on intellectual freedom was a Separatist named Roger Williams. Among other things, he believed in complete religious freedom for everyone, a conviction which, in 1636, forced him to flee from Massachusetts. Williams and those who shared his beliefs fled to the region of present-day Rhode Island. There they founded a settlement of their own called Providence, where religious freedom was a guaranteed right of every citizen.

Another man who found himself dissatisfied with the strictures of life in Massachusetts was Thomas Hooker, a Congregational preacher who, in 1636, traveled south down the Connecticut River with his family and his congregation, and settled at Hartford in the Connecticut Valley. Still others of Massachusetts' citizens, seeking to increase their land holding, moved north into New Hampshire and Maine.

But the New England expansion was hard on the Indians, who began to find themselves being driven out of their traditional

The figure of the Indians fort or Palizado in NEW ENGLAND And the maner of the destroying It by Captayne Vnderhill And Captayne Mason

Hear entera Captayne Vnder

The Indians houses

Hear Entera Captayne Mason

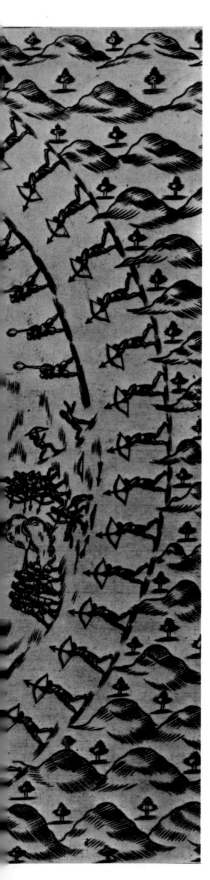

Left: the plan of the fortified Pequot village in Connecticut, showing the 1637 attack by Puritan soldiers and their Indian allies. More than 600 of the inhabitants were massacred.

Right: the Wampanoag chief, King Philip, who led a confederation of tribes against the settlements around Plymouth in 1675. The portrait is on a window shade, and may have been a curtain on a traveling Indian sideshow.

hunting and farming lands. In 1636, a Pequot Indian was accused of murdering a Massachusetts colonist. The colonists' response to this "outrage" was swift and terrible. They burned a Pequot village in Rhode Island. Then in 1637 a force of armed men from the Massachusetts Bay area, together with their Indian allies, marched to a stockaded Pequot village in Connecticut and set it ablaze, coldly shooting down any inhabitants who tried to escape from the inferno. In all, between 600 and 700 Indian men, women, and children died in this brutal massacre. For some 40 years thereafter, the New England colonists were not troubled by the region's Indians. But in 1675, a group of New England tribes, under the leadership of King Philip, the son of Massasoit, attacked settlements in Massachusetts. This started a full-scale war between the colonists and the New England tribes, which lasted about three years. In the end, the settlers routed the Indians, but not before more than 1,000 colonists had been killed and 12 towns destroyed.

During the late 1600's, several of Massachusetts' colonial offshoots received charters of their own, making them colonies on an equal basis with Massachusetts itself: Connecticut in 1662; Rhode Island in 1663 (its second charter—the first was granted to Roger Williams in 1644); and New Hampshire in 1680. Maine, however, remained officially part of Massachusetts until after the Revolutionary War.

And the Plymouth community? This, the first successful Puritan outpost in the New World, the Pilgrims' brave experiment in building a life of their own, never achieved separate status as a royal colony. Instead, it became a ward of the Massachusetts Bay Colony, and lost its distinctive identity entirely in 1691, when it was formally absorbed as part of Massachusetts.

Journael van Herry Hutſon,

Left: title page of Henry Hudson's journal, published in Amsterdam in 1663. Although an Englishman, his voyage in 1609 was for The Netherlands. Below: an imaginative version of Hudson's arrival on Manhattan Island. When they arrived ashore from the *Half Moon* Hudson and his crew were met by the kindly Algonkian Indians who made them very welcome. Originally, Hudson had been sent to find a Northeast Passage to China, but he changed his course in mid-voyage.

The Dutch in New York

6

When the pioneer farmers of Massachusetts began moving south and west into the Connecticut Valley, they found themselves face to face with a rival group of colonists—the Dutch. For England had not been the only seafaring nation to interest itself in America's Atlantic seaboard during the early 1600's. The Netherlands, too, had established outposts there—outposts that guarded the entire region between the Connecticut Valley and Delaware Bay.

Dutch claims to the mid-Atlantic coastline originated, curiously enough, in a voyage made for The Netherlands by an Englishman, Henry Hudson, in 1609. An expert sailor and navigator, Hudson had already made two voyages for England in search of a northeast passage to Asia around Russia's Arctic seas. Neither attempt had succeeded, but the merchants of The Netherlands, as eager as their English counterparts to discover a new water route to the East, had faith in his navigational skills. In January, 1609, the Dutch East India Company contacted Hudson and hired his services. According to the contract they drew up, the English captain was to "search for a northeast passage, sailing north around Russia until he shall be able to sail south to a latitude of 60°."

On April 6, 1609, Hudson set sail from Amsterdam in a small vessel called the *Half Moon*. Early in the voyage the Dutch and English members of his crew began to quarrel among themselves about how things should be done aboard ship. The English sailors objected to the fact that the cook was a Dutchman, and complained bitterly about the meals he prepared. For their part, the Dutch seamen were annoyed because they were not permitted to eat with the captain as was the custom on Dutch vessels. Hudson finally put an end to these squabbles. But he could not diminish the fears and foreboding that developed among all the members of the crew when the ship entered the northern seas.

Day by day, as the *Half Moon* struggled through increasingly icepacked seas, Hudson's men became more anxious and resentful. When the captain heard them muttering darkly about returning to Amsterdam, he knew that he must do something, and quickly, or he would be faced with a mutiny. Hudson had with him some maps and letters from his friend Captain John Smith that seemed to indicate the presence of a broad, navigable waterway somewhere along the coast of New England. Could this, he had often wondered, be the long-sought Northwest Passage? Hudson showed the docu-

ments to his restless crew and proposed that they abandon the search for the northeast passage and look for the northwest one instead. He also made it clear that he would have them all hanged as mutineers if they made him return to Amsterdam. Obviously, it was "westward or nothing," and the crew agreed to his plan.

Hudson proceeded across the Atlantic to Newfoundland, and from there sailed south, past Cape Cod, to Chesapeake Bay and on to what is now South Carolina. Although at one point he was only some 60 miles from Jamestown, he did not visit the English colony. He finally turned north again, closely following the shore until he reached the northern coast of present-day New Jersey. There, on September 3, 1609, he reached the large bay that is now called New York Harbor.

No European vessel had been in these waters since 1524, when, it is believed, Giovanni da Verrazano had discovered the bay during his voyage for France. Hudson explored the harbor with extreme caution, constantly taking soundings, and acutely aware that at

Above: a map of Manhattan Island showing part of Long Island, drawn about 1665. The cartographer has carefully drawn in the trees to show how richly forested the island was.

Right: the Indians of the area that is now New York. Both Hudson and the early Dutch settlers on Manhattan Island found the Algonkian Indian tribes living there very helpful.

276

any moment a strong breeze might blow the ship aground on the sandy bed of the bay. At last, however, he located a deep main channel, and entered the mouth of the great river that now bears his name. Here he sent a party of men ashore to investigate. They soon returned with the happy report that "the land is pleasant, with grass, flowers, and trees that fill the air with sweet smells."

A party of Indians had been seen on shore watching the ship and were invited aboard to trade. One of Hudson's officers later wrote that they were "very polite, [although] we dared not trust them." It was just as well, for a few days later, a group of braves attacked some of the crew, fatally wounding Hudson's mate.

The Indians on Manhattan Island, which Hudson visited on September 12, proved more genuinely friendly. Hudson himself later reported that they were "very good people, for when they saw that I would not remain, they supposed that I was afraid of their bows, and taking their arrows, they broke them into pieces and threw them into the fire." These Indians, an Algonkian tribe, were later to prove immensely helpful to the first Dutch settlers on Manhattan Island.

Hudson took the *Half Moon* some 150 miles up the Hudson River to a point north of present-day Albany. Along the way, he met with various tribes, some of them Iroquois, and did some very profitable trading, exchanging beads, knives, and hatchets for choice beaver and otter skins. But the Indians he encountered near Albany seemed suspicious of the white men. To forestall a possible attack, Hudson invited the local chieftains aboard the ship and, in the words of one of his men, "took them down into the cabin and gave them so much wine that they were all merry." Having thus disarmed the Indians' leaders, Hudson hastily concluded his trading negotiations, and sailed back down the river.

The English captain then made his way back to England, reaching Dartmouth on November 7, 1609. He sent a full report of his voyage to his Dutch employers, and received a request from them that he come to The Netherlands to discuss another journey. But he was prevented from doing so by an order from King James I that forbade all English sailors to hire themselves out to foreign companies.

Thus it was for England, rather than for The Netherlands, that Hudson made his next—and last—voyage in 1610. This time he sailed northwest, past Iceland and Greenland, and discovered

An aerial photograph from 35,000 feet of the ice pack breaking up in Hudson Bay. It was in this icy world that Hudson, his son, and seven of the loyal crew members were set adrift.

Hudson Strait and the immense bay in northeastern Canada now called Hudson Bay. But again the intrepid navigator was troubled by a rebellious crew, and this time neither threats nor promises availed to forestall a mutiny. In the middle of James Bay, a southern extension of Hudson Bay, the crew set Hudson adrift in a small boat with his son John and seven other men. None of the nine was ever seen again.

Meanwhile, the Dutch merchants were already making plans to capitalize on Hudson's explorations for The Netherlands. They had studied his report carefully, and had been quick to see the great fur-trading possibilities of the Hudson Valley. It was not long before many of these merchants were making westward voyages to trade with the Indians in the region that the Dutch now called "New Netherland."

One of these seagoing merchants was Adriaen Block, who journeyed to the mouth of the Hudson in 1614. There, while his

"Hudson's Last Voyage," by John Collier. Hudson appears to have had continual troubles with his crews, but no one will ever know exactly what happened on the ship in Hudson Bay, because the only eye witnesses were the mutinous crew members.

ship lay at anchor, it caught fire and was completely destroyed. Undismayed, Block ordered his crew to construct a new vessel for the voyage home. His sailors did their utmost, but could produce only a makeshift boat some 50 feet long. Afraid that it might not prove strong enough for the journey across the Atlantic, Block decided to stay close to shore for as long as possible. Accordingly, he sailed north through Long Island Sound, hugging the southern coast of Connecticut so that he might find ready shelter for his frail craft in the event of a storm.

Had Block not followed this course, he might have missed the narrow mouth of the waterway that the Pequot Indians called the *Quinnitukut* (meaning "the long, tidal river")—today's Connecticut River. Curious about this *versbe riviere*, or "freshwater river," Block sailed some 45 miles up it to the site of present-day Hartford, and all along the way marveled at the beauty and richness of the surrounding valley. When at last he reached home later in the year, he

GREENLAND

BAFFIN
BAY

LANCASTER SD.

4b

4b

4b

4b

B A F F I N   I S L A N D

FOXE
BASIN

ARCTIC CIRCLE

ICELAND

2b

1a,b

1c

4a

4b

1a,b

2b

1c

4a

RESOLUTION I.

1a,b

2b

4a

HUDSON   STRAIT

4a

2C

2b

1c

1c

2b

2b

L a b r a d o r

A T L A N T I C   O C E A N

H U D S O N

B A Y

2b

2C

2b

NEWFOUNDLAND

GULF OF
ST. LAWRENCE

CAPE
BRETON I.

JAMES
BAY

2B?

2b

2b

2C

Nova Scotia

2a

The Great Lakes

St. Lawrence

2a

2a

Fort Orange
(Albany)

Connecticut

Cape Cod

2a

3

Saybrook

3

Hudson

3

2a

Ohio

NEW NETHERLAND
New Amsterdam
(New York)
MANHATTAN I.

2a

2a

3

Wilmington

2a

DELAWARE BAY

CHESAPEAKE
BAY

2a

2a

Jamestown

2a

	Frobisher	1a,b	1576, 1577
		1c	1578
	Hudson	2a	1609
	Hudson (with Bylot)	2b	1610
	Hudson (after being set adrift)	2B	1610
	Mutineers (with Bylot)	2C	1610
	Block	3	1614
	Bylot & Baffin	4a	1615
		4b	1616

© Geographical Projects

0   100   200   300   400

Left: northeastern Canada and
United States, showing attempts made
by men such as Hudson and Baffin to
find a Northwest Passage to the East
in the years between 1576 and 1616.

Right: *Het West Indisch Huys,* West
India Company House in Amsterdam,
from which the orders went out to
govern New Netherland. In all their
colonization the main object of the
Dutch was to set up and protect
profitable trading.

produced a detailed map of the region, and urged the Dutch
authorities to assert The Netherlands' claim to it.

In fact, the Dutch were slow to take advantage of Block's explorations in the Connecticut Valley. But they wasted no time in establishing a foothold in the Hudson Valley. As early as 1624, a Dutch
fur-trading post called Fort Orange was established on the site
of modern Albany. And in 1625, the Dutch West India Company,
formed four years earlier, sent a contingent of settlers to found a
colony on Manhattan Island.

The Manhattan community, which the Dutch named "New
Amsterdam," soon flourished. In its first year, it returned the
company's original investment with a highly-profitable cargo of
4,000 beaver pelts and 700 otter skins. In 1626 the Dutch governor
of New Netherland, Peter Minuit, purchased the island of Manhattan from the Algonkian. The price he paid—trinkets worth 60
guilders—may have been worth more in the New World at that
time than the $24 so often quoted. It was, after all, in the colonists'
best interests to deal fairly with this tribe, who had not only brought
them gifts of food during the winter, but also kept them supplied
with furs for trade. Later, however, when the Dutch began to
profit more from their trade with the inland Iroquois, they turned

Below: ships leaving Amsterdam
harbor for the Atlantic Ocean, very
probably taking emigrants to America.
The Dutch West India Company tried to
strengthen Dutch claims to their
American territory by offering
enormous grants of land to settlers who
would agree to bring other colonists.

on their Algonkian friends, joining forces with the Iroquois when they made raids on Algonkian villages. The Dutch were first and foremost merchant-traders, and they saw their Indian alliances purely in terms of what was best for business.

To encourage colonization in New Netherland, the Dutch West India Company began offering huge tracts of land to any member of the company who would undertake to bring over at their own expense at least 50 families of settlers within four years. The first of these grants was made in 1629, and others soon followed.

Above: New Amsterdam in 1653, after a watercolor by J. Vinckeboons. At this point the settlement was huddled at the tip of the island, in the area that is now the financial center of the city, with forests covering the rest of the island.

Below: Manhattan today, a photograph by Malcolm Robertson and Alan Brooking showing an Aer Lingus Boeing flying over the city, now an international center of finance, business, and—in the U.N.—world government.

Individual men were given vast estates, rather like feudal manors, in what are now the states of Connecticut, Delaware, New Jersey, and New York. The system was based on the premise that each landowner, or *patroon*, should bring with him tenant farmers to work his land. However, few of the patroons were able to recruit— or to retain—enough farm laborers to work their estates. Nor is it any wonder. Each tenant farmer was required: to pay his landlord a yearly rent of $200; to do three days' service per week for the landlord with his own horse and wagon; to keep up the roads on the estate; and to keep the landlord's storehouse well-stocked with game, wheat, and firewood. Few Dutchmen were willing to subject themselves to this form of economic slavery in the New World, and only one of the patroonships (that of Kiliaen Van Rensselaer on the banks of the Hudson River) ultimately flourished.

New Amsterdam, however, continued to grow and prosper, and soon developed a genuinely cosmopolitan character. Merchants from many lands came to the port to trade, and by 1660 New Amsterdam was supporting a population of more than 1,000. But elsewhere in New Netherland, Dutch power was minimal, and the Dutch found themselves hard put to it to defend their territorial claims against "trespassers" from other nations.

In 1633, word reached the colony's governor, Wouter van Twiller, that Englishmen had been seen in the Connecticut Valley. Van Twiller set out post haste for the region, and built a fort called the "House of Hope" on the present site of Hartford. He also nailed up a proclamation warning the English that they would be severely punished if they tried to settle there. But, in the fall of the very same year, a shipload of Englishmen from the Plymouth Colony blithely sailed up the Connecticut River, ignored the posted warning, and passed directly under the noses of the Dutch gunners— who were so taken aback that they forgot to open fire.

The Plymouth group proceeded to build a settlement about a mile upriver from the fort. Although the two groups were hostile toward each other at first, they soon learned that they would have to cooperate if they were all to survive the winter, and peaceful relations were established. But, after Thomas Hooker and his followers arrived in the valley in 1636, the English settlement became much larger than the Dutch, and the Massachusetts pioneers took to heckling their neighbors in the fort. In 1649, a former governor of New Amsterdam reported that the English "have finally seized the whole of the [Connecticut] River. . . . They have belabored the Company's people with sticks and clubs [and taken] hogs and cows belonging to the fort. . . ." In his report, the ex-governor goes on to enumerate further outrages, and finishes with what must surely have seemed the final insult: "The English have torn down the Dutch coat of arms that had been affixed to a tree, and have carved a ridiculous face in its place!"

The Netherlands complained bitterly that England's colonists had acted "contrary to the laws of nations." But in America,

Below: Peter Stuyvesant (1610–1672) in a portrait on a wooden panel by an unidentified artist. Rigorous in maintaining the position of the Dutch in America, he helped evict the Swedish settlers on the Delaware.

possession was the law, and the Dutch could not hope to keep out the thousands of English settlers who streamed into the Connecticut Valley in the mid-1600's. The Dutch had more success against the Swedish "trespassers" to the south, who, in 1638, had founded a settlement on the Delaware River near the site of present-day Wilmington. In 1655, the Dutch attacked the little colony and ousted the Swedes without much difficulty.

The man who led the attack against New Sweden was New Netherland's governor, Peter Stuyvesant, a tall, stubborn ex-soldier with a booming voice and a wooden leg. Stuyvesant ruled the colony with an iron will, and was almost universally resented. His enemies mockingly called him "Old Silver Nails" for the decorative silver studs he wore on his peg leg. But Stuyvesant did much to promote order and prosperity in New Amsterdam and, if he had had his way, would vastly have increased Dutch power in the New World. The Netherlands, however, refused to grant him the military support he needed to defend Dutch claims in America, despite the obvious fact that New Netherland was rapidly becoming no more than a series of trading posts in English territory.

Nonetheless, the Dutch did control the vital harbor at the mouth of the Hudson. Moreover, their very presence there effectively cut off the English colonies in the north from those in the south. With these thoughts in mind, King Charles II of England took the deliberate step of granting the entire territory between the Connecticut and Delaware rivers to his brother James, Duke of York, in 1664. All that remained was to secure the grant. Accordingly, the Duke sent a fleet of warships to capture New Netherland and, early in September, 1664, after the English show of force, Governor Stuyvesant capitulated. Back in Europe, the Dutch retaliated by

Far left: the early Swedish settlements along the Delaware River, based on a map drawn by Peter Lindstrom in 1654–55. It was these settlements that were attacked by the Dutch in 1655, in an attempt to retain their territory.

Left: Swedish settlers from the Delaware River colony with the Indians. Many land-starved Swedish pioneers left their overcrowded homeland for a fresh start in the New Sweden colony. As with many of the settlements in America success depended largely on good relations with neighboring Indians.

Below: a town plan of Manhattan. Drawn in 1664, it shows The English fleet in the harbor, as Manhattan was taken by the English in that year. Note the street with the wall, which logically became "Wall Street."

declaring war on England—a war that they failed to win. And in 1667, by the Treaty of Breda, New Netherland was officially turned over to England.

Meanwhile, the busy commercial life of New Amsterdam continued unabated. Even after the city had changed hands and been renamed New York, many of the Dutch merchants opted to remain there. It was probably about this time that the name "Yankee" arose, and one theory is that it comes from the common Dutch name Jan Kees—short for Jan Cornelius.

Four new colonies were eventually carved out of New Netherland: New York, New Jersey, Pennsylvania, and Delaware. In 1664, the Duke of York granted the New Jersey region to two aristocratic friends of his, Sir George Carteret and Lord John Berkeley. Ten years later, Berkeley sold his holding to a group of Quakers who wished to escape religious persecution by founding settlements in what became known as "West Jersey." After Carteret's death another group of Quakers bought his section, then known as "East Jersey." In 1702, England united the two colonies as a single royal colony.

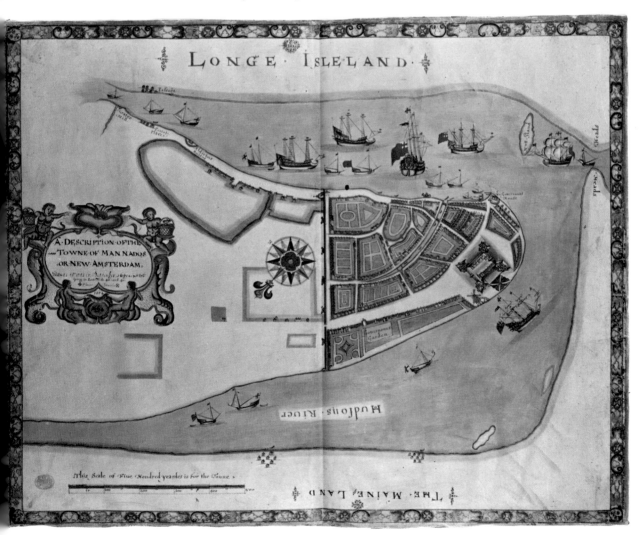

The Dutch Boare Dissected, or a Description of HOGG-LAND.

A Dutch man is a Lusty, Fat, two Legged Cheese-Worm: A Creature, that is so addicted to Eating Butter, Drinking fat Drink, and Sliding, that all the World knows him for a slippery Fellow. An *Hollander* is not an *High-lander*, but a *Low-lander*; for he loves to be down in the Dirt, and *Boar*-like, to wallow therein.

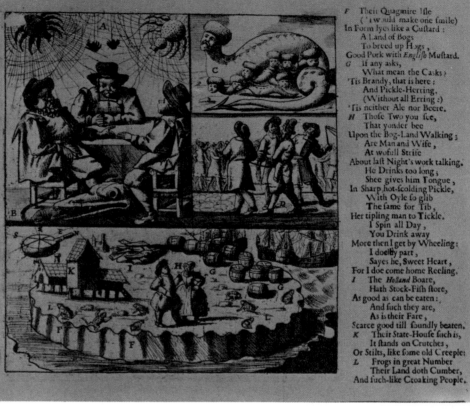

THe *Dutch* at first,
When at the worst,
The *English* did relieve them:
They now for thanks,
Have play'd base Pranks
With *Englishmen* to grieve them.
A Those Spider-Imps,
As big as Shrimps,
Doe lively Represent,
How that the States
Spin out their Fates
Out of their Bowels vent.
B The *Indian* Ratt
That runs in at
The Mouth of Crocodile,
Eates his way through,
And shews well how
All Nations they beguile.
C The Monstrous Pig,
With Vipers Big,
That Seven-headed Beast,
Shews how they still,
Pay good with ill
To th' *English* and the Rest.
The Vipers come
Forth of the Wombe,
With death of their own Mother:
Such are that Nation,
A Generation,
That rise by fall of Other.
D One of the Rout
Was Whipt about
Our Streets for telling lyes:
More of that Nation
Serv'd in such Fashion
Might be for Forgeries.
E Their Compass is
An *Holland* Cheese,
To steer a Cup of Ale-by:
The Knife points forth
Unto the North
The Needle these Worms sail-by.

F Their Quagmire Isle
('twould make one smile)
In Form lyes like a Custard:
A Land of Bogs,
To breed up Hogs,
Good Pork with *English* Mustard.
G If any asks,
What mean the Casks?
'Tis Brandy, that is here:
And Pickle-Herring,
(Without all Erring:)
'Tis neither Ale nor Beere.
H Those Two you see,
That yonder bee
Upon the Bog-Land Walking;
Are Man and Wife,
At wofull Strife
About last Night's work talking.
He Drinks too long;
Shee gives him Tongue,
In Sharp hot-scolding Pickle,
With Oyle so glib
The same for Tib,
Her tipling man to Tickle.
I Spin all Day,
You Drink away
More then I get by Wheeling:
I doe lye part,
Sayes he, Sweet Heart,
For I doe come home Reeling.
I The *Holland* Boare,
Hath Stock-Fish store,
As good as can be eaten:
And such they are,
As is their Fare,
Scarce good till soundly beaten.
K Their State-House such is,
It stands on Crutches,
Or Stilts, like some old Creeple:
L Frogs in great Number
Their Land doth Cumber,
And such-like Croaking People.

Above: *The Dutch Boare Dissected,* an anti-Dutch broadsheet published in 1665, during the period of Anglo-Dutch rivalry. Among other things, it describes the Dutch as "cheese-worms." The tension between the two countries was not limited to America: at this time the two nations were at war.

Meanwhile, in 1681, yet another Quaker, William Penn, had been granted the vast territory stretching west of the Delaware River between southern New York and northern Maryland. The grant was, in fact, in payment for a large debt owed by Charles II to Penn's father. Penn named the heavily-wooded region *Sylvania*—from the Latin word for "woods"—and Charles added the prefix "Penn."

Penn's idea was to establish a well-organized community where religious toleration and a humane legal code would prevail, and he set about his task with remarkable energy and thoroughness. He circulated an advertisement for his proposed colony both in England and Europe, stressing the fact that religious freedom would be guaranteed to all settlers who believed in God. Soon hundreds of German Lutherans and French Huguenots, who were hounded for their beliefs in their own land, were flocking to join the English, German, Dutch, and Welsh Quakers in the new colony. Settlers from the German Rhineland soon became known as the "Pennsylvania Dutch." They were called "Dutch" because the word "Deutsch" (meaning "German") was misinterpreted.

Even before the first settlers had arrived, Penn's surveyor had carefully chosen a site for the main city of Philadelphia, and drawn up plans for its construction. Last but not least, Penn went out of his way to make friends with the region's Indians, ensuring an interval of peace that was to last for about 75 years. Penn's original group of settlers dealt absolutely fairly with these Indians. But later settlers in Pennsylvania were not so scrupulously honest, and used the famous "walking purchase" system to cheat the Indians out of their land. According to this system, an Indian would agree to sell as much land as a white buyer could walk around in a day and a half. But unbeknown to the Indians, the white men all too often cleared a path through the woods in advance, and used trained "walkers" to pace off the course.

From their original settlement at Philadelphia, the Pennsylvania settlers gingerly explored the region to the north and west of them, the fertile Susquehanna River Valley. The first white man to follow this river to its source in central New York was Conrad Weiser, a second-generation Pennsylvanian who had lived among the Iroquois as a boy and spoke their language. In the winter of 1736, Weiser was sent on an urgent peace mission to the Iroquois center at Onondaga, in an effort to stave off an anticipated attack on Quaker settlements in northern Pennsylvania. Weiser almost died during

Above: William Penn, in a portrait by Francis Place. A Quaker, Penn was given a grant to vast territory in payment for a debt the king owed his father. It became a haven for religious dissenters. Below: Penn's treaty with the Indians, by Benjamin West. Penn, determined to make friends of the Indians with his policy of justice and honor, created a peace that lasted 75 years.

Right: "On the Susquehanna," by Joshua Shaw. The Quakers gradually explored the rich valley through which this river flowed. The peace between the Indians and settlers that existed in Pennsylvania was extended here mainly through the work of Conrad Weiser, a second-generation Pennsylvanian who knew the Iroquois Indians very well.

the journey, the snows were deep, the game scarce, and the forest trails all but invisible. When, despite everything, he reached Onondaga, even the Iroquois were deeply impressed, and agreed to his proposal of peaceful coexistence with the Quaker settlements in the Susquehanna Valley.

The colony of Delaware was originally part of Pennsylvania, but its legislature separated from that of the larger colony in 1701. Nevertheless, it did not become fully independent until 1776, just over a year after the outbreak of the Revolutionary War. By that time, of course, there were 13 English colonies along the Atlantic seaboard. The last three of these were North Carolina and South Carolina, which originated as land grants to a group of titled Englishmen in the late 1600's, and Georgia, which began in 1733 as a haven for England's debtors. The Georgia refuge was the idea of a noted English humanitarian named James Oglethorpe, who had devoted his life to helping the poor and oppressed. But Georgia, like North and South Carolina, soon became a land of opportunity for the rich, rather than for the poor, as wealthy Englishmen began establishing large plantations there and importing African slaves to work the land.

By 1750, there were more than 1 million persons living in the 13 colonies along the Atlantic coast from Maine to Georgia. New towns and homesteads sprang up everywhere, and increasing numbers of colonists began to move inland, driven by an unflinching pioneer spirit that was to become a hallmark of the American character. In doing so, they spread the English sphere of influence far and wide through the eastern wilderness, and gave their French and Spanish rivals in North America increasing cause for alarm.

Right: immigrants on their way to America being welcomed in Leipzig in 1732. They were persecuted Lutherans, who were on their way to Georgia to find a place to live where they would be able to practice their religion.

288

A. DÉPÔT.
B. MONTÉE AU PARLOIR.
C. PETITE SACRISTIE.
D. PORTE EXTÉRIEURE DE LA CHAPELLE
DU COUVENT.
E. PARLOIR AU SECOND ÉTAGE SUR LE-
QUEL LA PLUPART DES RELIGIEUSES
ET DES ÉLÈVES, LORS DE L'INCENDIE
DU MONASTÈRE EN 1650 S'ÉCHAPPÈ-
RENT EN ROMPANT LES GRILLES.
F.F. DORTOIR DES RELIGIEUSES.
G.G. INFIRMERIE DES RELIGIEUSES.
H.H. DORTOIR DES ÉLÈVES PENSIONNAIRES.
J. CELLULE QU'OCCUPAIT LA MÈRE
MARIE DE L'INCARNATION LORS
DE L'INCENDIE.
K. BOULANGER.
L.L. RÉFECTOIRE DES RELIGIEUSES.
M. *ANTIQUE FRÊNE*, GÉANT
SÉCULAIRE, SOUS LEQUEL LES RE-
LIGIEUSES, DANS LES PREMIERS
TEMPS, INSTRUISAIENT, DANS CHA-
CUNE DE LEURS LANGUES SAUVA-
GES, ET PRÉPARAIENT AU BAP-
TÊME, LES NÉOPHYTES, AL-
GONQUINES, HURONNES, ET
MONTAGNAISES.
CE *FRÊNE* ÂGÉ AUJOURD'HUI
1847 D'ENVIRON 500, OFFRE EN-
CORE AUX SŒURS DU MONAS-
TÈRE SON OMBRE FRAÎCHE, ET
DES SOUVENIRS TOUCHANS.
N. MAISON DE MADAME DE
LA PELTRIE, BATIE EN 1642
ET DEMOLIE EN 1836.

PREMIER MONASTÈRE DES URSULINES DE QUEBEC
AVEC SES DÉPENDANCES BATI EN 1642, ET BRULÉ EN 1650.

The French Extend their Grasp

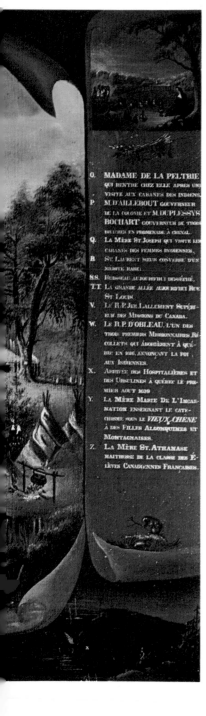

But what of New France during this period of rapid English colonization along the Atlantic seaboard?

In the early 1600's, Champlain's far-flung expeditions had put the French in a position to dominate both the Laurentian Valley and the entire Great Lakes region. But to take full advantage of their expanded sphere of influence, the French needed a strong colonial base on the St. Lawrence. And, after Champlain's death in 1635, New France simply failed to grow.

Unlike the English, the French tended to view the New World chiefly in terms of trade—fish, furs, and a possible westward route to the Indies—rather than as a place to build homes, towns, and a new life. For this reason, few French farmers and tradesmen came to settle in Canada, and by 1660, there were only 3,000 permanent residents there. More than that number of English colonists had settled in Massachusetts in a single year!

Among the brave few who did come to New France during this period were the priests, nuns, and missionaries of the French Catholic Church. Franciscan missionaries had been working in the colony since 1615, and in 1639, nuns of the Ursuline and Hospitalière

Left: the Ursuline Convent in Quebec, built in 1642. It was destroyed by fire in 1650. The Ursuline order has been at the center of life in Quebec since the first nuns arrived there in 1639, to begin their work as both teachers and nurses to the community.

Right: Louis XIV, the Sun King, who was the French monarch during the period after Champlain's death and was determined to keep his American colonies securely under French rule.

orders came to Quebec to teach the children and minister to the sick in the little settlement. In 1642, priests of the Sulpician order established a mission called Ville-Marie on the island of Montreal. Here, with the help of a handful of soldiers, they built and maintained a church and a hospital, despite persistent Iroquois raids.

But perhaps the most dedicated and courageous missionaries in New France were the French Jesuits. Traveling far and wide among the Indians to teach the faith, many of them met barbarous deaths at the hands of the hostile Iroquois. In 1649, for example, a Jesuit

named Father Jean de Brébeuf and his companion, Gabriel Lallemant, were captured and cruelly tortured for many hours with red-hot axes before being put to death.

In fact, Iroquois ambushes, attacks, and massacres were a frequent occurrence throughout the Canadian colony during this time. Nor were these the only hardships borne by the French settlers. Farming was a grim struggle in the stony soil and cold climate of the region, and even the French fur-trading company seemed to be on the

Above: the martyrdom of three of the Jesuits, Fathers Brébeuf and Lallemant at the stakes, and Father Jogues kneeling at the left. This painting by Pommier, a French priest, was made in 1665 from a picture that was part of a map by Bressani drawn in 1657, only eight years after the event.

brink of ruin. Disease swept through the colony in the early 1660's, and in 1663, the whole area was shaken by an earthquake. But that very year, just as the weary settlers were beginning to cry "Back to France!" King Louis XIV stepped in to save New France. Raising it to the status of a royal province, he equipped it with a regiment of highly-trained soldiers, and appointed a special officer called an *intendant* to head the colonial government and take charge of the colony's internal affairs. The colonial governor was mainly responsible for defense.

The first intendant was a remarkable man named Jean Baptiste Talon. At his urging, the governor instructed the soldiers to build forts all along the St. Lawrence and the southern shores of Lake Ontario to protect New France from the Iroquois. Meanwhile, Talon improved the colony's economic position by establishing local industries like shipbuilding and weaving. Then, to increase the population, he initiated a scheme whereby thousands of young French men and women were recruited to settle in Canada. He encouraged each young couple to have as many children as possible, promising a free grant of 100 acres of land to every father of 12 or more. This plan worked so well that some men eventually petitioned for 200 acres on the grounds of having had a family of 24 or more!

As New France began to revive, Talon turned his attention to exploration. Since Nicolet's voyage in 1634, he learned, only two Frenchmen had dared to venture far into the mysterious lands west of Lake Huron. These two were Médart Chouart, Sieur de Groseilliers, and his brother-in-law, Pierre Ésprit Radisson. Together, the two brothers (as they liked to call themselves) had journeyed farther into the western wilderness than any white men before them. But before they had joined forces, each had had adventures on his own.

Above: Jean Talon, the first *intendant* of New France. He was quick to see the importance of exploration in strengthening the position of the French in their American possessions. Below: Pierre Radisson in a canoe on one of his expeditions into the Great Lakes region. He made the journeys with his brother-in-law, Groseilliers.

In 1652, when Radisson was only 16, he had been captured and "adopted" by the Iroquois Indians in upstate New York. After two years as their prisoner, he had been rescued by some Dutch merchants, who sent him back to France. But once there, he had found European life unbearably tame, and he was soon back in Canada, taking part in a Jesuit expedition deep into Iroquois country.

It was on Radisson's return from this mission that he first met Groseilliers, who himself had just come back from a three-year fur-trading expedition into the interior. In the course of this expedition, Groseilliers had traveled as far as Green Bay on the western shores of Lake Michigan, and had explored the region around Sault Ste. Marie (the falls on the St. Marys River between Lake Huron and Lake Superior). Finding that they shared a love of the wilderness, the two young men began to make plans for a new journey into the interior.

Setting out in 1659, the pair journeyed beyond Sault Ste. Marie, paddling along the southern shores of Lake Superior to Chequamegon Bay. All along the way, they traded with the local Indians, and returned to Montreal in 1660 with a small fortune in furs. The following year, they set off again and this time traveled all the way to the western tip of Lake Superior. From there, they journeyed overland into present-day Minnesota, and became the first white men to meet and trade with the Plains Indians. They then turned north, traveling overland and by canoe as far as north Hudson Bay.

Some years after their return from this extraordinary journey, Radisson and Groseilliers quarreled with the French authorities, and offered their services to King Charles II of England. Under his patronage, they began a series of trading missions to the Hudson Bay region that led, in 1670, to the creation of England's highly-successful Hudson's Bay Company.

Meanwhile, Talon had heard the stories about the young men's wilderness exploits, and determined at once to claim the vast region they had explored for France. Accordingly, in June, 1671, a regal ceremony was performed at Sault Ste. Marie. In the presence of 14 Indian chiefs, a Frenchman called François Daumont, Sieur de St. Lusson, formally asserted France's claim to all the known lands of Canada, together with "all other countries, rivers, lakes, and territories contiguous and adjacent thereunto."

Just about this time, Talon began to hear tantalizing rumors about a great river that flowed south from the Great Lakes region. The priests in the missions that were then being built along the Great Lakes often heard the local Indians speak of this mighty river, though the Indians themselves could not say where it emptied out. A missionary named Father Allouez was one of those who had heard tell of the mysterious river, and it was he who first described it as the "Mississippi," from the Indian words for "great" (missi) and "river" (sipi).

The possibility of such a waterway was of enormous interest to the French authorities. If the river flowed southwest to the Pacific Ocean, it would provide the long-sought passage to Asia. If it

Above: the Mississippi, a vast expanse of water flowing south of the Gulf of Mexico. This view is near La Crosse in Wisconsin, north of the junction with the Wisconsin River where Joliet and his party entered the great river.

Right: Father Jacques Marquette and Louis Joliet meeting with Indians, from a Dutch history of exploration published in the early 1700's. Contacts with the local Indians were important on this kind of expedition, both to help replenish supplies and as a source of information about what lay ahead.

flowed south to the Gulf of Mexico, it would give the French another outlet to the sea for the furs of the Great Lakes region. In either case, French control of the river would serve to check both Spain and England's inland colonial ambitions, and open up the vast American heartland to French exploitation.

With these thoughts in mind, Talon and the new Canadian governor, Louis de Buade, Comte de Frontenac, commissioned an expedition to find and explore the Mississippi. To lead the expedition they chose an adventurous fur trader named Louis Joliet. He was an ideal choice, for he not only knew the Great Lakes area, but possessed the mapmaking skills of a trained cartographer. Joliet was to be accompanied by a party of five men and a Jesuit priest named Father Jacques Marquette. A courageous and dedicated missionary, Marquette had spent several years in the upper lakes area and was fluent in no less than six Indian languages.

Joliet's party set out from the Strait of Mackinac in Lake Michigan in May, 1673, traveling by canoe to Green Bay and thence along the Fox River. A portage of two miles took the men from the lower reaches of the Fox to the Wisconsin River, which they followed west to its junction with the Mississippi. Floating with the current, they proceeded smoothly down the great river, noticing fewer moose and more buffalo along its banks as the northern forests gave way to the open plains of the Midwest. Near the site of present-day St. Louis, their canoes picked up speed, swept along by the turbulent waters of the Missouri, which empties into the Mississippi at this point.

Along the way, the party saw few Indians, and those they did meet were friendly. But when they reached the mouth of the Arkansas River, they found the native peoples hostile and suspicious. Marquette was unfamiliar with the language of these Quapaw tribesmen, but he had the good fortune to find a young Indian who also spoke Illinois, a language he did know. Through this interpreter, he learned of "black gowns" to the south, who "rang bells for prayers." These were almost certainly Spanish priests, which meant that the expedition was nearing the Spanish outposts along the Gulf. Joliet and Marquette took counsel. If they should be captured by the Spaniards or killed by yet more hostile Indians farther south, the fruits of their voyage would be lost. Moreover, they had determined with almost complete certainty that the Mississippi River emptied into the Gulf of Mexico. In fact, they had accomplished their mission, and there was nothing more to do but head for home.

Paddling upriver proved a difficult task, and Father Marquette was taken ill. Anxious to make his report to Talon and Frontenac, Joliet left Marquette in the care of the Green Bay mission, and hurried on alone with his maps and charts. But, while shooting the Lachine rapids above Montreal, Joliet's canoe overturned, and all his precious records of the two-year journey were lost. Fortunately, he was able to make some new maps from memory. And in addition, Marquette still had the journal in which he, too, had recorded many of the expedition's discoveries and observations.

Right: Joliet and Father Marquette being entertained by Indians on their expedition. Until they reached the mouth of the Arkansas River—south of Memphis on what is now the Arkansas/Mississippi state line—all the Indians they encountered were friendly to them.

Above: Louis Henri Buade, Comte de Frontenac, the governor of New France from 1672–82 and 1689–98. He commissioned Joliet to explore the Mississippi and was instrumental in rewarding La Salle for his discoveries.

When Marquette recovered, he returned to the Illinois region to work and teach among the Indians. There, worn out and ailing, he died in 1675, near the shores of Lake Michigan. Joliet took to fur trading once more, ranging through the Canadian forests on expeditions that eventually took him as far north as Hudson Bay.

Perhaps, on one of his visits to the Laurentian colony, Joliet met the man who was destined to take up the thread of Mississippian exploration where he had left off. That man was the intrepid Robert Cavelier, Sieur de La Salle. Born in France of a wealthy family, La Salle had early shown a talent for science and mathematics, and his education had been taken over by the Jesuits. But he had grown up a proud and headstrong young man, with a character ill-suited to the religious discipline. At 21, he had left the priesthood, only to discover that, as a Jesuit, he had been disinherited under French law. Practically penniless, he had set off for the New World to seek his fortune in 1666, at the age of 23.

Soon after he arrived in Canada, La Salle opened a fur-trading post near Montreal. From the Indians he traded with, he learned about the existence of a large river to the southwest called the "Ohio." He became curious about this mysterious waterway, and anxious to

Above: Robert Cavelier, Sieur de La Salle. Born into a wealthy family in France, he spent most of his life in the American wilderness, where at last he realized Talon's vision of extending French power to the Gulf of Mexico.

explore it. Accordingly, in 1669, he sold his trading post and set off for the interior. For the next several years he crisscrossed the region south of the Great Lakes. In the course of his travels, which took him as far south as Illinois, it is reported that he succeeded in locating the Ohio River and in following it south to the rapids above present-day Louisville, Kentucky.

When young La Salle returned to Montreal, Governor Frontenac saw to it that he was amply rewarded for his exploratory efforts. He was honored at the French court and given a tract of land on the site of modern Kingston, Ontario. The location of this land, which included an outpost called Fort Frontenac, soon made La Salle a wealthy man, for all the fur-laden Indian canoes from the interior had to pass by his estate on their way to Montreal. This gave La Salle a chance to bargain for the choicest furs at the lowest cost before the Indian traders reached the buyers farther east.

But the stream of fur-laden canoes passing Fort Frontenac seemed a mere trickle to La Salle. He knew that a vast fortune in beaver pelts lay waiting in the interior. The problem was how to get them to the St. Lawrence faster and in greater bulk. What was needed, he felt, was a European-style vessel that could sail around the Great Lakes from Lake Erie to Lake Superior, trading with the Indians along the way. That such a ship could not travel back from Lake Erie into Lake Ontario, and thence up the St. Lawrence, La Salle already knew. Fear of the Iroquois had thus far prevented French exploration of Niagara Falls, but its existence had been common knowledge since Champlain's time. La Salle's plan was to establish an eastern depot for his ship near the mouth of Lake Erie. Although cargoes would have to be transported from there to the St. Lawrence by canoe, the total time required to get them from the upper lakes to Montreal would still be cut in half.

La Salle set out for Niagara in 1678, accompanied by his best friend Henri de Tonti, by a Franciscan missionary named Father Louis Hennepin, and by a party of workmen. When they reached the Niagara River, La Salle put all hands to work to build a ship and a fort. It was the middle of winter, and he had to urge his men on with threats and occasional rewards of gold pieces.

Above: "The Expedition leaving Fort Frontenac on Lake Ontario, November 18, 1678," by George Catlin. This was the first of Catlin's series on La Salle commissioned by Louis Philippe, king of France in the mid-1800's.

Left: the earliest picture of Niagara Falls, from Father Louis Hennepin's book published in Utrecht in 1697. The French had known about Niagara Falls earlier, but their bad relations with the Iroquois Indians had kept them from actually reaching the falls.

Below: "Portage around the Falls of Niagara, January 22, 1679," the third in the series of 26 paintings by George Catlin on the explorations of La Salle.

The party had brought with them a large quantity of supplies, but even so, La Salle was forced to return to Fort Frontenac for additional materials. There he found himself confronted by his creditors, who angrily demanded payment of the many debts he had already incurred in outfitting his expedition. Putting them off with the promise to pay up as soon as his ship returned from the Great Lakes, La Salle set off once more for Niagara.

During his absence, work on the boat had continued under the watchful eyes of a few hostile Iroquois. While the bulk of the tribe had gone south to fight the Erie Indians, a few of these Iroquois warriors had stayed behind to keep an eye on the strange doings of the white men. The Iroquois continually prowled around the vicinity of the boat, and one day even attacked the smith, who was forced to defend himself with a red-hot iron. This hostile atmosphere had one beneficial result, however, for as Father Hennepin wrote later, it "encouraged our workmen to go on with their work more briskly!" In fact, by the time La Salle returned, in August, 1679, the ship was all but finished, needing only the heavy anchors that he brought with him from Fort Frontenac.

With its heavily-caulked flat bottom and its makeshift deerskin sails, the 60-ton vessel was hardly the pride of the French fleet. Nevertheless, this "winged canoe," as the Indians called it, was about to become the first sailing ship on the Great Lakes. La Salle named it the *Griffin,* in honor of the Comte de Frontenac, whose coat of arms bore two griffins. And, as soon as the last supplies were on board, he weighed anchor and set sail, undeterred by the grumblings of the ship's pilot, who swore that La Salle had brought him into the wilderness "to die in fresh water."

Covering as many as 100 miles a day when the wind was right, the *Griffin* sailed into Lake Erie, Lake Huron, and then into Lake Michigan. Frequent stops were made along the way to trade with the Indians, and soon the ship's hold was bulging with a rich cargo of beaver pelts. La Salle, delighted with the success of his project thus far, began to envisage a whole fleet of ships to ply the inland waterways. Nor did his ambition stop there. He wanted to travel down the length of the Mississippi. He proposed to establish a direct shipping link to the sea and, at the same time, carry out Talon's dream of extending authority as far south as the Gulf of Mexico.

With these thoughts in mind, La Salle ordered some of his men to sail the fur-laden *Griffin* back to Lake Erie, while he, Tonti, and a few of the others made preparations for the journey down the Mississippi. As the *Griffin* sailed away, La Salle and his party left the southeastern shores of Lake Michigan, paddled up the St. Joseph River, and followed the Kankakee River to the Illinois River. Near the site of present-day Peoria, they landed, built a stockade called Fort Crèvecoeur (Fort Heartbreak), and began work on the boat that would take them down to the Gulf.

La Salle had given the *Griffin's* crew orders to return to Lake

Above: "Launching of the *Griffin*," by George Catlin in his La Salle series. Although most of the Iroquois Indians had gone south for a war with the Erie Indians, there were a few who remained as a menacing presence, and the expedition was relieved to get the ship finished and safely underway.

Right: the building of the *Griffin*. It is unlikely that La Salle's workmen had ever built a ship before, much less one furnished with deerskin sails. La Salle's idea was to bring furs from the upper lakes in his ship to the mouth of Lake Erie, thus cutting in half the time that had been required previously to bring furs to Montreal.

Michigan with supplies for the Mississippi venture as soon as they had seen the cargo safely on its way north from Niagara. But three months passed with no word of the *Griffin's* return. La Salle decided to go to Niagara to find out what had happened. Leaving Tonti in charge of Fort Crèvecoeur, he set out in March, 1680, with six Frenchmen and an Indian guide.

The spring thaws were just beginning, and jagged ice floes in the streams and rivers made it impossible to travel by canoe. Patches of slush covered the soggy ground, and even the men's snowshoes became useless. Sinking ankle deep with every step they took through the marshy woodlands, La Salle and his men struggled on until they reached the southeastern shores of Lake Michigan. Here, at the mouth of the St. Joseph River, the *Griffin* was to have made its first stop. But the Indians of the region had seen nothing of the ship. More and more anxious, La Salle hurried on, trudging mile after weary mile until he finally reached Niagara. But alas, there was no sign of the *Griffin* here, either. With a heavy heart, La Salle left his exhausted companions at Niagara, and marched north through the spring rains to Montreal. Here his 1,000 mile journey ended with a confirmation of his worst fears: word had reached Montreal that the ship had gone down in Lake Michigan.

The loss of his fur fortune meant that La Salle once more had no money. But he was persuasive and ambitious, and he managed to borrow enough cash to stave off his creditors and purchase fresh supplies for his Mississippi venture. However, before he could complete his preparations, two coureurs de bois reached him with news of a further disaster. Tonti's men had mutinied. La Salle's absence, the imminent threat of an Iroquois attack, and word of the *Griffin's* fate—which meant that the men would not receive the two years' back pay owed to them—had made them turn on La Salle's lieutenant. Tonti and a few loyal men had been driven into the woods, while the mutineers had destroyed the fort, taken as many supplies as they could carry, and thrown the rest into the river.

Above: "The Chevalier De Tonty Suing For Peace in the Village of the Iroquois," by George Catlin. Tonti was stabbed by one of the warriors as he tried to persuade the Iroquois to let them go. Eventually the wounded man and his companions were released, and managed to make their way north into friendly Ottawa territory.

Above: Henri de Tonti, 1650?–1704. He was nicknamed "Iron Hand" on account of the artificial metal hand he wore. He and La Salle became friends in France in 1678 and came to Canada together. The two of them managed to extend greatly the territory of New France through their explorations. Courtesy Chicago Historical Society.

Below: "The Expedition Arriving at the Mouth of the Mississippi; La Salle Erects a Cross and Takes Possession of the Country 'In the Name of Louis Le Grand, King of France and Navarre,' April 9th, 1682," by George Catlin.

La Salle set off immediately to find his friend. By August, 1680, he was back in Illinois country. There, in a recently-abandoned Illinois village, he found a scene of devastation. An Iroquois war party, frustrated and vengeful at finding their intended victims gone, had dug up and mutilated all the bodies in the Illinois' cemeteries. But La Salle found no trace of a white man, which gave him hope that Tonti might still be alive. He hurried 50 miles down the Illinois River to Fort Crèvecoeur. There, amidst the ruins, was the half-finished hull of the boat. On the side of the vessel, one of Tonti's mutinous crew had scrawled the bleak words, "We are all savages."

La Salle scoured the surrounding territory for some sign of his friend, traveling down the Illinois River to the point at which it joins the Mississippi. Once on the mighty river, he must have been sorely tempted to begin his long-awaited journey to the Gulf of Mexico. But this was not the moment for such a venture. He had with him only four men and meager supplies—and, even more important, he had yet to find Tonti. Sadly, La Salle turned away from the Mississippi and paddled 273 miles back up the Illinois. Then, hoping daily for some word of Tonti, he set out overland for southern Michigan.

But it was to be many months before La Salle learned—through an accidental meeting with some Indians from Wisconsin—that his friend was safe and well. Tonti and his men, they told him, had been captured by the Iroquois, who, for a time, had threatened to murder them. But in the end, Tonti had convinced the Iroquois to let them go, and, half starved and feverish, he and his men had made their way north to Wisconsin. There, they had been taken in and nursed back to health by a friendly Ottawa tribe.

Below: a map of the early 1700's showing the Mississippi region. The expanse of the French possessions at that time is impressive. Through the exploration of Joliet and La Salle, the course of the Mississippi River is quite accurately charted, complete with its main tributaries. The Great Lakes are also reasonably well defined. Compare them with the obviously stunted shape of the Florida peninsula and the uncertainty about the position of the mountains in the "Pays des Apaches"—the land of the Apache.

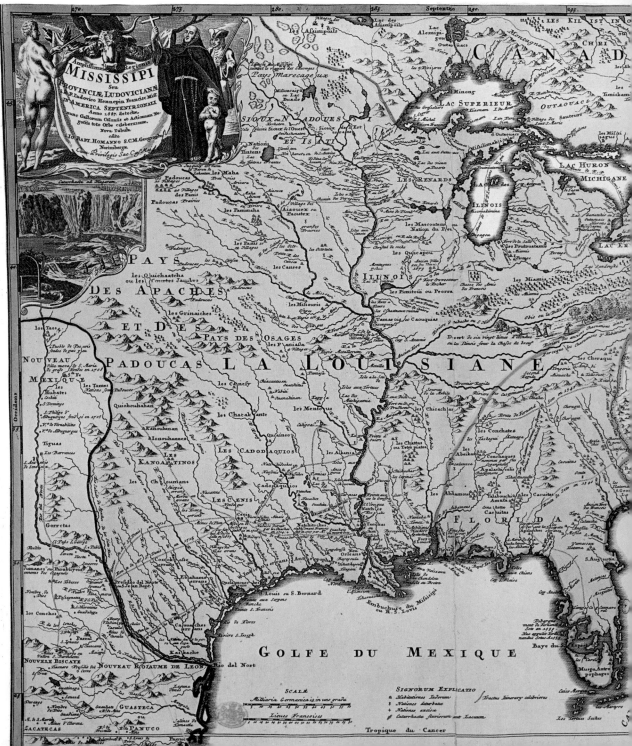

Left: "Wreck of the *Aimable* on the Coast of Texas," 1685, by George Catlin. The *Aimable* was the unlucky supply ship of La Salle's fleet that ran aground.

Reunited once more, La Salle and Tonti made preparations for the long-delayed Mississippi expedition. La Salle traveled through the Illinois and Ohio region, recruiting Indians to take part in the venture. At last, with a party of 23 Frenchmen and 18 Indian men and their families, La Salle set out from Fort Miami in December, 1681. It was the dead of winter but, as usual, La Salle was too impatient to wait for better weather. The canoes and supplies were placed on sledges and dragged along the frozen surface of the Illinois River to the Mississippi. Then, in mid-February, 1682, the party began its voyage down the mighty river. Like Joliet and Marquette nine years before, La Salle met only friendly Indians as he proceeded south. But unlike his predecessors, he did not stop when he reached the Arkansas River, but continued south to the Mississippi delta. There, as his men paddled on between the low marshes, La Salle found the water growing gradually saltier. And suddenly, on April 8, 1682, the broad horizon of the Gulf itself appeared before him.

La Salle landed, planted a large wooden cross, and fired off a volley of musket shots. Then, in the name of Louis XIV, he formally took possession of the entire Mississippi Valley for France. But the small party of men he had with him was not enough to establish a permanent post at the mouth of the Mississippi. La Salle decided to go to France to seek royal backing for a large expeditionary force.

La Salle made only one major stop on his way back to the Great Lakes. That was at a point along the Illinois River, where he built a trading post he called Fort St. Louis. Then he returned to the Laurentian Valley and sailed for France. At the French court, his action in claiming the Louisiana territory excited enormous interest. And his heady vision of French supremacy in the American heartland soon won him the king's support for a major expedition to build a port on the Gulf coast.

In August, 1684, La Salle sailed from France with "4 vessels, which had on board 280 persons, including the crews, 100 soldiers with their officers, about 30 gentlemen volunteers, some young women, and the rest hired people and workmen of all sorts necessary for founding a settlement." These are the words of Henri Joutel, a young man who signed on as La Salle's personal aide, and who kept a detailed journal of the voyage—a journal that was to record an almost unending series of disasters.

Quarrels between La Salle and the admiral of the fleet, Beaujeu, began early in the voyage, and soon the two men were completely at odds. When they reached the Caribbean, Spanish pirates captured one of the vessels, and La Salle was taken dangerously ill with some unknown fever. He had recovered by the time the fleet reached the Gulf, but here, a new series of mishaps occurred. The expedition's supply ship ran aground and was destroyed in a storm. Far more serious, the expedition was unable to locate the mouth of the Mississippi. Several shore parties—one of which was led by La Salle himself—went inland to find the main channel of the river. But each time they were misled by the maze of streams, foggy swamps, and

Above: the murder of La Salle, from Father Hennepin's book. La Salle had sent several discontented men on a routine duty. When they didn't return, he sent his nephew after them. They killed the nephew, and when La Salle came to investigate, he was shot through the head so that, according to Joutel, "he dropped down dead on the spot, without speaking one word."

Above: Father Louis Hennepin, 1640–1701, in an anonymous oil portrait painted in 1694. Father Hennepin was a Franciscan missionary in New France.

shallow bays that so effectively hide it. Both officers and crew began to doubt the very existence of the river, and La Salle's honor and credibility were called in question. At last, Beaujeu decided to sail for home, and many of the men opted to go with him. But La Salle refused to give up. He knew his river was close by, and he insisted on remaining behind with a few others to hunt for it.

But the place where La Salle and his party were eventually put ashore was hundreds of miles west of the Mississippi delta—on the Texas coast. Here, at Matagorda Bay, unaware of their true position, La Salle and his followers built a small fort and began a series of fruitless attempts to locate the banks of the Mississippi. At last, in January, 1687, La Salle set off to make one final, desperate search for the great river. With him he took 17 men, including his faithful scribe Joutel. He left behind 20 men to hold the fort at Matagorda.

La Salle's party marched a distance of some 200 miles through bush and swamplands, under the watchful eye of hostile Indians.

After several weeks of this torturous progress, the men began to despair of ever finding the Mississippi. Desperate and frightened, several of them turned on La Salle and, early one morning, shot their commander through the head. Thus, still seeking his river, Robert Cavelier, Sieur de La Salle, died in the wilderness.

For a while, Joutel's life, too, hung in the balance. But he succeeded in getting back to Matagorda and, the following May, set off from there with six other men in an attempt to reach Canada. With the help of an Indian guide, they managed to reach a small French outpost on the Mississippi that had been set up, long before, by the faithful Tonti to greet La Salle and help him on his way up the river. Upon hearing Joutel's story, Tonti made a heroic effort to save the stranded people at Matagorda Bay, but was prevented from reaching them by hostile Indians south of Arkansas. Meanwhile, La Salle's murderers—who knew that they could never return to any area under French control when the truth about them was known—

Above: Father Hennepin captured by the Iroquois Indians, in a plate from his book. His captors, however, were sufficiently impressed by the "magic" of his compass and his silver chalice so that they did not dare to kill him.

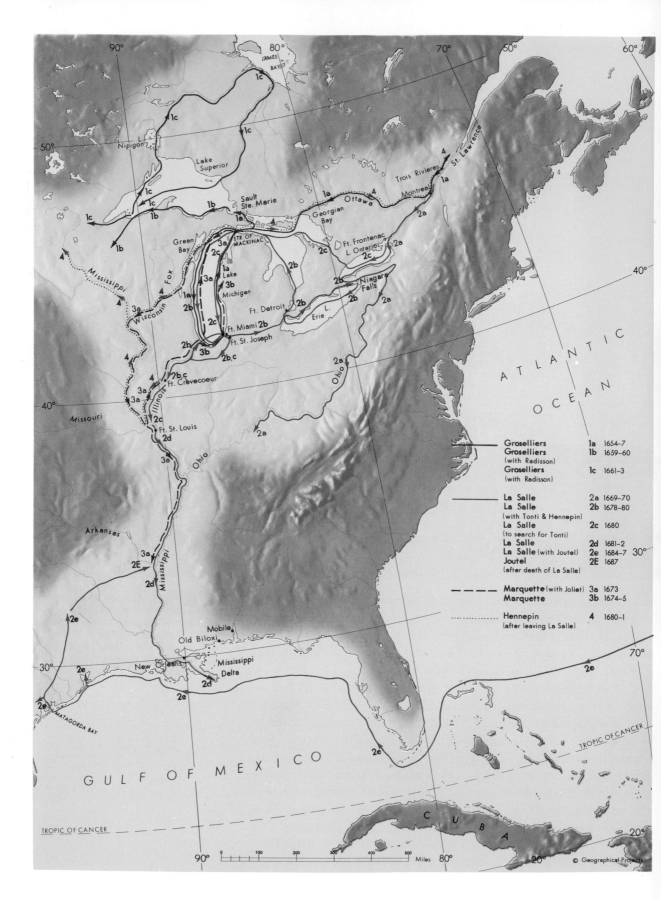

90° 80° 70° 50° 60°

JAMES BAY

1c

1c

1c

1c

L.
Nipigon

Lake Superior

1c

1c

50°

St. Lawrence 4

Trois Rivieres

Montreal 1a

1a Ottawa 4

1b Sault Ste. Marie

1b

1a

Georgian Bay

1b

1b

Ft. Frontenac 2a
L. Ontario 2a

2c

1a STR OF MACKINAC

3a

Green Bay

2c

2c

2b

2b Niagara Falls

40°

Mississippi

4

4

Fox

3a

1a Lake Michigan

3a 3b

2b

2b

L. Erie

2b

ATLANTIC

Wisconsin 4

4

3a

1a

2b

Ft. Detroit 2b

2c

2a

OCEAN

4

Ft. Miami 2b

Ft. St. Joseph

2b,c

4

2b

3b

Ohio 2a

40°

3a
3a

Ft. Crevecoeur

Ohio

Missouri

Illinois

2c
Ft. St. Louis

2d

2a

3a

Groselliers   1a 1654-7
Groselliers   1b 1659-60
(with Radisson)
Groselliers   1c 1661-3
(with Radisson)

Arkansas

3a

2E

Mississippi

2d

La Salle   2a 1669-70
La Salle   2b 1678-80
(with Tonti & Hennepin)
La Salle   2c 1680
(to search for Tonti)
La Salle   2d 1681-2
La Salle (with Joutel) 2e 1684-7
Joutel   2E 1687
(after death of La Salle)

30°

2e

Mobile
Old Biloxi

Marquette (with Joliet) 3a 1673
Marquette   3b 1674-5

70°

2e

New Orleans
Mississippi Delta

2e

Hennepin   4 1680-1
(after leaving La Salle)

2d

2e

2c

MATAGORDA BAY

TROPIC OF CANCER

2c

GULF OF MEXICO

CUBA

TROPIC OF CANCER

20°

A

20°

90° 0 100 200 300 400 500
Miles 80°

© Geographical Projects

Left: the central and eastern United States, showing the routes of French explorers such as Groselliers and La Salle up and down the Mississippi River between 1654 and 1687.

were captured by a hostile tribe, who first enslaved them, and then turned them over to the Spanish. The Matagorda settlement vanished without a trace.

The failure of La Salle's expedition, however, did not put an end to French attempts to expand their sphere of influence in North America. Even before La Salle's death, Tonti's cousin, Daniel Greysolon, Sieur Duluth, had explored the upper reaches of the Mississippi and claimed much of the country beyond it for France. A curious sidelight of Duluth's expedition was his rescue of Father Hennepin who, in 1679, had set off to explore the southern Illinois River and been captured by the Sioux. The Indians had starved and taunted him, but had spared his life because they believed he could summon supernatural forces with his magnetic compass and his silver chalice. Duluth's fortuitous arrival with a party of armed men in 1680 released the missionary from his miserable captivity.

In the 1690's, the French increased the number of their outposts in the Great Lakes region and began building forts southward along the Mississippi. The northern anchor of this system of fortifications was Fort Pontchartrain, commonly called Fort Detroit, a post established by Antoine de la Mothe Cadillac in the Michigan region west of Lake Erie. In 1699, a French-Canadian explorer named Pierre le Moyne, Sieur d'Iberville, established an outpost at Old Biloxi (now Ocean Springs), on the Gulf Coast, and three years later, another French fort was built at Mobile. Finally, in 1718, La Salle's cherished dream of a port at the mouth of the Mississippi was realized with the building of New Orleans, capital of Louisiana and southernmost citadel of the French in North America.

But for how long could the French maintain their grasp over these vast regions of the American continent? Already there had been clashes with the Spanish to the south and with the English to the northeast. Sooner or later, there was bound to be a monumental collision as the various territorial claims made by the three nations—and particularly those made by France and England—began to overlap and conflict.

Below: New Orleans in 1726, only eight years after its founding, in the earliest known picture of the city.

Fighting for the Land

8

Above: "The Death of Wolfe," a painting by Benjamin West (1738–1820). The battle for Quebec cost the lives of both the British and French generals. It was only one of the battles over possession of the American continent.

Left: James Wolfe. His conquest of Louisbourg not only safeguarded New England, but opened the way to Quebec. When Quebec fell in September, 1759, Canada had been won for the British.

In the late 1600's, as the exploration and colonization of North America gathered momentum, an important question began to be asked in the courts of Europe: Which of the great powers would ultimately control the vast American continent? Spain, France, and England had all made territorial claims there, and those claims had begun to conflict dangerously. In the 1690's, there were clashes between the French and the Spanish on the Gulf Coast, and between the Spanish and the English south of the Carolinas. But the most serious conflict of interests was between the English and the French, whose rival claims in New York, New England, and the Hudson Bay area provoked many a bloody skirmish during the late 1600's. These skirmishes were part of a desultory and inconclusive struggle called "King William's War," which dragged on from 1689 to 1697.

Anglo-French territorial conflicts came to a head in a series of major wars during the 1700's. Ostensibly, the wars originated in purely European issues. But each Anglo-French war in Europe was used as an excuse to pursue the territorial struggle in America. And significantly, all of the treaties which ended the wars included provisions stating exactly who had won what in the American provinces. Of course, the French and British frontiersmen in those provinces paid little attention to the treaties. It took a long time for European news to reach America, and even when it did, orders from abroad were not likely to stop the farmers and fur traders from fighting for their land.

The first of the wars in the 1700's was the War of Spanish Succession (1702–1713). In America, where it was called "Queen Anne's War," the struggle took place in New England and in the Florida and South Carolina regions. Both in the north and in the south, the French—aided by the Spanish—fought hard, but were defeated. Great Britain emerged triumphant from the conflict, having added the Hudson Bay region, Newfoundland, and Acadia (as the French then called Nova Scotia) to the American regions under her control.

To counter these losses, the French stepped up their fort-building activities east of the Mississippi, with the idea of keeping the English boxed in behind the Appalachians. But the French could not hope to contain their British rivals, they simply did not have the strength. To begin with, by 1760 the entire population of New France was only about 60,000, while the population of the 13 British colonies numbered over 1,500,000. Moreover, unlike their British counterparts, the French settlers had developed no home industries, and were heavily dependent on an unreliable supply of provisions and equipment from abroad. New France prided itself on its permanent force of professional soldiers. But the average French-Canadian lacked the fierce spirit of independence and self-reliance that made even the improvised citizen militias of the British colonies formidable opponents. Last but not least, the French had never succeeded in winning over the hostile Iroquois, who, as early as the mid-1600's, had begun siding with the British in their quarrels with the French.

A new European conflict, the War of the Austrian Succession, broke out in 1744. In America, where it was called "King George's War," the struggle led to the British capture of Fort Louisbourg on Cape Breton Island. The sudden conquest of this major port, surprised the British as much as it did the French. Nevertheless, the British deeply resented the provision in the Treaty of Aix-la-Chapelle that forced them to relinquish their prize in 1748.

Perhaps this was why, the following year, the British king gave his blessing to a scheme that was certain to anger the French. The crown granted 200,000 acres of land in the upper Ohio Valley to a

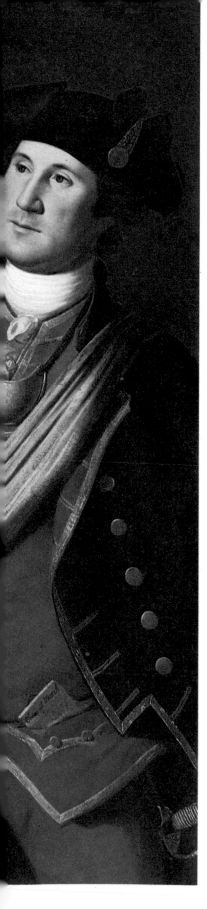

Left: a portrait of Colonel Washington of the Virginia militia, by C. W. Peale. Even early in his military career he had a fine tactical sense and could adjust his strategy to unorthodox situations.

Below: Newfoundland in 1692, a chart of the coastlines, with the fishing districts marked. Note how the fishing grounds have fleets marked English, French, and Maine (American). Not only was the land jealously claimed but the sea, also, was under dispute.

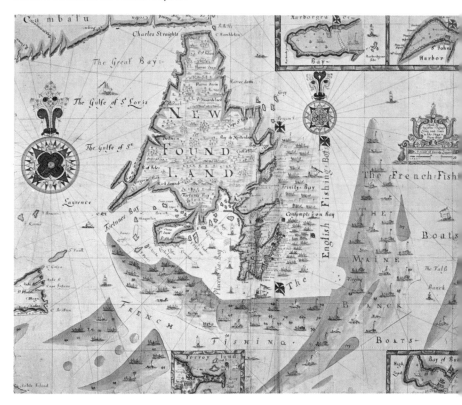

group of Virginians and London merchants who wished to trade and settle there. This was the very region to which French fur traders were already staking their claims. Not surprisingly, the French resented the Virginian interlopers, and sent an armed force to oust them. Moreover, the French began building a chain of forts from Lake Erie to the Ohio River to secure their own claim to the area. One of these forts, built in 1754 on the site of present-day Pittsburgh, was Fort Duquesne. The very next year, Virginia sent a group of volunteer soldiers under General Braddock to attack the French stronghold. One of the officers was a young Virginian named George Washington. He strongly urged Braddock to use the Indians' own guerrilla tactics against the French and their Indian allies. But Braddock insisted on relying on traditional European fighting methods. The result was a disaster, in which the general and many of his men were killed. Only young Washington's courage and cool-headedness saved the rest.

The battle at Fort Duquesne took place, in fact, between wars. The next major European conflict, the Seven Years' War, did not begin until 1756. Nevertheless, the Americans saw this third war as a continuation of the Ohio Valley struggle, and simply called it the French and Indian War.

The effect of this Anglo-French confrontation on the balance of power in North America proved decisive. In 1758, the British retook Louisbourg, the key to the St. Lawrence River and to the safety of New England. The news of the event was celebrated with giant bonfires in London, Philadelphia, Boston, and New York. In the same year, Fort Duquesne was captured by a British force—again one that included George Washington, much to his satisfaction. But the most important British victory in America was the capture of Quebec in 1759. Under the leadership of General James Wolfe, a large British force sailed down the St. Lawrence to Quebec. After a

Below: North America in 1700. By this time three European powers—France, Spain, and England—were firmly established in the south and east of the continent. But it was between France and England that the great conflict for supremacy took place in a series of major wars in the 1700's.

British possessions 1700

French possessions 1700

Spanish possessions 1700

Areas claimed by British & French

© Geographical Projects

siege of almost three months, Wolfe's army stormed the Heights of Abraham above the city. Quebec, guarded by a smaller force of French soldiers under Marquis de Montcalm, was at last forced to surrender, but not before both generals had been fatally wounded. Wolfe lived just long enough to know that he had won Canada for Britain. British supremacy there was further assured the following year when Montreal was captured.

By the Treaty of Paris in 1763, France formally turned over to Britain not only Canada but also all her possessions east of the Mississippi River, with the exception of New Orleans, which France ceded to Spain in return for the help Spain had given the French during the war. Spain also received all French land west of the Mississippi. But, on her side, Spain was forced to turn over all her Florida holdings to Britain.

The year 1763 marked a momentous turning point in American

Below: North America in 1763. After a series of victories over the combined armies of France and Spain in both America and Europe, Britain now reigned supreme over the whole eastern half of the continent. It was not until 1776, when the Thirteen Colonies rebelled, that Britain's supremacy was challenged.

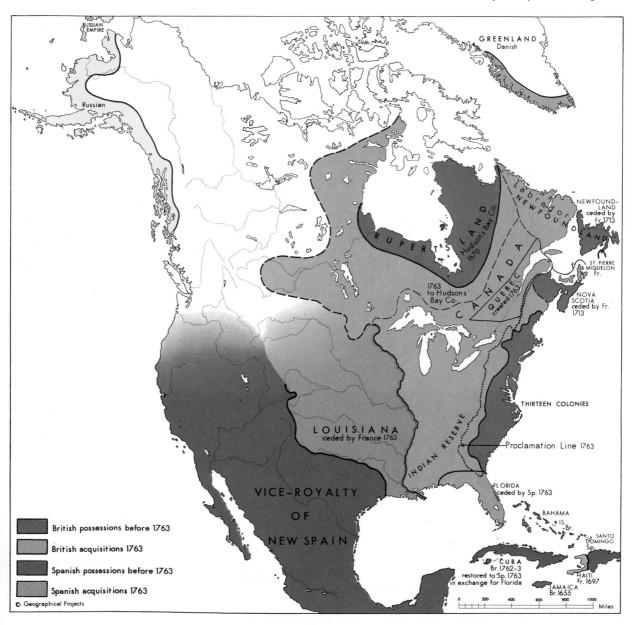

history. Britain now reigned supreme over the whole eastern half of the continent, and her right to do so was not again challenged until 1776, when the Thirteen Colonies themselves rebelled against British rule.

Meanwhile, British colonial expansion continued at breakneck speed, both along the Atlantic coast and westward, toward the foothills of the Appalachians. Everywhere in the fast-growing colonies—from New Hampshire to Georgia—there were land-hungry men eager and willing to seek their fortunes in the virgin wilderness beyond the existing frontiers. Moreover, after 1763, the British colonists who wanted to travel beyond the Appalachians might do so without fear of reprisals from the French. Even so, the men and women who set out to tame the primeval forests of the interior had to be both strong and courageous, for the life of the pioneer was one of unremitting hardship, backbreaking labor, and the constant threat of Indian attack.

One man who proved himself eminently successful in dealing with all the problems and perils of the wilderness was Daniel Boone. Born in a log cabin in Pennsylvania in 1734, Boone spent his boyhood years learning the ways of the woods: how to stalk every kind of game; how to survive in the open in all weathers; and, perhaps most important, how to outfox a hostile Indian. When young Daniel was 16, his family moved to the wild frontier country in North Carolina, where it was his job to keep the family larder well stocked with game. In 1755, Boone took part in the struggle to wrest Fort Duquesne from the French, and it was on this campaign that he first heard tales of the beautiful Kentucky wilderness beyond the Appalachian highlands. Then and there, Boone became determined to see this wonderful region, but almost 14 years elapsed before he was finally able to do so.

In 1769, Boone set out from North Carolina with a few friends,

Below: "A View of Part of the town of Boston in New England and British Ships of War Landing their Troops 1768." The troops were landing in an attempt to enforce duties and taxes imposed on the colonists. This was one of the acts that infuriated the Americans, and led to their rebellion against the British in 1776.

Above: the colonial settlements had very different patterns of life in different regions. Here a southern plantation is shown, painted by an unknown artist in 1825. These plantations relied mainly on crops of rice and tobacco until the invention of the cotton gin in the late 1700's made cotton the most profitable crop.

and followed the centuries-old "Warriors' Path"—a well-worn Indian route snaking through the dense woods—over the Cumberland Mountains at Cumberland Gap and into Kentucky. Boone was delighted with the richness and wild beauty of the region, and spent two years, often on his own, exploring it. Back in North Carolina, Boone was chosen to lead a group of pioneers over the mountains into Kentucky in 1755. The route he and his party followed soon became known as the "Wilderness Road," and began to be used by countless numbers of pioneer settlers on their way west. Boone himself brought his own family out from North Carolina and settled several miles south of present-day Lexington. But in 1799, he was off again, seeking a new, still-virgin wilderness farther west. For Daniel Boone was a true pioneer, a man driven by a restless spirit of adventure and an irrepressible belief in the opportunities that might lie just over the horizon.

But as the colonists streamed west, blazing trails, clearing fields, and setting up homesteads, they seemed to forget that the lands they were carving out of the wilderness rightfully belonged to another people—the Indians. All along the Atlantic seaboard a single, tragic pattern had emerged from all the contacts between the white men and the native tribes. The Indians' initial friendship and cooperation made it possible for the colonists to survive, but then, as the colony became self-sufficient and began to expand, the colonists rejected the Indians and began driving them out of their lands. Some tribes retreated quietly as their traditional tribal lands were put to the plow. But others fought back, burning and pillaging the British settlements. For such Indians there could be no compromise. They could not accept the white man's insistence on personal property. Their orientation was to communal living and communal property. To them individual ownership of the land was a sacrilege.

But the colonists paid no heed to the Indians' protests. The westward movement was in full swing, and the "heathen natives" must be driven out to make room for the new settlers. Sometimes Indian territories were simply confiscated. Sometimes they were "bought" for a jug of brandy or a few hatchets. Sometimes the colonists bullied and threatened the Indians to make them leave, sometimes they simply massacred them. The most horrible and effective means of eliminating the Indians was the "scalp bounty"—a system by which colonists were paid sums of money for Indian scalps. Any frontiersman in need of cash could easily earn what he needed by scalping a few Indian women and children.

Some of the Indians in eastern and central North America became converts to Christianity, and adopted the white man's way of life. But by doing so, they fired the special hatred of the frontiersmen, who viewed them as a competitive threat. Huddled in European-style villages, such Indians proved an easy prey for murderous white farmers and hostile Indians alike. Those who survived these vicissitudes were cut down by European diseases, to which they were especially vulnerable. The remaining Indians were driven westward. But as they moved away from their traditional lands, their social fabric often disintegrated. The eastern tribes scattered and began to forget their heritage of legends, customs, and beliefs. Even the powerful Iroquois—whose 10,000 warriors had once controlled the giant triangle of land from the Great Lakes and the upper St. Lawrence to the junction of the Ohio and the Mississippi rivers—were ultimately contained and subdued by the thousands of settlers who swarmed west after 1763.

Nothing, it seemed, could stop these new "Americans" once they had set their hearts on going west. Daniel Boone had explained his restless search for virgin lands by saying, "I want more elbow-room!" Many other men felt the same way and, as the fertile river valleys of the east filled up with farms and townships, more and more pioneers pulled up stakes and set out for the wilderness beyond the Appalachian mountains. Many of them began their westward trek on the very rivers that had already played such an important part in the early exploration of America: the St. Lawrence and the Hudson, the Connecticut and the Susquehanna, the Delaware and the James, the Ohio and the Illinois. These and others of the many rivers east of the mighty Mississippi had provided America's first explorers with a gateway to the interior. Now, as they began to provide the pioneers with a stepping-stone to lands yet farther west, these vital waterways more than ever deserved to be called "Rivers of Destiny."

Below: "Daniel Boone Escorting Settlers Through the Cumberland Gap," by George Caleb Bingham. Daniel Boone was typical of many restless American frontiersmen, always pushing over the next line of hills to see what lay in the valley.

Above: Indian chiefs visiting the trustees of Georgia in London, 1734–5. In the early days of several colonies the Indians were treated with respect and many of the early settlers depended heavily on their friendly advice. It was later, when the expanding settlements needed room to grow, that the relationships tended to deteriorate.

Right: "Osceola as a Captive, in a tent Guarded by a Sentry," as painted by Seth Eastman. All too soon the need of the new Americans to move farther west was reason enough for moving the Indians out of the way and ruthlessly punishing any who dared to protest.

Acknowledgments

© Aer Lingus-Irish International Airlines 282(B); Biblioteca Nacionale, Madrid, courtesy American Heritage 197; Courtesy of The American Museum of Natural History 174; Photo F. Anton, Munich 195; Archives Nationales du Québec 192, 225(B); Archives Nationales, Paris 309; Barnaby's Picture Library 189, 263(L); Bibliothèque Nationale, Paris/Photo C. Burland 196; Reproduced by permission of the Trustees of the British Museum 186, 213, 226(T)(B) 224, 248, 249(T), 251(R), 270, 276, 277, 286, 312; British Museum/ Photo R. B. Fleming © Aldus Books 171(R), 173(B), 181, 185(B), 201, 202, 204–05, 206, 208, 222, 228, 229, 230 231(T), 232, 238–39, 240, 250(T)(B), 251(L), 252(T)(B), 253(R), 257, 262(T) (B), 263(R), 266(R), 272, 274(T), 281(T), 284(TL)(TR), 285, 293(B), 295(B), 297(T), 300, 304, 306(L), 307; British Museum/ Photo John Freeman © Aldus Books 175, 176, 203, 236; Canadian Government Travel Bureau 231(B); Canadian Land Forces Command and Staff College 296; Colonial Williamsburg 259; Seth Eastman, *Lacrosse Playing Among the Sioux*. In the collection of The Corcoran Gallery of Art 182–83; Photo John de Visser 221, 237; Ferdinandeum Museum, Innsbruck 216–17; Photo R. B. Fleming © Aldus Books 173(T), 184, 187(R), 190, 198, 234, 249(B), 265, 299(T); Geographical Projects Limited, London 170, 177, 210–11, 256, 280, 308, 314, 315; From *Discovery and Exploration*, produced by Geographical Projects Ltd., published by Paul Hamlyn 191; Gilcrease Institute, Tulsa 178; The Historical Society of Pennsylvania 254(R), 287(T); Hôtel de Dieu, Québec/Photo W. B. Edwards 292(B), 293(T); Reproduced by permission of the Hudson's Bay Company 235; By permission of The Huntington Library, San Marino 218; The John Judkyn Memorial, Freshford Manor, Bath/ Photo Mike Busselle © Aldus Books 194, 207(R), 212, 215(B); The John Judkyn Memorial, Freshford Manor, Bath/Photo R. B. Fleming © Aldus Books 215(T); Photo Hank Lefebvre 243; The Mansell Collection 187(L), 227(L), 258; Massachusetts Historical Society, Boston 269; The Metropolitan Museum of Art, New York 317; The Metropolitan Museum of Art, New York/Picturepoint, London © Aldus Books 169; Minnesota Historical Society 306(R); Josef Muench, Santa Barbara 278; Musée du Louvre, Paris/Photo Giraudon 219, 291; Musée du Seminaire de Québec/Photo W. B. Edwards 222–23, 233; M. and M. Karolik Collection, Courtesy, Museum of Fine Arts, Boston 288–89; Museum of the City of New York 282(T); National Collection of Fine Arts, Smithsonian Institution, Washington, D.C. 168, 185(T), 253(L), 268, 274(B), 318; National Collection of Fine Arts, Smithsonian Institution, Washington, D.C./Photo USIA 171(L); National Cowboy Hall of Fame, Oklahoma 319(B); Paul Mellon Collection, National Gallery of Art, Washington, D.C. 166, 298, 299(B), 301, 302, 303, 305; The National Gallery of Canada, Ottawa 179, 290; The National Gallery of Canada, Ottawa/ Canadian War Memorials Collection 310–11; National Portrait Gallery, London 287(B), 310; National Portrait Gallery, London/ Photo John Freeman © Aldus Books 245; National Trust (The Vyne)/Photo Jeremy Whitaker 264(B); The New York Historical Society 220, 227(R), 267(B), 284(B); The New York Public Library 287(T), 289, 316; The Ohio Historical Society 180; Old Jesuit House, Sillery, Québec/Photo W. B. Edwards 239, 292(T); Courtesy of the Pennsylvania Academy of the Fine Arts 287(B); Picturepoint, London 193, 199, 295(T); Courtesy of Pilgrim Society, Pilgrim Hall Museum, Plymouth, Massachusetts 264(T), 267(T); Dr. L. H. Hurrell/Photo Jeremy Whitaker 260; Dr. A. Welker/Photo Jeremy Whitaker 266(L); Private Collection, London 281(B); Public Archives of Canada 224, 225(T), 297(B); Reproduced by courtesy of the Marquess of Salisbury K.G./Photo John Freeman © Aldus Books 286; The State Historical Society of Wisconsin 207(L), 240–41; The Tate Gallery, London 279; Courtesy U.S. Capitol Historical Society/Photo George F. Mobley 208–09; Wadsworth Atheneum, Hartford, Connecticut 271, 312–13; Reproduced by permission of the Trustees of the Wallace Collection 255; Courtesy of the Webb Gallery of American Art, Shelburne Museum, Shelburne, Vermont 273; The Wellcome Foundation, London 254(L); Courtesy, The Henry Francis du Pont Winterthur Museum, Delaware 319(T).

Left: Raising of the flag; Louisiana Transfer Ceremonies. The new nation of the United States of America took a great leap westward when Jefferson bought the Louisiana Territory, gaining with it the brave tradition of the Spanish, French, and English men who first took the twisting forest paths and followed the shining rivers into the heart of the unknown continent.

PART THREE

*Bridging a
Continent*

Below: wild mustangs, many of which were once tame horses, can still be seen galloping across the Nevada desert. Horses were brought into America by the Spanish.

Bridging a Continent

BY MARTIN HILLMAN

Right: an early photograph of a wagon train that is moving slowly along a narrow mountain trail through the Ute Pass, Colorado.

Foreword

In 1763, France lost her lands in North America, when the Treaty of Paris divided her possessions between Britain and Spain. Now Britain ruled America from the Atlantic coast to the Mississippi, while Spain controlled the western part of the continent. Britain's good fortune was, however, only short lived, for in 1776 her Thirteen Colonies rebelled. Their determination to win independence was great, and the American Revolution was successful. In 1783, the Thirteen Colonies became the first states of the United States of America. North of the Great Lakes, however, in what is now Canada, British rule continued. From this time on, two North American nations would develop side by side.

In 1783, although the United States, Spain and Britain between them laid claim to the whole of North America, vast stretches of the continent remained to be explored. Whole areas were still unknown, and even in those regions that had been traveled, many blanks had still to be filled in on the map. The story of exploration now became one of a drive to the westward as, from their Atlantic coast beginnings, the nations expanded to the Pacific shores. At first, the search for trade and land were supreme motives for the pioneers' journeys but, in time, another force appeared in the United States. Labeled as "Manifest Destiny", it was the doctrine that the United States had the right to rule from the Atlantic to the Pacific, and it became the American dream. Through the journeys of exploration that this part of the book relates, the dream would be fulfilled.

The Spirit of Expansion
1

In 1801, Napoleon Bonaparte, the Emperor of France, worked out a secret treaty with Spain—a treaty that placed over 800,000 square miles of North America's heartland in French hands. That territory, called Louisiana, embraced the vast spread of unexplored wilderness from the northern edge of present-day Texas north to Canada, from the Mississippi west to the Rocky Mountains. It also included the mouth of the Mississippi, and the seaport of New Orleans on the Gulf of Mexico. It was about 17 times as large as what we now know as Louisiana.

The treaty seemed to be all to Napoleon's advantage. By trading off a small Italian kingdom for the vast territory of Louisiana, he had re-established France on the North American continent. But, for the American president, Thomas Jefferson, who had just taken office, the dealings between France and Spain posed a threat. Louisiana lay next to the western boundary of what was then the United States. Jefferson would much rather have weak Spain as a next-door neighbor than powerful, warlike France. Spain had let the young American republic use New Orleans harbor. Since the great river and its tributaries formed a principal route for outgoing goods, New Orleans was crucial to America's prosperity. But just before giving up control of

Left: in 1801 Louisiana comprised more than 800,000 square miles of virgin territory. Exploration there had been the work not of Americans but of Frenchmen, Spaniards, and British and French Canadians. Much of the land was forested, rimmed with mountains, veined with rivers. Only the Indians traveled it regularly. They lived, as they had always done, by hunting, and at this stage of their relationship with white men were, for the most part, friendly and helpful, willing to trade and to provide guides.

Right: Thomas Jefferson, third President of the United States, was possessed by the great American dream of opening up the West. It was thus appropriate that it was he who, as President, was responsible for the purchase of Louisiana from France, which had acquired the territory originally from Spain.

329

Louisiana, Spain had closed the port to the United States. That was serious enough. Much worse was having a stronger and ambitious nation such as France in control. For this reason, President Jefferson rattled a few threatening sabers and sent an envoy to France to see whether Napoleon could be talked into opening New Orleans again. Jefferson told his envoy to hint that the United States would happily buy the city outright, harbor and all.

Fortunately for the United States, Napoleon's plans for a new French empire in North America ran into trouble. He had just suffered the loss of 50,000 troops trying to suppress a rebellion of former slaves on the French island of Santo Domingo in the West Indies. Those were the troops he had planned to use in the occupation of Louisiana. And in Europe, Napoleon was threatened by war with Britain. The emperor knew that he would soon be too busy in Europe to worry about protecting American colonies, even if he could have sent soldiers and supplies past the British Navy. He also knew that he was going to need money. Jefferson's envoy—James Monroe, soon himself to be President—was indeed taken aback by an offer from the French

Above: when Napoleon decided to offer Louisiana to the American plenipotentiaries Livingston and Monroe, its boundaries were far from clear. He simply offered the territory as he had acquired it from Spain. When asked to define the bounds of this cession, Napoleon's foreign minister Talleyrand said: "You have a noble bargain, make the most you can of it."

Right: the covered wagon was the classic vehicle by which men, women, and children opened up the American West. There were three wagon trails across the trans-Mississippi West. The first was the Santa Fe trail, and the first American wagons reached Santa Fe in 1822. By 1831 one caravan of a hundred wagons carried over two hundred thousand dollars' worth of goods to the New Mexico capital.

to sell not only New Orleans, but the entire territory of Louisiana.

The United States had soon parted with about $15 million and had received ownership of a tract of land that doubled the size of the Amercan nation. Some countries might have found such an enormous gulp of new territory a little hard to swallow, but not the United States. The Louisiana Purchase seemed to stir in the American people and their leaders an appetite for more. Previously, exploration and colonization of the New World had been left chiefly to the European powers. It had been nearly 200 years since the first British settlers established themselves in Virginia. Now the Americans, some of them having been settled in the New World for six generations, began to realize they had a vast area at their disposal. So the push westward and the expansion of the American frontier began.

The problems which faced these pioneer explorers were many. Just as they were basically unaware of the kind of country they would have to cross, they often lacked the equipment or the skills to do so. The emptiness of the continent was a spur, but the scattered Indian population had influenced the way of life of the settlers. They learned from the Indians how to grow corn, sweet potatoes, and other foods, and how to farm the land. Others took up the rich fur trade and became woodsmen. The settlers were adjusted to the kind of climate and territory they found where they settled and were unprepared for the great differences they would encounter. For example, the Virginians were accustomed to easily navigable rivers, but in the northern parts no network of inland waterways existed. To the west the huge range of the Rocky Mountains and the variation in the climate around them presented new hazards as did the central regions of the recently acquired territory, mistakenly considered the "Great American Desert" for years and years.

Apart from natural difficulties, the farmers knew only the most

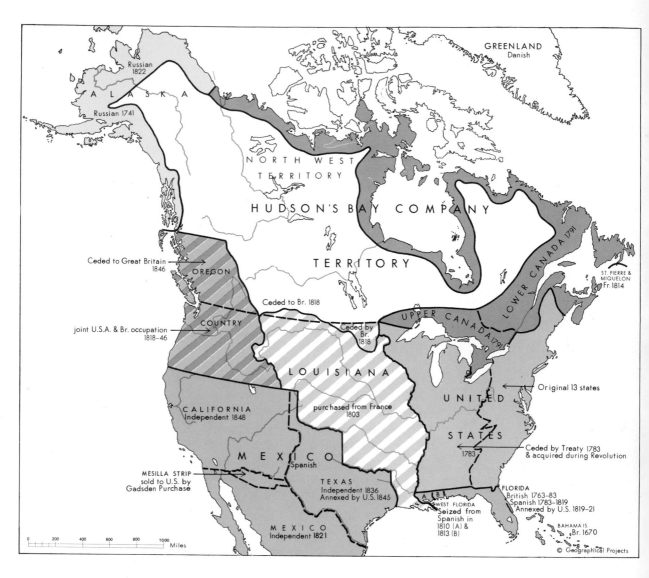

Labels on map:

GREENLAND
Danish

Russian 1822

Russian 1741

ALASKA

NORTH WEST
TERRITORY

HUDSON'S BAY COMPANY
TERRITORY

Ceded to Great Britain
1846

OREGON

Ceded to Br. 1818

joint U.S.A. & Br. occupation
1818–46

COUNTRY

Ceded by
Br.
1818

LOWER CANADA 1791

ST. PIERRE &
MIQUELON
Fr. 1814

UPPER CANADA 1791

LOUISIANA

purchased from France
1803

UNITED

Original 13 states

CALIFORNIA
Independent 1848

STATES

1783

Ceded by Treaty 1783
& acquired during Revolution

MESILLA STRIP
sold to U.S. by
Gadsden Purchase

MEXICO
Spanish

TEXAS
Independent 1836
Annexed by U.S. 1845

FLORIDA
British 1763–83
Spanish 1783–1819
Annexed by U.S. 1819–21

A B
WEST FLORIDA
Seized from
Spanish in
1810 (A) &
1813 (B)

BAHAMA IS.
Br. 1670

MEXICO
Independent 1821

0 200 400 600 800 1000 Miles

© Geographical Projects

Above: North America in 1803, at the time of the Louisiana Purchase. The pink areas were British, orange were Spanish, yellow, Russian, and green, United States.

basic methods of farming, which worked adequately on the virgin fields but tended to exhaust the soil rapidly. And there was an inborn tendency to move on to new pastures before agricultural methods had been improved. In addition the characteristics of the various Indian tribes varied greatly from region to region. Some were helpful and friendly, but others, viewing the white man with dread and suspicion, were hostile and dangerous.

There was friction among fur traders in the Louisiana territory. A border dispute soon arose because no one knew where the borders lay. Spain argued that Louisiana's southern boundary lay on the Red River. The United States claimed it was farther south, on the Rio Grande in Texas. Before a settlement could be reached, American adventurers raided into Spanish territory to trade, and Spanish soldiers charged out from their southwest strongholds to capture and imprison these "trespassers."

Spanish Florida then became the scene of further conflict. A band of American freebooters took over a piece of that area, asked for an-

nexation to the United States, and promptly got it. Eventually the United States were to buy the rest of Florida. But the same treaty which permitted them to do so drew Louisiana's boundary in such a way that Texas remained Spanish. Spain tried appeasement by inviting Americans to colonize portions of Texas. This was inviting the robbers in to share the feast. Soon, however, Mexico fought and won its independence from Spain. The newly independent nation of Mexico promptly took over Texas. Within a few years, America's Texans went to war with Mexico and declared their own independence. Later, the United States took up arms against Mexico, and pushed the Spanish-Mexican borders still farther to the southwest.

The main obstacles to United States growth, then, needed no explorers to report on them. To the north and northwest, the British settlements in Canada stood in the way of American advance. To the south and southwest, outposts of the Spanish empire sat tight in Florida, in Texas, and beyond the western mountains in California. The United States had snatched Louisiana from the jaws of both of these

Above: the St. Lawrence River was one of the waterways which was used as a highway for expansion by traders and the settlers who followed in their footsteps. The St. Lawrence forms a natural boundary between what have now become the United States and Canada.

Above: the fur trade in North America had been important since the 1600's, but it was to reach its peak by the 1840's, after which it rapidly declined. The bulk of trade was in beaver skins. The trappers went out far beyond the farthest fringes of settlement and civilization to trap and trade furs with the Indians. They returned to the frontier outposts to sell their pelts, often drank and gambled away the proceeds, many returning to the wilds having lost every penny they had gained.

colonial powers: Spain had ceded it to France on the condition that it would not fall into American hands. But if France had kept Louisiana, the British might have invaded it and taken it over in the war against Napoleon.

Many Americans resented the fact that any part of North America should be British, especially when the biggest piece, Canada, was populated by Loyalists who had deserted the United States during the War of Independence. Other, more practical men also resented the British control of the fur trade and their competition with American fur companies in the forests around the Great Lakes and in the Columbia River Valley.

In the late 1700's, the Canadian fur trade was dominated by two giant companies. The older of the two, the Hudson's Bay Company, founded in London in 1670, controlled the west coast of the great bay, traded with northern Indians, and made few forays into the interior. Its Canadian-based rival, the North West Company, had grown out of a combine of many small enterprises. The Northwesters, as they were called, had found the pickings rich enough to join forces and abandon their often brutal competition.

They collided twice with the Americans when they went southward in force to trap and to trade during the 1780's. Extending all the way to the central Missouri region, they thwarted both Spanish and American fur seekers. They, and some Hudson's Bay men who followed them, ignored the treaty that placed the American border north of the British posts on Lake Superior. They stayed on United States soil well into the 1790's. During this time the Indians of the Ohio country went to war against American settlers all along the frontier, to some extent with British aid and encouragement.

But British help to the Indians did not go far enough. The American General, "Mad Anthony" Wayne—a hero of the Revolution—defeated the tribes at the Battle of Fallen Timbers, in 1794. In the process he laid claim to much new frontier land for the United States. Then, out of British-American efforts to make peace on the border, Jay's

Treaty evolved. This treaty was signed in England in November 1794, and was ratified the following June. It finally evicted the British from their Great Lakes posts. But this treaty also allowed Canadian traders full use of waterways south of the border, which gave them new freedom to operate in American territory. Wayne's victory may have ended an Indian war, but it did not lessen the fierce rivalry of the fur traders or put an end to trouble between Britain and the United States.

By the time of Jay's Treaty, both the Americans and the Canadians were struggling for the fur trade in the Pacific Northwest. Alexander

North America. Relief coloring shows the broad central plains and the more rugged coastal and far northern areas.

Above: "Mad Anthony" Wayne and a small American force defeated the Indian tribes of the old northwest at Fallen Timbers in 1794. He made them sign away their lands to the Americans in a series of treaties, beginning with that of Greenville in 1795. This picture, painted by a member of Wayne's staff, shows American leaders and a group of Indians. Picture by courtesy of the Chicago Historical Society.

WHO'S AFRAID?

OR, THE OREGON QUESTION.

Left: the northern boundary of Oregon was the subject of dispute between America and Britain during the 1830's and 1840's. James K. Polk won the presidency in 1844 on the slogan "Fifty-Four Forty or Fight," referring to the American boundary claim. But the British had no wish to fight and the claim was settled amicably in 1846.

Mackenzie, the Canadian explorer and trader, was the first white man to cross the continent and reach the Pacific. A few years later, Meriwether Lewis and William Clark paved the way for Americans. The Northwesters and American companies raced for control of the rich territory in the valley of the Columbia River. That region, soon to be called Old Oregon, was to be hotly contested until the 1840's. When the boundary was drawn at last to end the dispute, the Columbia Valley became American. Until that time, however, Canadian fur traders continued to harass the American frontier.

Slowly, during the first half of the 1800's, the Americans were to take for granted the idea that theirs was to be a transcontinental nation—that it would stretch to the Pacific. They were to see territorial expansion as the American destiny. During these years, too, the first wagon trails westward were to be established. Some Americans even dreamed that Canada and Mexico would also become part of the United States. And, by the 1840's, the idea of expansion had been glorified in the popular slogan "Manifest Destiny." The phrase was invented by John L. Sullivan, the editor of a New York City newspaper. In 1845, Sullivan wrote, "It is our manifest destiny to overspread and

Above: the Alamo, originally the chapel of the San Francisco mission in San Antonio. It was the scene of a famous last stand, when a tiny force of men, including Davy Crockett and Jim Bowie ("the Knife"), fought to the death against a superior Mexican force during the Texan revolution against Mexican rule. The revolution led to Texas becoming a republic and joining the Union in 1845.

337

Right: in 1800, the American West belonged to the Indians who had lived there for thousands of years fishing and hunting buffalo. They had found the best trails across the mountains and rivers and had discovered many mineral deposits. Their methods of travel on water and land were ideally suited to the conditions and they taught the explorers how to live in the open country. But by the end of the century the white men had settled the plains, the buffalo were destroyed, and the Indians had been forced into reservations.

Right: the arid Southwestern territory was entirely different from the broad plains of the prairies across which the early western explorers and settlers moved. This picture shows typical country to the southwest of the Rockies, in Arizona.

possess the whole of the continent which Providence has given us."
But even before the politicians picked up the phrase, the spirit of expansion was to push the American frontier toward the Pacific Ocean.

Settlers carried their sense of destiny with them like a banner, as did cattlemen, miners, land speculators, railroad builders, and all the tens of thousands of Americans who pioneered the West. But first of all, it was the explorers who advanced the cause of Manifest Destiny. As soon as Louisiana had been purchased, they began a half-century of route-finding, map-drawing, and learning the hard way about the obstacles that faced their country's westward growth.

The story of America's half-century of growth and the story of western exploration blend into one. Obviously, explorers and adventurers such as Lewis and Clark, Pike, Frémont, and the rest opened the way for the bearers of Manifest Destiny following in their wake. Traders of all sorts, competing hotly with one another and with foreign interlopers, opened up virgin territory, and in the process helped to claim it for the United States. The United States Army galloped across the West to deal with Indians (who neither knew nor cared who claimed Louisiana) and while doing so opened up the trails and wagon routes to the West. Early pioneers set out on agonized marches to Oregon or Utah or California long before the spread of settlement had even crossed the Mississippi, and often took side trips—sometimes by accident—into unexplored wilderness.

Below: from the Indians with whom
they bartered for furs and skins to
send back to England, the men of the
Hudson's Bay Company learned a
great deal. One very important
lesson was the technique of fishing
through the ice in winter, shown
here on the Red River of the North.

Forerunners
2

The Louisiana Purchase may have raised the curtain on the drama of westward exploration, but before the end of the 1700's there had been a prelude of heroic proportions. And it was performed almost entirely by the footloose fur traders of French and British Canada.

America's fur men had stayed content for some time with the lush forests of their old frontier east of the Mississippi, using that river's eastern tributaries as their highways. But traders in Canada had access to the St. Lawrence and Hudson Bay, both of which offered routes deep into the west. The Hudson's Bay Company began an immediate drive in that direction by sending Henry Kelsey inland in 1690 to become the first white man on the Canadian prairies. Fifty years later Anthony Henday was sent to penetrate into Blackfoot country within sight of the Rocky Mountains. The Company's French rivals, the Vérendryes, De la Corne, and others, also joined in the competition of exploration. And, following the British takeover of Canada in 1763 as spoils of the Seven Years' War, new rivals filtered out from the east—English-speaking Canadians, most of them backed by Montreal trading firms, and sneeringly called "Pedlars" by the Hudson's Bay Company.

The Pedlars fanned out across the west, plucking furs from Indians who had previously traded with the Hudson's Bay Company, and forcing the older company to take action. The Hudson's Bay Company responded by focusing on the north, where the Pedlars had not yet penetrated. In the late 1760's, they sent William Stewart to their most northerly fort to open up trade with the Chipewyan Indians. He plodded 800 miles across the bleak barrens northwest of Churchill before reaching his destination. Upon his return, he related Indian tales of a great river running past a mountain of pure copper. Because the Pedlars had already seriously reduced the Hudson's Bay Company trade with the Woods Cree and other tribes of the Saskatchewan River Valley, the thought of a northern copper mine seemed rather attractive. For this reason, the Hudson's Bay Company decided to go north again—in the person of Samuel Hearne.

Hearne was a sturdy Londoner, skilled at navigation and surveying, but too new to the fur trade to know about Arctic survival. In 1769, he set out northwest from Churchill with a wholly inadequate supply of food, clothing, and equipment. He was guided by Indians who did not really know their way. As a result, within a month he was back at Churchill, chagrined. But by early 1770, he was ready to make another

Left: Samuel Hearne, whose contact with the Chipewyans was of immense value to the Hudson's Bay Company. Hearne built their first inland post, Cumberland House, on the Saskatchewan River.

Right: a trapper and his wife, with their dog pulling the sledge loaded with partridges. Many trappers married local women and their way of life became a mixture of European and Indian patterns.

trip, with more experienced Indians and more suitable equipment. This time, however, bad weather and a shortage of game forced him into long halts along the way before he had halfway reached his objective. Again he turned back.

On the journey back to Churchill, in 1771, he met up with a Chipewyan leader named Matonabbee who knew about the Coppermine River (as it is now known), and he volunteered to take Hearne there. Hearne's knowledge of Arctic survival had improved, so he did not find it necessary to wait for spring to begin the trip. In December of the same year, he set off with Matonabbee and his Chipewyans. He learned a great deal from these Indians. They gathered birchbark along the way for canoe-making so that they could enter navigable waters when necessary. And they also led him to forests where herds of deer wintered, and these supplied the party with food during the cold season.

Their march northward that spring was direct and uneventful. And in July, 1772, they finally reached what Matonabbee informed them was the Coppermine River. But Hearne was terribly disappointed. The river was barely navigable by canoes, and thus useless to the Hudson's Bay Company coastal shipping. The "mountain of copper" did not exist, and, though Hearne found samples of the metal, mining it was not an economic possibility for the mining techniques of the time.

A dejected Hearne began to retrace his steps. He was not even impressed by the fact that when his canoe drifted into the mouth of the Coppermine River, he became the first white man to reach the Arctic Ocean overland. He felt that the journey had been futile, and it seemed only appropriate that on the way home he should lose his watch, his quadrant, and (briefly) his way.

But at least Hearne had improved the Hudson's Bay Company's contacts with the Chipewyans, which were badly needed to offset the Pedlar threat. Because of his experience, the Hudson's Bay Company

…ife returning with a load of Partridges from their Tent. — By Wm Richard…

343

Left: a Chipewyan warrior. The pioneers of the Hudson's Bay Company and their rivals, the "Pedlars," were very dependent on the local Indians, who acted as their guides.

Above right: a drawing by Samuel Hearne of Lake Athabasca, which illustrates the account of his journey from Prince of Wales Fort around the Hudson Bay region.

Bottom right: the Governor of Red River, Hudson Bay, in a canoe in 1824. The early explorers very quickly adopted the canoe as a convenient means of transportation through the network of rivers which crisscrossed the country.

sent Hearne westward in 1774 to the Saskatchewan River (60 miles above The Pas in present-day Manitoba), to build their first true inland post, Cumberland House, in a key position on the Indians' forest and river routes. The Hudson's Bay Company's trader Matthew Cocking had first located this site during an inland journey to examine the spread of Pedlar influence. But Cumberland House had been constructed too late. For great fur-trade figures, such as the Frobisher brothers, Alexander Henry, James Finlay, and above all Peter Pond, were already pushing deep into the west.

Pond had drifted from the fur forests south of the Great Lakes to join in the rush into the Saskatchewan Valley. He had heard accounts of a very rich fur country farther north. In 1778, he decided to try the trek himself. He took four canoes and a few French-Canadian *voyageurs* (travelers), the superb woodsmen and canoeists who made up the main labor force of the Canadian fur trade. They reached a point some 40 miles south of Lake Athabasca before the rivers froze.

Pond became, then, a major contributor in opening up the northwest's richest fur country. He also tried making maps of the entire Athabasca region, and became the first fur man to learn the value of *pemmican,* the dried and pounded buffalo meat that was easily transported, and that kept indefinitely.

When the other Pedlars realized that the riches of Athabasca meant plenty of furs for all, they began thinking of transforming their competition into a cooperation. By 1783, the arrangements were made, and the North West Company came into being. But Pond backed off, returning to the United States with his maps of Athabasca and a dream of discovery. As an American, he wanted the new United States Con-

Above: a French Canadian voyageur. The term *voyageur*, meaning a traveler, was used to describe the trappers who hunted in the wilderness. It was also used in New France to describe trappers who operated without a licence. The King of France granted rights to men to engage in the fur trade and these men, in turn, had the right to hire voyageurs to do the actual trapping for them.

Right: a list from the York Factory account book of 1714—1715, which sets out approved trading prices for various commodities. This shows an early attempt that was made to bring some organization to the fur trade.

346

gress to subsidize him on an expedition that would search for a route from Athabasca over the mountains to the Pacific. But the Canadian northwest must have seemed too far away, then, to interest the young republic; Pond was turned down. He returned to Canada, joined the North West Company, and moved back into Athabasca.

The Northwesters called themselves "Lords of the Lakes and Forests," and usually made good their boast. Every fall, fleets of birchbark canoes, paddled by tireless French voyageurs, fanned out across the whole of the Canadian West. They moved south of Superior to challenge American traders, and near Hudson Bay to challenge the British company. And when the Canadian explorer Alexander Mackenzie had shown the way, they moved out and beyond the Rockies to the Pacific coast.

Meanwhile, in Athabasca, Pond found another famous fur trader, Peter Pangman, who headed a rival company. Pangman sent a group to build a post near Pond's in order to drain off some of the American's trade. One of Pangman's men was killed in a fight with Pond's employees. This alerted the rival traders to the danger of the new rivalry, which could easily have degenerated into a shooting war. As a result, in 1787, the North West Company talked the Pangman group into an amalgamation under the North West Company title. Among the new members was a young Scot who had been Pangman's man in the Churchill area, and who was now sent to complete his fur-trade education with Peter Pond in Athabasca. His name was Alexander Mackenzie,

Above: a painting by Samuel Hearne of Prince of Wales Fort, Manitoba. This was the earliest fort built by the Hudson's Bay Company and became the prototype for those built later. It was surrounded by a stockade (a line of stout posts firmly set into the ground) which protected the buildings from Indian attack.

Left: Sir Alexander Mackenzie (1764?—1820), Scottish-born Canadian explorer. In 1789 he made a remarkable journey from Fort Chipewyan along the Great Slave Lake and down the river—later called the Mackenzie River — to the Arctic. Three years later he crossed the Rocky Mountains from Fort Chipewyan to Cape Menzies, reaching the Pacific coast overland.

Right: an outer trading station at Moose Factory, in the lowlands of Ontario, bordering James Bay. This is a typical inland station and show fortifications built to protect Hudson's Bay Company men stationed away from company strongholds.

a man in his early twenties who was experienced in the fur trade and fired with restlessness and ambition.

Pond shortly went east to face trial for his alleged involvement with the killing. He was acquitted, but the stain on his name drove him from Canada in 1790. Before he left, though, he had told Mackenzie about the areas of the northwest. Mackenzie soaked up Pond's geographical knowledge, studied his laboriously scrawled maps, and was infected by his obsessive belief in the existence of a route to the Pacific.

In 1789, Mackenzie set off from Fort Chipewyan on Lake Athabasca to lead a group of French Canadians into the north. Fiercely cold weather (though it was June) and ice on the waterways slowed his progress through the Slave Lake region. But in a few weeks, he had crossed the Great Slave Lake itself, leaving it by way of a very wide and terrifyingly swift river. On July 12, he and his men were swept into the tidewaters of the Arctic Ocean. Mackenzie had hoped the river would lead him to the Pacific. As Hearne had done, he retraced his steps

filled only with disappointment and with no sense of achievement.

When Mackenzie returned to Fort Chipewyan, other disappointments awaited him. New navigational measurements which had been compiled at Fort Chipewyan indicated that the Athabasca region was a great deal farther away from the Pacific than Pond or Mackenzie had realized. Mackenzie felt that he needed better preparation for another attempt. He took some leave from his Northwester duties, and went back to Britain to improve his geographic and navigational education.

In 1792, Mackenzie again left Fort Chipewyan to explore. This time he led a group of six voyageurs, two Indians, and a Scot named Mackay. When they approached the Peace River, they began to travel westward by canoe. After having gone some distance, Mackenzie chose a place for a winter camp to wait until the thaw. While there, he asked the local Indians about the western mountains. His men spent their time building a special birchbark canoe, which was 25 feet long and

Above: the Rockies, a chain of
mountains—in places 350 miles
wide—extending 3,000 miles down
western North America, from northern
Alaska to northern New Mexico.
Several rivers have their source in the
Rocky Mountains, among them the
Columbia, Missouri, Arkansas,
Colorado, and the Rio Grande.

Left: copper kettles and blankets such as these were among the most common articles which the Hudson's Bay Company traded with the Indians.

4 feet 6 inches at the beam. It could carry 3,000 pounds of supplies and equipment and 10 people. Yet, empty, it was light enough to be carried by two men on a *portage* (French for "carriage," which came to mean carrying a boat overland). Mackenzie and his men embarked in this canoe toward the Rocky Mountains in May, 1793.

On paper, Mackenzie's plan seemed simple. He intended to work up to the headwaters of the Peace River in the Rockies, and then seek out a navigable river flowing down the mountains on the westward side. But unexpected difficulties arose. The current of the river was so strong that it taxed every ounce of the voyageurs' strength and canoemanship. The new canoe leaked, causing delays for extra caulking, and the Indians seemed unhappy and likely to desert at any time.

As the days passed, it became harder and harder to make their way up the river. At times the voyageurs had to force the heavy canoe through rocky cascading rapids, or portion out the cargo into enormous packs, staggering on portages through tangled forests and over dangerously steep slopes. It was not long, though, before the mountains were sighted. This encouraged Mackenzie, but he had believed that the Rockies stood like a single wall which sloped down to level ground on the west side. When the expedition clawed its way up to the narrow headwaters of the Peace, they found instead that these mountains were only the most easterly of a series of parallel ranges, with mile after mile of jagged granite peaks and crags.

Near the Peace River's head, Mackenzie found that it was formed by two streams, known today as the Finlay and the Parsnip. The Finlay seemed to be flowing in the right direction and to be the least torrential. But an Indian had told him that the other stream, though apparently flowing from the south, would later turn in the direction he wanted. Mackenzie took the chance and chose the Parsnip.

Several days of slow progress followed because of the powerful stream currents. Mackenzie had also been warned, by Indian friends, of nearby tribes who might be dangerous. But the first mountain Indians they met were poor Sekani, half-starved and terrified at their first sight of white men. Mackenzie soon won their confidence with food and gifts, and began asking about the river route ahead. One Sekani had heard of a great waterway to the west, which seemed accessible by a short march from the Parsnip's head. Encouraged by this news, the group struggled on up the Parsnip. They were cold and exhausted, but they were not too tired to realize that they had crossed the Great Divide (the highland in North America that separates waters flowing into the Atlantic from those flowing into the Pacific). From that time on any river they traveled would flow westward and they would be traveling with the current.

They soon found their way by a short portage to a narrow waterway that flowed frighteningly fast and was cluttered by trees and rocks. Hidden sandbars added further dangers, and even the voyageurs' skill was not enough to avoid them all. Their canoe finally struck a sandbar, ricocheted onto rocks, and was seriously damaged. Men and cargo were spilled into the torrent. They were luckily washed up into

Above: the type of fast-flowing, tree- and rock-strewn river which the early explorers forced their way along as a matter of routine.
Below: an Indian salmon trap. Such traps take advantage of the fact that salmon swimming upstream can freely enter the first line of nets, but once inside they are unable either to go past the second line of nets and escape upstream, or return the way they have come.

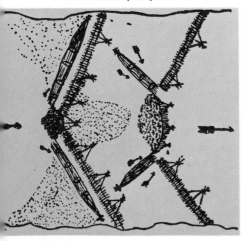

shallow water, and no one was drowned. But most of the stores had been lost, including all of their ammunition.

Every shred of Mackenzie's leadership was needed to raise the morale of his men. He had his group hastily patch the canoe, which was to carry some of the men and part of the remaining stores down the river. The others hacked their way about two miles a day through the tangle of mountain bush. By June 17, they had forced their way to the banks of the great river mentioned by the Sekani.

In better spirits, the company swept down the new river and found it was tributary to a still greater waterway known now as the Fraser. Mackenzie had no idea what lay ahead of him in the mountain canyons of that river. But he was more concerned just then with the local Indians. He had seen houses, salmon traps, and other signs of Indian habitation. He soon found that these tribes, called Carriers, were as warlike as they were civilized. The first band of Carriers that Mackenzie met threatened his party with death if they landed. Mackenzie promptly landed—by himself, and unarmed.

His courage impressed the Indians; they let him approach, and they listened to what he had to say. Within a short time, he won them over and delighted them with gifts of trinkets. They conducted him to their camp, and told him fearful tales of the Fraser River's impassable rapids and the perpendicular rock walls of its canyons. They also told him of fierce Indians along those canyons who killed strangers first and inquired about them afterward. But Mackenzie suspected exaggeration, and was stubbornly determined to go on.

When he returned to the river, he met another band of Indians, who were more friendly but just as full of dire warnings about the river. Mackenzie considered continuing overland, partly because his great canoe had been so badly damaged. But he delayed his decision and continued downriver until July 4, encountering frequent rains and clouds of tormenting sandflies along the way.

By then the treacheries of the Fraser had begun to make themselves known, so the group took to the land and cached the canoe and a supply of pemmican on the riverside. They plodded for 10 days in the face of grueling scrambles up the steep sides of the Coast Ranges, while their food supply and their energy were rapidly diminishing. They stumbled through a hailstorm and through drifting snow in a mountain pass; they slid down into a valley and found it clogged with forest. But their luck finally changed when they met up with some Bella Coola Indians, who fed them with salmon and told them in sign language that the river flowing past their village led to salt water. Mackenzie had come far closer to the sea than he had dared to dream.

The Indians provided Mackenzie and his men with two canoes, and the party returned to the river once more. A day later they reached over the sides of their canoes to find that the water was salty. They were in a narrow fiord-like inlet (North Bentinck Arm). Gulls flew overhead, and the men saw porpoises and seals in the water. Mackenzie was torn between his desire to reach the open sea and the pressing need to begin the return trip as quickly as possible. For food supplies were running low, and it was a long way back to Fort Chipewyan.

Mackenzie was also nervous about some Bella Bella Indians camped in the inlet whom he believed to have been ill-treated by some seafaring fur traders. He had heard that, as a result, they were hostile toward the white man. This soon proved to be true, for the Indians began to harass Mackenzie's men, steal from their camp, and threaten an all-out attack. At one point, while Mackenzie was on land alone, several of them rushed him with spears. But they stopped and backed away when he coolly raised his gun.

Above: a Plains Indian *parflêche* (an envelope made from dried rawhide) used to store pemmican. Pemmican was made of diced lean meat, dried in the sun, pounded, and mixed into a paste with melted fat. Sometimes flavored with berries, pemmican would keep indefinitely in these containers.

Although Mackenzie kept the threatened Indian attack from materializing, it was clear that he had to leave the inlet for home. So the group returned upstream to the friendly Bella Coolas, and then marched back over their former path to their cached canoe. In better spirits now, and with their food stores replenished, the men rapidly forced their way up the Fraser and its tributary. Not even their extreme weariness, the numbing cold of the water, or an unexplained injury to Mackenzie's ankle could hold them up.

On August 16, they crossed the Great Divide, and soon portaged

their way to the Peace River. The weather was warm, great buffalo herds grazed beside the river banks, and the current swirled their canoe at high speed toward Lake Athabasca. In one day they had covered a distance that had taken them seven days to travel going the other way.

On August 24, in a flurry of flag-waving and rifle fire, Mackenzie's group swept up to Fort Chipewyan. Fifteen hundred miles behind them lay the evidence of the first overland crossing of the continent, a rock bearing the following inscription: "Alex. Mackenzie from Canada by land 22d July 1793."

Left: Canada, with the vast northwest highlighted in green, showing the routes of the men who explored there in the years between 1650 and 1811.

Above: Mackenzie's Rock, commemorating the first overland crossing of the continent. The rock bears the inscription: "Alex. Mackenzie from Canada by land 22d July 1793."

355

Corps of Discovery
3

President Thomas Jefferson may have been startled when France offered the whole of the Louisiana Territory for sale in 1803, but he was far from unprepared. In 1792, he had been instrumental in sending a French scientist westward up the Missouri River, although nothing concrete had developed from that journey. Then, a few months before his envoy went to Paris to discuss Louisiana, Jefferson had quietly directed his private secretary to undertake certain studies. These included geography, navigation, and other subjects that would be needed on an exploring trip to the Pacific.

Jefferson's private secretary was a man named Meriwether Lewis, a 29-year-old Virginian, frontiersman, and soldier. He had served in the army in Ohio with a former Army captain and friend, William Clark. They had enormous respect for each other as soldiers and woodsmen, and were now going to work together again as partners for Jefferson. The two were to share joint command of the expedition, though, in fact, Lewis became the overall leader.

News of the Louisiana Purchase speeded up their preparations. Lewis had copies of most of the available maps of the northwest, which included those of Captain Vancouver and Alexander Mackenzie. He had abundant supplies and equipment ready, among which was a collapsible canoe he had invented himself (but which turned out to be impracticable). Boatbuilders were adapting—to Lewis' designs—a 55-foot keelboat, which could be sailed, rowed, poled like a raft, or, as a last resort, towed from the riverbank. The boat carried two wooden canoe-like rowing boats called pirogues. In addition, it was to hold instruments, weapons and ammunition, tools, provisions, spare clothing, 21 bales of goods for trading with Indians, and more than 40 men.

Lewis recruited some of his men in Pittsburgh, and took them down the Ohio River in August, 1803, to join Clark. The trip was interrupted by the usual obstacles of river travel such as shallows, fogs, and squalls. But in late October they reached Louisville, where they picked up Clark and his Negro servant, York.

Clark had done some recruiting, too. A group of tough young Kentuckians had signed on, of whom the brothers Reuben and Joseph Field were the most outstanding frontiersmen. But the expedition's most valuable acquisition was George Drouillard, half French and half Shawnee, an expert with a rifle, as well as being a scout, a tracker, and a woodsman. He made even the Field brothers seem like novices. Aside from a few French-Canadian rivermen who were to run

Below: (right) Meriwether Lewis (1774—1809) and (left) William Clark (1770—1838), leaders of the first United States overland expedition to the Pacific. From May, 1804 to September, 1806, the expedition covered over 4,000 miles, meeting Indian tribes never previously seen by white men, and keeping a valuable record of scientific observations. Despite the hardships and exposure they suffered, only one man died on the expedition. Lewis was made governor of northern Louisiana in 1807. Clark was made superintendent of Indian affairs at St. Louis in 1807 and territorial governor of Missouri in 1813.

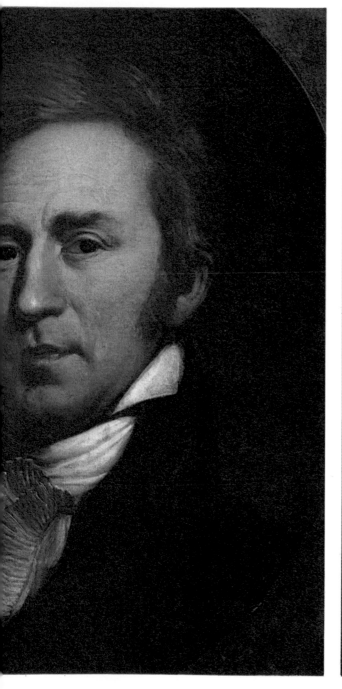

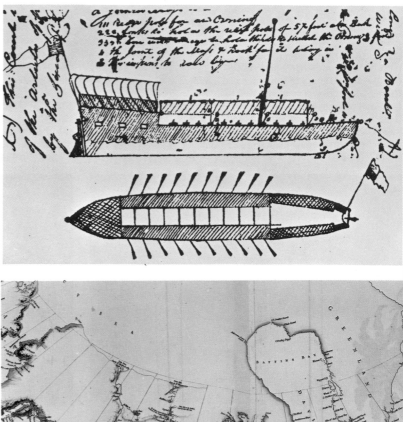

Above right: sketch from the "Field Notes" of Captain William Clark, showing the expedition's Missouri River keelboat. A keelboat is a long, shallow craft, pointed at both ends, which is either sailed, rowed, poled, or towed from the riverbank.

Below right: a map of America by Aaron Arrowsmith dated 1804. This would have been the type of map taken on the expedition and shows how little information was available at the time. The western part of the continent is almost completely blank, with only a theoretical range of mountains sketched in to the west of the Mississippi River.

the boat, the remainder of the expedition's strength was made up of regular soldiers.

Jefferson had made it clear to Lewis that his job would be to explore the upper Missouri region for a water route linking with the Columbia River; to make maps and charts of the river and its valleys; to contact the Indians of the region; and to examine the soil and the animal and plant life. In other words, the exploration was to be of a scientific nature.

In late 1803, Lewis and Clark took their men and their boat up the Mississippi to St. Louis, where they spent the winter. Waiting for spring and for the formal transfer of Louisiana to the United States, Lewis remained in St. Louis to attend to diplomatic business while Clark took the party up the river to St. Charles. Clark wrote the following description of St. Charles: "This village is about one mile in length, situated on the North Side of the Missourie at the foot of a hill from which it takes its name *Peetiete Coete* or the *Little hill*. This Village Contns about 100 houses, the most of them small and indefferent and about 450

Below: a lithograph by Felix Achille St. Aulaire showing a keelboat under sail on the Mississippi in 1832.

inhabitents Chiefly French, those people appear Pore, polite & harmonious."

On May 21, 1804, after Lewis had joined the party, the keelboat was launched on the Missouri. As Clark wrote in the journal: "All the forepart of the Day arranging our party and procureing the different articles necessary for them at this place. Set out at half passed three oClock under three Cheers from the gentlemen on the bank and proceeded on to the head of the Island (which is Situated on the Stbd. Side) 3 miles. Soon after we Set out to day a hard Wind from the W. S. W. accompanied with a hard rain, which lasted with Short intervales all night."

Clark managed to push the boat on the average 15 miles a day, while Lewis wandered the shore making scientific observations. In late

Below: Sioux Indians moving camp. The Indians of the Sioux tribe became well-known for their courage and fighting ability and were particularly feared by the early explorers because of their ferocity.

May, they reached La Charrette, the most westerly fragment of civilization on the river. Beyond that tiny settlement lay the unknown wilderness.

By July, they were deep into wild Indian country, but had not met up with any Indians. Then, during a halt at the junction with the Platte River, Drouillard came in from hunting accompanied by a Missouri Indian. A few days later a large company of Oto and Missouri came to visit. Lewis spoke to the assemblage about the United States control of Louisiana and the need for peace between Indians and Americans. And he was delighted and encouraged by the Indians' cordial acceptance of these sentiments. But Lewis also knew that the unpredictable Sioux were out there, too, and might not receive him so cordially. He made an attempt to invite the Sioux for a gathering: "We set the Praries on fire as a signal for the Soues to Come to the River," but there was no response. Drouillard, though, encountered some Omaha Indians, and through them Lewis made contact with the Sioux nation. On August 31 (at Council Bluffs), he opened his first council with the most feared Indians in the Missouri country.

Lewis saw little of the legendary ferocity of the Sioux in this first contact, and the expedition parted from the Indians on the best of terms. But Lewis kept his perspective. He had originally planned to send his soldiers back to St. Louis in the pirogues in the autumn, but now he decided to keep them where they were for the winter, in case of Indian

hostilities. Besides, extra hands were needed to prepare their winter camp.

For a while, the Corps spent some idyllic days, hunting the abundant autumn game, while Lewis was happily engrossed with natural history. He wrote about his observations in great detail: "Having for many days past confined myself to the boat, I determined to devote this day to amuse myself on shore with my gun and view the interior of the country lying between the river and the Corvus Creek.... One quarter of a mile in rear of our camp which was situated in a fine open grove of cotton wood passed a grove of plumb trees loaded with fruit and now ripe, observed but little difference between this fruit and that of similar kind common to the Atlantic States... a great number of wolves of the small kind, halks [hawks] and some pole-cats were to be seen... to the West a high range of hills, strech across the country from N. to S. and appeared distant about 20 miles; they are not very extensive as I could plainly observe their rise and termination no rock appeared on them and the sides were covered with virdue similar to that of the plains this senery already rich pleasing and beatiful was still farther hightened by immence herds of Buffaloe, deer, Elk, and Antelopes which we saw in every direction feeding on the hills and plains."

But the mood was shattered by the keelboat's approach to another Sioux camp, which turned out to be far from peaceable. When Lewis tried to begin a council, the chiefs reacted with suspicion and belligerence. He made an attempt to change their attitudes by inviting them to the keelboat for gifts of whiskey, but to no avail. Clark escorted the chiefs back to shore in a pirogue, and at that point the warriors menacingly surrounded the boat. Clark could not return, they said, until further gifts were made and more respects were paid to the Sioux leaders. No one knows whether the Indians were just testing the white man's mettle or actually planning violence. But Lewis and Clark handled the moment perfectly with calm and counter-threat. Clark, alone on the beach, drew his sword and stood firm. On the keelboat, Lewis ordered his riflemen to the ready, but withheld the order to fire. And the Sioux, with spears and arrows against rifles, backed down and released the pirogue. Clark related this incident in the journal as follows: "Met in Council at 12 oClock and after Smokeing, Cap. Lewis proceeded to Deliver a Speech which we (were) oblige(d) to Curtail for want of a good interpreter ....

"Envited those Cheifs on board to Show them our boat and such

Above: an Azimuth compass of about 1770, a surveyor's compass of the type available to Lewis and Clark. Below: a pocket sextant made in the late 1700's. Using a compass, a sextant, and a watch, the explorers were able to make rough maps, chart rivers, and fix their positions.

Left: an illustration showing
Captain Clark and his men building
a line of huts, from "a journal of
the voyages and travels of a corps
of discovery, under the Command of
Captain Lewis and Captain Clark of
the Army of the United States, from
the mouth of the River Missouri
through the Interior parts of North
America to the Pacific Ocean during
the years 1804, 1805, and 1806,''
by Patrick Gass, published in 1807.

Curiossities as was Strange to them, we gave them ¼ a glass of whiskey which they appeared to be verry fond of, Sucked the bottle after it was out & Soon began to be troublesom, one the 2d Cheif assumeing Drunkness, as a Cloake for his rascally intentions I went with those Cheifs *(in one of the Perogues with 5 men—3 & 2 Inds.)* (which left the boat with great reluctiance) to Shore with a view of reconsileing those men to us, as Soon as I landed the Perogue three of their young Men Seased the Cable of the Perogue, *(in which we had pressents &c)* the Cheifs Soldr. Huged the mast, and the 2d Chief was verry insolent both in words & justures *(pretended Drunkenness & Staggered up against me)* declareing I should not go on, Stateing he had not receved presents sufficent from us, his justures were of Such a personal nature I felt My self Compeled to Draw my Sward *(and Made a Signal to the boat to prepare for action)* at this Motion Capt. Lewis ordered all under arms in the boat, those with me also Showed a Disposition to Defend themselves and me, the grand Chief then took hold of the roap & ordered the young Warrers away, I felt My Self warm & Spoke in verry positive terms.

"Most of the Warriers appeared to have ther Bows strung and took out their arrows from the quiver. as I *(being surrounded)* was not permited to return, I Sent all the men except 2 Inps. [Interpreters] to the boat, the perogue Soon returned with about 12 of our determined men ready for any event. this movement caused a no: of the Indians to withdraw at a distance, Their treatment to me was verry rough & I think justified roughness on my part, they all lift [left] my Perogue, and Councild with themselves the result I could not lern and nearly all went off after remaining in this Situation Some time I offered my hand to the 1. & 2. Chiefs who refusd. to receve it. I turned off & went with my men on board the perogue, I had not prosd. more the [than] 10 paces before the 1st Cheif 3rd & 2nd Brave Men Waded in after me. I took them in & went on board.

"We proceeded on about 1 Mile & anchored out off a Willow Island placed a guard on Shore to protect the Cooks & a guard in the boat, fastened the Perogue to the boat, I call this Island bad humered Island as we were in a bad Humer."

For a while the Sioux seemed pacified, even friendly. But a flurry of trouble arose again when Lewis finally decided to set sail. For the Sioux had been piratically terrorizing river traders and they did not want a powerful force of white men so deep within their country. But again the explorers' combination of coolness and firepower kept

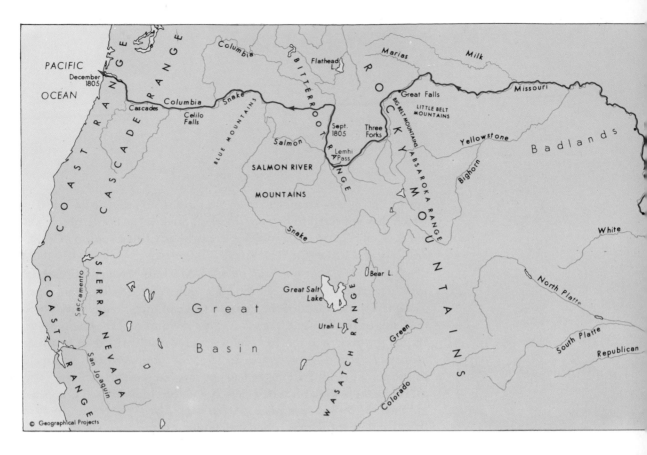

the Indians from starting a fight. As a result, peace had been preserved, and the Corps of Discovery sailed on.

Because the weather had turned cold, windy, and wet, a winter campsite was urgently needed. One was found on Mandan country by the time of the first snow, and its construction was begun in November. A stout log cantonment called Fort Mandan was soon put up, and the Corps settled in for the tedious winter wait.

There were some minor diversions during those winter months such as hunting parties, Christmas festivities, and the like. Lewis made contact occasionally with North West Company fur traders, among them being Antoine Larocque, probably the first white man to explore into the Yellowstone River Valley. Of more importance, though, was a freelance French trader who joined the Corps. He brought with him two Indian wives. One of them, a Shoshoni girl (Sacagawea), was later to prove to be of help to the expedition.

When spring freed the keelboat from river ice, Lewis sent it back east with some of the soldiers. The narrowing river demanded smaller craft, and so the Corps, with Mandan help, made six dugout canoes to supplement the two pirogues. On April 7, 1805, Lewis and Clark and about 30 men moved out again northwestward.

"So far," Lewis wrote in a letter at this time, "we have experienced more difficulty from the navigation of the Missouri than danger from the savages...." And those difficulties worsened as they passed into Dakota badlands, where even fur traders had not traveled. But by late

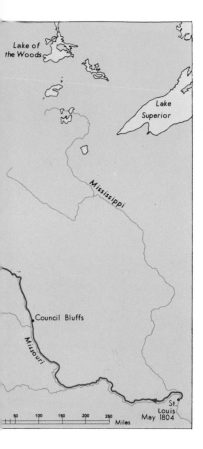

Above: the route followed by the Lewis and Clark expedition westward from St. Louis across the Great Divide to the coast of the Pacific.

April they had reached the junction with the Yellowstone River, which was located in rugged foothill country. This region held some animals which were strange to them: mountain sheep, mules, deer, and grizzly bears. The Corps had heard terrifying tales of the ferocious bears; they soon found them to be no exaggeration. When Clark and Drouillard were hunting, they encountered a grizzly that pursued them back to the river even though the hunters had shot the bear several times before it died. Later, another grizzly chased six hunters out of the forest and into the river in spite of eight bullet wounds.

While bears were keeping the hunters busy, the Missouri was occupying the rivermen. On a number of occasions, squalls nearly upset the canoes. The strengthening current forced the men to give up rowing and turn to towing. And, in June, the Corps reached a fork in the river, for which they had been entirely unprepared. They had no idea which branch to take. Clark decided to explore a short distance up the northern branch while Lewis took the other. Their men felt that the northern branch (which Lewis called the Marie River, now the Marias) was more navigable than the other. Understandably, they clamored that it was the true Missouri. Lewis was convinced otherwise. But the expedition's esprit de corps showed itself when the men followed Lewis without a murmur even though they disagreed with him. Lewis was very soon proved right, though, for the boats came within earshot of the Great Falls, which they knew were a feature of the true Missouri. In Lewis' words: "I retired to the shade of a tree where I determined to fix my

Right: an American explorer up a tree to escape a bear. Clark originally reported that the stories of the ferociousness of the grizzly bear were exaggerated. However, on further acquaintance he found the tales were true and that the grizzly would attack without provocation.

Above: a scene, showing a typical camp in the moonlight, which became part of the legend of the West. For almost a hundred years from the time of Lewis and Clark, such scenes were enacted nightly in the wilderness.

camp for the present and dispatch a man in the morning to inform Capt. C. and the party of my success in finding the falls and settle in their minds all further doubts as to the Missouri."

They began a grueling portage around the 90-foot cascade. Lewis, roaming the countryside as usual, almost idly shot a buffalo for camp meat—and very idly neglected to reload. In nearly cost him his life, for out of nowhere came a grizzly bear at full charge. Lewis ran for the river while trying to reload, but the bear was gaining on him too rapidly. His only weapon was his *espontoon* (a short pike widely used at that time). At the water's edge, Lewis clutched it and turned to face the onrush of the grizzly. For no good reason the bear stopped short, and then wheeled and galloped off into the bush. And Lewis, puzzled but hardly shaken, reloaded his gun and wandered peacefully back to the camp at the Falls.

There he found his men making a crude wagon to carry the boats on the portage. They had to repair the wagon constantly, because deep mud and rough ground weakened its structure. But finally, in mid-July, the back-breaking, 18-mile detour was over, and the Corps went back on the river to force their way up into the Rocky Mountains.

The expedition now found itself in the country of the Shoshoni (or Snake) Indians, the people of Sacagawea, the wife of the French trader. But though there were plenty of signs of Indians, they still had not met up with mountain Indians from whom they needed advice about travel through the Rockies. Lewis and Clark had been shocked, as Mackenzie was, to find that the Rockies were not a single wall of mountains. They still believed that the Columbia headwaters would be waiting for them, after a short overland trek across the Continental or Great Divide.

By late July, they had reached another expected landmark, the Missouri's Three Forks. They camped there for some time in order to rest the men who were worn out from towing the boats against the shallow but violent mountain stream. As was written in the journal: "The men were so much fortiegued today that they wished much that navigation was at an end that they might go by land." But they continued on the southwest branch of the river (Lewis called it the Jefferson). Lewis, with Drouillard and others, left the party, to forge ahead on land and look for the Shoshoni. They roamed the river valley for days while Clark and the others dragged the boats up the now unnavigable stream. Soon the Jefferson itself forked, and Lewis thought that the boats would never be able to pass that point. He also realized that the Corps had climbed high up into the mountains, and had come near to the source of the Missouri and the Great Divide: "the mountains do not appear very high in any direction tho' the tops of some of them are partially covered with snow. this convinces me that we have ascended to a great hight since we have entered the rocky Mountains, yet the ascent had been so gradual along the vallies that it was scarcely perceptable by land." In fact, two more days of climbing and wandering brought Lewis through what is now known as Lemhi Pass. He found a rivulet on the other side, and was ecstatically convinced that it fed directly into the Columbia. Unfortunately, the river was not navigable. Now the need for Indian help grew even more desperate. The day after crossing the Divide, Lewis met a band of Shoshoni.

Drouillard was sent to bring back Clark and the rest of the company with all possible speed. When they arrived, it was discovered that the leader of the Shoshoni band was Sacagawea's brother. On account of this family connection, the Corps acquired anything they wanted from the tribe, such as horses, some Shoshoni guides, and information

Above: this picture of the San Juan mountains, Colorado, shows the gradual slopes by which they can be climbed. The explorers were surprised at the heights they attained without being aware that they had been climbing.

Right: a mural by E. S. Paxon shows Sacagawea pointing out the country of her childhood to Lewis and Clark at Three Forks, western Montana.

about westward routes. Because of the oncoming August frosts and autumn snows, the expedition hastily left the Shoshoni to continue their journey.

They cached their canoes and some equipment on the Jefferson River, and then struggled off on heavily laden horses over underbrush-choked mountain trails looking for navigable water. But in September they decided to turn north to the Bitterroot Valley in order to strike an Indian trail described by the Shoshoni. The trail was rocky and precipitous; horses crippled themselves and some even fell down the slopes. The hunting grew poor and the men grew hungry. Once or twice the men killed and ate one of the more useless horses; the rest of the time they ate leftover bits of bear grease, scraps of corn, or nothing. They were now 6,000 to 7,000 feet up, and on September 16, they suffered the first heavy snowfall of the mountain winter, which caught them on a rugged and treacherous ridge: "began to Snow about 3 hours before Day and continued all day the Snow in the morning 4 inches deep... at 12 oClock we halted on the top of the mountain to worm and dry our Selves a little as well as to let our horses rest and graze a little on Some long grass which I observed, I have been wet and as cold in every part as I ever was in my life, indeed I was at one time fearful

my feet would freeze in the thin Mockirsons which I wore."

They soon found before them lower, less rugged terrain, and a creek which they were sure would lead to the Columbia River. A headlong descent by the starving, weakened men brought them to a hospitable Nez Percé camp, where the Indians fed them on dried salmon. Here the weather was warmer and game more plentiful.

After they had been fed and had rested, the Corps began to travel again. Within a few days they had reached the Clearwater River, a tributary of the Snake which led to the Columbia. On October 7, they

Right: a typical peril of river travel is shown in this illustration from Patrick Gass's Journal of 1807. The canoe has struck a tree and overturned, spilling the occupants out into the swirling water of the river.

Right: when the Corps of Discovery
finally reached the estuary of the
Columbia River it was this shoreline
that confronted them—the Oregon
coast, which stretches from the
Columbia River in the north to
California in the south.

Above: a sketch map by Clark showing
the mouth of the Columbia River, from
the original journals of the Lewis
and Clark expedition 1804—1806.

embarked in their canoes on the river. They battled through the rapids
without pause and stopped only briefly to buy fish and dog meat from
riverside Indians.

From the Clearwater they paddled into the Snake River, which had
even more rapids. But Lewis refused to hesitate. He even ordered his
men to run the risk of rocks and cascades rather than make a portage.
Several times canoes overturned and sank, but always, miraculously,
the men in them survived. They managed to salvage the canoes, repair
them, and keep going.

On October 16, almost without warning, the canoemen found themselves on the broad waters of the Columbia, rushing toward the sea:
"after getting Safely over the rapid and haveing taken Diner Set out
and proceeded on Seven miles to the junction of this river and the Columbia which joins from the N.W. In every direction from the junction
of those rivers the country is one continued plain low and rises from
the water gradually, except a range of high Countrey on the opposit
Side about 2 miles distant from the Collumbia." They were continually
held up because of the rapids and dangerous stretches of water which
ran through the Cascade Mountains. And yet Lewis and Clark urged
their men on because of the approaching winter.

When they reached the Narrows of the Columbia, Lewis saw the
water "boiling and whorling in every direction" over jagged rocks,
but the impatient Corps flung their canoes through the obstacles,
without any damaging effects. A longer portage then had to be made
around the ferocious waters of the Cascades. Needless to say, the men
resented the waste of another few days. By early November, though,
the Cascades were behind them; they had overcome the last mountain
obstacle and were moving through tidewater.

Within a few days, the river widened into a broad bay. The Corps
thought (mistakenly) that they could see the Pacific. "Ocian in view!
O, the joy!" wrote Clark in his journal, but that joy turned to misery
when rough water and torrential rain drove them to camp under the
bay's sheer cliffs. They huddled there for days, with their soaked
buckskin shirts rotting on their backs, until quieter weather allowed
them to embark again. Within a short time, they had paddled into the
Columbia's estuary, with the open sea almost anticlimactically spread
before them.

Later, while a spot for a winter camp was being chosen, Clark carved
on a pine tree a message that consciously echoed Alexander Mackenzie:

Above: one of the great successes of
the Lewis and Clark expedition was
the friendly relationship it maintained with the majority of the
Indian tribes it encountered. Clark
particularly had a special gift for
dealing with the Indians and he
remained an "ambassador" to and for
Indians long after the expedition.

Right: "The Captive Charger" by the
American artist Charles F. Wimar,
records one of the many hazards that
Lewis and Clark, like other explorers,
had to face—the fact that the
Indians were immensely interested
(often in an acquisitive way) in their
belongings, especially their horses.

"William Clark, December 3rd, 1805. By land from the U. States in 1804 and 1805."

Wintering on the coast brought rain, boredom, and swarms of curious Chinook Indians. Needless to say, the men were all delighted to start out on the return trip. Before leaving for home, though, the party distributed some lists of their names to the Indians in the area. The object of such lists was stated as follows: "The object of this list is, that through the medium of some civilized person who may see the same, it may be made known to the informed world, that the party

Above: lithograph published by Julius Hutawa in St. Louis, Missouri, showing St. Louis in the mid-1800's. The small pictures around the edge show the principal buildings of the city at that time. Lying between the Appalachian Mountains and the Rockies. St. Louis is on the main course of the Mississippi. In 1806, when Lewis and Clark finally returned to St. Louis, it was a great fur-trading center. Picture by courtesy of the Chicago Historical Society.

consisting of the persons whose names are hereunto annexed, and who were sent out by the government of the U'States in May 1804 to explore the interior of the Continent of North America, did penetrate the same by way of the Missouri and Columbia Rivers, to the discharge of the latter into the Pacific Ocean, where they arrived on the 14th November 1805, and from whence they departed the [blank in MS] day of March, 1806 on their return to the United States by the same route they had come out."

On March 23, they began their fight upstream against the Columbia's swollen torrent, hugging the bank and portaging often. But in spite of all caution, their canoes suffered constant damage. And when they found the roaring narrows wholly impassable by water, they abandoned canoe travel and transferred their baggage to horses, which they acquired from the Indians.

Throughout April, they marched overland, painfully but steadily, toward the Clearwater River and the Bitterroot Valley beyond it. During the winter, Lewis and Clark had rightly decided that their original route, through Lemhi Pass, had taken them too far southward. Therefore, they intended to head straight across the mountains (overland) from the Bitterroot and, hopefully, to come to the Missouri in the vicinity of the Great Falls.

Friendly Nez Percé and Walla Walla Indians kept them supplied with food, a few extra horses, and information about adequate mountain trails. The march progressed with little drama, except for constant and careful negotiations for food and other assistance at various Indian villages. In late June, they reached the Bitterroot Valley and stopped to take stock.

They decided to divide the party and carry out some necessary explorations. Lewis, Drouillard, the Field brothers, and a few others were to set out on a likely route across the Divide, head straight for the Missouri, and then descend to the Great Falls. Lewis would leave a few men there, and turn north with the rest to explore the Marias River, the north branch of which had puzzled them before. Clark was to set out with his party south through the mountains to the Jefferson River. He would then send some men by water to the Great Falls and take the others overland to explore along the Yellowstone River.

Clark's party moved off on July 3, on a usable trail, and crossed the Continental Divide through Bozeman Pass to reach the Missouri's Three Forks. A sergeant took some men downriver to the Falls, while

Above: a medicine man of the Black-foot tribe. Medicine men knew a little simple medicine; they could set broken bones and understood the value of herbs. But most of their "medicine" was based on the Indian belief that illness was brought about by evil spirits and the medicine man's cures involved charms, incantations, magic rituals, and elaborate ceremonies. He would wear the mask of the particular spirit involved so that he could speak with the spirit directly himself.

Clark (whose group included Sacagawea) traveled easily over-land to the Yellowstone River. Their exploration proved un-eventful, except when some Crow Indians stole half of their horses. But the group managed comfortably to reach the Missouri again in early August.

Lewis and his party chose a suitable easterly trail that brought them over the Divide by a pass now called Lewis and Clark Pass. The Little Sun River then carried them down the Missouri. Toward late July, Lewis, Drouillard, and the Field boys set off up the Marias River, wondering whether it would bring them as far north as the Saskatchewan Valley. They were also wary because they had now entered the hunting ground of the notorious Blackfoot Indians.

Before the end of July, their fears proved justified, for they met up with a band of eight Piegans (one of the three main tribes of the Blackfoot Confederacy). The Piegans seemed cool but not hostile. Lewis rashly invited them to camp with his party and to hold council. During the night, however, the Blackfoot tried to steal the whites' rifles. A scuffle broke out as the explorers awoke. Reuben Field saw one Blackfoot running off with two of the rifles. Both Field boys were famous for their running and Reuben easily overtook the Indian. They fought, and Reuben killed the Blackfoot with his knife. The other Indians had raced out of the camp to drive off the whites' horses. Lewis and Drouillard ran after them, and a fight developed. Lewis shot an Indian, retreated to the camp, and quickly gathered his men. They were soon galloping at high speed for the Missouri. With only brief rests, the expedition traveled over 100 miles in the next 24 hours. There they met up with the soldiers awaiting them, and set off downriver, on July 28, to meet Clark near the mouth of the Yellowstone. They moved at top speed, for they knew a large force of Blackfoot would be scouring the region for them.

Lewis and the main body of the Corps met Clark's party in mid-August, and within a few days they re-entered Mandan country (what is now North Dakota). The return was eased by the mountain shortcuts, and they traveled 1,900 miles in less than five months.

On September 20, 1806, they paddled into La Charrette. Three days later, more than two years after the start of their 8,000-mile journey, the Lewis and Clark expedition made a triumphant entry into St. Louis: "we rose early took the Cheif to the public store & furnished him with Some clothes &c. took an early breckfast with Colo. Hunt

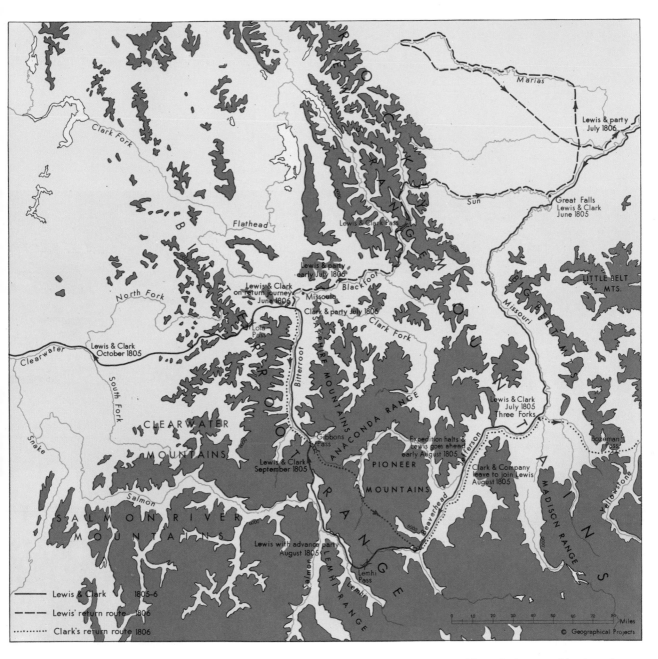

Detail from the journey of Lewis and
Clark, showing the separate routes
taken by the groups on their return
east through the mountains. The
green shows the lower-lying ground,
the brown the mountains themselves.

and Set out decended to the Mississippi and down that river to St. Louis
at which place we arived about 12 oClock. we Suffered the party to fire
off their pieces as a Salute to the Town. we were met by all the village
and received a harty welcom from it's inhabitants &c."

Lewis and Clark had not found a wholly manageable, all-water route
to the Pacific (i.e. a Northwest Passage), or anything remotely re-
resembling one. Like Alexander Mackenzie, they felt disappointed.
But they *had* found a northwest region vastly larger and richer than
anyone had visualized. Now, thanks to them, the United States knew
a great deal more about those invaluable lands, and proceeded to lay
claim to them. In the next four decades, swarms of explorers, traders,
and settlers were to spend their efforts consolidating that claim.

Edging Toward the Southwest

4

While Lewis and Clark were battling with the Missouri River in northwest Louisiana Territory, an expedition to blaze a trail into the southwest was being planned. It was to be led by a young army lieutenant named Zebulon M. Pike. The idea for the expedition arose out of a political situation contrived by two ambitious men.

When Louisiana had been formally purchased, an army general named James Wilkinson had been appointed its first governor, and commander of the western army. The general was an ambitious schemer and opportunist, as was Aaron Burr, a politician who had helped Wilkinson become governor. Burr may have had dreams of power that involved getting Spain and America into war, during which he hoped to peel off a piece of Spanish America as his own independent nation. Wilkinson found these plans parallel to his own, and knew that he was in an excellent position to implement them. He was the governor, and he was also in the pay of the Spanish—to inform them about any United States' threat to the southwest.

In order to further his ambitions of a possible takeover of the whole of Louisiana, Wilkinson decided to have the territory investigated

Left: deserted cliff dwellings common in the southwest, originally inhabited by Indians who proved particularly vulnerable to the white men.

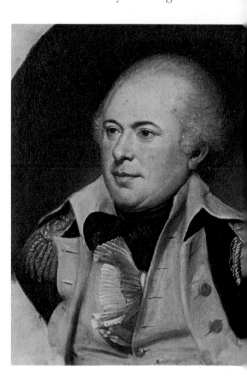

Right: James Wilkinson (1757–1825), American soldier and adventurer. He became governor of the part of Louisiana above the 33rd parallel in 1805. In his joint roles of army commander and governor, he attempted to fulfill his ambition to conquer Spain's Mexican provinces and to set up his own independent nation.

Above: Zebulon Pike (1779–1813), American explorer and soldier. He led the expedition which explored the upper Mississippi region in 1805. Then in 1806 he headed an expedition to the headwaters of the Arkansas and Red rivers. Pike was military agent in New Orleans in 1809–1810 and Deputy Quartermaster General in 1812. He saw active service in the War of 1812 and was killed by a falling rock as his victorious soldiers were breaking into a British garrison at York (now Toronto), Canada, in 1813.

in greater depth before exploring the southwest. For this reason, he first sent Pike north to find the source of the Mississippi and to locate likely sites for United States Army posts in the region. He was also to report on British fur trading there. In August, 1805, Pike began his trip up the Mississippi from a settlement near St. Louis. Pike wrote in his journal: "On the 9th day of August, 1805, the exploring party, consisting of Lieutenant Pike, one sergeant, two corporals and seventeen privates, left their encampment near St. Louis in a keelboat, seventy feet long, provisioned for four months; in order to make a survey of the river Mississippi to its source."

At that time Lewis and Clark were in Shoshoni country, struggling across the Rocky Mountains. By comparison, Pike's journey was uneventful. His meeting with Indians along the way proved satisfactory; even the Sioux treated him with courtesy.

Rain and fog brought discomfort and reminded them that winter was approaching. Therefore, in mid-October, Pike set his men to work on a winter camp near what is now Little Falls, Minnesota. By the time the camp was finished and provisioned, the river had begun to freeze. Pike had sleds made and in early December he and some of the men set off on foot along the river. Mishaps were frequent, but more or less trivial. The main problem was that sleds toppled into stretches of open water, or broke down. The journals of Pike's expedition reported the difficulties: "Whilst proceeding up the river, the foremost of the sleds, which contained all the ammunition, and the baggage of Mr. Pike, fell through the ice. The men had to get into the river, up to their middles in water, to recover the articles; and on an examination of them it was found that all their cartridges, and several pounds of battle powder [gun powder] was spoilt, what they happened to have in kegs was saved, or they must have given up... the voyage for want of the means of supplying themselves with provisions."

When the expedition had reached a fork in the upper Mississippi, Pike chose the branch now called Leech Lake River as being the true course to the source of the Mississippi. But he was proved wrong. For this branch led him to Leech Lake, when, in fact, the other branch led farther north to Lake Itasca, the river's true source. Of course, Pike was tracing a frozen river in mid-winter, with numerous small rivulets and obscure channels from which to choose. At that time, apparently only one white man, a trader named Morrison, had been to Lake Itasca, and he was not aware that it had any connection with the Mississippi.

Right: much of Pike's exploration was undertaken during the winter months in conditions such as these. Difficulties due to the unfamiliar terrain were made even more hazardous by the bitter mountain conditions and inadequate food supplies.

None of the Northwesters living in the area had been able to fix the source either. Therefore, Lake Itasca was left in obscurity until 1832 when H. R. Schoolcraft was finally to proclaim it as the Mississippi's origin and give it its current name.

Pike retraced his steps along the river, and on April 30th, 1806, the expedition floated into St. Louis. The journal account says: "At daylight on the morning of the 30th of April they reached the portage de Sioux, where Capt. Mancy's men were landed, and directed to march across the land to the cantonment. Mr. Pike walked through the village, which has not more than about twenty houses, built of squared logs. They arrived at Saint Louis about noon, after an absence of eight months and twenty two days," By then, Governor Wilkinson's plans for the southwest were beginning to come to a head.

The Spanish holdings in what is now the United States included Arizona, New Mexico, most of California and Texas, and parts of Utah, Colorado, Nevada, and Oklahoma. But then there were no fixed bound-

Above: Mandan Indians crossing the frozen Missouri. The Indian method of travel on frozen rivers was one of the skills that the white men were forced to learn. Although they did not travel in winter from choice, circumstances often made it necessary.

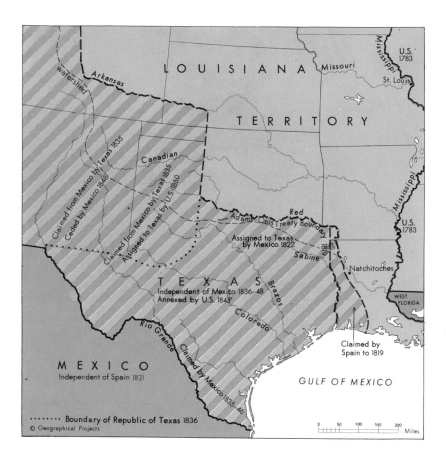

Above: the American flag of 1795, with
fifteen stripes and fifteen stars,
and the Spanish colonial flag of the
same period. The flags represent
the powers facing each other in the
southwest during Pike's explorations.

Above: the southwest of what is now
the United States and Mexico, showing
the disputed area between the Red
and Rio Grande rivers, where Pike
was exploring in the years 1806-1807.

aries, so that the enormous central and southern region where the South
Platte, Arkansas, and Red rivers flowed became violently disputed
territory. By the time Pike returned from the north, frontier tensions in this region had almost reached a state of war. Much of the conflict had been created by the explorers who had been sent to this
controversial territory by the President. For instance, in October, 1804,
Jefferson sponsored two scientists, William Dunbar and George
Hunter, on a voyage up the Red River. But hostile Indians had diverted
them to the Ouachita River (Ozark plateau), and in the end they covered
little ground and brought back information of secondary value. In 1806,
Jefferson tried again, sending an army captain named Sparks and a surveyor named Thomas Freeman with 37 men up the Red River. They
covered 600 miles before being turned back by the Spanish cavalry.

Wilkinson was now ready to explore the southwest of Louisiana.

He authorized Pike to form and lead this expedition. Pike was to look for the headwaters of the Red River, by way of the Arkansas. But his trip was to begin by escorting some Osage Indians to their home (on the Missouri-Kansas border) and to mediate in an Osage-Kansas Indian war. On no account, Pike's official orders said, was he to venture into Spanish territory. But it was likely that Wilkinson had given Pike additional, secret orders to look at as much of the Spanish southwest as he could.

Wilkinson informed the Spanish authorities that Pike was on his way into their territory. Undoubtedly he knew that Spanish soldiers would rush out to capture Pike. In this way, Pike would be certain to reach Santa Fe, though as a prisoner, and would then be able to do some close-range spying. Or his capture might create an international incident that would further the Wilkinson-Burr plans—or both. It seems

Above: Pawnee Indians migrating. The Indian tribes were moved about by both the Spanish and Americans whenever it suited the governments' convenience. Indian wars and Spanish/American rivalries were both occasions for voluntary or involuntary movement of the Indians.

Above: Pikes Peak, Colorado, found by Zebulon Pike in 1806, in the Rampart range of the Rocky Mountains.

Below: Mexican soldiers, typical of those that Pike would have seen.

quite probable that Pike was completely unaware of this intrigue.

Pike set out from the Mississippi on July 15, 1806, heading for Osage country in the company of 22 men, including Governor Wilkinson's son James, also an army lieutenant: "....We sailed from the landing at Bele Fontaine about 3 o'clock P.M., in two boats. Our party consisted of two lieutenants, one surgeon, one sergeant, two corporals, 16 privates and one interpreter. We had also under our charge chiefs of the Osage and Pawnees, who, with a number of women and children, had been to Washington. These Indians had been redeemed from captivity among the Potawatomies, and were now to be returned to their friends at the Osage towns."

They rowed and poled two barges up the Osage River and duly delivered their 51 charges. After addressing the Indians on the subject of United States displeasure with Indian wars, Pike acquired horses and set off *north*west toward the Republican River. This brief detour was made in order to contact the Pawnee and to inform them of America's ownership of their territory.

The Pawnee proved none too friendly because some weeks earlier a large detachment of Spanish cavalry had visited the region (probably looking for Pike), poisoning the Pawnee minds against American interlopers. When Pike informed the Pawnee that they now owed allegiance to the Stars and Stripes and not to Spain, the Indians grew uncooperative and menacing. They threatened to stop Pike by force from traveling west: "Wednesday, October 1st. Paid a visit to town and had a very long conversation with the Chief, who urged everything in his power to induce us to turn back. Finally, he very candidly told us that the Spaniards wished to have gone further into our country, but he induced them to give up the idea; that they had listened to him and he wished us to do the same; that he had promised the Spaniards to act as he now did, and that we must proceed no further, or he must stop us by force of arms. My reply was that I had been sent out by our great father to explore the western country, to visit all his red children, to make peace between them, and turn them from shedding blood; …I had not seen any blood in our path; but he must know that the young warriors of his great American father were not women, to be turned back by words; that I should therefore proceed, and if he thought proper to stop me, he could attempt it; but we were men, well armed and would sell our lives at a dear rate to his nation; that we knew our great father would send his young warriors there to gather our bones and revenge our deaths on his people when our spirits would rejoice in hearing our exploits sung in the war-songs of our Chiefs." In spite of this grand oration, Pike was disturbed by the Chief's threats of force. But Pike did as he said he would and rode off toward the Arkansas River. He impudently followed the broad swathe of a trail that the Spanish cavalry had made on their way back to Santa Fe.

By October 18, Pike reached the Arkansas. Lieutenant Wilkinson then returned with some men to the Mississippi with reports. Pike took the remaining men and pushed westward up the Arkansas, toward the mountains—and the Spanish possessions. The headwaters of the Red River, his ostensible goal, lay almost due south.

Wilkinson's party traveled in coracle-like canoes, which had to be dragged over miles of shallows on the lower Arkansas, and which he finally abandoned when an autumn frost brought ice to the river. With his clothing in tatters and his ammunition running short, the young lieutenant grimly refused to stop and build shelters for the winter. Instead he forced his way along the unpredictable waterway to the Mississippi, and on to New Orleans. At the Arkansas' other extreme Pike had been meeting as much difficulty with equal determination.

Pike's group rode on horseback along the bank of the river. The valley deepened into a gorge, and the trail grew rougher; their

Above: the sort of clothes worn by most western trappers and explorers. Although made of buckskin, the material used by the Indians, the style shows strong European influence. The skins held in the body warmth, and protected the wearer from wind.

tired horses began to give out fast. Then, on November 15, the men saw what looked like a small blue cloud to the west. A spyglass revealed it as a thrusting mountain peak, and the men cheered aloud at having come in sight of the Rocky Mountains: "At two o'clock in the afternoon I thought I could distinguish a mountain to our right, which appeared like a small blue cloud; view it with the spy glass, and was still more confirmed in my conjecture, yet only communicated it to Dr. Robinson, who was in front with me; but in half an hour they appeared in full view before us. When our small party arrived on the hill they with one accord gave three cheers to the Mexican mountains [the main chain of the Rocky Mountains]. Their appearance can easily be imagined by those who have crossed the Alleghenies; but their sides were whiter, as if covered with snow, or a white stone."

By November 25, they were camped at the vast peak's base, or so they thought, until they set out to climb it. They found that they had climbed a spur, and that the "Grand Peak" lay a day's march away. Pike asserted that it would never be climbed by man, for he judged its height at over 18,000 feet above sea level.

This side trip to the mountain, which later became Pikes Peak, was beset by the fierce Colorado winter. As freeze-up settled in, the march became agony. The horses grew weaker because of the lack of grass. The men were numb with cold and had frostbitten feet. Still following what he thought was the Spanish trail, Pike struck northward, cross-country, and on December 13 came to a frozen river, which he correctly identified as the Platte (i.e. the South Platte). The expedition struggled south again, but when they found themselves back at the Arkansas River, Pike concluded that it was the Red: "After pointing out the ground for the encampment, the doctor and myself went on to make discoveries, as was our usual custom, and in about four miles' march we struck what we supposed to be Red River… which here was about 25 yards wide, ran with great rapidity, and was full of rocks. We returned to the party with the news, which gave general pleasure. Determined to remain a day or two in order to examine the source."

But the men were in no condition for clear thinking. They were freezing in their cotton rags and had been sleeping on snow and frozen ground. Many were without blankets because they had cut them up to wrap their feet in. Horses were collapsing under them at a rapid rate. In these circumstances, geographical inaccuracy can be forgiven. At least the buffalo remained plentiful, so that they did not starve.

Above: the kind of environment in which Pike and his party found themselves during the winter of 1806, in the mountains of Colorado. The rugged, snow-covered mountain passes, with no grass for the horses to eat, and little or no shelter for the men, did not stop them, however, and most of the party survived the ordeal.

Within a short time, though, Pike realized his mistake about the Arkansas. He decided, therefore, to build a winter camp, deposit some of the supplies and two men there, and go on foot to find the Red River.

During the grueling march, two of the men developed such badly frozen feet that Pike, reluctantly, had to leave them behind. He left ample provisions and promised to send help as soon as he could. Snow, weariness, and 70-pound packs slowed his progress, but despair changed into elation when he came to a creek (the Medano), and found near it a large river flowing southeast. Pike jubilantly announced that they had found the Red. In fact, they had circumvented the source of the Red and they were now on the Rio Grande's northern headwaters.

The party built a stockade there and settled in for the winter, with

the exception of Dr. Robinson. The doctor had been commissioned to find the fur trader Baptiste Lelande in Santa Fe, to get some money that Lelande owed his backer in Kaskaskia.

Shortly after Dr. Robinson set out, some Spanish soldiers rode up to announce that he had been picked up by outriders, and that Pike was trespassing on Spanish territory. The Spanish commanding officer addressed Pike as follows: "Sir, the governor of New Mexico being informed you had missed your route, ordered me to offer you, in his name, mules, horses, money, or whatever you might stand in need of to conduct you to the head of Red River; as from Santa Fe to where it

Left: Spaniards escorting Pike into
Santa Fe after his arrest for trespassing onto Spanish territory. From
Santa Fe, Pike and the men arrested
with him were taken to Chihuahua
and then by a roundabout route to
the American frontier.

is sometimes navigable is eight days' journey, and we have guides and
the routes of the traders to conduct us."

"What," said I interrupting him, "is not this the Red River?"

"No sir! The Rio de Norte."

"I immediately ordered my flag to be taken down and rolled up,
feeling how... I had committed myself in entering their territory,
and conscious that they must have positive orders to take me in."

"He now added that he had provided 100 mules and horses to take
in my party and baggage, and how anxious his Excellency was to see
me at Santa Fe." In February, 1807, Pike was escorted into Santa Fe

Below: a typical settler's room in New Mexico in the 1800's. Such rooms were sparsely furnished, the dim light contrasting severely with the brilliant sunlight outdoors. Despite the intense heat outside, the room was very cool due to the thickness of the exterior adobe walls.

Below: Aaron Burr (1756—1836) the politician who joined with Wilkinson in a bid to conquer Mexico. When the scheme failed, Wilkinson betrayed Burr and he was tried for treason in 1807. Though officially cleared, public opinion was against him and he fled to Europe for five years.

by the Spanish. He was treated with courtesy, but his notes and papers were confiscated and he was clearly in custody.

At that point, Pike's journey of exploration ended. The Santa Fe authorities sent him to Mexico, and from there he was escorted through Texas back to the frontier settlement of Natchitoches. He returned home on July 1, 1807, to find himself in the center of a political storm.

During Pike's journey (in 1806), border tensions had deepened in the delicate area between the Sabine and Red rivers. Governor Wilkinson was ordered to lead the western army to Natchitoches; he reached the frontier in September, ready to profit by the coming war. But he was thwarted. The Spanish did not arrest Pike that year, no international incident sparked off hostilities, and the government had begun to probe into the doings of Aaron Burr and his associates.

Wilkinson, therefore, cut his losses. He betrayed Burr to Jefferson, revealing the whole plot—except for his own role. Then he negotiated with the Spanish, setting up a neutral zone west of Natchitoches that would prevent quarreling until a boundary treaty could be agreed upon. In February, 1807, Burr was charged with treason. And though the charges did not stick (he was acquitted in late 1807), his reputation

was greatly harmed. Wilkinson, too, was affected and became the object of an investigation. He was officially cleared, twice, but was replaced in March, 1807, as governor of Louisiana by Meriwether Lewis.

Pike's denial of any knowledge of the conspiracy seems to have been generally accepted, and he remained something of a popular figure. But the shadow of Burr and Wilkinson, to some extent, prevented his achievement being as widely hailed as that of Lewis and Clark. And yet history shows that Pike's exploration proved just as valuable to United States expansion. His detailed descriptions of the Kansas-Colorado area, New Mexico, and Texas opened the way for other explorers and traders.

At the same time, Pike's journey had one invidious, long-range effect. He had called the Arkansas River region "sterile." In the published account of his findings he described the *entire* central plains region as "incapable of cultivation" and likely to become "as celebrated as the sandy deserts of Africa." Pike, therefore, made the first authoritative statement of an idea that was to hold currency for years: the idea of the "Great American Desert." Others after him echoed this phrase, thereby focusing attention on the more obvious riches of the Far West.

Above: the painting of Stone City, Iowa, by Grant Wood, suggests the immense fertility of the area, and completely refutes Pike's idea that the central plains were not worth cultivating. One of the reasons why settlement jumped from the east coast to the west coast was because of the great myth that the prairies were an uncultivable desert.

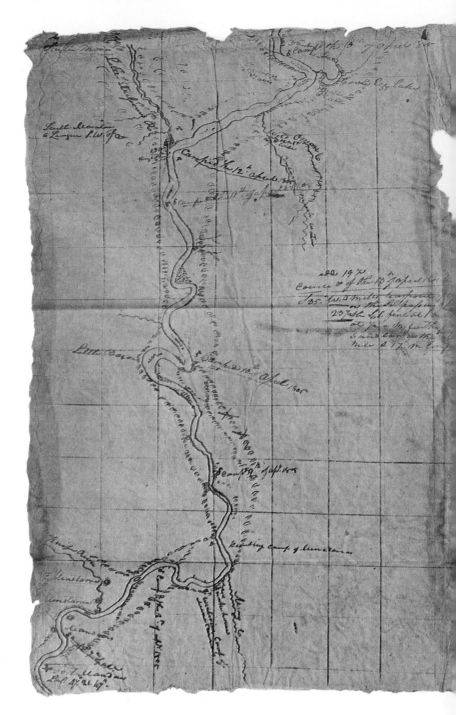

Right: this page from Lewis and Clark's journal, in which they described what they saw and drew illustrative maps, shows the sort of detailed information that the early expeditions produced on various parts of the Great West.

Fur Traders and Mountain Men
5

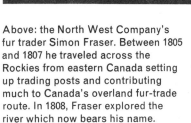

Above: the North West Company's fur trader Simon Fraser. Between 1805 and 1807 he traveled across the Rockies from eastern Canada setting up trading posts and contributing much to Canada's overland fur-trade route. In 1808, Fraser explored the river which now bears his name.

The northwest Rocky Mountains take in an enormous area—the states of Oregon, Washington, Idaho, parts of Wyoming and Montana, and Canada's British Columbia. Alexander Mackenzie and Lewis and Clark brought back information in abundance about this region. But the picture as a whole was still very sketchy. People were still guessing about the geography of the area. Some of the guesses proved rather far-fetched, like Clark's idea that the Yellowstone River would lead neatly south to Santa Fe.

It was necessary, therefore, for other explorers to venture into the

Below: a "Universal Instrument," surveying equipment available in the early 1800's. Such instruments were used to measure the horizontal angle between two far objects, or angles of elevation or depression. They had a simple graduated scale providing the tangent of the angle.

high country to fill out the geographical picture. And they came, all of them, not as government-backed expeditions, but as fur traders who were looking for beaver. The Canadians concentrated first on the area Mackenzie had passed through, and then they gradually moved south. The Americans went to the upper Missouri first, and gradually moved west. Both groups collided briefly on the Pacific coast and later shifted their main operations southeast, down around the headwaters of the Snake River.

Simon Fraser first led the traders of the North West Company into what is now British Columbia. From 1805-1807, he roamed the northern Rockies, building forts and trading. In 1808 he set out to follow the turbulent river that Mackenzie had thought was the upper Columbia.

The river seemed to be nothing but mile upon mile of rocky narrows and rapids, cascades, and whirlpools, which occurred in unbroken, exhausting succession. Fraser's voyageurs labored heroically to keep the expedition's four canoes afloat, but the strain proved too great. When the precipitous canyons allowed, Fraser took his men off the

river. They marched alongside it, through fiercely tangled forest, and walked along rock-strewn trails where only mountain goats and Indians knew of secure footholds. Finally, after hundreds of miles and near starvation, they reached the navigable stretch of the river. They took to canoes again and headed down river toward the Pacific.

Even then Fraser did not reach the open sea. Hostile Indians turned him back in the Strait of Georgia. But before retracing those painful steps, Fraser checked his instruments and found that according to Mackenzie's calculations he should be at 46° latitude. Instead he was far north of that latitude on which he knew the Columbia lay. He had proved Mackenzie wrong, and found another river, now the Fraser.

At about the same time, David Thompson, a brilliant surveyor as well as a fur trader, had crossed the mountains to look elsewhere for a Northwester route to the coast. Thompson traveled many southbound waterways, including the Kootenay River down into Idaho, and had soon formed a clear picture of British Columbia's southern rivers. He had also located the headwaters of the Columbia.

Above: a painting by Paul Kane in 1847 of the falls at Colville on the Columbia River. Rising in the ice fields of the Rockies, the Columbia is the largest river that flows into the Pacific Ocean from the North American continent.

But Indian troubles and fur trading kept him from embarking on that river until 1811. He then fought his way down the river, with five voyageurs and four Indians in an oversized canoe. They traveled through the narrows and cascades that Lewis and Clark had conquered. When Thompson reached the Pacific in July, he had shown that the Northwesters could travel by water across the continent from the St. Lawrence to the Columbia.

The Northwesters in British Columbia were the first fur men to carry the trade west of the mountains. In America, their counterparts concentrated on the upper Missouri. A shrewd St. Louis businessman, Manuel Lisa, had seen the potential of the high country even before Lewis and Clark had finished their expedition. In April, 1807, Lisa led 42 men, with George Drouillard as guide, up the Missouri. They overcame all the obstacles of that river, including the truculent Sioux and Arikara Indians. By late October, they had erected a fort on the Yellowstone River, near its junction with the Bighorn. Lisa then sent his men out into the wilds to trap and to trade.

Among those men was John Colter, who had trapped that region widely after leaving Lewis and Clark, and who had met Lisa's party on their way upriver. But the Yellowstone Valley held no further interest for him. So he left Lisa's fort to begin a looping route that would take him over approximately 500 miles of rugged mountain country, where no white man had been before. And Colter went alone, in the dead of winter, carrying only a handgun and a 30-pound pack on his back.

He roamed the Bighorn, and then explored up the Yellowstone. There he stumbled on the steam-spouting geysers and pits of bubbling mud in what is now Yellowstone National Park. Colters Hell it was called, but few people believed his story. He also crossed the Great Divide in the towering Teton Mountains, becoming the first white

Above: "Escape from Blackfeet" by Alfred Jacob Miller, about 1837. The Blackfoot, a group of Plains tribes living between the Mississippi River and the Rocky Mountains, were the strongest and most aggressive tribe on the northwestern plains, as many of the early explorers (particularly John Colter) came to realize.

Left: Grand Teton mountains, part of Grand Teton National Park, established to preserve an area of unusual scenic beauty in northwestern Wyoming. John Colter, an American trapper turned mountain man, was the first white man to explore the region and the reports of his exploits have formed the basis of information about America's frontier expansion in that area.

man to look down into Jackson's Hole. It was an amazing achievement, which was made all the more heroic by his brushes with hostile Indians, struggles on improvised snowshoes against mountain blizzards, and long periods of hunger when game was scarce.

After his solo journey south along the Bighorn, Colter trapped around the upper Missouri, and at one point fell in with a group of Flathead Indians. He was with them when a superior force of Blackfoot ambushed the group. Colter was hit in the leg, but managed to pour such a withering fire into the Blackfoot ranks that he turned the battle against them. He made his way back to Lisa's fort, recuperated, and returned to the wilderness.

Upon his return, he was immediately captured by the vengeful Blackfoot. By way of a slow death, they disarmed him, stripped him naked, and let him run, with the whole Blackfoot band screeching after him. Colter ran, pushing himself to the limit. He outdistanced all his pursuers but one. Turning suddenly, Colter grabbed the Indian's spear and killed him instantly. Running again, he reached the Madison River, plunged into the freezing water, and hid under a cluster of driftwood.

Above: German-born John Jacob Astor, who emigrated to New York in 1783. Picture by courtesy of the Chicago Historical Society.

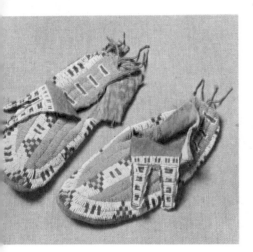

Above: moccasins of deerskin or mooseskin, with elaborate beadwork embroidery. These are typical examples of Indian footwear which the mountain men quickly adopted.

Meanwhile, the furious Indians scoured the riverbanks for him. After some hours, Colter emerged from the driftwood, clambered up a sheer cliff, and began walking on gashed and bleeding feet to Lisa's fort about 200 miles away. In spite of underbrush, thorns, rocky terrain, swarms of insects, freezing nights, and barely any food, in less than 11 days he reached the fort. Soon after, Colter left the fur trade for the comparative peace of a Missouri frontier farm.

By 1810, a great many mountain men were roaming the Rockies of Idaho. They were the leftovers from Lisa's group or newcomers connected with a new venture that took the United States fur trade to the coast. The venture was owned by a New York merchant named John Jacob Astor. He sent a group of men by ship—the *Tonquin*—around the Horn of South America to build Fort Astoria at the mouth of the Columbia. While the ship was en route, another Astor employee, named Wilson Price Hunt, led a party of 60 men westward out of St. Louis for the same destination.

Their journey was sheer disaster. Recruiting difficulties delayed them, and ice on the Missouri forced them to stop for the winter after only a few hundred miles. Fear of the Blackfoot then kept them off the river, so they started, with only enough horses for carrying baggage, across South Dakota and Wyoming to the Bighorn Mountains. They reached Wind River (a branch of the Bighorn) in the fall of 1811.

Game grew more scarce as they passed from the Wind to the Green River and over the mountain ranges to the Snake. Finding that stream unnavigable, they continued on foot. The group decided to split, scattering in smaller groups to find food and a passable route. Some men dropped out, hoping to survive on their own. The others went on, at times eating their own moccasins, wandering lost in the deepening canyon of the Snake, and trying, in vain, to run canoes down that ferocious torrent.

In spite of a winter's torment in the mountains, most of the party reached Astoria by early 1812. They found the place in a sorry state. The *Tonquin* had been blown up during an Indian attack farther up the coast, and during the previous summer, David Thompson had floated down the Columbia to announce that Canada, i.e. the North West Company, claimed that river's territory. Astor had to be informed, so in June, 1812, young Robert Stuart set off with a group of men to retrace Hunt's overland path.

Stuart was out in the wilds when the War of 1812 broke out. He knew

nothing of the arrival at Astoria (in early 1813) of a Northwester force demanding the fort's surrender and threatening the Astorians with the imminent arrival of a British warship. In fact, the warship did not arrive until November of that year, by which time the Astorians had saved face and cut their losses by selling the fort to the North West Company.

As a result, Stuart's ordeal turned out to be pointless. But it resulted in a discovery that would revolutionize all travel to and through the western mountains. For when they reached the Bear River, Stuart's group drifted southeast where they came upon a broad vista of low, rolling hills with mountains looming on either side. They had found South Pass, which was no narrow corridor but a 20-mile-wide gap in the eastern mountain range, which led out to some of the great central rivers. This discovery proved to America that the Columbia was accessible by means other than laborious boat-and-portage river travel. Wagons would now be able to roll all the way to the coast through this low-elevation doorway through the mountains.

But wagons were not yet ready to roll, and the fur traders had not yet finished with the region. With the Canadians firmly in charge of the Columbia Valley, the American emphasis shifted back to the mountains. And even there they met strong competition from the North West Company, especially after the region had come under the leadership (in 1816) of a dynamic, 300-pound Scot named Donald McKenzie.

McKenzie had been an Astorian with Hunt's party and knew the region well. As a Northwester, he fanned his men out through the Columbia Valley, and then led a thrust into the rich beaver country of Idaho (roughly between the headwaters of the Snake, Wind, Green, and Bear rivers). McKenzie himself thoroughly explored the Snake River country, firmly locating that river's navigable parts and some

Above: Fort Astoria in 1813, the central depot set up by John Jacob Astor in 1811 at the mouth of the Columbia River. It was seized by the English two years later.

Below: Northwester Donald McKenzie, who organized the Canadian company's fur-gathering operations in the West. Instead of fixed posts, he introduced mobile trapping brigades.

Above: the aptly-named Snake River has its source in Wyoming, just to the south of Yellowstone Park. It leaves Wyoming and flows sinuously westward through Idaho, turning northward at the Oregon border to form a natural boundary between the two states. Flowing westward again, it joins the Columbia River near Pasco, Washington, 1,038 miles from its source. This was the area that McKenzie explored so thoroughly. No longer known for beaver hunting, it is now predominantly a farming area.

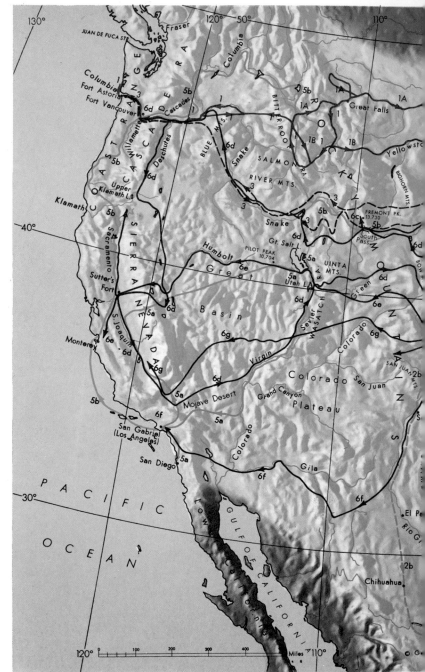

Right: The United States, and the routes of the most important explorers from Lewis and Clark to Frémont. The green highlights the area of exploration.

shortcuts (such as the Boise River). Meanwhile, other Northwesters ranged all over the region of the Snake and Green rivers, penetrating as far south as Bear Lake, the most southerly exploration in the mountains up to that time. Against such rivals, the slow-moving, conservative Hudson's Bay Company lost every battle in the wilderness. The rivalry between the companies continued for several years, during which time they opened up Canada as far as the Pacific.

McKenzie retired in 1821, the year that the North West Company amalgamated with the Hudson's Bay Company under the latter's ban-

Lewis & Clark	1	1803-6
Lewis' return party	1A	1806
Clark's return party	1B	1806
Pike	2a	1805-6
	2b	1806-7
Astorians (Hunt & Stuart)	3	1811-3
Long	4	1819
Smith	5a	1826-7
	5b	1828-31
Frémont (with Nicollet)	6a	1839-40
Frémont	6b	1841
	6c	1842
	6d	1843-4
	6e	1845-7
Frémont (after resigning from Army)	6f	1848-9
	6g	1853-4

ner. His successors found that American competition was stepping up. In 1824, the Northwester Alexander Ross, operating north in the Clearwater River region, met a group of American mountain men led by a youth named Jedediah Smith. Ross did not know it, but this young man represented the most dangerous competition of all.

Smith, only 26 years old at that time, was to become as legendary a mountain man and explorer as John Colter. He had come west as part of a major fur-trading assault, which was organized by William Henry Ashley out of St. Louis. In 1822, the Ashley men went west in two

Above: early in the 1820's the fur trade became more highly organized. Annual rendezvous (gatherings of trappers) were established, at which furs were traded for ammunition, food, and other commodities. The first of such rendezvous took place on the Green River, near the Wyoming/Utah border, in 1824. These gatherings became an important annual event, not only for trading, but as a social event and a time for exchanging news.

parties, one headed for the Yellowstone and the other, led by Smith, through the heart of the Black Hills into Bighorn country. With Smith went other mountain men, only slightly less famous, such as Thomas Fitzpatrick, James Clyman, and William Sublette.

Smith and his men fought their way through fierce rains, murderous rocky canyons, and bleak waterless plains. Smith had a hand-to-hand fight with a grizzly bear that nearly tore his face off, but it only briefly delayed the trek. In early 1824, they continued their struggle, running up against mountain blizzards, cold, and hunger. By March, they had located Sweetwater Creek through South Pass. They were the first men since Stuart to traverse the pass and find the trail along the creek that provided the easiest access.

Smith's expedition ranged through the mountains between the Snake and the Green rivers, which were now the center of the mountain fur trade. It was there that a new Hudson's Bay trader named Peter Skene Ogden countered the American threat with a "scorched-earth" policy — sending his men rampaging through the wilderness and clearing it of beaver. As furs grew scarcer, both Canadian and American

traders ranged farther south, and the exploration emphasis shifted to Wyoming and Utah.

Trappers continued for years to range the northwestern mountains, still finding enough beaver to justify the effort. But even in the 1820's, other people, not traders, developed an interest in the northwest. Ashley's reports on the South Pass and its environs naturally led to dreams of overland wagon trains and of settlers on the rich Oregon soil.

In the 1840's the Oregon Trail was used by early squatters moving into Oregon to homestead the land. And shortly thereafter, they began to clamor to Washington to give them territorial status. British Canada had hoped that the boundary would be drawn at the Columbia, but Canada had failed to follow up her fur traders with settlers. And she had failed to reckon with American Manifest Destiny, which by the 1840's anticipated the Stars and Stripes flying from Alaska all the way south to California. For by then American trail-breakers had forced their way into the Spanish southwest, had found it enticing, and had made all America hunger for it.

Above: a photograph of the 2,000-mile-long Oregon Trail, which looked much like this for miles of its length. It wound its way from Independence, Missouri, across prairies, deserts, and mountains to the northwest Pacific coast. It was the longest overland route used by settlers in their movement west. The deep ruts made by the wagon wheels can still be seen today. The covered wagons took six months to make the journey, often across flooded rivers, and with the ever-present threat of attack by Indians hanging over them. Always short of water and food, and facing the possibility of an outbreak of disease, the settlers' trek was a great feat of endurance.

Below: the Plaza and Church of El Paso. The largest city standing on the Mexico/United States border, El Paso (Spanish for "the pass") is known as the gateway to Mexico. Spanish priests founded a mission there in 1659, thus establishing an important Spanish foothold in the then-unexplored southwest territory.

The Road to Santa Fe

6

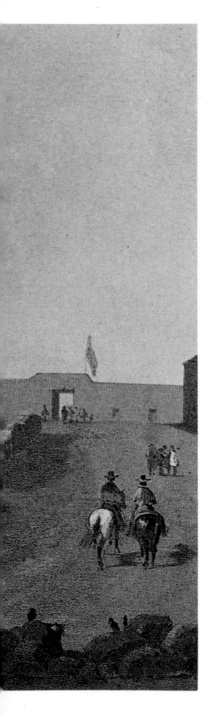

As traders rushed off up the Missouri once Lewis and Clark had shown the way, various entrepreneurs poured into the southwest in the footsteps of Zebulon Pike. Although the traders were aware of Pike's arrest and Spain's jealous protection of its mountain frontier, most of the adventurers seemed willing to take their chances—with varying consequences. In 1809, for instance, Anthony Glass reached as far as the upper Colorado River, in Texas, to trade with Indians, and returned to Missouri safely. In the same year, three traders named McLanahan, Smith, and Patterson tried to make a profit from the Indian trade on the Red River, but the Spanish came out and arrested them. And in 1812, another trio, Baird, Chambers, and McKnight, rode straight to Santa Fe with a pack train of trade goods. They were stopped by the Spanish and spent the next nine years in a Chihuahua jail. In 1814, a profit-seeker named Joseph Philibert took some trappers to the head of the Arkansas River to investigate the beaver population. They profited not only from the beaver skins but from buffalo hides as well. Fortunately, they were never bothered by the Spanish during their first hunting expeditions. But in 1816, the Spanish evidently thought that these Americans had been tapping Spanish resources for much too long, and proceeded to carry off Philibert and company to the Santa Fe prison. They were treated fairly leniently, however, and released in a few days.

In the words of one modern historian, Spain had dropped an "iron curtain" across the mountains in front of Santa Fe. They did not want trappers and traders to open the door for American expansionism. But this policy of isolationism only enhanced the American adventurers' desire to explore the Santa Fe region. The individual probes and thrusts might have continued for years if the Mexican revolt against Spain had not altered the situation.

Before that disruption, however, the United States and Spain had come to an agreement about the boundary of Louisiana. According to the Adams-Onis Treaty of 1819, the boundary line was to be drawn from the Sabine River northward to the Red. It would continue west along that river to 100° longitude, and then north to the Arkansas up to the 42nd parallel, which it followed to the Pacific. Because of this settlement, the United States decided that an official expedition ought to be conducted to bring back maps, charts, and descriptions of the natural resources of the area.

The decision to send troops to that area coincided with a wish to try out steamboats on the Missouri. As a result, in 1819, five poorly-built

Right: Karl Bodmer's "Unloading of the Steamboat *Yellowstone*, April 19, 1833." Steamboats were first used on the Missouri in the early 1800's and Stephen Long's experiments with these craft started what turned out to be a very successful method of transportation.

Right: these New Mexico religious statuettes of the 1800's were carved from wood and were used by the missionaries in their attempts to make Christian teaching more comprehensible to the Indians.

boats steamed off up the river with 1,000 men, while a sixth boat trailed behind bearing a handful of scientists under the command of Major Stephen Long. Unfortunately, the soldiers were inadequately supplied and began dying in their winter camp of scurvy, and assorted fevers. Major Long, however, took his scientists east again. It was there that he received his orders to take the group on a governmental scientific expedition into the southwest.

Long took with him some army topographers, a zoologist, a botanist, a naturalist, and a painter named Samuel Seymour. Their main concern was to examine the terrain, the natural resources, and the wildlife. They were also to perform a fairly full exploration of the headwaters of the Red River, the United States' new southwestern extremity.

The group rode out along the Platte River in June 1820, and achieved a fairly quick crossing of the plains. By late June they had come within sight of the mountains. They continued to ride toward the mountains, proceeding southeast and then south along the South Platte.

The expedition continued south toward the Arkansas, still having explored no new ground. Balked by the mighty Royal Gorge of the upper Arkansas, the group split in two. A Captain Bell took some men down the Arkansas. Long took the others south in the direction of

the Red River. Bell's group entered Plains Indian territory—Arapaho, Kiowa, Cheyenne—and met harassment enough to drive three men to desertion. The deserters took with them most of the expedition's journals and scientific notes, and neither men nor papers were ever seen again. Meanwhile, Long marched across the Cimarron River and came upon a sizable waterway which he confidently identified as the Red. Following it east, the group underwent its first serious hardship, a scarcity of game that drove them to kill their horses for food. But in spite of their troubles, the men forged ahead. Eventually the river joined another waterway, which was clearly the Arkansas. Their time had been spent, then, following the Canadian River and not the Red.

In every way, Long's journey was a disaster. And he later compounded his failure by reiterating Pike's view of the central plains as the "Great American Desert... almost wholly unfit for cultivation." We may enjoy the irony that hindsight reveals. But some modern historians have pointed out that, in a sense, Long was right. The great plains *were* uncultivable in terms of the agricultural techniques employed in the United States at that time. In 1821, however, no one had time to listen to Stephen Long because of the upheavals in the Spanish southwest.

An American trader named William Becknell was fortunate enough

Above: a view of the chasm through which the Platte River issues from the Rocky Mountains. The Platte—in some places a mile wide—is the United States' shallowest river. It winds across central and southern Nebraska and was one of the main features of the settlers' route across the plains. The name Nebraska comes from the Oto Indian word "nebrathka," meaning flat water, the Indian name for the Platte.

to reap the benefits from that upheaval. He had organized a pack train
at Franklin, Missouri, which he led out across the plains to the great
bend of the Arkansas River. He headed west into Colorado, looking
for Indians to trade with, but instead was confronted by a detachment
of Spanish soldiers near the Canadian River. Becknell expected to be
arrested, but the soldiers told him that there had been a revolution.
They explained that the Spanish southwest was now independent
Mexico, and that the new nation welcomed (and needed) trade with
the United States. Becknell immediately headed toward Santa Fe,
sold his goods for huge profits in Mexican silver, and hurried back to
Franklin with the news.

Left: Stephen Long holding a council with Pawnee Indians. A United States Topographical Engineer, Major Long led his army expeditions to the Upper Mississippi, the Rockies, and the Great Lakes, where he had many clashes with Indian tribes. This picture shows a more tranquil episode in his dealings with Indians.

Above: a Hopi Indian water bottle, of Spanish shape, but with Indian decoration. Water carriers such as this were very necessary to survival in the central plains, where scarcity of water was a continual problem.

In 1822, Becknell went out again. But this time he left the pack-horses at home and took wagons, the first wheels to roll onto the central plains. Osage Indians created some trouble in the journey's early days, and the wagon train was delayed in Kansas by floods. A wagon train usually consisted of about 25 wagons. Each could carry approximately 7,000 pounds weight. When Indians attacked, they could protect themselves, to some extent, by forming a circle to shield the livestock and provide a screen for the defenders. However, they were cumbersome vehicles and Becknell's main concern was finding a route through the mountains. For this reason, he diverged from his previous route from the upper Arkansas River and cut southwest across arid prairie,

Right: typical wagon train of the 1800's moving along the Santa Fe Trail. Hundreds of families joined together to form such trains and they were guided by a scout who knew the route. The wagons, pulled by oxen or mules, had white canvas tops, which from a distance looked like sails—the famous "prairie schooners."

hoping by this means to come to a more passable mountain gateway.

The wagon train went through unbearable days of blinding sun and heat. Their water gave out several times, and the mules began dropping one by one from thirst. Because of the men's own thirst, they resorted to drinking the dead mules' blood to keep themselves alive. But eventually Becknell's determination brought the exhausted party to the banks of the Cimarron River—which led almost due west to Santa Fe. Becknell achieved his goal and made his profits. But of prime importance was the fact that he had carved out the basic route to be used by traders and travelers for years to come—the Santa Fe Trail.

Legions of traders and trappers followed Becknell's wagon trail to Santa Fe in succeeding years. But the Americans had no sooner reached Santa Fe when they began looking farther west.

Etienne Provost may have been one of the first white men who entered the Great Salt Lake country of present-day Utah. In 1824, he worked his way up the Green River Valley and came to one of the small mountain rivers flowing into the Salt Lake. Whether he actually saw the lake is still debatable, even though he claimed to have done so.

Some historians seem to feel that the mountain man Jim Bridger was the first man to see the lake. In late 1824, when he had been trapping with a group near the Bear River, two trappers began to wonder where that river led. They sent young Bridger downstream to investigate. He arrived at a huge body of water, tasted it, and hurried back to announce that he had found an arm of the Pacific.

Bridger may have first tasted the Great Salt Lake, but it was Peter Skene Ogden, the Hudson's Bay Company's "Scourge of Oregon," who took the first thorough look at it. In December of 1828, after having explored unknown regions of Oregon and northern California, Ogden reached the shores of the Great Salt Lake. He explored the lakeshore to some extent, but of more importance, he moved through inhospitable desert to the west of the lake where he located a sizable western river. Ogden called it the Unknown, but today the river is known as the Humboldt. Its valley was to form one of the major highways to California and the Pacific coast.

In the late 1820's, both Jedediah Smith and Ogden went farther afield into the desolate terrain of Utah, and separately, both explorers reached down through the mountains into the badlands of Arizona. Eventually they went their own ways, westward into the heart of California.

Above: the Great Salt Lake, Utah. Though fed by freshwater streams, the lake is very salty. This is due to the high rate of evaporation and the fact that the lake is extremely shallow.

Right: frontiersman Jim Bridger.
Hunter, trapper, trader, and guide,
he was possibly the first to see the
Great Salt Lake, and the first man in
the Yellowstone area. He became
a semilegendary figure in the West.

Reaching for California
7

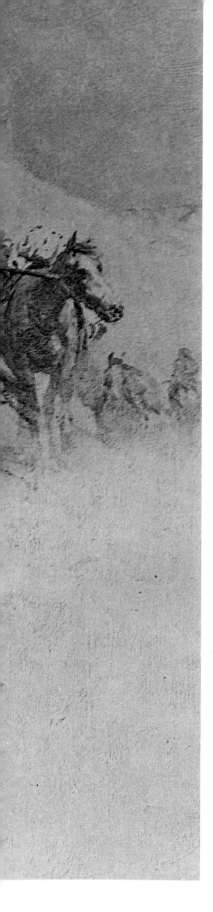

By the middle of the 1800's three routes penetrated through the south-western mountains into the promised land of California. Basically they followed old Indian trails or Spanish routes which still required rediscovery by Americans. The first route to be established—called the Old Spanish Trail—emerged from the determination of Jedediah Smith, the enthusiastic young mountain man who was second to none in his eagerness to explore the land about him. Smith's trapping journeys in southern Idaho and northern Utah made him keen to press on into the unknown regions of the southwest in the hope of finding un-exploited trapping country, and possibly setting up new trade routes to California and from there into the Pacific northwest. In August, 1826, he and 16 trappers went to investigate the area.

The group moved along the Wasatch Mountains to the Sevier and Virgin rivers. The going became difficult as they had to drag themselves through a dry, dusty land that Smith called a land of starvation. Pushing on to the Colorado River, they followed it southward through the starkly rugged Black Mountain region of Arizona. By now the struggle was for survival. Their horses weakened and died, and the men resorted to eating the leathery flesh.

Then suddenly they emerged out of desolation and into plenty—the green fields of the Mojave Indians near what is now Davis Dam. The Indians made them welcome and helped the explorers regain their strength during a two-week stay. The men learned that California lay nearby, and Smith had no hesitation in going on. In November, with Mojave guides, the party crossed the Mojave Desert on an ancient Indian trail that led into and through the San Bernardino Mountains. They became the first Americans to enter California overland.

The Spanish authorities in San Gabriel (later part of El Pueblo de Nuesta Senora la Reina de Los Angeles de Porciuncula, now simply Los Angeles) were not pleased with this new American break-through, but they let the Americans depart without interruption in January, 1827. Smith's party moved out north to the San Bernardino Valley, and then went on to the San Joaquin Valley. By spring they were in

Left: Jedediah Smith, American trader and explorer, who set out from the Great Salt Lake to find trade routes to California. This picture shows him crossing the desert from Green River to the Spanish settlement at San Gabriel.

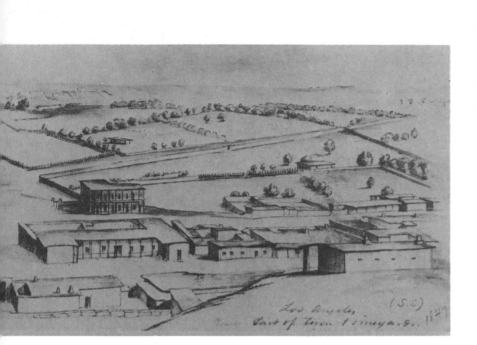

Los Angeles (S.C)

Above: sketch by William Rich Hutton showing San Gabriel, Los Angeles, in 1847. Los Angeles was the second village established by the Spanish in California and when Jim Bridger and his party arrived there in 1826 they were not welcomed by the Spaniards, who saw the Americans' arrival as a threat to their control. Mexico took over government of Los Angeles in 1835 and American troops captured it in the war of 1847.

Above right: the Great Basin, a desolate, waterless valley in the Nevada desert. This arid, infertile area is true desert, entirely different from the "Great American Desert" which Pike and Long said was uncultivable, but which has become the great farmland of the United States.

northern California. Smith tried to cross the still snow-clogged passes of the High Sierra, but killed five horses in the attempt, and very nearly killed his men. He finally left some of them in a camp to wait for a thaw, and with two others forced his way over the mountains. After the long journey, they approached the vast Nevada desert called the Great Basin.

The three men decided to cross the desert. Had they known the hardship to be faced, they might have decided otherwise. The hot glare of the sun and the desolation were unbearable. Several of the horses that had survived the mountain passes weakened and died in the desert. The men were again forced to eat horsemeat and the few stringy, desert rabbits they could catch. Their water ran out. One of the men lay down to die. But Smith and the other man went on until, at last, they stumbled upon a waterhole. Revived, they returned for their companion, and the three of them somehow managed to stagger forward. After 32 days of desert travel they arrived, in late June, at the exact spot that they had left the previous year—the south shore of the Great Salt Lake.

The fact that Smith arrived at his exact destination shows his remarkable sense of direction. He had no instruments, no guides from San Gabriel onward, and no trails of any kind to follow. Yet he had circled through the California interior and had come over the most inhospitable mountains and the widest desert in America.

Smith also demonstrated the mountain man's stamina and restlessness by setting off again, after only 10 days in camp, to pick up caches of furs left along the way. With 18 men, he followed more or less the same route southward to the Mojave villages. But when they reached those villages, they found that the situation had changed. Since their last visit, the Indians had fought with a party of white trappers from Taos, with the result that the Indians turned hostile toward Smith and his men as well. When Smith's party began a crossing of the Colorado River, the Mojaves attacked, killing 10 men and leaving Smith and the other 8 stranded on a makeshift raft in midstream. But the stranded men safely crossed the river and escaped into the desert, where Smith led them back to his old route and the Mojave River. They went northward, and reached the mouth of the Sacramento River where they struggled through the wilderness along its banks in order to winter in the Sacramento Valley. In July, 1828, they found themselves in Oregon, where they trapped along the Umpqua River.

One day, Smith and two men took a canoe to reconnoiter up a nearby stream. In their absence, a band of forest Indians sprang from the bushes and brutally massacred every man in the camp but one. The survivor fled through the forest, and Smith and his two men fled as well. All four eventually reached the Hudson's Bay Company's Fort Vancouver.

Below: a water canteen made of ribbed metal, now rusty, dating from about 1860. This was probably used in the Civil War, but is almost certainly like those carried earlier in the century, which would have been used by people like Jed Smith.

Below: Fort Vancouver, built in 1825 on the Columbia River, near the mouth of the Willamette (opposite today's Portland), as the Pacific headquarters of the Hudson's Bay Company. Surrounded by a stockade 318 feet square, the fort consisted of warehouses, stores, offices, dormitories, a brick powder magazine, and a dock for ocean-going ships. There were herds of livestock, grainfields, and orchards. To Jed Smith, on his arrival there in 1828, the fort was a symbol of the great power of the Hudson's Bay Company, which he called "all grasping."

From the Fort, the group made their way north, almost to the present Canadian border. They trapped as they went. By 1830, they had returned to their own territory around Wind River.

That year, Smith retired from the fur trade to farm in Missouri. In 1831, though, he decided to try one more trek into the West. This time he went with a wagon train going to trade in Santa Fe. On the Cimarron Cutoff, Smith rode out alone to look for water and was attacked by a band of Comanche. In true western fashion, he accounted for at least two Indians before he was killed.

Smith's achievements were not merely adventures. He is remembered not as an Indian-fighter, but as a brilliant explorer. He penetrated unknown wilderness and mapped and reported on much of the ground he covered. In this way he vastly extended the United States' knowledge of and appetite for its riches. In addition, Smith

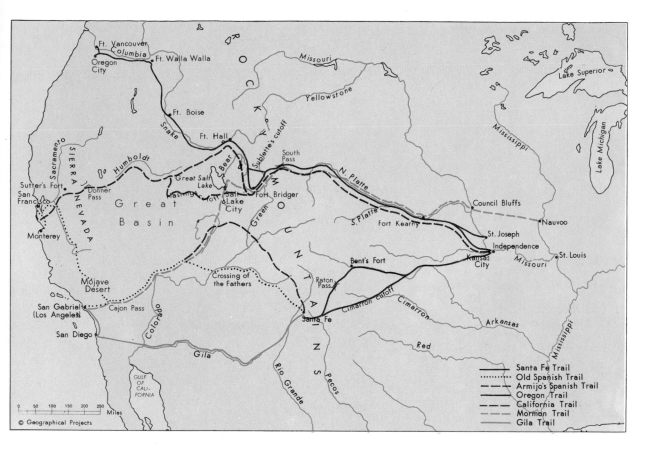

Above: The western trails that first the explorers and then the settlers followed on their way west. Some of the trails were established by individuals or groups — such as the Mormon Trail — but others, like the Old Spanish Trail, were traditional routes that had been used for years.

carved out the Old Spanish Trail, although Mojave hostility caused the route to be altered later.

By the early 1830's, the southerly overland links between Santa Fe and California had been completed. The making of the Gila Trail by James Pattie and Ewing Young and the alteration of the Old Spanish Trail by William Wolfskill opened the way southwest. The trappers and traders were the first arrivals of the American influx that was yet to come to California. Before that wave of settlers took place, though, the special routes of the trappers had to be developed out in the east.

This process of opening up routes was a slow one. The old routes used by the mountain men had almost to be *re*discovered, and official fact-finding explorations to be organized. For example, the South Pass into the Green River Valley offered a perfect wagon route to both Oregon and California. But as yet no one had defined the easiest and quickest way from the pass into California's unpopulated central valleys. Settlers could never have traversed the difficult southern trails laid down by Smith and Pattie. And, unfortunately, no one had located a better, more northerly route.

A start had been made, however, in 1828, when Peter Skene Ogden found the Humboldt River. The next year Ogden retraced his steps to the Humboldt, cut across a portion of the Great Basin, and pushed south to the Colorado River. When he eventually reached the Colorado, he then took his men along the river to the Gulf of California, and so became the first white man to cross the American West from north to

Above: trappers and Indians forming
a cavalcade. Groups such as this
opened up the footpath trails of
the mountain men and made them
negotiable by the settlers.

south. But he did not leave a complete trail behind him. He left only
the beginning of one, following the Humboldt River.

Two years later, the government sent out an army captain named
Benjamin Bonneville to have a good look at the settlement possibilities beyond the mountains, disguising his researches as fur trading.
Bonneville produced little new knowledge about the Indians or the
terrain. However, he did contribute indirectly to the opening up of
the Far West. In 1832 he set out with 110 men from his post on the
Green River on an exploring expedition into California. One of the
party was Tennessee frontiersman Joseph Reddeford Walker, who
later established the basic settler route into California.

The party traveled west from the Salt Lake to the marshy headwaters
of the Humboldt River, as Ogden had done. At that point, they had a
brush with some Digger Indians, killing many of them. The Diggers
had gathered in great numbers, but the trigger-happy explorers did
not wait to find out if they were really hostile or merely curious.

After this far-from-noble victory, Walker's party moved into the
mountains, probably up the Walker River, over the Divide into what
is now Yosemite National Park. As usual, heavy snow in the Sierra
made for a grueling passage. But conditions improved as the party
made the descent into California. They were the first white men to see
and describe the Yosemite Valley, the giant redwoods, and the general
richness of the land. By December, 1833, Walker and his companions

were standing on the coast of the Pacific south of San Francisco Bay.

The expedition began the journey back in January, and this time Walker moved through the San Joaquin Valley, where he discovered the low-altitude gap through the southern Sierra to be named "Walker Pass." It was a vital discovery because it completed a suitable route for settlers, which came to be called the California Trail.

Meanwhile, more and more Americans were using the Old Spanish and Gila trails to reach California. Others, particularly those who had already established shipping companies on the coast, traveled by sea. And in the late 1830's, traders regularly moved in and out of California from Santa Fe, thus emphasizing the United States' presence. Many of these Americans settled in California, which at that time belonged to Mexico. Although the settlers proclaimed loyalty to Mexico, they did, in fact, form a nucleus of United States' expansion. Several of the settlers managed to obtain land grants from Mexico. Swiss-born John

Right: watercolor by Alfred Jacob Miller, painted in 1837, of Captain Joseph Reddeford Walker, the Tennessee frontiersman who established the route for settlers traveling to California. He is followed—at the correct distance dictated by etiquette—by his Indian wife.

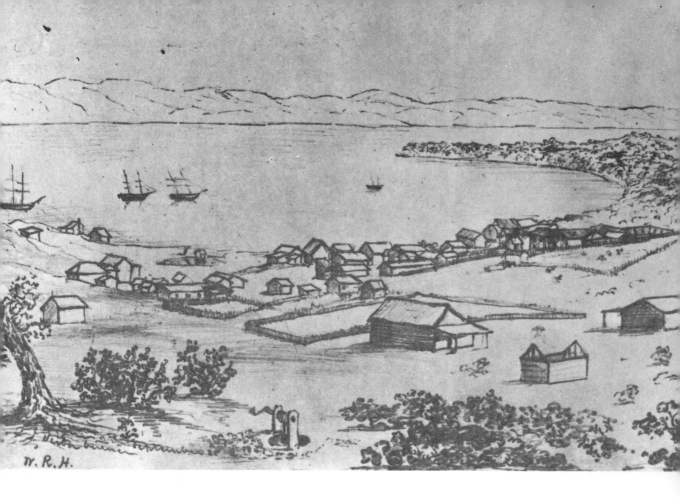

W. R. H.

Sutter was given a huge area in the Sacramento Valley, where he established a fort. Near Sutter's Fort was the enormous ranch of John Marsh, another new "Mexican" and a fugitive from justice in the east.

These establishments, and others like them, were in some of the richest land in the west. In addition they were far away from the eyes of the Mexican authorities. News of such properties reached the Missouri frontier and groups of pioneers gathered to launch a small-scale invasion of California.

The first group from Missouri crossed the prairies in 1841. It consisted of 69 people, including women and children, and was organized for the journey by John Bartleson and John Bidwell of Missouri. The mountain man Thomas Fitzpatrick guided their wagon train, which was made up of 14 covered wagons and a number of assorted carts. They traveled along the Platte River and through South Pass to the Bear River Valley. There, in August, part of the group split off and headed for Oregon. About 30 remained intent on making for California, among them Nancy Kelsey, the 18-year-old wife of Benjamin Kelsey, and their baby daughter. They were the only woman and child to complete the journey overland.

They set off without maps or guides to the region, leaving Fitzpatrick to go his own way. Having exchanged their wagons for pack animals they found themselves stumbling around in the desert of the Salt Lake region for weeks, subsisting on mule meat and coyotes. At

Left: San Francisco as it would have looked to Joseph Walker and his party when they arrived in 1833. Although the Bay was located by explorers in the 1500's, it was not until 1782 that a few Mexican families settled there, near the Spanish mission of St. Francis of Assisi, founded in 1776. The village that grew, El Paraje de Yerba Buena (the little valley of the good herb), was taken by the Americans in 1846 and a year later was named San Francisco.

Above: the sort of Mexican ranch owner who would have formed a large part of the population of California in the 1800's. His clothes were elaborate. The cape, called a manga, is an oval of blue or green material, lined with painted percale (fine, closely-woven cotton). The velvet collar is overlaid with gold lace, and a gold fringe decorates the shoulder. His hat is of Vicuña felt decorated with gold lace. His chamois vest reveals a shirt of fine fabric pleated at the front.

last the party reached the Humboldt River. There some Indians gave them vague directions, and the company moved into the mountains. Hardship, caused in part by ignorance, continued to test their endurance, but the pioneers were determined to go on. The expedition went too far south before crossing the Sierra, but finally made its way along the Walker River and through the high mountain passes. Emerging in late October into intractable canyon country, they almost despaired of ever reaching California. But still they pushed on, and after a few days their perseverance was rewarded. They descended into the greenery of the San Joaquin Valley. Many of them, like Marsh, were able to acquire land from Mexico.

One of the party, Joseph Chiles, returned to Missouri for more emigrants, and led a large party westward in 1842. Chiles took some of them on a circuitous route northwest into Oregon and then swung down into California. But he did not find a better route that way. In 1843, Joseph Walker led a wagon train via the Humboldt River to find Walker Pass, although they had to abandon the wagons in order to cross it. But in 1844, a group at last took covered wagons all the way from Missouri to California.

That group contained some 40 people, including 8 women and 15 children. It was led by Elisha Stevens and guided by at least two mountain men. One of the guides found a shorter route from South Pass to the Bear River, known as Sublette's Cutoff. From the Bear, the party

Above: the Sierra Nevada, the range of mountains which forms the eastern boundary of California. After many weary months of travel across desert and plain, the pioneers were faced with these mountains to cross. Wagon trains followed the trails blazed by trappers and explorers, widening them to make a way possible. Many of them failed and the early trails were littered with signs of their failure. It was never easy to get a loaded wagon through the steep and rocky passes.

entered Oregon and rested at a fur-trade post. In mid-August, they went south to rejoin Walker's California Trail at the Humboldt River. An old Indian told them about a useful pass to the west—some distance away from Walker's southbound route. The new route led to the two-day horror of the Forty Mile Desert between Humboldt Sink and Carson River in Nevada. This tract of land was strewn with dead animals' stinking, rotting flesh, and was littered with abandoned wagons, cooking pots, camping equipment, and anything that trappers had discarded to lighten their loads. They moved on to Truckee River, and traveled through the location where present-day Reno, Nevada, is situated. With winter coming on and food running short, the party struggled up into the mountains.

After laboring with the oxen and the laden wagons up mountain slopes and battling across icy, rock-strewn streams they found the

pass Indians had told them about. It was barely traversable by wagons. They might have turned back had it not been for Stevens' leadership and the party's high morale. But by early December, the wagons were through the mountain corridor and into California near Sutter's Fort.

It was the first time that a wagon train had crossed the continent into California. But this great achievement in surviving the long trek, and the importance of discovering the pass, were overshadowed by the tragic fate of the Donner party in the same pass in 1846-47. The party was badly organized and rife with dissension among its members. They were caught by early snowfalls in the California Sierra and forced to camp there. Food ran out and it is thought some members resorted to cannibalism. And today that vital gateway to the Californian valleys is called Donner Pass, commemorating the grisly failure rather than the heroic success.

Above: a typical pioneer family with their wagons. Most of the men and women who pushed the frontiers westward were simple people who faced the hardships and privations because they wanted a chance to improve their lives in the virgin lands of the West. Frontiersmen had to be farmers, hunters, and trappers, handy with an ax and able to build a shelter, boat, wagon, or sledge, and to mend a broken plow. Their lives were hard and the rewards were seldom great for the first settlers.

"The Pathfinder"
8

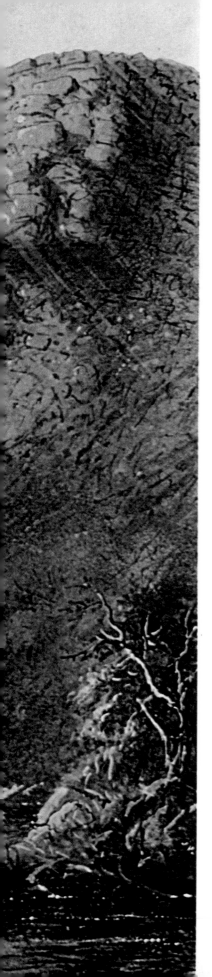

During the early 1840's American expansion rapidly increased. Droves of American adventurers and settlers moved west along the Oregon Trail or over the Sierra on the California Trail, while Britain and Mexico watched helplessly. Britain's hands were tied by an agreement that established joint Anglo-American occupation of Oregon, with a boundary settlement yet to be made. The British at first had hoped that the boundary would eventually follow the Columbia River. But the Hudson's Bay Company soon grew pessimistic and anticipated that the Americans would settle into territory beyond that line. For this reason, in 1843, the Hudson's Bay Company built a new Pacific headquarters on Vancouver Island to be assured of their hold in the area. That same year, 1,000 Americans moved into Oregon, calling themselves the "Great Immigration." A sizable number had invaded the valleys of California, too, and the Mexican authorities had become sufficiently dependent on American trade to forestall any anti-American moves.

From then on, American exploration became almost exclusively an explicit investigation of the Oregon and California regions prior to their takeover. The War Department had formed a Corps of Topographical Engineers for this purpose. Among them was a young lieutenant named John Charles Frémont, whose travels were to earn him the title of "the Pathfinder."

Frémont was a handsome, energetic, and romantic figure. He had a way with the ladies and a flair for publicity, but he also had well-defined qualities of leadership that attracted the loyalty of the roughest

Left: the "Devil's Gate," a notable landmark on the Oregon Trail, where the Sweetwater River—a branch of the North Platte—flows through a ridge of granite mountains.

Right: John Charles Frémont (1813—1890), American soldier, explorer, and politician. He became known as "the Pathfinder" during the course of his explorations of the greater part of the country between the Rockies and the Pacific coast. Frémont was the first Republican candidate to be nominated for the presidency in 1856 but he was defeated by Buchanan by 60 votes.

427

Above: map, published by R. H. Laurie in 1830, showing the "Probable Course" of the Buenaventura River. This mythical river was regularly shown on maps of this period because people believed that such a river *should* be there. The fact that any- one who had traveled there knew quite well that it was not, made little or no difference.

of mountain men. Frémont had gained his first exploring experience around the Mississippi. He had done such a good job that he was chosen by Senator Thomas Hart Benton as the leader of a large-scale exploration west of the mountains.

In 1842, Frémont went into Oregon in the company of a cartog- rapher named Charles Preuss and a handful of mountain men, includ- ing Kit Carson. They broke no new ground, except when Frémont climbed one of the Wind River mountains to perform the symbolic act of planting the American flag.

The next year, Frémont took his mapmaker and his mountain men (Thomas Fitzpatrick as well as Carson) on a careful investigation of Oregon, as far as the coast. His instructions, which referred to "the interior of *our* continent," made it clear that the exploration was to define the best areas for further American settlement. They discovered many promising areas, taking special note of the Bear River Valley and finding suitable territory in the environs of the Great Salt Lake. From the lake, Frémont moved by way of the Snake River up to the Columbia to complete his task. But he impulsively exceeded his orders when he decided to go south to look for that mythical river, the Buenaventura (believed to link the Pacific and the Salt Lake, and placed on most maps of the west in spite of the fact that no one had ever seen it).

With the rapid approach of winter, the expedition set out in November and moved south to the Deschutes River. Within a short time, they were struggling up the slopes of western mountains in the first deep snowfalls of December, and inching down rugged terrain to enter the Great Basin of Nevada. Cutting across its western edge, they began (near Lake Tahoe) a foolhardy winter assault on the Sierra Nevada.

Driving snow, fog, and interminable rocky slopes would have been bad enough, but Frémont complicated his ascent by dragging along a small cannon that he had begged from the Army to impress the Indians. The group's horses and mules weakened, their supplies ran low, and their Indian guide deserted. Feet froze, eyes were blinded from snow-glare, men collapsed from hunger, and one man went mad. But Frémont drove them on, and by mid-February they had crossed the Divide. They continued the struggle through heavy snow and dangerous mountain terrain until they emerged into the "perpetual spring," as Frémont called it, of the Sacramento Valley.

In March, they left that valley, where they had recuperated at Sutter's Fort, and moved south through the San Joaquin Valley in order to cross the Sierra through the Tehachapi Pass. They continued south to the Old Spanish Trail and turned east, where they met Joseph Walker, whose mountain skills eased their passage the rest of the way to the Sevier River and eastward into Colorado.

Frémont wrote a brilliant report of this epic journey, and Preuss drew up the maps of it. It was widely circulated in the east, and had enormous influence over would-be emigrants. Frémont may not have located many easy or tempting paths, but he fully awakened the spirit of Manifest Destiny. In 1844, President James K. Polk was elected

Below: an Indian guide presenting a prospective employer with his "certificate." The success, or otherwise, of an exploratory mission depended largely on the skill and reliability (or lack of it) of the Indian guides. Their certificates were probably no more than a letter from a previously satisfied customer.

on the platform of expanding Oregon all the way north to Alaska ("54° 40′ or Fight"). And in the same year, the United States successfully managed to pick a fight with Mexico in order to launch an expansionist war. Frémont, as it turned out, helped to promote that war.

In 1845, he was sent west again to make surveys of the Arkansas and Red rivers, and to examine the Salt Lake region and much of the Sierra Nevada for useful military routes in case of war. He assigned a young lieutenant to make a survey of the rivers while he plunged back into the southwestern mountains, accompanied by Kit Carson, Joe Walker, and a tough contingent of soldiers and mountain men. His route led them through the Tennessee Pass, across the Grand River, and along the White River to the Great Salt Lake. From there they marched across the wastes of the Great Basin to Pilot Peak. Frémont then took some of the party southwest to the Humboldt headwaters, while Joe Walker guided the others southward to cross the Sierra at Walker Pass.

Frémont arrived at Sutter's Fort in California in December, having found the Sierra unusually open and free of snow. He had located a useful and reasonably quick route into the Californian interior, and lost no time in reporting it to the American consul in Monterey. But routes were to be the least important result of this entry into California.

Mexico was alive with the talk of war. Texas had already been snapped up by the United States' annexation in 1854, and the Mexicans feared that California could easily be taken in the same way. Understandably, the Californian authorities objected to the presence of Frémont and his 60 well-armed men. As a result, in February, 1846, Monterey's General Castro ordered Frémont out of California. The Pathfinder fortified himself on Hawk's Peak and dared the Mexicans to make him go. But after a few days without being troubled, Frémont and his men slipped away by night, heading north for Oregon.

At about that time, General Zachary Taylor and his troops had massed near the Rio Grande, hoping to tempt Mexico into striking the first blow. Sure enough, in May, 1846, Mexico succumbed to temptation, killed some of Taylor's dragoons, and started the war.

Meanwhile, a group of American rebels who had no idea that the war had started began a revolt of their own. In June, they took over Mexican headquarters in Sonoma. They celebrated their success by raising a makeshift flag picturing a bear over the words "California Republic." This event came to be known as the Bear Flag Revolt.

The real conquest of California, though, was conducted by Frémont and General Stephen Kearny. Frémont marched south at the head of 150 mountain men and American pioneers, while Kearny effortlessly took New Mexico with his motley Army of the West. Eventually, Frémont's revolutionaries joined forces with the United States military, and by mid-August California was American. Frémont was named as the first governor of this new United States acquisition.

The United States had now managed to acquire the southwest and the northwest, which enlarged its territory immensely. Settlers by the hundreds poured through South Pass each year, branching out to the north and the south. They were not deterred by the Indian men-

Above: James Knox Polk (1795—1849), 11th President of the United States from 1845—1849, when territorial growth was at its height. During his term the Star-Spangled Banner was raised over Texas and most of what are now the nine western states.

Right: map showing the Far West, with the routes of the trappers, the mountain men, and explorers who mapped the area west of the Rocky Mountains.

Astorians   1   1811-3
  Hunt   1A   1811-3
  Stuart   1B   1812-3

Ogden   2a   1824-5
               2b   1825-7
               2c   1828

Smith   3a   1826-7
               3b   1827-30

Walker   4   1832-4

Frémont   5a   1843-4
               5b   1845-7

Frémont (after 5c   1848-9
resigning from Army) 5d 1853-4

Above: while General Kearny took New Mexico, a side expedition under General Doniphan went into Mexico itself. Here American troops storm the bishop's palace in Monterrey, in a drawing by a private in the army, Samuel Chamberlain.

ace in Oregon, nor by postwar dislocations in California. They were not distressed by the tales of the Hastings and Donner parties, both of which had suffered terribly in their attempts to reach California.

In 1846-47, Brigham Young translated Frémont's glowing words into the reality of the Mormon migration to the Salt Lake. The Mormons were followers of a new religion they claimed was based on revelation. They had been surrounded by hostile neighbors in Illinois and Missouri, who had eventually shot their original leader and burned their towns and houses to the ground. The Mormons traveled across the plains ignorant of frontier rigors but unswervingly determined to make the desert bloom. They hoped to gain a worthwhile

Right: war was declared between the United States and Mexico in May, 1846, but in June of that year a band of American settlers, not knowing that war had been declared, staged the Bear Flag Revolt. After capturing the fort at Sonoma, Mexico's headquarters in northern California, they raised this flag—a homemade banner, bearing a star, a grizzly bear, and the words "Californian Republic."

home of their own which would be located a long way from eastern persecutors. Because of this hope, many Mormons starved, froze, and crippled themselves during the long journey "home."

Elsewhere, in Oregon and California, the living was easier, and the wagon trains kept plodding across the prairies. This increased the populations of those regions considerably, but the great determining factor that flooded the west with swarms of newcomers was the gold found in the mountains of California.

The frenzy began in early 1848, when a man helping to build a saw-mill on the property of John Sutter noticed a sparkle of yellow in a mountain stream. Throughout the spring, various workers scraped up bits of the yellow stuff, tested it, and proved it was gold. In May, the traditional cry went up in San Francisco, "gold in them thar hills!" By June, the city had been virtually deserted, and the news was spreading east like a prairie fire. All of California seemed to be grubbing in the Sierra foothills. Oregonians left hard-won homesteads and hurried south for their share. In the beginning of 1849, thousands of easterners mortgaged their futures to pay profiteering ships' passage fees to California. Many thousands more pinned their hopes on the overland trails. One estimate numbers the overlanders in 1849 at 50,000. Most of them were channeled through the South Pass and were directed by hastily written guide books that seldom mentioned the hazards to be

Above: Brigham Young (1801–1877), the Mormon who led his followers from Illinois to Utah when anti-Mormonism forced them to leave first one place, then another. They reached the Great Salt Lake valley in 1847.

Right: a facsimile of an entry in the diary of William Bigler, who was at Sutter's Mill, California, when gold was discovered. Bigler was a member of the Mormon Church, working his way from Los Angeles to the Church's new home at Utah in 1848. He had reached Sacramento where he was employed by John Sutter when the first nuggets of gold were found by James Marshall.

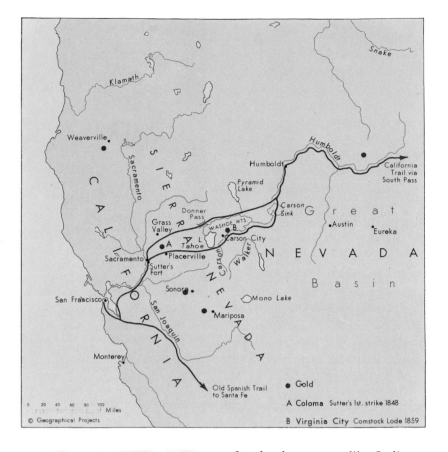

Left: gold strikes made in the areas that are now California and Nevada.

Right: details from "Grant and His Generals" by Balling, showing Generals Devin, Custer, and Kilpatrick. Although Custer (detail at top) is shown as a Civil War general, his greatest fame came as an Indian-fighter, and especially through his famous Last Stand on the Little Bighorn River, where Custer and his entire regiment were killed by the Sioux.

A Coloma   Sutter's 1st. strike 1848

B Virginia City   Comstock Lode 1859

Above: the California gold rush brought many different nationalities to the shores of America. This engraving shows a Chinese man going to the mines in 1853.

faced—deserts, warlike Indians, or the difficult mountain pathways.

The struggles and miseries of the "forty-niners," as they were called, have only minor relevance to western exploration. Most of them followed the settlers' trails as best they could. Others blithely decided on Jed Smith's Old Spanish Trail, and met the greater horrors of the Mojave Desert and other neighboring wastelands. One group discovered a blazing basin below sea level, walled in by mountains seemingly without exits. They called this basin Death Valley. A more useful discovery was made by a company of Mormons trekking eastward from their successful gold diggings. They located a pass through the Sierra along the Carson River that neatly linked the goldfields (Placerville especially) with the Humboldt River headwaters. This route and, to some extent, the Donner Pass, became the most popular for gold-seeking emigrants during the rush.

The Californian gold rush reached its peak in 1852, by which time the mountains seemed overrun with men of every nationality, including a major influx of Chinese. The miners began to scatter through the mountains in the 1850's, hoping to find a repetition of the rich veins of California. They risked Apache attacks along the Gila River and eastward into Arizona. They then filtered into Nevada, up unknown rivers and canyons, digging and panning along the way. Their searches were rewarded by the fantastic wealth of the Comstock Lode near Virginia City, Nevada, on the edge of the Great Basin.

Exploration, of course, continued to be incidental and haphazard, but new western regions began to open up when precious metals were found in their soils. Miners fanned out later into Colorado, into British Columbia in the famous Cariboo rush of the 1860's, and eventually into more northerly states such as Montana and the Dakotas. As late as 1874, gold turned up in the Black Hills of South Dakota. Although this area had been crossed before, it was given a thorough, scientific survey by an expedition under the leadership of Colonel George Armstrong Custer. The expedition was typical of the general overrunning of the west by engineers, topographers, and surveyors, who were busily seeking out the small unknown areas that remained. Their work was often difficult, but the unknown areas were now linked by established trails and outposts. The blank frontier was vanishing, and a more complete picture of the west was being built up.

The Fact-finders
9

As western gold created something of a population explosion and Americans rushed westward in hundreds of thousands, the United States wanted to know more about the newest additions to its transcontinental nation. Those early settlers also began yearning for better links with home than dusty prairie trails and cruel mountain passes. As a result, the era of exploration of the 1800's ended with the same kind of government-backed, fact-finding expeditions that had begun it.

Some of these parties went looking for improved routes for settlers, with an eye to transcontinental communications. Others went to perform scientific surveys of the wilderness. By the late 1840's, the days of original discovery were past. Any discoveries yet to be made were incidental and comparatively trivial—a small river, a low range of hills, or a useful mountain pass. But even though the scientists and surveyors were not discoverers, they were still important explorers. For their comprehensive and systematic examination of the West formed a necessary prelude to its wholesale settlement.

Oddly enough, even before stagecoaches had begun operating routes into California, and before the steam locomotive had lost the sheen of novelty in the East, Americans began talking about transcontinental railroads. Many put their words into action by looking for routes. In mid-winter 1848-1849, Frémont organized a party to scour the mountains for a usable pass. But the fierce snows accounted for the loss of 11 men and doomed this last pathfinding attempt to failure.

The army (i.e. the Topographical Engineers) instigated other searches for routes in the Gila River region and the plains of west Texas. Similar teams looked in New Mexico, while Captain Howard Stansbury examined the Salt Lake region and the Mormon settlements, locating the valuable Cheyenne Pass. Much of Stansbury's route eventually formed the path of the Union Pacific Railroad, but no one paid much attention to it at the time (1850). Railroad plans had become excuses for eastern financial and political machinations. No one was really ready to build a line, and so geographical facts tended to be ignor-

Left: prospectors washing gold from the Calaveras River in northern central California. The "forty-niners," as these men were called, flocked to California from all over the world and by the end of 1849, the population of California had increased from 20,000 to over 107,000.

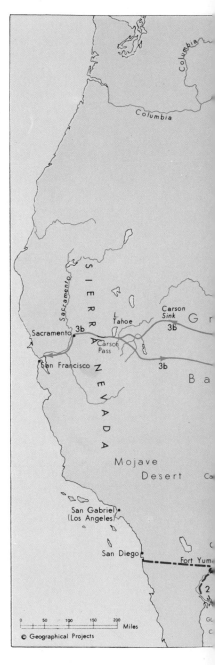

Above: a 50-foot linen measuring tape, with book-form leather carrying case, which also holds a note pad and pencil, as used by the surveyors in the 1800's.

Left: a prismatic compass by Andrew Yeates. Made in the late 1800's, this instrument has a spirit level, a small telescope, and a tripod clamp. These allow more accurate bearings to be taken.

ed. Surveyors were still looking for railroad routes in the early 1860's.

Before then, the army began a series of surveying expeditions into the West, called, by the historian William H. Goetzmann, the "Great Reconnaissance." Some of these centered on Utah because of the Mormon War of 1857, a war set off when the Mormon church clashed with the federal government over who really ruled the territory. As a by-product, Lieutenant J. C. Ives made a notable exploration along part of the Colorado River, though the river's extent remained a mystery for years. In 1859, Captain J. M. Macomb systematically explored the wilderness northwest of Santa Fe, emerging eventually into the Green River Valley with the first clear idea of that region's drainage. Captain J. H. Simp-

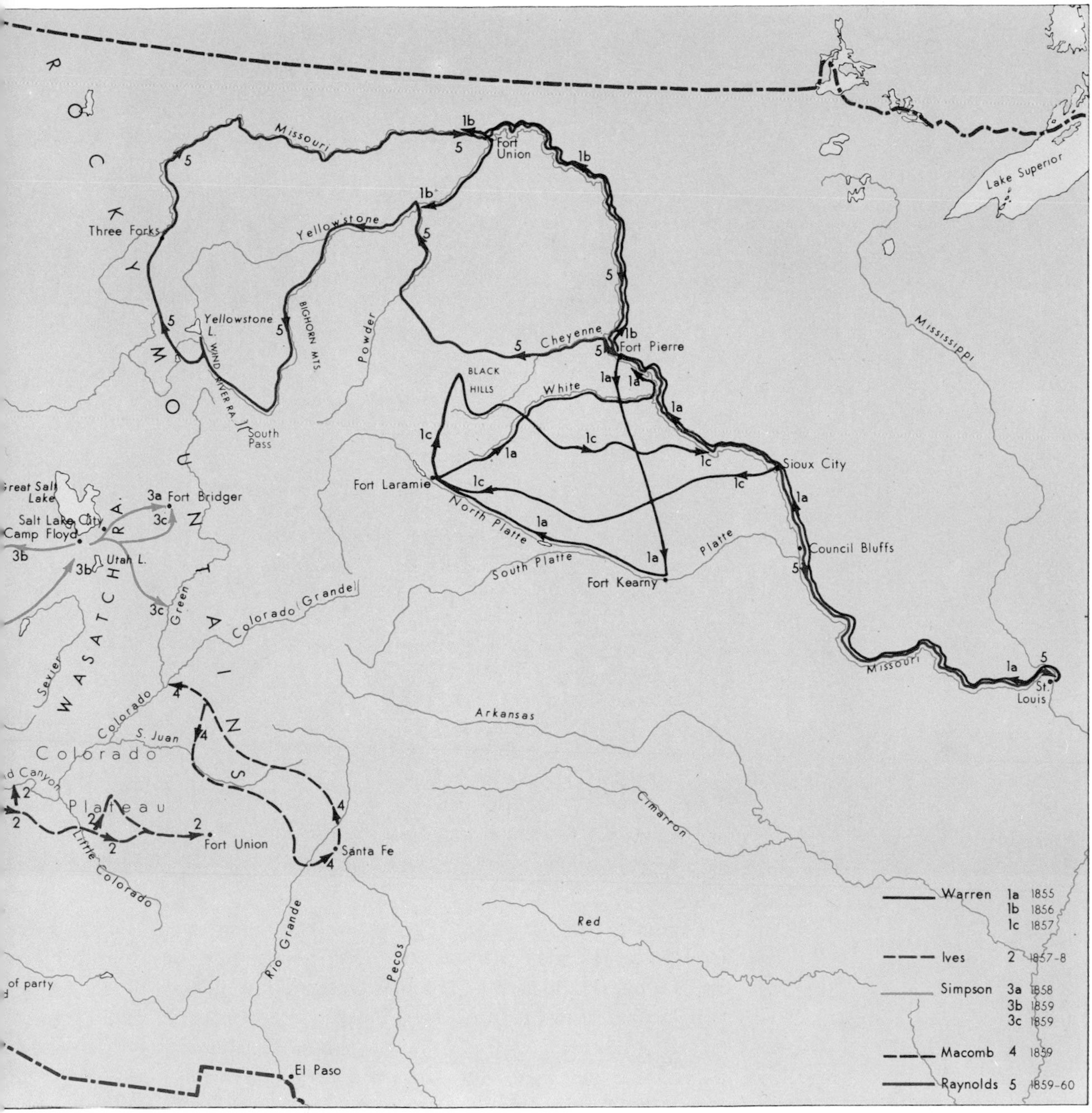

R O C K Y M O U N T A I N S
W A S A T C H R A.
Missouri
Fort Union
Three Forks
Yellowstone
Yellowstone L.
WIND RIVER RA.
BIGHORN MTS.
Powder
South Pass
Cheyenne
Fort Pierre
BLACK HILLS
White
Lake Superior
Mississippi
Sioux City
Fort Laramie
North Platte
South Platte
Platte
Fort Kearny
Council Bluffs
Missouri
St. Louis
Great Salt Lake
Salt Lake City
Camp Floyd
Fort Bridger
Utah L.
Green
Sevier
Colorado Grande
Colorado
S. Juan
Colorado Plateau
Little Colorado
Fort Union
Santa Fe
Rio Grande
Pecos
Arkansas
Cimarron
Red
El Paso
Warren 1a 1855
1b 1856
1c 1857
Ives 2 1857-8
Simpson 3a 1858
3b 1859
3c 1859
Macomb 4 1859
Raynolds 5 1859-60

son roamed the Great Basin and the Wasatch Mountains. Captain G. K. Warren made an overland foray into the Dakotas, partly to find military routes for operations against the Sioux. Captain W. F. Raynolds wandered the Wind River region looking for a southern access into the rugged terrain of what is now Yellowstone Park. He failed to find one, even with the expert guidance of Jim Bridger.

At about the same period, the British began to show interest in the Canadian west. The Hudson's Bay Company seemed doubtful whether the Canadian west was suitable for settlers, but its view could hardly be called objective. For this reason, in 1857, Britain sent Captain John Palliser and some scientists to examine the Canadian west.

Above: routes of the surveyors Warren, Ives, Simpson, Macomb, and Raynolds, who worked out the details of the topography of the western United States.

Palliser's topographical reports were praiseworthy, but, oddly enough, he returned with the strongest warning about the aridity of the prairies, or the Great Canadian Desert. This attitude to the American plains, as put forward by Pike and Stephen Long, had already been discredited by Frémont and others. Revaluations of Canada's magnificent wheat-growing areas had yet to be made.

And so inquiries into the West continued. Reports cascaded onto government desks, with maps of exceptional accuracy accompanying them. Frémont's map of this route in 1843-44 was the first map to represent the western regions comprehensively. But Lieutenant Warren's map of the entire trans-Mississippi west (completed in 1857) took the prize for accuracy and comprehensiveness. Reports of scientific observations became as numerous as those of the topographical explorations. Geologists rushed to the West, and many became involved in examining the stratified canyons of Colorado. Paleontologists joined them after John Evans returned from South Dakota with a treasure-hoard of fossils. Botanists and zoologists scattered across the wilderness to study plants and animals. Archeologists searched among the leftovers of prehistoric tribes, mainly in New

Mexico. The West, then, became filled with excited and eager scientists.

One of the busiest groups concentrated on the mountain-strewn terrain of the southwest. Led by Josiah D. Whitney, from 1860 onward, the California Survey made a massive assault on that region's geology. Its scientists encountered the dramas of mountain exploration—such as floods, snows, and crippling cold. Many of these explorer-geologists became expert mountain climbers. Whitney and company inched up to the 14,162-foot summit of Mount Shasta, in 1862, where they nearly collapsed from lack of oxygen. A dynamic Yale graduate named Clarence King joined them in 1863, and attempted to stand "on the top of California." With only a bowie knife, a geologist's hammer, and a rawhide lasso, King ascended Mount Tyndall and climbed within a few hundred feet of the region's great peak, Mount Whitney, so named for Josiah Whitney.

Meanwhile, far to the east, the Confederacy's secession had launched the war between the States. Congress was now northern-controlled, so that it could overcome some of the sectional politics that had blocked a decision on a transcontinental railroad. An engineer named Theodore D. Judah had located what seemed to be a useful route through the

Left: Pueblo Indians and their dwellings. These are modern descendants of the ancient Pueblo tribes, who still live in much the same way as their forefathers.

Sierra. And though it was to be some years before a comparable route could be found through the Rockies, the transcontinental railroad got under way in 1862. The Central Pacific was to build over the Sierra, and the Union Pacific was to cross the plains and the Rockies to join the Central. (By the mid-1860's several smaller railroad lines were crisscrossing the Midwest.) The two lines were built in frantic competition. The Union Pacific only caught up when, in 1866, a young engineer named James Evans located an ideal pass through the Rockies, near present-day Cheyenne, Wyoming.

By 1869, California had its steel link with the east, and in the 1870's and 1880's, other railroad companies rushed to throw their competitive lines across the mountains—the Kansas Pacific, Texas Pacific, Southern Pacific, Northern Pacific and, of course, the Atchison, Topeka, and Santa Fe. By then, too, newly confederated Canada was dreaming of transcontinental rails. It spent much of the 1870's looking for a route across the fearsome topography north of Lake Superior, and across the jagged Canadian Rockies. The railroad engineer Sandford Fleming led hosts of surveys in these inhospitable regions. By 1880, the

Right: a rawhide lasso, the frontiersman's most valuable and versatile tool, was used for anything and everything, from catching cattle and pulling wagons over muddy swamps, to killing a snake or tying a pack.

Left: by the 1860's a transcontinental railroad had been started, with two companies working toward each other—the Central Pacific across the Sierra, the Union Pacific across the plains and the Rockies. This picture shows the workmen building the track across the Nevada desert in 1868.

Right: the Canadian Rockies, showing the terrain through which the Canadian Pacific railroad engineers forced their steel link with the West.

Below: transcontinental railroad lines laid across North America.

Canadian Pacific Railway began construction. It overcame monumental financial obstacles thanks to the business genius of its president, George Stephen. And it overcame constructional obstacles because of the American engineer William Van Horne, its general manager. He believed that nothing was impossible and laid 500 miles of track one summer to prove it. He finished the job by 1885.

The railroads, of course, brought not only settlers but a measure of civilization to the West. Even so, during the days of the Union and Central Pacific's construction, exploratory reconnaissances went on. The army, after the Civil War ended, shifted its cavalry out west to protect settlers from Indians and to conduct a "mopping-up" program of topographical surveys. Some civilian ventures went on as well, such

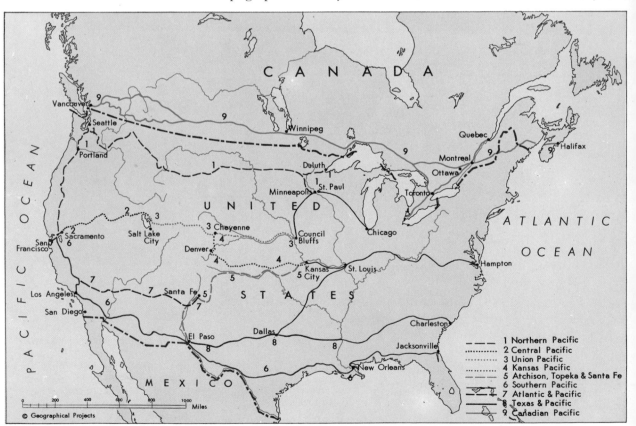

1 Northern Pacific
2 Central Pacific
3 Union Pacific
4 Kansas Pacific
5 Atchison, Topeka & Santa Fe
6 Southern Pacific
7 Atlantic & Pacific
8 Texas & Pacific
9 Canadian Pacific

© Geographical Projects

as the one that made a successful tour of the Yellowstone region in 1869. By the early 1870's, Captain W. A. Jones had found the elusive southern entrance to Yellowstone Park (Togwotee Pass, from the Wind River Valley). By that time the region had become a national park, thanks to the good offices of many military and civilian explorers who wished to save it from exploitation.

Clarence King returned to the West in the late 1860's to undertake a full-scale survey of the mountainous region along the 40th parallel in northern Nevada, Utah, Colorado, and southern Wyoming. King needed all his boundless energy to keep the reconnaissance going in the face of a summer heatwave, malaria among his men, and his own temporary collapse after being struck by lightning. His survey was spectacularly successful in its mapping of some of America's most treacherous terrain (including the Black Rock region and the Great Basin). In 1870, having taken a new approach to Mount Shasta, King was the discoverer of the first active glacier to be seen in the United States. It was of major importance in the flurry of geological theorizing about the West's prehistoric development.

King continued his worthwhile discoveries, while, at the same time, a less famous man, Lieutenant George M. Wheeler of the U.S. Army, explored some Nevada and Arizona byways with notable results. He and his men performed a systematic exploration of Death Valley (in heat up to 120°F). They also made a difficult and partial exploration of the Colorado River, because they chose—quixotically—to move

Above: the party that went west with John Stevens, one of the many settlers who traveled to and established themselves in the Midwest. Seen here, the party is piling grass over a swamp to form a bridge.

*up*stream against torrential currents and rapids. Wheeler continued his widespread surveys of isolated and wild areas into the 1870's. By then he was joined by the civilian explorer and geologist F. V. Haydon, whose work almost eclipsed that of Wheeler.

Many of Haydon's discoveries were paleontological and not geographical, though no less noteworthy in their own context. For instance, he was the man who first dug up the prehistoric ancestors of the modern horse, although anti-evolutionists dismissed these finds as implied blasphemy (in the same way as Darwinism was dismissed). His work in the Yellowstone area contributed much to the establishment of the national park, as did his other work (in Colorado, for example) to the data-gathering by railroad builders.

And so this pattern of western exploration continued. Men traveled west on hard-living expeditions, and encountered all the difficulties of terrain, weather, wildlife, and Indians then existing. But, as Wheeler said in 1871, "the day of the pathfinder has ... ended." The paths were there, not as ragged Indian trails, but as stagecoach routes and railroad tracks. Towns were built, and ranches, farms, mines, and mills were in operation. But exploration of the West did not stop suddenly. It gradually slowed and mingled with the scientific fact-finding that began in the wild 1840's, and went on long after the West had been wholly tamed and won.

Left: a mining tramway in Death Valley near the Nevada border in California. The heat and aridity make Death Valley virtually intolerable during the long hot summer.

Above: Virginia City, Nevada, the
liveliest ghost town in the West.
Once the richest city in America,
it remained an important tourist
center after its famous mines—from
which more than $1,000 million in
gold and silver was extracted from
the Comstock Lode—were exhausted.
The Church of St. Mary's of the Mountains is among the best of the period.

449

The Disinherited
10

The early explorers of North America must be regarded as the first spearhead of American western expansion. Even the traders and mountain men saw themselves that way, however businesslike or individualistic their primary motives might have been. They believed that the wilderness they roamed rightfully belonged to the United States, and that the aboriginal inhabitants had no more claim to the land than the grizzly bears or coyotes. The Indians were merely part of the landscape and one of the many obstacles that expanding America had to overcome to fulfill its destiny.

This attitude affected every contact between explorers and west-

Above: "The Song of the Talking Wire" by Henry F. Farney. The utter dejection of this Indian, leaning against a telegraph pole as though listening to voices speaking through the wires, outlines the problem, which still exists today, of finding a place for the Indian in modern America.

ern Indians. Of course, these contacts played a relatively minor part in the long, tragic story of America's dealings with the Indians. The actions of explorers had much less impact on Indian relations than full-dress governmental policy, which developed over the decades without any noticeable humanitarian improvements.

Perhaps the process of western expansion must be seen as an unavoidable culture clash, and one which the Indians could only lose. But it can also be argued that the clash might have been less violent, and that the loss might have been diminished. Instead, American attitudes toward the Indians led inexorably to bloodshed and treachery. Whether or not the explorers and Indians met first as friends, or circled each other suspiciously, the end result was the same. The Indian was alienated, and the likelihood of a peaceful settlement between the two groups was made more remote.

From the beginning, white attitudes toward Indians grew out of two primary concepts. First, the Indian was considered an inferior being. He was thought of as not only culturally inferior, but also somewhat less than human in his wild savagery, amorality, and godlessness. These views originated from the eastern frontier, where Indian wars had been going on for generations before the Louisiana Purchase. Men who had fought to expand America into Ohio or Kentucky later went into the West with feelings of hate and contempt for all Indians. And even the more thoughtful frontiersmen who admired the Indian peoples upheld the second of these concepts—that the Indians lived on vast areas of valuable land which was rightfully American. Therefore, whether the approach toward the Indian was one of loathing or admiration, the first westerners agreed that the Indian would eventually have to be pushed aside.

Beforehand, however, the frontiersmen also decided that the Indians could be exploited through trade. Because of this exploitation, the Indian's attitude toward the white man was one of fear and bitterness. Various conflicts on the old frontier also helped to create inter-tribal rivalries, which pitted Indians against Indians on the front lines. The Iroquois learned to hate the French, and the Cherokee, who were fighting for the British, were terrified by the American revolutionaries. The explorer-traders also profited by these traditional Indian enmities, arming some tribes against others. In Canada, the Cree obtained firearms from fur traders and carried out wars against the Blackfoot. In the United States, traders armed the Crow and Flathead tribes against the Blackfoot and sometimes the traders themselves took an active part in the battles that followed. It was not surprising that the Blackfoot struck back against whites as well as Indians, once they too had guns.

At other times, the traders enraged Indians by trying to cut out the middlemen, Indians who had traditionally gathered furs from the deep interior and passed them on to the whites in the Mississippi Valley. The Sioux's attitude toward Lewis and Clark stemmed partly from a fear of being cut out in this way. The Blackfoot, too, opposed the idea of anyone but themselves trading with the mountain tribes.

Below: the tribal Indian areas of North America, with the Eskimos in the far north, showing the Indian migrations and movements in the 1800's.

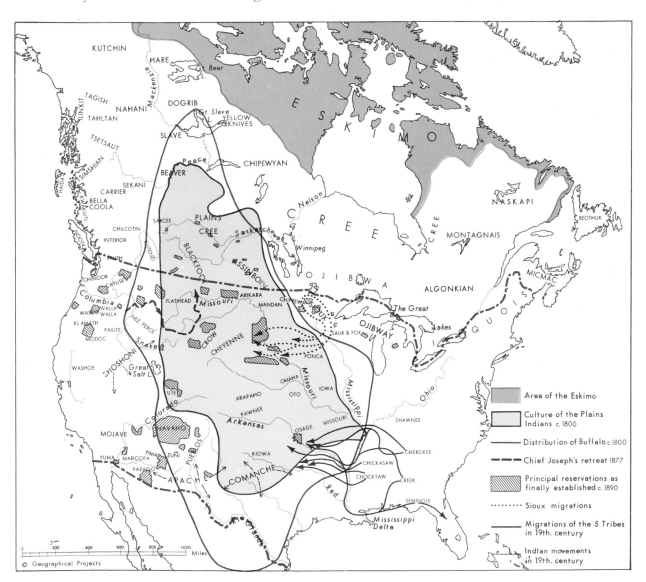

Area of the Eskimo

Culture of the Plains Indians c. 1800

Distribution of Buffalo c.1800

Chief Joseph's retreat 1877

Principal reservations as finally established c.1890

Sioux migrations

Migrations of the 5 Tribes in 19th. century

Indian movements in 19th. century

© Geographical Projects

453

Above: however much the early traders may have despised the Indians for their lack of culture, not one of them could deny the great part that the tribesmen played in western trade; either directly by supplying the furs to be traded, or indirectly by acting as guides to the white men.

The trading techniques were also at fault, because many of the traders were ruthless men. For instance, the North West Company thought nothing of cornering a market by extortion, threatening Indians with violence if they dared to trade with rival companies.

Added to these forms of exploitation and alienation were the complications brought by the white man into the West. For instance, the effect of white men's goods on the tribes undermined the traditional Indian skills in a relatively short time. With the availability of iron for axheads and arrowheads, the Indians lost their ability to work stone and flint within a single generation. Therefore, their dependence on the whites, and thus their potential degradation, began almost overnight. Needless to say, the traders were delighted with the situation.

This dependence was further enhanced when the traders offered alcohol to the Indians in exchange for furs. Indian chiefs were well aware of the effect of drunkenness on the tribesmen and loathed the white men because of it. Even worse was the result of diseases which occurred in mild forms in whites but slaughtered the non-immune

Indians by the thousands. In the 1780's a smallpox epidemic killed about one-third of Canada's Plains Indians. Between 1835 and 1860, the United States Plains Indians suffered a similar epidemic, at the time of the first onrush of miners, topographical explorers, and early pioneers. At least half of the Kiowa and Comanche tribes died of a mild cholera in 1849. In the 1870's, another smallpox epidemic swept through the Blackfoot and other tribes, accompanied by rumors that it had been purposefully begun by whites who included infected blankets and clothing among trade goods.

It is not hard to believe that such an early use of biological warfare might have occurred to the white men as an easy and final solution to the Indian problem. Many theorists quite readily suggested extermination of the Indians as a practicable policy to deal with the situation. Certainly the extermination of the buffalo in the late 1800's was explicitly a means of controlling (or wiping out) the Plains Indians.

No one denies that many of the great warrior tribes were given to atrocity (as whites termed it) as normal techniques of war. And no one

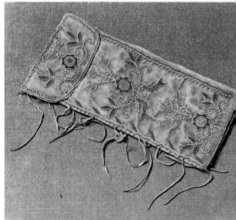

Above: knee-leggings with beadwork, a craft practiced by the Indians, whose traditional handicrafts are only now being fully appreciated.

Left: scalping, one of the Indian "skills" most feared by white men. These sketches demonstrate various gruesome aspects of the art. Pictures show dried scalps being used as decoration on wearing apparel, a horse's harness, and on tepees; the head of a "lucky" victim who has survived the ordeal; and how the scalp was taken.

Below: an attack such as this, by Comanche on a wagon train, became part of the legend of the West. The reasons for such sudden and unprovoked attacks were frequently obscure and those poor unfortunates who were attacked were often the innocent victims of ill-feeling caused by the tribes' previous encounters with hostile white men.

denies that peaceable parties of whites were attacked and massacred for no reason— at least no apparent reason. But it should be remembered that atrocities occurred on both sides. The British anthropologist Peter Farb has suggested that scalping was introduced to the Indians by the whites of the eastern colonies. The colonial authorities actually paid bounties for Indians who were killed, and scalps were taken as proof of the money earned. The practice appeared very early, when New York was still Dutch. By the mid-1700's an Indian scalp taken in Pennsylvania earned the scalper $130.

As for the unwarranted attacks by Indians, it can be understood, if not condoned, that Indians failed to distinguish between dangerous and friendly whites. If a tribe experienced only brutality, contempt, trading swindles, and violence at the hands of the whites, they most likely decided to alter the pattern by violence. Jedediah Smith's men were excusably enraged and embittered by the sudden, unforeseen assault on them by the Mojave (in 1827) who had been friendly the previous year. But Smith's men had no way of knowing about the earlier clash between the Mojave and James Ohio Pattie over a minor trading disagreement, which resulted in an unexpected attack by Pattie on the Indians. Perhaps the Oregonian Indians who jumped Smith's men

The Herald.

EXTRA.

A Massacre

11 Persons Murdered

AT A

Conference at Frog Lake.

Fears Entertained for Battleford.

NAMES OF THE KILLED.

Russian News.

WINNIPEG, April 13.—Telegraphic communication with Battleford was resumed last Thursday, April 8, and news came of a massacre at Frog Lake on April 2 According to it, the Indians invited Acting Sub-Indian Agent Thomas T. Quinn and others to a conference in their camp, and shot them as soon as they entered. Eleven persons were killed.

Father McCombe and some ten settlers are entrenched in the Hudson Bay buildings at Fort Pitt and are surrounded by large numbers of savages. Big Bear's band is amongst them. Great fears are entertained for their fate as well as the fate of the besieged at Battleford who are holding out, but according to the telegram on Thursday were very anxious.

The names of the killed at Frog Lake as far as can be learned are:
Rev. Father Faford.
Rev. Father Terrarch.
Indian Agent Quinn,
Farm Instructor Delaney.
John Goninlock and wife.
J. Williscraft.
Charles German, and three others, names unknown.

Messrs. Delaney, J. K. Simco and two men of the H. B. Co. were taken prisoners

There are 25 police at Fort Pitt. The Stony Indians fired on the police while going to the river for water. In the skirmish which followed two Indians were killed. No whites were injured.

The latest reports say that the situation is unchanged.

Gen. Middleton's force camped yesterday 32 miles from Humboldt, and 10 miles on Salt Plain. Col. Otter has orders to go across the country to Battleford, if the boats are not ready at the mouth of Swift Current to take him down the Saskatchewan.

The York Rangers and the Simcoe Foresters went west to Qu'Appelle and Swift Current last night, and the 9th battalion arrived here. Col. Williams will reach here to-morrow with the Toronto cavalry. The Seventh of London is a day or two behind.

LONDON, April 12—The Russian force attacked the Afghans at Peijdeh on March 31, and drove them from their position. The Russian accounts say the attack was provoked by the Afghans, but it is believed that the Russians were the aggressors. England is awaiting a satisfactory explanation before declaring war.

Above: a typical report of an Indian massacre which made front-page news in an Extra issued by the Calgary *Herald* on April 13, 1885.

later—or the Comanche who eventually killed Smith—had similar experiences of white violence and treachery festering in their tribe's memory.

But westerners seldom bothered to consider the Indians' provocations. Generally they saw only the horrible results of savage Indian massacres—which sensation-mongering newspapers on the frontier liked to play up, perhaps to justify the United States' policy of pushing Indians out of the way of settlement. But massacres of Indians by white westerners were probably just as great. Sometimes retaliation went to the extreme, such as the infamous Massacre of the Marias in 1870, in Montana. A detachment of U.S. cavalry pursuing some Blackfoot horse thieves encountered a village of that tribe and killed well over 100 men, women, and children before they realized that they were firing on the wrong band of Blackfoot.

Of course, these ugly stories do not portray the Indian-Westerner situation in its entirety. In addition to the friendships that grew between certain explorers and western tribes, there were a few early missionaries who went into the northwest to try to pacify the tribes of the region. Men such as the Methodist Jason Lee helped to prepare the Nez Percé and other tribes for the onrush of settlers on the Oregon Trail—and the Nez Percé remained friendly to Americans longer than any other western tribe. It was not until the Nez Percé became exasperated by land-grabbing and encroachments that Chief Joseph reluctantly led his warriors onto the warpath in the late 1870's. This was one of the last of the desperate and futile uprisings that accompanied the entrance of the railroads and the exit of the buffalo.

But good relations between Indians and whites in the United States were always the exception, whereas in Canada they tended to be the rule. Two factors kept them that way—the terrain of Canada and the Hudson's Bay Company policy.

This terrain included the forbidding landscape of the Canadian Shield, which presented an impassable barrier to overland travel above the Great Lakes. Lines of communication for anything larger than a fur trader's canoe simply did not exist between east and west. The Canadian West, then, was the sole preserve of the fur men far longer than in the United States. And while the North West Company may occasionally have provoked Indian wrath, the Hudson's Bay Company laid down an explicit policy of pacification and good relations. Their policy was a paternalistic one through which they hoped to keep

the Indians in a fairly dependent position. Above all, the Hudson's Bay Company had no dreams about a Canadian Manifest Destiny. It actively avoided any general policy of settlement, and the Indians, therefore, had no fears for their land.

The Indians also came to respect British justice, and the British Army, a colonial army which did not have plans or ideas of expansionism. After 1821, when the Hudson's Bay Company ruled the West monopolistically, peace reigned unbroken for decades. Only a trickle of settlers had gone West by the 1860's, and most of them stayed on the fringes of the wilderness. Many missionaries brought the pacifying influence of their religion to the West, and the Northwest Mounted Police maintained law and order and an unswerving tradition of justice. All of this happened long before any massive movement of settlers began to threaten Indian rights and drive them onto reservations. That sort of threat did not materialize until the 1880's, after Canada's transcontinental railroad had thrust into the prairies. By then the familiar missionaries and Mounties had established traditions of peaceful interrelationships that the tribal chiefs found hard to break.

Furthermore, Canada's widespread fur trade had produced a uniquely powerful separate community in its wild west—the *métis* (people of mixed blood). They were predominantly French-speaking, Catholic people who were once wild buffalo-hunting nomads. By the mid-1800's the métis had settled in many areas and held responsible positions in the Hudson's Bay Company. They formed a valuable link—and a buffer—between Indians and white authorities, and were respected and listened to by both sides.

In 1885, though, the métis were led by Louis Riel in Canada's last, and perhaps worst, Indian uprising. There were a number of reasons

for this revolt. Indians were starving, the buffalo were gone, and governmental policy had grown callous and inept. Nevertheless, many tribes stayed quietly on their reserves during the fighting. Even the Blackfoot remained peaceful—partly through the influence of mounted police and missionaries, and partly because some of the chiefs saw only futility and despair in any attempt to resist the inevitable.

Further warnings about American land-hunger and expansionism existed in abundance east of the Mississippi. On those older frontiers, the spread of American settlement took the invariable form of land grabbing, which included driving out the Indian by force. More usually,

Above: Louis Riel was born in St. Boniface, Manitoba, in 1844. He followed his father as leader of the *métis* and led their protests against the government in 1869 and 1885. After the first uprising failed, Riel was outlawed and fled to the United States for several years. He returned to Canada and was elected to the House of Commons in 1873 and 1874, but was denied his seat. Riel was committed to an insane asylum in 1876 but was freed in 1878. The second rebellion was also a failure and Riel surrendered. He was hanged for treason and his death in 1885 caused an upsurge of religious and racial hatred all over Canada.

though, a quasi-legality was imposed on the acquisitions of Indian land by means of treaties. Treaties were drawn up to conclude frontier hostilities, or they were peaceful agreements by which Indians "ceded" a certain amount of land while retaining portions of their traditional hunting grounds. But, of course, an Indian tribe was more than a little naive in the face of the treaty's "small print." Or, if more shrewd Indian leaders balked at signing, a lesser chief could usually be bribed or coerced into signing away his tribe's lands. If the tribe disowned his authority and tried to reclaim the land, that was considered overt treaty-breaking answerable by force—and a clear American conscience.

Gradually, then, the eastern tribes were pushed farther and farther west as the frontier rolled on. By the late 1700's, the frontier line was being pushed back across the Mississippi. Indians who had given up their ancestral lands in one place were now being shifted off their reserves (set aside by treaty) for smaller, poorer reserves. Some fought, as Tecumseh did in the early 1800's trying to unite the small tribes of the Great Lakes region. But they were crushed, and the broken tribal remnants were more thoroughly dispossessed.

By that time, the removal of Indians had become standard practice. The ruthless idea developed of removing all eastern Indians—what

Above: the life of the Plains Indians was dominated by the buffallo. Their traditional ceremonies honored these animals as the providers of shelter, food, and clothing. Buffalo dances were performed to attract the animals to the hunters, with the men wearing buffalo heads and skins. The arrival of the white men completely changed the way of life of the Indian peoples and their own culture was sharply altered.

there was left of them after the frontier wars—west of the Mississippi. They were to be moved onto unclaimed land in order to join the tribes already wandering there, thereby forming one big Indian Territory. The explorers depended largely on these plans of relocation to deal with the Indians to their own advantage. It was Zebulon Pike who launched this project with his report on the agricultural uselessness of the Great Plains. He stated it bluntly: the pioneers should "limit their extent in the west to the borders of the Missouri and Mississippi, while they leave the prairies incapable of cultivation to the wandering and uncivilized aborigines of the country." In short, the Indians should be pushed into an area that was considered completely useless to the white settlers.

Major Stephen Long's echo of Pike in 1820 speeded up the formulation of this policy. The usual quasi-legal treaties somehow found Indian signatures, and removal of the Indians was rapidly speeded up. The removal remains one of the most brutal and appalling episodes in the history of race relations anywhere. Eastern Plains tribes such as the Osage were pushed off their ancient stamping ground to make way for tribes from Illinois or Kentucky. The Cherokee, who had consciously made themselves a neat little civilized community in Georgia, which included industry, schools, and newspapers, were uprooted by means of deception and force. They were sent west in their "Trail of Tears," a forced march that killed some 4,000 of them. The Great Lakes tribes were pushed westward to meet the same fate. The Seminoles of Florida refused to budge. They vanished into the swamps and fought a bitter guerrilla war made sordid with American atrocity and treachery.

In the end, the eastern frontier was virtually free of large concentrations of Indians. The Plains tribes naturally resented the arrival of "foreign" Indians. And skirmishing made survival even more difficult for the dispossessed forest Indians trying to adapt to prairie life. By the mid-1800's, traders, mountain men, and miners were cluttering the mountains, and the Indians began to feel the pressure of the white presence in the Far West. It was a pincer movement. The Indians saw encroachment and dispossession coming from both sides, and out of bitter desperation, they rose in arms in a last hopeless attempt to turn back the tide.

As tribe after tribe went to war, the railroads and pioneer settlements crept onto the grasslands. The buffalo finally vanished under the

Above right: the lush green, wooded landscape of the Blue Ridge Parkway in North Carolina. About 35,000 Indians lived in North Carolina when the white men first arrived, among them the Cherokees, who lived in the Blue Ridge Mountains. Their reserves were gradually overrun by the white settlers and the tribes were forced to move to smaller, poorer reserves.

Below right: the sort of arid desert terrain to which the Cherokee Indians were moved as the frontiers were pushed farther and farther west.

Below left: Alcatraz Island, once a federal prison in San Francisco Bay, was taken over by Indians after the United States Government found it uneconomic as a penal colony. The new possessors have erected signs establishing the island as "Indian land," to which all Indians are welcome. Below right: San Francisco from Alcatraz Island, the sky-scrapers of the modern city contrasting sharply with the tepee in the foreground.

slaughtering rifles of hunters and soldiers. The army fought with brutal power, inevitably defeating the Indians who were herded onto reservations of poor, worthless land. The Indians even lost some of that in years to come, for Indian policy remained—and to some extent still remains—wide open to bureaucratic mismanagement, and general lack of understanding.

These were the end results of a process that began—in the West—when Lewis and Clark fired their rifles and cannon to impress riverside tribes with American power, or when Pike casually bought the present site of Minneapolis from a local chief. The explorers, government surveyors, scientists, traders, and mountain men perhaps would not have wished such a fate to befall the West's Indian population. But they brought with them the seeds of those inevitable horrors.

The Inheritors
11

By the end of the War of 1812, expansion of the American frontier settlement had taken in Indiana, Ohio, Illinois, and Missouri, and the Mississippi and lower Missouri valleys. The movement then leaped across 2,000 miles to re-establish itself in the empty wilderness of the western mountain states. Expansionism and land hunger may have provoked such a gigantic step, but it actually had been motivated by the fantastic tales of the explorers.

The grand image of the Far West took some time to develop, though, because only a general, rather hazy picture of that area filtered out to the public. This lack of information was partly due to the fact that reports from explorers were given directly to their government sponsors, who did not relay details in their entirety. In addition, the fur traders who followed the forerunners often kept their acquired knowledge to themselves. John Jacob Astor, for instance, did not release the Astorians' reports and maps for many years. As a result it was necessary to rediscover places such as South Pass. For these reasons, the pressure of advancing settlement on the eastern frontiers did not really build up to explosive proportions until a good many years after the War of 1812 was over.

By the time the need to conquer new lands had become irresistible, a sizable bulk of information had been made available. Much of it was highly romanticized, if not downright false. Semifictional accounts of life in the fur trade appeared in quantity. J. O. Pattie's *Personal Narrative,* published in 1831, was one of the most popular, and contained its own set of misrepresentations. None of these publications could be termed adequate guides for would-be settlers of the 1800's. Many of their most notable errors occurred in the geographical data and the maps that accompanied them, and yet such errors often had enough authority behind them to ensure that later cartographers would perpetuate them.

During the 1820's, then, most maps of the West followed William Clark's example of placing the headwaters of the Bighorn and Yellowstone rivers within a stone's throw of the Rio Grande and its Spanish strongholds. Zebulon Pike, too, imposed his idea on several maps that

Left: this picture of golden wheatfields on the Palouse Hills near Colfax, Washington state, shows how settlement and cultivation of the Far West has been established today.

Above: the life of the fur trader was romanticized by many contemporary painters, among them George Caleb Bingham. "The Trappers' Return," which he painted in the mid-1880's, shows trappers returning from a trip, with their canoe laden with skins, watched over by the cat tied securely at the bow of the boat.

somewhere in the central Rockies lay one grand mountain origin of all the Plains rivers. In the same way, certain leading Spanish explorers had earlier believed in the Buenaventura River and had placed it on their maps, and American explorers scoured the West in search of it.

In the 1830's, the professional romanticizers began writing about the wondrous events of the West. The emphasis of such books and newspaper articles was firmly placed on heroism. Publishers saw profits in tales of western adventures, thereby initiating the creation of the western myth. Mountain men and Indian-fighters became immortalized in these literary works.

The trappers and explorers themselves were still publishing their journals and reminiscences. And though these may have glossed over errors and sordid episodes, details of the West were beginning to crystallize and to fire the imaginations of pioneer leaders in the East. For instance, Jedediah Smith wrote a detailed report to the government on the fertile lands of the Columbia Valley, which stated that settlers' wagons could readily be taken through South Pass and northwest into Oregon. This report pointed the way to the creation of the Oregon Trail. At about the same time, the fur trader Joshua Pilcher, head of the Missouri Fur Company, added further stimulus to emigration by

Above: "A new map of North America from the Latest Authorities" by John Cary, Engraver, 1824. This is a fine example of early mapping, showing how the mountains of the Far West were increasingly well-known and accurately shown. Compare the map of 1804 on page 38 to see the progress.

Right: a wagon train crossing the Ute Pass, Colorado. The reports given to the pioneers before they started on their journeys did not prepare them for the hazards they would meet. The passes and rivers to be crossed often necessitated manhandling the wagons, and some trails were so narrow there was barely room for a wagon.

Above: Joseph Reddeford Walker, a sheriff in Missouri, was one of the great names among mountain men. His finest achievement was his expedition to California in 1833 when he became known as one of the notable pathfinders of the Great West. His party was the first to see and describe the Yosemite Valley. He also acted as a guide to the second overland party to cross the mountains to California.

warning about a possible British takeover of the Oregon region, if the United States did not get there first. These reports gained national circulation, as did the later *Narratives* of the clerk Zenas Leonard, who had marched with Joe Walker during the laying out of the California Trail.

By Leonard's time, the reality of a Manifest Destiny had become apparent. His sentiments clearly paralleled those of the majority of his countrymen in their bland assumption that the United States would shortly take over the Far West and civilize it. J. C. Frémont's writings also demonstrated the need and inevitability of such a move. His own dashing image served to accentuate the glamour, excitement, and taste of the West.

But in spite of this new clarity about the West, errors and falsifications still occurred. Landford Hastings, whose distorted geography helped to lead the Donner party into their fearful trap, poured out equally distorted propaganda about the perfections of California. Richard Henry Dana, in *Two Years Before the Mast,* also glorified that region, but, like other versions of the "guide" to western travel, it contained innumerable inaccuracies. It played down the Indian menace, rarely mentioned the wide deserts or cruel mountain passes, and offered only vague or incomplete information about trails.

At the beginning of the 1850's, one of the most far-reaching misapprehensions about the West still remained firm, that of the Great American Desert. After 1825, according to the historian R. A. Billington, "every literate American believed the region west of the 95th meridian to be a great, unusable desert." Therefore, the explorers were directly responsible for the "leapfrogging" movement of the settlement frontier, from the Mississippi Valley to the mountains.

The leapfrogging process was not readily halted. Although traders, trappers, and early colonists drew groups of settlers to California and Oregon, no nucleus of settlement existed on the central plains. Only millions of buffalo and thousands of wandering Indians were located there. And after mid-century, the American policy of the relocation of Indians to the prairie "wastelands" accentuated the leapfrogging by imposing an even greater barrier to settlement of the plains than climate and topography.

Only when the restless American appetite for unclaimed land and the "taming" of the Plains tribes were satisfactorily fulfilled did settlers begin to encroach on those flat, open grasslands. Previously, they

Right: this page from a geologic map of the United States shows the wealth of detail now available compared to the early maps. This is, to a large extent, due to the foundations laid by the explorers. The different colors indicate different geologic formations.

not only would not, but decidedly could not make the move. For agricultural techniques of the early 1800's demanded rich loamy soil, a humid atmosphere, and abundant wood. More sophisticated techniques were needed before Americans could turn in any number to "dry farming." Therefore, the cattlemen moved onto the prairies first, realizing that if they could support the gigantic herds of buffalo they could certainly support a few straggly, lean-shanked steers.

The ranchers followed the explorers and early colonists into Texas, Wyoming, and Montana. They left a few ramshackle prairie towns in their wake, and those, plus new farm methods and machinery, opened the doors to full-scale settlement. The settlers learned to build houses and barns of sod, and took advantage of the newly invented barbed wire for their fences. They found out how to use windmills to pump water up from deep-drilled wells and how to plow the shallow soil. Above all, they started to take full advantage of new machinery, and to make greater use of far larger acreages than was ever possible in eastern farming areas.

Meanwhile, of course, the age of exploration had faded away. But the settlers were indebted to the explorers in many ways. The explorers had opened up vast reaches of good land and had determined their extent and main features. Scientists had gathered fine details of terrain and resources which contributed necessary information to

Above: before the Spanish introduced horses into America, the Indians could hunt buffalo only on foot. This they did with moderate success. Sometimes they reasoned that to disguise themselves as wolves gave them an advantage over their huge adversaries. Once they had horses, however, in the 1700's, their prowess as hunters was increased and so began the decimation of the buffalo herds.

Right: settlement of the prairie regions, previously considered infertile and uncultivable, reached its height in the early 1900's. Many of the settlers built their homes from sods, the material most readily and cheaply available. The sods were cut from plowed furrows 12—14 inches wide. A sod-house wall could be anything from 24—30 inches thick. If possible, the roof was made of poles laid across the walls, covered with hay, and the whole thing overlaid with more sods. Sod houses were cool in summer, warm in winter, fire-proof, and would last 20 years or more. They had few windows so were dark inside.

hopeful pioneers. The trails that were laid down by the explorers provided geographical data which helped cartographers to map out accurate routes for the pioneers to come.

Then, too, the early explorers had left in their wake tiny focal points of civilization that later burgeoned into full settlements. From Lewis and Clark's Council Bluffs to the Astorians' trading post on the Pacific and to Sutter's Fort in California, way stations had been scattered across the wilderness. Pioneers going west sometimes stopped at those stations, thereby causing their enlargement. In the northwest, places such as Laramie and Boise dropped the prefix of "Fort" that was used in fur-trading days, and became thriving towns. Santa Fe and Taos swelled into major centers, and Salt Lake City sprang up along an important pioneers' thoroughfare.

And, similarly, old fur-trade posts of the Canadian West rapidly transformed themselves into settlements. The Hudson's Bay Company

moved its Pacific headquarters to Fort Victoria on Vancouver Island, when it saw the inexorable advance of Americans into the Columbia Valley. By the 1850's, it had become western Canada's second true settlement (after Selkirk's colony in what is now Manitoba). Gold seekers in British Columbia, like their earlier counterparts in California, built crude shanty towns to accommodate themselves and their pleasures. When the mining boom died down, some of these towns avoided the slide into ghost-town status and gathered settlers. Trading posts in the interior supported themselves extensively by limited farming of the surroundings. This farming proved the agricultural worth of the land and attracted a trickle of pioneers from eastern frontiers of Canada. The far-reaching explorers of Canada had left behind them the same kind of colonies-in-embryo as had dotted the western United States.

In less than 100 years, therefore, two small clusters of settlements on the eastern seaboard of North America had metamorphosed into

Above: not all settlements prospered, especially those which sprung up quickly around mines. Once the mining boom was over many towns dwindled, and ghost towns like this one at Bodie in California are not an uncommon sight in the West today.

479

Index